About the Author

John Fox is a retired international civil servant, having worked as a publications officer for both the BBC in London and UNESCO in Paris and Geneva.

He is the author, with Marit Fosse, of three books:
The League of Nations: From Collective Security to Global Rearmament.
Nansen: Explorer and Humanitarian.
Sean Lester: The Guardian of a Small Flickering Light.

He has also written a brief biography of Lord Robert Baden Powell (2013) published in English and French in the international educational journal Prospects.

Talleyrand

John Fox

Talleyrand

Olympia Publishers
London

www.olympiapublishers.com
OLYMPIA PAPERBACK EDITION

A CIP catalogue record for this title is
available from the British Library.

ISBN: 978-1-78830-888-5

First Published in 2021

Olympia Publishers
Tallis House
2 Tallis Street
London
EC4Y 0AB

Printed in Great Britain

PREFACE

The Canton of Geneva in Switzerland is closely surrounded on three sides by lines of mountains and it might have seemed perfectly normal to an outsider that the cantonal border—actually, the border of Switzerland—should run along the crests of these mountains. In fact, the frontier wanders aimlessly across open fields, hills and forests, along small streams and around vineyards ignoring the topography in a splendidly indifferent manner, isolating one village in Switzerland from its almost identical neighbour in France a few hundred metres away. I became intrigued by the arbitrary nature of this boundary and decided to find out the reason that lay behind its irregular course.

As it stands today, the border was established in 1815 by the second Treaty of Paris following the Napoleonic Wars and its line had been decided by the Genevan politician Charles Pictet-de-Rochemont on grounds that were important to him at that time—whether the population of a village had a majority of Protestants or of Catholics. Geneva, having been a bastion of Protestantism for more than 250 years, did not wish to adulterate its citizens with the wrong sort of Christians. Pictet-de-Rochemont had attempted to carry out this policy in the previous year when Napoleon had first been defeated by the Allies but his ambitions had been thwarted by a wily French politician named Talleyrand. One year later, following Napoleon's unsuccessful return to power during the Hundred Days, France was in an extremely weak position and Talleyrand was unable to resist Pictet-de-Rochemont's demands.

I decided to find out more about this "wily French politician" and soon discovered that, given the large number of books about his life and epoch, this subject could be described as "an already well-ploughed field". Eventually, I became so overwhelmed in making sense of the sequence of historical events in which Talleyrand was involved that, in order to grasp the essentials, I decided to write the story of his life for my own understanding.

I am extremely grateful to Sarah Webborn, who read the manuscript and made a number of important observations.

INTRODUCTION

Talleyrand was widely admired throughout Europe as the greatest diplomat of his era and set the standard for conducting international negotiations. He was also particularly renowned for his witty conversation and teasing charm. Far from dwelling on what a wonderful person he was, it is customary for many books about him to start by listing his many faults: the worldly priest, the wayward bishop, the barefaced liar, the false friend, the inconstant ally, the surreptitious plotter, the expedient turncoat, the destroyer of evidence, the inveterate gambler, the stock-market inside dealer, the bad payer, the shameless seeker of the financial kickback, the ultimate survivor—the list goes on. On the other hand, these less recommendable traits of his character can be contrasted with the shrewd, witty, well-educated, well-mannered, well-dressed, well-connected, charming aristocrat and representative of the *Ancien Régime*, a lifelong friend to the devoted members of his "harem" and generally recognized by his peers as a far-sighted politician and diplomat who sought peace and international economic development through the introduction of wise and enlightened policies into post-Revolutionary France and to Europe as a whole. This was the man who, for fifty years, influenced the political life of a continent recommending policies of political and economic cooperation—particularly with England—during decades of conflict, who managed to survive the tightrope of the French Revolution, who outmanoeuvred Napoleon and Tsar Alexander I of Russia, and who was twice instrumental in restoring the Bourbon dynasty to the throne of France. Despite the fact that Talleyrand pursued policies that were designed to ensure the happiness and prosperity of the French nation, he was often scorned by the general public, distrusted by his peers and vilified by the press. Throughout his life, through good times and bad, his sound advice was mostly ignored in France and in 1792, 1799, 1807 and 1815 he found himself in the political wilderness.

Talleyrand lived towards the end of the Age of Enlightenment and was influenced by its liberal tendencies. This was a cosmopolitan worldview, inspired by such French writers as Voltaire and Rousseau, promoting science and reason to examine how the world actually functioned and rejecting magic, the supernatural, dogma and authoritarianism. Although he was trained as a priest and never actually opposed Roman Catholicism, Talleyrand was sceptical about religion and strongly favoured freedom of conscience. In France, the period from 1789 to the 1830s witnessed a roller-coaster ride for the Roman Catholic priesthood and the Papacy as different political regimes followed one another, alternately forbidding and endorsing religion in general and Christianity in particular, trying to introduce some kind of spiritual alternative, seizing and restoring the church's property, and even holding hostage two different Popes. Prior to the French Revolution many intelligent young men, such as Talleyrand himself, were trained for the priesthood since it was seen by their noble families as a sure avenue to prestige and financial security. It was a matter of minor importance whether they took their religious vows seriously, particularly those concerning celibacy. In the era when Talleyrand lived, even a priest's vows of fidelity to the church presented no obstacle whatsoever to a stream of love affairs with pretty women. Following the Revolution, a remarkable number of these priests gravitated to politics and became Talleyrand's friends and colleagues—and enemies. The qualities required to be a politician and a priest are not the same, although many of them, often due to their training, rose to be competent government ministers in a succession of regimes. The more able ones like Talleyrand served the Revolution, the Directory, the Napoleonic Empire, the Bourbon Restoration and the July Monarchy with perfect equanimity and skill. Talleyrand lived to be 84 years old and during a long and active career that spanned the 1770s to the 1830s he came into contact with hundreds, even thousands, of influential people including French and foreign monarchs, emperors, princes, archbishops, politicians, generals, journalists, ministers, members of the aristocracy and the diplomatic corps, not to mention an enormous number of ladies, friends, wives and mistresses of the above, many of whom had been hostesses of salons in eighteenth century Paris and/or who described the remarkable events of these times in their diaries. Through much of his adult life, he occupied posts of political power and, under the enormous variety of regimes that governed France during this epoch, he always pursued liberal policies and sought peace through a balance among the European powers.

Faithful to his liberal tendencies, Talleyrand was an advocate of freedom of the press. This may seem an extraordinary paradox when confronted with his need to quash rumours about the huge under-the-table bribes that he is known to have received when in office, as well as the numerous occasions when he lied unashamedly or destroyed the evidence implicating himself in equivocal affairs. Sometimes the press or his political opponents—even Napoleon—got wind of some of these discreditable scandals but he would simply deny any involvement or pass the blame disingenuously on to one of his irreproachable colleagues. The more it looked like he would be caught red-handed in some outrageous affair, the more he managed to wriggle out of all responsibility for his participation in it. In total contrast, there were also numerous occasions when he would be the victim of slanderous, illogical and entirely fabricated accusations in the press, which he habitually shrugged off without comment. As the restored Bourbon monarchy stumbled to its demise in the 1820s with increasingly harsh press laws accompanying its collapse, Talleyrand would become an even greater advocate of freedom of the press. Inevitably, the government paid no heed to his wise policies.

Talleyrand was motivated by money. When he was in positions of power, he augmented his salary thanks to under-the-table "sweeteners" with foreign representatives who expected to have their interests pursued as a priority. He was also known to syphon off part of any national revenues passing through his office. It was a period of corruption and his justification for this unlawful practice was that his salary was not sufficient reward for the services he provided and—one may add—to maintain the profligate lifestyle he conducted. The money was no sooner acquired than spent, for he lived in a multitude of rented mansions, purchased property, offered extravagant banquets to large numbers of people on a regular basis, habitually gambled and provided generous pensions and dowries to members of his family, as well as sharing the bounty with other long-term political acquaintances. Furthermore, because of his physical infirmity, it was always necessary, when travelling around Paris and elsewhere, for him to possess a private horse-drawn carriage.

When referring to the huge sums of money passing through his hands, authors refer to "livres" (everyday money up to 1795), the "louis" (= 20 livres) and the "golden louis" (= 24 livres). Following the Revolution and after some experiments, the "franc" was reintroduced as the coinage in 1795. It had a value of just over 1 livre, having previously been the currency in earlier times but had gone out of use during the seventeenth century. In the ten years on either side of 1800 both of these terms were employed indiscriminately and are used in this way in this text. Thus, in 1800 a salary or a gift of 100,000 francs or livres would give a modern figure of very approximately £350,000 or US$450,000. More than 200 years later, it is meaningless to state what these figures actually represented in purchasing power but they are sufficient to indicate that we are dealing with very considerable sums of money. It is remarkable to note that already in the early nineteenth century, government revenues could be counted in billions.

Talleyrand's clubfoot gave rise to one of his many nicknames corresponding to the general public's view of his reputation for venality, cynicism, corruption—and survival: "the limping devil". At different moments and often at the same time he was detested in France: by the Royalists and foreign governments who considered him a dangerous revolutionary; by the Republican authorities, who took him for a Royalist and counter-revolutionary; by the Roman Catholic Church, who scorned him as a renegade bishop and role model for delinquent priests; and by the Bonapartists, who believed—with good reason—that he was a traitor. At the very same moment in February 1793, he was banished from England as an international anti-Royalist revolutionary and facing arrest in France as an enemy of the Revolution and supporter of the French Royal Family. This can be contrasted with the attitude of many important political figures who admired him as a realistic and visionary foreign minister, seeking equilibrium and prosperity on a European scale. Like many of the greatest politicians, throughout his life he pursued his own policies independent of political parties and of tidal changes in regimes.

Inevitably, the events of these years triggered changes in society, culture, customs and fashion setting in motion the advances of the nineteenth century. From our twenty-first century perspective, it is noteworthy that some of the customs that society found normal at that time would now appear strange, even deeply shocking or criminal, to the modern reader. For instance, many of the women appearing in this story were married at the age of 13, 14 or 15, sometimes with much older men but also sometimes to boys of their own age, typically being obliged to accept an expedient family decision without having any say in the matter. For royal families, this was a common practice to cement political alliances, while for the aristocracy it was frequently associated with the very crudest financial transactions for these girls were often heiresses in possession of large dowries. Nowadays, even taking into consideration that some people mature earlier and some later, such girls (and boys) would be considered as juveniles and very far from being of a marriageable age. As they grew up, it was not uncommon for their lives to fall apart as they developed into people who shared nothing in common with their partners. The outcomes could easily be predicted: upon reaching adulthood, they would often have experienced great unhappiness involving the breakdown of their relationship, separation and divorce. The resulting rate of unwanted pregnancies, women dying in childbirth and infant mortality was perfectly appalling by modern standards. It should also be understood that, in some of these arranged marriages, the couple had lots of children and—as they say—lived happily ever after.

A second accepted form of behaviour that arrests our attention was the belief that duelling was a very fitting way to settle a dispute. There are events described in this book where duels take place leading to the death, one could even say the murder, of one of the participants. Among the most tragic was Alexander Hamilton dying at the hands of Aaron Burr, both of whom Talleyrand counted among his friends. Contemporary literature describes numerous other cases of people being killed or mutilated in duels, quite independent of any system of justice, but they have only been included on these pages when they directly affected Talleyrand's story. Nevertheless, it is striking to note that there were two duels involving serving British Prime Ministers mentioned in this narrative: William Pitt faced George Tierney on Putney Heath in 1798, while Arthur Wellesley, the Duke of Wellington, challenged

George Finch-Hatton, Earl of Winchelsea, on Battersea Fields in 1829. In some cases, reason intervened and the protagonists fired their pistols harmlessly into the air or decided that it would be undignified to fight to the death—such as Tsar Alexander I and Clemens Metternich's quarrel over the Duchess von Sagan in 1814. Due to Talleyrand suffering from a clubfoot, this handicap must have rendered him immune from such incidents for at no time was he involved in a duel (although the same is not true for the members of his family). It was also very much his practice not to confront adversaries but to manipulate them to his advantage.

It was a time when society was dominated by men while women, if we adopt Napoleon's attitude, were expected to accept a subordinate role and to bear children. Nevertheless, this period brought to the fore a series of extraordinary women who marked this epoch with their personalities. Amid many names mentioned on the following pages, one could draw attention to Marie-Antoinette, the Princess Liéven, Juliette Récamier, the Countess de Brionne, Aimée de Coigny, Félicité de Genlis and, of course, Dorothea, the Duchess de Dino. What these ladies had in common was that they managed to dominate and out-perform their menfolk on the social and political scene. However, the most outstanding representative is the troubling personality of Germaine de Staël, whose convoluted existence was intertwined with that of Talleyrand in a number of different ways. She was renowned on a European scale as a leading thinker of the age, an idealist whose actions and words confounded society's norms of female decorum and male authority.

Although I have not dwelt on the battles that took place, Talleyrand's lifetime included a period of twenty-two years of almost uninterrupted warfare, leading to terrible loss of life during the fighting and, particularly, in its aftermath. Estimates of the casualties during the Revolutionary and Napoleonic Wars vary so wildly that there does not seem to be any point in citing figures. However, what is clear is that hundreds of thousands of soldiers, sailors and civilians died during this period and that knowledge of hygiene was so rudimentary that the vast majority of them died not on the battlefield but from infected wounds, exposure and disease. On this subject, it is interesting to note that, after the disastrous French retreat from Moscow in the autumn of 1812, huge numbers—the figure of 150,000 is mentioned—of French soldiers who were cut off in Russia actually survived as prisoners-of-war or as beggars.

A situation that will face the English-speaking reader is the nature of French aristocratic names and titles—one might mention Lucy Dillon who became Mme La Marquess de La Tour du Pin-Gouvernet. More particularly, changes occurred to a person's title as they advanced in their careers—by way of example, we can cite Louis Stanislas Xavier, Count de Provence, who became "Monsieur" (the king's brother and heir to the throne) and finally Louis XVIII. Although I have tried to limit the occasions for confusion, the reader's attention is drawn to the need to take note of these progressions. Talleyrand himself changed his appellation completely five times during his lifetime. Some nationals of the British Isles will also be disappointed by the abundant references to England and the English; this is the way Talleyrand and members of the French Government of that time referred to the country and its inhabitants located on the other side of the Channel. I have also made a number of decisions on typographical difficulties and French spellings. This concerns particularly a person's rank (count, baron, duke, prince, etc.), which is written in English followed by their family or noble name written in the language of the country he/she comes from, hence the Duke d'Artois, Prince von Trauttmansdorff, Countess Tyszkiewicz, etc.

Following the French Revolution, there were many admirable efforts to sweep away the paraphernalia of the *Ancien Régime*—some more successful than others. The Republican Government sought, among other reforms, to decimalize the currency, the system of weights and measures, as well as the calendar, achieving success with the first two. As regards the decimal calendar, in September 1792, the Constituent Assembly decided that all public documents would in future be dated Year I, etc., and beginning in late 1793 to the end of 1804, the French Republican calendar was used. It has become standard practice for the major historical events of this eleven-year period in France to be expressed according to this calendar. Thus, for example, Napoleon's coup d'état is known as *18 Brumaire Year VIII*. This remarkable system consisted of twelve months, each divided into three ten-day weeks called *décades*. The tenth day, *décadi*, replaced Sunday as the day of rest. The five or six extra days needed to approximate the solar year were placed at the end of each year and called complementary days. The month is divided into three "weeks" of ten days. Each day was divided into ten hours, each hour into 100 decimal minutes and each minute into 100 decimal seconds. For better or for worse, Napoleon abandoned this system at the beginning of 1805.

How does one concentrate the events of daily life over several decades into a coherent narrative? Each day of each person mentioned in this book would be filled with conversations and incidents that they obviously found so passionately important and interesting that many of them wrote them down—one has only to read the voluminous diaries of the Baron de Vitrolles, Lucy Dillon and Gouverneur Morris to understand the situation. There may be times when quite lengthy conversations are recorded verbatim, while in other cases months or even years are dismissed in a couple of sentences or are simply ignored. I have been guided by the authors mentioned in the bibliography to select the important events in Talleyrand's life, but the final selection is my own.

In his novel *A Tale of Two Cities,* Charles Dickens contrasts the social and political events taking place in Paris and London during (and prior to) the events of the French Revolution. Dickens draws disconcerting contrasts between the two cities, from the leafy, sunlit lanes of Soho in London to the turmoil of denunciation, arbitrary arrest, the semblance of a trial and summary execution at the height of the Reign of Terror in Paris. Dickens presents both the cruel indifference of the French upper-classes prior to the Revolution and the subsequent blood-thirsty reaction of the lower-classes in equally damning terms. Through his simplified version, his story portrays an avaricious aristocracy that shamelessly oppresses the nation's poor while the revolutionaries take their revenge through pitiless capital punishment on a massive scale. Talleyrand made sure that he was absent from France during the Terror for, as a proud member of the aristocracy, there is no doubt whatsoever that he would have perished. However, living in the Age of Enlightenment, Talleyrand realized that profound political and social reform was desperately required—but how was it to be achieved? Ultimately, Dickens agrees with Talleyrand that the actions of the French Revolution were so far-reaching and horrifying that they eventually became hostile to its own ends. It took more than 150 years for France to find once again a strong and stable form of government.

During the 1770s, France had tried to undermine England by supporting the American revolutionaries in their War of Independence. The British had their revenge when the debt-ridden French monarchy collapsed following the recall of its parliament after a gap of 175 years, while English merchants conducted a roaring trade with the newly independent United States. As a result, from 1789 to 1815 there was a tussle to seize control of the rudder of the French ship of state by different political factions reflected in wild changes of course as different power groups eclipsed each other, often resorting to the guillotine, the firing squad or banishment to Guyana (an almost certain death) to enforce their power. Sometimes those in charge would be seemingly incorruptible politicians, like Robespierre, who nevertheless got it all hopelessly wrong; at other times, there were immoral leaders, like Barras, whose time in government was not admired then or now. The latter-day policies of the belligerent Emperor Napoleon were no exception. If there is one lesson to be learned from all this turmoil—still true today—it is that some radical factions sincerely, earnestly and passionately believed that they had that magic to defend the only true and right policies for the successful government of the nation and yet, with the advantage of hindsight, one can see that they were wretchedly, despairingly and ridiculously misguided. These situations can be contrasted with Talleyrand's approach, which from 1789 to the 1830s sought a France living within its natural frontiers and governed by a constitutional monarchy controlled by a democratically elected two-chamber parliament that encouraged peace, prosperity, education, justice and freedom—but rarely was his advice followed.

CHAPTER I
EARLY DAYS

Charles-Maurice de Talleyrand-Périgord was born at 4 Rue Garancière on 2 February 1754 in what is now the sixth *arrondissement* of Paris. He was the second son of Charles-Daniel, a 20-year-old colonel in the king's grenadiers. His mother, Alexandrine d'Antigny, aged 26, was a lady-in-waiting at the court of Versailles, ruled by the shy, secretive and lecherous King Louis XV. The baby was baptized the same day in the parish church of Saint-Sulpice, which lay immediately opposite the family home. The name Talleyrand was a derivative of the word *taille-rang* [he who cuts a swathe through the enemy's ranks], supposedly awarded to one of his warrior ancestors in historic times. The first part of his given name, Charles, had been a male first name in the family over many generations. Since Maurice de Saxe's victory at the Battle of Fontenoy in 1745, it was the mode at that time to give the name Maurice to boys in military families—the Talleyrand family succumbed to the fashion. His closest companions usually addressed him by this name.

While the family proclaimed its origins and its ancient alliances lost in a feudal past, contemporary genealogists threw doubt on the continuity of the name, particularly "Périgord" which seems to have gone out of use for some 200 years in the mediaeval period. Not long before his death Talleyrand commissioned a genealogist called Saint-Allais to establish the true family tree, which he accomplished to the titleholder's satisfaction, only for the proposals to be thrown out almost immediately as nonsense by experts. Nevertheless, Charles-Maurice never concealed the pride he found in being the descendant of a supposedly ancient and noble family that had produced civil servants fulfilling high offices for the crown for generations. In 1817, he hung a series of (fictitious) portraits of his ancestors in his country château starting with a certain Adalbert de Périgord who lived in the tenth century.

Although the family name was Talleyrand, his parents' noble title was the Count and Countess de Périgord. Charles-Daniel and Alexandrine considered themselves as part of the high aristocracy who, since time immemorial, revered the royal family and perpetuated the ancient traditions at the court of Versailles, but the wealth that would normally be associated with their rank eluded them. Their fortune had drastically waned in the second half of the eighteenth century. Charles-Daniel was 16 when he married 22-year-old Alexandrine; he was not rich but his lineage was impeccable and his career prospects good. They formed a happy couple, belonging to the small number of families at the court of Louis XV who occupied the limelight. Although Alexandrine brought with her a modest dowry and her family owned a château in the countryside, maintaining a standard of living that required a mansion, servants and a carriage in Paris was a strain on the family's resources. His father's step-brother, Gabriel-Marie de Talleyrand, was a highly placed army officer who enjoyed the king's confidence. Charles-Daniel also followed a classical military career at the royal court, including in 1759 becoming an equerry to the Dauphin, the heir to the throne, well known for his rigorous conservatism. However, Gabriel-Marie rose high in the court hierarchy and gained considerable wealth, while Talleyrand's father Charles-Daniel did not. The family's total income was only one-third of what Charles-Daniel's brother Alexandre-Angélique, Archbishop of Reims, spent on his kitchen and stables. From time to time, Louis XV's attention was drawn to the financial plight of "this poor family" with the result that they were awarded handouts from the royal purse. This largesse was irregular, so that Alexandrine was forever writing to her mother about their parlous financial position. When Charles-Daniel died in 1788, it would be his saintly brother Alexandre-Angélique who discharged the greater part of his debts.

A further blow to their finances was that Louis, the Dauphin as the heir to the throne was known, in whose entourage Charles-Daniel served, died in 1765 and his wife two years later, weakening the Talleyrand family's position at the court of Versailles. Alexandrine, with the reputation of a busybody, sought to become a lady-in-waiting to the new Dauphine—Marie-Antoinette—but the official post was actually occupied by her mother-in-law, the Marquess de Talleyrand, who would not die until 1788. So, at this time she was merely a "friend" of Marie-

Antoinette and, when off duty, occupied a tiny apartment in the attic of the palace. There were always hierarchical scuffles at court to obtain the favour of the royal family and by October 1782 relations with Queen Marie-Antoinette had deteriorated. Charles-Maurice would never forget his parents' money difficulties and, when he was in a position of power, made sure that his brothers and his nephews benefited from rapid and financially beneficial promotions in the military hierarchy.

To the high aristocracy in the middle of the eighteenth century there were two opposing forms of conduct concerning the upbringing of children—family pride and parental neglect. Small children mattered little and often died in infancy. The long-term duty of upper-class parents to their children came, if they survived childhood, through finding positions at court and arranging good marriages—both of which might bring them wealth—but this would not happen at least until they became teenagers. Jean-Jacques Rousseau did not write the ground-breaking *Émile* until 1762 and it would be another thirty years before the austere attitude to parenting young children would evolve. As the Prince de Ligne observed: "It was fashionable in this world to be neither a good father, nor a good husband." While aristocratic parents sought to promote the wealth and honour of every family member, they did not believe that this would be achieved by close involvement during early childhood. Talleyrand states that he did not remember meeting his parents until he was 4 years old and then rarely slept under the same roof. He claims in his—not particularly reliable (doubt has even been thrown on their authenticity)—memoirs that he was placed in the care of a lady who lived in the suburbs and that one day he fell off a chest of drawers and broke his foot leaving him lame for the rest of his life. It took until 1988 for this legend to be definitively dismissed. Examination of his shoes preserved at the Château de Valençay showed the left foot to be abnormally long, the right leg truncated with an iron support designed to be attached to it—he was born with a clubfoot. We also know that, when he was in his 60s, many people attended the ceremonial of his *levée*— the public ceremony of rising from the bed and getting dressed in the morning—with one of his colleagues noting that "He showed for everybody to see the claws that served as his feet." This physical deformity was a blow to the family's prestige that the parents were reluctant to admit. A contemporary portrait of his military uncle Gabriel-Marie suffering from exactly the same problem indicates that the condition was hereditary.

Individuals in aristocratic families were expected, often compelled, to make sacrifices that would lead to benefits for the whole family. When his elder brother Alexandre died suddenly as a child, Charles-Maurice became the rightful heir to the family estate—however financially ill-endowed. The eldest son of an aristocratic family was destined for a military career. Even though his uncle Gabriel-Marie had been born with a clubfoot and achieved the rank of lieutenant-general in the king's army, Charles-Maurice was not considered suitable material for the same profession. According to the conventions of the *Ancien Régime,* children's careers were decided by their parents and in Charles-Maurice's case, despite being the eldest child, as their principal heir he would not benefit from the rights of primogeniture as an officer in the army but would rather be directed to the priesthood. Since throughout his diplomatic life he pursued policies of pacifism on a European scale, this decision by his parents was most fortuitous, although at the time it appeared to deny him his rightful inheritance. Charles-Maurice had two younger brothers, Archambaud and Boson, who lived at home with their parents in a perfectly normal family setting and who both grew up to serve without distinction in the military. Their elder brother must have asked himself for what reason he was treated differently and excluded from the household. The only account of his childhood that we possess is taken from Talleyrand's memoirs, where it is believed that he exaggerated parental indifference for we know that his mother took him on several occasions for treatment of his legs at the spa town of Bourbon-l'Archambault.

According to these same memoirs, at about the age of 4 he was living with his carer, in a suburban neighbourhood and hobbling around on a crutch when one of his sea-faring uncles became curious as to his whereabouts. Since his older brother Alexandre had now died and the younger children were not yet born, Charles-Maurice was the family's only child, apparently living in isolation and squalor. This uncle rescued him and took him to the family home to meet his father and mother again, requiring them to provide an explanation and an adequate solution about the neglect of their son, the heir to the family's name. It was very fashionable at that time to consider a period spent in the countryside as positive for the health and, given the recent death of his elder brother, Charles-Maurice was shipped off to stay with his great-grandmother, the Princess de Chalais, who lived in the Périgord region in what is now the Charente *département* of France. Accompanied by his nurse, Mlle Charlemagne, it took them seventeen days to reach the Château de Chalais by an old bone-shaker stagecoach—a journey that nowadays can be completed in a few hours.

The recently widowed Marie-Françoise de Rochechouart-Mortemart was 72 years old in 1758 when her great grandson arrived. He would live with her for almost two years in a kind of enchanted idyll that would make a tremendous impression on him. For the first time in his life a member of his family loved him and he blossomed. "She made me aware of a kind of gentleness that I had never experienced before. She was the first woman in my family who showed me tenderness ... I liked her very much. Her memory is very dear to me." Marie-Françoise had been a lady-in-waiting to Louis XV's wife, Marie Leszczynska, at the Château de Versailles and she ran her home according to the same courtly routine reminiscent of a bygone era. She reigned over a number of elderly retainers who each carried out their functions with a grand dignity. Every Sunday, Charles-Maurice would accompany the Princess de Chalais and her entourage to church to celebrate mass sitting on a small chair by her side next to her personal pew. Back at the sombre château, he would assist the great lady while she said a few kind words, distributing medicines and dressings to those members of the local community who were not well. Here he learned that the cure for a head cold was to ingurgitate warm water through the nose and to snort it out into a bowl—a practice he would adopt throughout his life, even in the presence of the most noble company! The rural people of Chalais showed affection for his family in a setting that had remained unchanged for generations. It was here that he learned to read and write and even to speak some of the local dialect. Here too he learned what it was to be a representative of a proud noble family, impervious to public opinion, insults, flattery, threats and revolutions. Decades later at Valençay, he would seek to emulate this court of good manners by creating this miniature and charming world around him.

And then it all changed. In August 1760, the Bordeaux stage coach picked him and Mlle Charlemagne up dropping them off in Paris after the same seventeen-day journey. A servant of the family met them and took the 6-year-old Charles-Maurice straight to a boarding school called the Collège Harcourt, only a stone's throw from his family home. At Harcourt he would become associated with Auguste de Choiseul-Gouffrier, two years older than himself, and a nephew of the Duke de Choiseul, one of Louis XV's ministers. They would remain friends until Auguste's death in 1817. He would also remain faithful to one of his teachers, M. Langlois; sixty-eight years later his name appears on a list of guests invited to Talleyrand's Parisian residence! By then, Langlois was an agreeable old soul to whom Charles-Maurice paid a subsistence allowance. During these years at college, he was allowed to visit his parents, the Count and Countess of Périgord, once a week for Sunday lunch in the company of M. Langlois. Parental indifference was reflected in mediocre results at school.

While at the Collège Harcourt, Charles-Maurice caught smallpox, the disfiguring disease that would kill Louis XV some years later. He was taken to the house of a woman who cared for the sick on the nearby rue Saint-Jacques. He was very lucky; smallpox was a killer disease. When he was cured, his face had not been disfigured as happened to so many, among them his future political partner Mirabeau.

Another nasty surprise awaited him: "I understood that my parents had decided, according to what they considered as the family's interest, to direct me towards an occupation for which I had no disposition." This profession was to be a member of the clergy. As he mentions several times in his memoirs: "My feet made me a priest" and, one could add, threw him into the arms of the French Revolution and Napoleon Bonaparte. His parents were keen to point out to him that the high clergy of the Catholic church benefited from great wealth, respect, luxury and rapid advancement—and that their decision was final. All he had to do was to learn the rites of the Christian rituals. It was also well known that the church was a worthy dumping ground for superfluous sons of the nobility, at the same time providing them with financial independence. Inevitably, it would permit his younger brother Archambaud to assume the legacy of the eldest child—a military career. Never did he display any form of reproach towards his brothers or his brothers' children, although he felt that his parents had made a great error.

Talleyrand's uncle Alexandre-Angélique de Talleyrand-Périgord had already become a highly respected minister of the church occupying at that time the role of Bishop coadjutor to the Archbishop of Reims. He willingly followed a textbook career in the church, which he would pursue for several decades into the future, eventually becoming head of the French Roman Catholic church as Archbishop of Paris. Uncle Alexandre-Angélique obviously believed that nepotism was not a sin. Among his many functions, the Archbishop of Reims at that time, Cardinal Charles-Antoine de La Roche-Aymon, was responsible for distributing a number of ecclesiastical benefices and passed much of its administration to his assistant. The Archbishopric of Reims was one of the richest in France and, when La Roche-Aymon came to the end of his life, Alexandre-Angélique was designated as his successor. He had already begun to think about who would be his own heir. Of the children of his brothers and sister, at this time there was only one whose intellectual ability stood out—Charles-Maurice.

Without further explanation from his parents, when he completed his studies at the Collège Harcourt at the age of 15, Charles-Maurice spent 1769 in the cathedral of Reims bearing the name of Abbé de Périgord as a novice attendant to his uncle. Outwardly, Charles-Maurice was a handsome youth: blond, fresh-faced, well-mannered. Because of his clubfoot, he often stood still and held himself modestly to one side, which was considered a sign of merit in the ecclesiastical world. It was during this year that he met for the first time Félicité de Genlis, also known as Mme de Sillery, who would later become one of his mistresses and then a political companion throughout his life. It was said of her: "To avoid the scandal of flirtation, she gave way easily." During his residency in Reims, he would live either in the archbishop's palace or in his uncle's residence at the Abbey de Hautvillers, where Dom Pérignon had contributed to the development of the Champagne region's sparkling wine. Here he would live in noble style being served at table by servants in the company of eloquent companions and even be graced from time to time by the presence of his parents. However, he had not chosen an ecclesiastical career, was not convinced by the religious ceremonies conducted by La Roche-Aymon and, as a teenager, was indifferent to the opulent standard of living. At the age of 16, he found the ways of the world repugnant. He was dissatisfied about the discord between what was being preached, what his parents expected of him and his sincere unease with the empty hypocrisy taking place before his eyes.

Despite the many dramatic events over the next forty years that would send their careers down different paths, the nephew always displayed the greatest respect for his uncle's goodness and unswerving devotion to his ecclesiastic duties, while Alexandre-Angélique remained a faithful ally of Charles-Maurice in the most contentious circumstances. The church evidently presented opportunities for an ambitious young man seeking the fast-track to wealth and it is clear that for his uncle, for his parents and for himself his conviction about conducting religious services was not the primary consideration. Life in the church was not as restricted as religious duties might suggest and many bishops ignored the sacred vows of celibacy. Indifferent to church practices, resigned to his parents' wishes and not wishing to be the cause of a family scandal, he agreed to take the next step—to enter the seminary of Saint-Sulpice located equally close to his family home in Paris.

Except for his visit to Chalais and the year in Reims, Charles-Maurice would spend his entire youth in the same quarter of Paris: near the Rue Garancière where he was born; at the Collège Harcourt in the Rue de la Harpe; and in the Saint Sulpice seminary in the Rue Vieux-Colombier. He was swallowed up by the ecclesiastical world towards which he had been directed but for which he had no vocation. The young aristocrats who attended Saint-Sulpice wore black knee-breeches with black silk frock coats and were destined to become bishops—and wealthy bishops at that. He soon learned to educate himself by reading the works of historians and explorers in the college library: "I devoured the most revolutionary books I could find, feeding on history, rebellion, sedition and upheavals galore." He claims in his memoirs that he was unhappy and hid his sadness behind a façade of reserve. However, in other conversations with colleagues he paints a different picture saying: "When I want to be happy, I think of Saint-Sulpice and recall the memories of that time." It is true that he was among a group of young men of his own age and from his own social strata. Although it was walled in on all sides, the seminary of Saint Sulpice was located in the fashionable left-bank district of Saint Germain and there were no restrictions to prevent the students from stepping out onto the busy streets full of traffic, shops, townhouses and government ministries. His influential uncle managed to obtain a special dispensation so that he passed his bachelor's degree ahead of his companions. On 22 September 1774, at the age of 20 (even though the minimum age was 22), he obtained his *baccalaureate* in theology. He would forever be grateful to his teachers, ensuring that two of them were awarded bishoprics following Napoleon's Concordat with the Pope in 1801. After the Bourbon Restoration in 1814, Abbé Charles Mannay, one of his tutors, had his own private apartment in Talleyrand's town house.

In 1771, at the age of 18, he discovered love. He had noticed at the church of Saint Sulpice a beautiful young lady whose air of modesty pleased him. After mass one day there was a shower of rain, so he offered her half of his umbrella. She did not refuse and allowed him to hold her hand while descending the steps of the church. She lived close by in the Rue Férou near the Jardin du Luxembourg and he accompanied her to her apartment, the rent of which was paid by a rich gentleman friend. His relationship with Dorothée Dorinville, a young actress at the Comédie Française whose stage name was "Luzy", lasted for two years. Dorothée was of Jewish origin but had been brought up as a Christian. She played small roles at the Comédie Française yet had no disposition for the theatre. They had something in common; they were both obliged to participate in activities in which they were not really interested. Talleyrand did not bother to hide this romantic liaison, walking with his girlfriend through the streets beneath the seminary's windows, while at the same time making it clear that he had no particular vocation for religion either. His superiors became upset with this relationship and his attitude, considering excluding him from the college but hesitated to do so. He came from a noble family that did not merit being humiliated and the scandal would have been a terrible blow to the prestige of his worthy uncle, a former pupil destined for an impressive career in the church. Furthermore, with or without his mistress, his parents had decided he would be a priest so they closed their eyes to this relationship. The fact that he was allowed to pursue and complete his studies at the seminary would lead to unimaginable complications that lasted until his dying day: "They forced me to become a priest; they will live to regret it."

Talleyrand had been ordained as a junior priest on 1 April 1775 and was now officially referred to as the Abbé de Périgord. No member of his family, not even his mother, was present when he took Holy Orders listening to the sacramental phrase: "Until now you have been free… Once you have received this order you cannot break the commitments and you will be for evermore required to serve God." A few days later he received the post of sub-deacon of Paris with the official name of Carolus Mauricius de Talleyrand-Perigor [sic]. The die was cast for the next fourteen years. During this time, he lived a life of a young man at complete liberty in Paris.

King Louis XV having died the previous year of smallpox, the coronation of Louis XVI took place in the Reims Cathedral on 11 June 1775, where the kings of France had been crowned for a thousand years. As a member of the court, Talleyrand's father was honoured by fulfilling one of the principal ceremonial roles. His uncle Alexandre-Angélique, assistant to the Archbishop of Reims, also played a central part. Here, the cynical Abbé de Périgord saw for the first time the king's brothers: Louis Stanislas Xavier, Count de Provence—thirty years hence he would conduct and lose a battle of wills with the devious Louis XVIII; and the awkward Duke d'Artois, whose coronation as Charles X Charles-Maurice would attend fifty years later. Among the other royalty present were Philippe, the Duke de Chartres, later to become the Duke d'Orléans and, later still, during the Revolution, after adopting the name of Philippe-Égalité, he would sign the death warrant of the king they were now crowning. Nevertheless, in the treacherous political arena of 1793, Philippe would himself die on the guillotine. There was the Prince de Condé with a 3-year-old boy at his side, the Duke d'Enghien, the future victim of a grim Napoleonic tragedy in which Talleyrand would play a role so equivocal that it would still be haunting him half a century in the future.

Although the Abbé de Périgord did not wish to miss the coronation and had had to pull a few strings with his uncle to find a place, he was unimpressed by the grandeur of the ceremony establishing Louis XVI as

God's instrument on Earth. What did particularly attract his attention though were three graceful and perfumed young ladies from the royal court: the Duchess de Fitz-James, the Duchess de Luynes and the Viscountess de Laval, all renowned for their intelligence and beauty. He would eventually become very close friends with all three of them and, decades later, they remained among his most devoted disciples.

His friendship with these ladies would give Charles-Maurice his entry into high Parisian society. Laure, the Duchess de Fitz-James, had been married young to the Duke de Fitz-James, the great grandson of the exiled British King James II. She was the same age as Charles-Maurice and would soon be appointed as a lady-in-waiting to Queen Marie-Antoinette. Likewise, Guyonne-Élisabeth-Josèphe de Montmorency married the Duke de Luynes when she was 13. At the age of 20 in 1775, she became a lady-in-waiting to the queen and remained in this position until 1789. While the Duchess de Luynes was "built like a gendarme,... with a voice like a stevedore and the attitudes of a man", she was inseparable from her sister-in-law the Princess d'Henin, Viscountess de Laval, who was petite, feminine and graceful. Mme de Laval was the mother of Mathieu de Montmorency, who would later become a very good friend of both Mme de Staël and Talleyrand. All three of the young ladies he saw in Reims cathedral hosted salons in Paris, the one held by the Duchess de Fitz-James taking place on the Rue Saint-Florentin in a mansion that would many decades later become the Hôtel Talleyrand. However, the most popular destination for the intelligentsia was the salon of the Duchess de Luynes on the Rue Saint-Dominique, who later ran her own printing presses there. The only one of these ladies who was indisputably Talleyrand's mistress was the Viscountess de Laval. The Prince de Ligne described Parisian society before the Revolution: "Ceaselessly one looked for new conquests."

As we have seen, like Voltaire, Talleyrand was partial to the company of women. Beyond the worth of their companionship, they could also be devoted allies when pursuing one's ambitions. The most fashionable ladies played a role in politics, not necessarily in the court of the king at Versailles but in their Parisian salons where French society, politics and court gossip were analysed in great detail. In the company of a select circle of friends in their own drawing rooms, they exercised influence over the lives of men and the fate of nations independent of and often in opposition to that of the royal court. Each salon was a political and social world in its own right and Charles-Maurice frequented a myriad of them filled with light and varied feminine forms. In the more noble league of salons his company was also appreciated. His presence, his charisma and his repartee made him welcome in these mansions where he would enjoy the company of delightful young women, some of whom would become his mistresses.

In navigating Parisian society, one of the most fashionable places to be seen was the salon of Louise de Rohan, the Countess de Brionne, the very incarnation of eighteenth-century elegance and one of the most attractive and intelligent ladies in society. In Louis XV's court she had been a close friend of the king's mistress, Mme de Pompadour. She had also been the mistress of her cousin, Cardinal Rohan, and then of the Duke de Choiseul, following him into banishment at Chanteloup. Except for an ambiguous remark by Talleyrand's manservant Courtiade many years later, we can never be sure of the exact association between Talleyrand and Mme de Brionne. His reputation as a sophisticated pleasure-lover may have led him briefly into the beds of the Countess de Brionne, her two daughters Anne Charlotte and Marie Josèphe, as well as a stream of other married ladies including two who will later play a fundamental role in Talleyrand's life: Adélaïde de Flahaut and Germaine de Staël. What is certain is that he became the lover of Mme de Brionne's daughter-in-law, the Princess de Vaudémont, who would remain his most intimate correspondent until her death in 1832. Mme de Brionne admired the young Abbé de Périgord so much that she took it into her head that he should become a cardinal, but Marie-Antoinette and Louis XVI thought her enthusiasm was misplaced and this suggestion even left his own parents cold. Their unfavourable attitude is easily understood because he frequented the most disreputable salons and the most notorious gambling dens, whereas his attendance at his post in Reims had been sporadic and at no time did he conduct religious services—with consequences that we shall discover. Due to his involvement in the French Revolution, his relationship with the Countess de Brionne would be among the rare ones with his female acquaintances that eventually turned sour, although he visited her before she died in Vienna in 1815.

Mme de Brionne would play a supporting role in "the Affair of the Queen's Necklace". In 1772, Louis XV had decided to make a special gift of a spectacular diamond necklace to his mistress Mme du Barry. It would take the jewellers several years and a great deal of investment to amass an appropriate set of diamonds. In the meantime, Louis XV died of smallpox and Mme du Barry was banished from court. A confidence trickster, Jeanne de La Motte, conceived a plan to use the necklace to gain wealth and royal patronage. In March 1785, Jeanne became the mistress of Cardinal Rohan, a former French ambassador to the court of Vienna. Queen Marie-Antoinette disapproved of the cardinal, holding him responsible for spreading rumours about her behaviour at Versailles to her formidable mother, the Austrian Empress Maria Theresa. Borrowing large sums of money from Rohan, Jeanne de la Motte gained entrance to the French royal court and persuaded the credulous Rohan that she had become a close acquaintance of Marie-Antoinette and benefited from the queen's favour. She took advantage of the cardinal's gullibility to send him letters supposedly written by the queen, to which he replied. The tone of these letters soon became very passionate, and the cardinal begged Jeanne to arrange a secret tryst with the queen. The supposed meeting took place one dark night in August 1784, where the imprudent cardinal met a prostitute whom he believed to be Marie-Antoinette. Meanwhile, the jewellers resolved to use Jeanne as an agent to sell their valuable but unsold necklace to a member of the aristocracy. Imitating Marie-Antoinette's handwriting, Jeanne sent several letters to Rohan requesting him to purchase Louis XV's necklace on the queen's behalf. A little while later, Rohan negotiated the purchase of the necklace for 2 million livres to be paid in instalments. Claiming to have royal authorization, he showed the jewellers the letters he had received in the queen's handwriting. Rohan took the necklace to Jeanne's house where a man, whom the foolish cardinal believed to be the queen's valet, took possession of it. The diamond necklace was promptly broken up by the swindlers and its parts sold on the black markets of Paris and London. Having received no payment the jewellers complained to Marie-Antoinette, who told them that she knew nothing about it, having neither ordered nor received the necklace. The cardinal was arrested in the Hall of Mirrors at Versailles and taken to the Bastille. After a trial, he was declared innocent but Jeanne de La Motte and her accomplices were imprisoned. Even though Marie-Antoinette was herself entirely blameless, the affair of the diamond necklace was important in definitively tarnishing her public image. The affair reached the headlines at a time when Mme de Brionne, who had stood by her cousin, Cardinal Rohan, actively sought a cardinal's mitre for the Abbé de Périgord. Marie-Antoinette let the Austrian representative to the Vatican know that he should oppose any candidacy proposed by the Countess de Brionne.

Each salon had its own character. In some of them one would hear the latest gossip as if reading the morning news; elsewhere, the Abbé de Périgord was made welcome because of his witty banter and would be invited to stay for supper. He could be found in all those places where one meets well-informed, opinionated and polite company: around a fireplace, in a window alcove, at the supper table, in the back of a coach, in a bedroom. One's image and reputation were enhanced by being well dressed. Sometimes he wore his priestly garments and at other times city clothes consisting of a frock-coat, white waistcoat, chamois leather breeches, silk stockings, buckled shoes and a white cravat tucked high under the chin.

His education took place as much in the salons and boudoirs of these ladies as it had in the lecture halls of Saint-Sulpice and the Sorbonne. At the age of 21 he was the perfect example of the worldly priest, seen at the royal court and invited everywhere in Parisian society. He discovered that a priest who did not believe in God was a matter of small importance and raised no eyebrows in society if he was discreet, intelligent and well-mannered. He explored the boundary between flattery and impudence and found that the best way to be impertinent was "first of all to behave with the most exquisite politeness".

However, what is most relevant about his relationship with his female friends is the use that he would make of them later in the construction of his personality. The stories of his successes with women and the deliberately cultivated air of idleness and lack of seriousness tend to conceal the ambitious and hard-working young man. Forty years later, the Baron de Vitrolles describes Talleyrand's character: "He had all the weakness, the fragility and the softness of another sex. Temperamental in hatred as in friendship, in his preferences and his annoyances, there was in him much of the spoiled old flirt." Many of the lady friends that he had known before the Revolution, and not necessarily those who he had slept with, remained faithful to him—and he to them—until their deaths. To become lifelong friends needed qualities other than that of sexual conquest, such as discretion, affection, charming manners and most particularly shared intelligence. Many of the passions of 1787 would distil into devotion that would last a lifetime, so that forty years later Talleyrand would still be sharing gossip and reminiscences with his be-wigged, be-powdered and be-perfumed conquests of yesteryear.

Having diverted their eldest son into a career in the priesthood, the Talleyrand family focused all of its attention on his brother Archambaud. The plan was disarmingly simple: he would follow a military career as an officer and marry a rich heiress. One of Alexandrine's distant cousins had a daughter called Sabine de Sénozan de Viriville who, upon the death of both her parents, her uncle and her grandmother, had become one of the richest heiresses in France. After three months of negotiations, Archambaud, aged 17, married Sabine, not yet 16, at the beginning of 1779, with the marriage contract signed by King Louis XVI and Queen Marie-Antoinette. The marriage ceremony was conducted by Charles-Daniel's younger brother, Alexandre-Angélique, who had in the meantime advanced to the position of Archbishop of Reims. Archambaud's new wife was not good-looking, but this was considered no handicap when compared to her fortune. Archambaud himself was still an adolescent and had not yet found his true vocation in life: women, gambling and debt. The couple would have six children, of whom two boys and a girl would reach adulthood. Their two sons—Louis and Edmond, Talleyrand's nephews—will appear frequently on the pages to come, particularly and regrettably the latter.

Among the guests at Archambaud and Sabine's wedding, there were at least thirty titled members of the high aristocracy, but it is remarkable that the Abbé de Périgord was not among them. In his memoirs, he does not mention this major family event. When later he had become the undisputed head of the family, his absences will reveal a great deal about his feelings. In future years, as a diplomat, he will elevate silence to the level of a science, an extremely succinct manner of making one's opinion known. It would seem at this point as if Archambaud had stolen a march on him but the 24-year-old Charles-Maurice had boundless self-confidence and ambition.

CHAPTER II
THE BISHOP

In his *Memoirs* Talleyrand declares that life in Paris in the decades of the 1770s and 1780s was very agreeable. He belonged to a clique of aristocratic young men-about-town who pursued a carefree existence. With the gift of being able to parry his friends' questions with witty, elegant and nonchalant answers he became their leader. Among his privileges he also had access to the Château de Versailles where he formed part of Mme du Barry's entourage—one of King Louis XV's former mistresses and one of Marie-Antoinette's staunchest enemies.

The king had the power to bestow the revenue from wealthy church domains on suitable candidates, whose prospects were enhanced if they were actually present at Versailles. If the beneficiaries were fortunate enough to obtain one of these sinecures it meant that, without being obliged to perform any religious functions or even to be present at these churches, they would never be short of money again. In September 1775, at the age of 21, Louis XVI granted Charles-Maurice the living of the Abbey of Saint-Denis in Reims. The intervention of his uncle Alexandre-Angélique lay behind this windfall, the result of which was that he already earned more money than his parents. Alexandre-Angélique de Talleyrand-Périgord had clear ambitions to achieve what many of his religious companions were doing at this same time—to magnify the wealth and power of the Talleyrands by establishing a dynasty of family members in the most lucrative ecclesiastical posts. Besides, the Abbé de Périgord did not have to live in Reims since he could delegate his religious duties to a local *procureur général*. The outcome was that he would receive 18,000 livres per year for doing nothing (the actual amount far exceeded this official estimate)—his first substantial income on the way to a career that would see vast sums of cash pass through his hands. One may commend the fact that this money was used first of all to pay off his outstanding school fees to the Collège Harcourt, which his parents had somehow overlooked, as well as settling the remaining debt owed to his former teacher M. Langlois. While his uncle—a future archbishop—was revered as a saint in his own lifetime, to satisfy his ambition to establish a successor he would have to brave the remorseless delinquent behaviour of his nephew.

While Reims offered opportunities for financial reward, there was only one place where life was worth living and that was in Paris. Financially independent and free of responsibilities, the Abbé de Périgord found a house to let on a quiet and verdant corner of the Rue de Bellechasse just off the Boulevard Saint-Germain on the left bank of the River Seine. It was adjacent to the Hôtel de Guerchy rented by his parents, while his brother Archambaud and sister-in-law Sabine soon came to live nearby. His prestige as an ordained priest brought him closer to the members of his family and rather contradicts the impression in his memoirs of distancing himself from them. Mme de Genlis would soon become a neighbour in a new house built by the Duke d'Orléans, her former lover, in order for her to educate his children, the eldest of whom would in 1830 become Louis-Philippe, King of the French. Charles-Maurice furnished his house to his own taste, which inclined towards luxury, investing heavily in furniture and valuable books on literature, history and politics. In times of trouble, he could sell his books in order to obtain cash—there would be several such occasions.

It would be here that Talleyrand would entertain his friends with an early luncheon. They were mainly young, intelligent, confident, well-educated, debonair nobles who spoke their minds on any subject under the sun. This was the age of conversation and to talk well was then considered among the highest attributes that any person could possess. It was about this time that Joseph Courtiade became his valet and would remain so for the next fifty years. A year older than his master, he would be responsible for providing ample amounts of clean linen, as well as the necessities of a fine table. First among his guests was the acquaintance from his school days, Auguste de Choiseul-Gouffier, a traveller, scholar of Ancient Greece and a future French ambassador to the Ottoman Empire. Talleyrand described him as "noble, good, reliable, sincere" and would always address him in the warmest terms.

Then there was Louis, Count de Narbonne-Lara, a brilliant,

cultivated, charming, handsome politician, soldier and rake, an illegitimate son of Louis XV. He flitted through life like a charmed spirit with few moral principles, changing mistresses and political regimes carelessly. Talleyrand warned him not to commit himself passionately to liberal policies, nor to devote himself so wholeheartedly to the pursuit of women, but the flippant Narbonne was too fond of his own pleasure and ambitions to pay any attention.

A third friend at the Rue de Bellechasse was Armand Louis de Gontaut-Biron, another charming, good-looking, romantic philanderer and soldier of fortune. He was some years older than the others having already fought in the American War of Independence. In these days of relaxed morals, he was the lover of Aimée de Coigny, a famous beauty who will play a significant role in the Bourbon Restoration in 1814. Like Talleyrand, Biron would participate enthusiastically in the French Revolution, in his case as a general in the army, but would end up displeasing the Committee of Public Safety and dying nonchalantly on the guillotine on 31 December 1793.

There were also older guests at Talleyrand's breakfast table who nowadays would bear the label of "technocrats", two of whom he listened to with rapt attention. One was Pierre Samuel Du Pont, a fountain of ideas on business, industry, politics, physics, agriculture and the economy, and particularly how to combine them so as to multiply one's fortune a hundredfold. Later, Du Pont would emigrate to the United States where his youngest son founded a gunpowder factory that eventually became the manufacturing giant Dupont de Nemours. But the person whom Talleyrand admired unreservedly and from whom he learned the most was the Swiss banker Isaac Panchaud. After a chequered career during which he had made and lost several fortunes through financial speculation, Panchaud had learned a universal truth that Talleyrand would adopt as his creed: "Peace is the foundation of civilization because it encourages the accumulation of wealth through trade." As with Panchaud, throughout his life Talleyrand sought a constitutional monarchy for France (like that in the United Kingdom), peace and free trade. Panchaud was also in favour of the creation of a national bank and was aware that: "Financiers prosper when states are in trouble." He disagreed with everything that Jacques Necker, the French

Minister of Finance, had done during the American War of Independence. France was facing huge debts since Necker had borrowed heavily at rates of interest likely to bankrupt the government. Panchaud, on the other hand, favoured interest rates set as low as possible and keeping the money supply high. A subsequent Minister of Finance, the Abbé Louis, summed up Panchaud's philosophy: "A state that wants to borrow money must honour its debts, including its mistakes." Panchaud told anyone who was prepared to listen that, between France and England, the state that followed his financial scheme most closely would end up dominating the other. Panchaud was a risk-taker and speculated on currencies, bills of exchange, government credit and movements of capital. Following Panchaud's example, Charles-Maurice grasped the essentials of the financial markets and became a big player on the Parisian stock exchange. Sadly, Panchaud would die of natural causes on that fateful day, 14 July 1789—Bastille Day.

Nevertheless, the central character of proceedings at the Rue de Bellechasse was the politician Honoré Gabriel Riqueti, Count de Mirabeau. He was not at all like his other acquaintances since he was not rich, not charming and not at all good-looking, having been disfigured by smallpox. He was a passionate nobleman from the south of France who had already spent time in several French prisons. Mirabeau was, however, a brilliant orator bursting with charisma and energy who would later come to dominate the early proceedings of the French Revolution.

The cynical attitude of Charles-Maurice to religion was counterbalanced by the realisation that, for an ambitious young man, a religious career could become the stepping stone to the higher echelons of prosperity and political power—and not necessarily within the church itself. There were precedents in the form of Cardinals Mazarin and Richelieu, who had both been chief ministers ruling France in the early part of the seventeenth century. Many of the lesser prelates were wealthy rulers of their episcopal domains, while some bishops held political influence as the presidents of regional assemblies and were called upon to act as ambassadors and advisors to the king. Even Talleyrand's uncle Alexandre-Angélique would eventually live in princely comfort as the Archbishop of Reims in a sumptuous palace in that city, as well as possessing an elegant residence in Paris. It was obvious that the church was the shortest road to influence and opulence.

It was in his capacity as an ambitious priest that the Abbé de Périgord was nominated as one of the representatives for the province of Reims at the quinquennial Assembly of the French Church in March 1775. While his nomination was once more the work of his uncle, it is evident that the nephew's powerful intelligence, good looks and air of distinction made him stand out from the crowd, even if his faith in religion and his social life did not bear close examination. Following his official nomination as a canon in the Reims Cathedral, he became assistant to Monsignor de La Roche-Aymon, the president of the assembly appointed by the king. Among the purposes of the assembly was establishing the amount the church would pay to the royal purse each year in the form of a "free gift". Together with his colleague the Abbé Vogüé, Charles-Maurice's role was to defend ecclesiastical property from the perquisites of the royal tax collectors. Since some of the documentation dated from mediaeval times, the opportunities to claim ancient exemptions were many. In total contrast with his attitude some years later, the Abbé de Périgord's point of view at this time was that all clerical property should be immune from taxation. The assembly of the Roman Catholic Church in France considered his report on measures to protect the church's property as admirable and expressed confidence in his financial skills—far more than in his religious ones.

Despite his disdain for religion, at this stage the ambitious Charles-Maurice was only a sub-deacon and had not yet reached the level of a fully ordained priest. There was still time to give up the priesthood, but his religious career was unlikely to blossom until he was promoted to the rank of bishop. Benefiting from two letters that his uncle persuaded the king to write, he enrolled in the theology degree programme at the University of the Sorbonne. He passed his time in pursuit of the casual life of a bachelor in Paris. Participating with him on the university course were five young nobles of excellent pedigrees and abominable morals—to the horror of the faculty, they played cards during the lectures. A generation earlier, the philosopher Abbé Morellet had written that the studies at the Sorbonne "can well be regarded as extremely useless and little worthy of taking up men's time." In this atmosphere of "an unbelievable futility", the idea of a political career was taking root in the hearts of these rebel seminarists who had an appetite for the fire of reform. While the content of the course was largely devoted to religious sophistry, it provided an opportunity for Charles-Maurice to develop his debating skills to a high level. He graduated early with a *baccalauréate* in theology three years later. This was followed by a two-year master's degree—an essential step for a priest aspiring to be a bishop. On 2 March 1778, aged 24, he graduated top of the six priests who received their diplomas that year. He would form an enduring partnership with the person who came sixth in the list of laureates: the Abbé Desrenaudes.

Martial Borie Desrenaudes became adept at assuming and implementing other people's ideas. When, a couple of years later, the Abbé de Périgord became the Agent-General of the Clergy, he quickly came to appreciate Desrenaudes's ability to shoulder different responsibilities as a secretary, an administrator, an intermediary. He was smart, wrote with style and could turn his hand to almost anything: history, finance, law, politics. Some twenty years later, he would even write the little daily notes that Talleyrand would send to his intimate inner circle. Talleyrand paid him a great backhanded compliment: "He must know his country very well for he has never been arrested."

In the spring of 1778, the philosopher Voltaire, a major figure in the Age of Enlightenment, came to Paris from his residence in the village of Ferney, which lay near the French border on the edge of the city of Geneva. He had not set foot in the capital since he was banished over twenty-five years previously but returned at this moment to direct the rehearsals of his latest play *Irène*—and to die. The Abbé de Périgord was a great admirer of the Sage of Ferney who had directed his pen at human stupidity in general and religious bigotry in particular. Voltaire advocated freedom of religion and speech, and separation of the church and state, policies that Charles-Maurice would share—but was the world ready for such radical ideas? The young priest knelt before the author of *Candide* and received his blessing amid loud applause. Later, as one of the functions of the Agent-General of the Clergy, the Abbé de Périgord would be required to protest about the complete works of Voltaire flooding into the country spreading their "dangerous lessons of impiety." While it is doubtful if these books appealed to the general literate public, the pen of Abbé Morellet claims that a good many bishops "knew by heart the greatest part of Voltaire's short works and many sections of his poems and tragedies."

The Abbé de Périgord was accused of being an opportunist and an enemy of the faithful since he seemed only interested in pursuing his own ambition, in indulging his own pleasures and was indifferent to the irritation and scorn of his peers. He made no effort to conceal his self-indulgent way of life, nor did he seem to care who knew about it so it was not surprising that reports of his behaviour reached Monsignor Christophe de Beaumont, Archbishop of Paris, who placed his name on the index of delinquent priests. Although he had been ordained in Paris and belonged to this diocese administratively, one simple solution to this dilemma was for Charles-Maurice to be transferred to Reims where, since 1777, his uncle Alexander-Angélique had become the archbishop. The two archbishops were in agreement, so on 17 September 1779 he arrived in Reims ready to assume the next step in his spiritual career.

His childhood friend Choiseul discovered him one morning in a terrible state. The man who never showed any emotion was in tears about his forthcoming ordination as a priest. Choiseul advised him that he did not have to go through with the ceremony. If he was in doubt about his religious commitment, he should quit the church, but the distraught Abbé de Périgord insisted that he had no choice. Why did he take this step when it was obvious that he was not destined for the priesthood? Talleyrand did not confront situations, nor did he try to stop events from happening. He did, however, attempt to exploit them to his advantage. If he were to break with the church, he would earn the scorn of his family, lose the very considerable income deriving from his sinecures and therefore be unable to maintain the life-style that he considered his due. He was ready to conform to society's and his family's expectations for what was to him a passing inconvenience that could be tolerated and would perhaps lead to satisfying his ambitions. He was promoted to deacon in a solemn ceremony conducted by a friend of the family, the Bishop of Beauvais, François-Joseph de La Rochefoucauld-Bayers, at his uncle's private chapel in Paris. Normally, one could not be promoted again in less than six months but, once again by special derogation, he was soon ordained as a full priest at the age of 25 by the Bishop of Noyon, Louis-André de Grimaldi, on 19 December 1779. On the same day, as was the custom with so many other archbishops, his uncle granted him extensive administrative and spiritual powers in the diocese of Reims—respecting the unwritten rules of nepotism. However, at each of these stages, in the eyes of the church his vows became more binding and eternal, whereas we shall discover that, throughout his life, Talleyrand gradually came to consider the swearing of an endless series of pledges before bishops, revolutionary leaders and monarchs as totally meaningless. He did nothing that would frankly compromise his career but he paid no heed to the swearing of oaths, since they did not necessarily serve his ambition. This disdain also included situations when others were obliged to swear their allegiance for some cause or other in front of him.

The reason for this haste was that, now fully ordained and having previously shown his financial mettle in managing the church's affairs, he was a candidate for the post of Agent-General of the Clergy—the chief executive of the church—a choice that would be made at the next quinquennial General Assembly to be held in Paris in May 1780. In fact, as was the tradition, the Abbé de Périgord had already been potentially earmarked for this position as early as 1775. The clergy formed the First Estate of the kingdom, with its own legal and structural identity, as well as an autonomous and effective central administration. The church had its own system of representation—forbidden to other orders of the nation—and clung jealously to its privileges, particularly those concerning exemption from taxation. Since the time of Henri III in the sixteenth century, the General Assembly had exercised broad legislative and financial authority over the religious community of France, consisting of some 130,000 members located in 40,000 parishes. The post of Agent-General required high intellectual standards, patience, diplomacy and a grasp of law, finance and administration. It also called for discipline and hard work. By this time the function of Agent-General had become reserved for the clerical sons of the high nobility, which, while some of them may have had no particular gift for administration, was sure to guarantee them great wealth. Since the agents were in continuous contact with the king and government ministers, no candidate inimical to the House of Bourbon was likely to be elected. Neither in 1775 nor in 1780 did the Abbé de Périgord actually fulfil all the legal conditions to assume this function. Furthermore, a further handicap was that the bishoprics of Tours and Aix-en-Provence had been designated to submit a candidate to become the next Agent-General in 1780. Thus, in order to qualify, in early January the Abbé de Périgord was quickly awarded the living of the Church of Saint-Venant in Tours. One can only admire the deftness with which the manoeuvre was accomplished.

In May, he was appointed Agent-General of the Clergy for the next five years responsible for the vast and intricate administrative machinery of the church and for protecting its rights and privileges. He had barely installed himself in Reims when he was required to return to the church's headquarters in Paris. Although the Abbé de Périgord had not acquired much experience in administration, he was to carry out his new functions in an exemplary manner. He worked hard and had the ability to cut to the quick of matters, taking decisions not so much on religious grounds as on practicality. However, public opinion was increasingly hostile to the power and privileges of the church in a country where the clergy owned property equivalent to a quarter of the national wealth, generating revenue greater than that of the royal treasury. With the rank of state councillor, he was the church's representative to the king and had the right to participate in the royal council, particularly when it dealt with religious affairs. The post was handsomely rewarded with a high salary and numerous allowances and subsidies exempt from taxation. It was particularly noteworthy that appointment as a bishop was usually the reward of Agents-General after their five-year term of office—some candidates receiving this promotion even before the end of their mandate.

The administrative offices were located in the Convent des Grands-Augustins near the Pont-Neuf in Paris, where he was assisted by an experienced and devoted staff. The buildings dated from the mediaeval era and were in a ruinous condition. Crowded, inadequate, unhealthy and with its structural timbers rotting away, the humidity of the premises and the danger of fire threatened its extensive archives. The headquarters of the French clergy was never destined to see a new home before the entire question of premises was eclipsed by the Revolution a few years later.

In theory, Charles-Maurice was not alone in directing affairs since the post was shared between himself and the Abbé Thomas de Boisgelin, who had likewise been nominated by an uncle, the Archbishop of Aix-en-Provence, and who also belonged to that small community of young, worldly priests who frequented the Parisian salons. However, the work was not divided equally since within a year the handsome Boisgelin became involved in a torrid love affair with Anne Couppier, the Marquess de Cavanac, seventeen years his senior and another one-time mistress of Louis XV. The connection between Boisgelin and Cavanac became a public scandal when her husband caught the couple in *flagrant délit* and the two men came to blows. The husband was banished and Boisgelin discredited as a priest. His uncle, the Archbishop of Aix, was furious since his efforts to advance the career of his nephew were rendered null and void. Prime-Minister Maurepas reproached Boisgelin for having "chosen this moment for a tête-à-tête with such a pretty woman", to which the priest replied unabashed "[He] could do no better than to follow the example of a prelate who [he was] prepared to name." The net result was that the Abbé de Périgord had to assume the direction of the agency almost alone. He did not have solid grounds to reproach Boisgelin for, before long, he too made the acquaintance of another married woman, Adélaïde de Flahaut. Boisgelin died alongside hundreds of other priests in the Paris massacres of September 1792.

A thorough examination of the Agent-General's correspondence between 1780 and 1785 indicated that over 90% was attributable to Talleyrand written in his almost indecipherable handwriting, while Boisgelin's contribution was negligible. The Abbé de Périgord was remarkable for the role he played and the experience he gained in finance, legislation, law, diplomacy and politics. As a loyal public servant, he had an unswerving sense of duty to upholding the church's interests and the many archbishops and bishops who wrote to him or visited his office thanked the Abbé de Périgord for his invaluable assistance. He also established cordial relations with many government ministers, secretaries of state, presidents of parliaments, magistrates and political leaders. He demonstrated huge personal energy and excellent administrative ability, quickly identifying the heart of the problem, discarding the unimportant and devising simple and effective solutions. Avoiding lofty precepts, uplifting messages or innovative philosophies, he displayed rare skill in finding traditional remedies to traditional problems.

Since 1777, France had been providing military and naval support to the American struggle for independence from the British. Unfortunately, although fighting on the winning side, the French were to be the main losers in the war. Due to heavy borrowing, at the beginning of the 1780s a crisis struck the royal finances. While Anglo-American trade revived after the war, the French were to be left out of a prosperous economic relationship with the new United States. Instead, the cost of the war helped ruin the French Government, so it could be said that the American Revolution was a direct cause of the French one.

With national bankruptcy impending, the French Government was looking at all avenues to increase its revenues; its attention was particularly attracted by the wealth of the church. The religious authorities of France were of the opinion that it was illegal for the government to impose taxes on it except by its own consent. The clergy was powerful enough to bargain the conditions under which it would pay any royal subsidies, with the result that its contribution fell far below its ability to pay. In his role as Agent-General, Talleyrand addressed notes, memoirs, letters and reports written in an elegant style and flattering language to the most eminent members of the king's council in an attempt to prevent the church's income being used to resolve the debt crisis. In this way, he established official contact with a large number of important personalities, some of whom we will meet again, including La Rochefoucauld, Calonne and Necker. For example, on 28 June 1782, Charles-Maurice wrote a long letter in a cloud of fragrant flattery to Charles Gravier, Count de Vergennes, the Minister of Foreign Affairs, requesting that he should use his influence to protect the church's interests. Vergennes replied that he had no ill intentions towards the clergy. As a safety measure, a few months later, at an extraordinary meeting of the senior clergy, a grant of 15 million livres was awarded to the crown on condition that it did not make any further demands of the church until 1785.

One of the most pressing problems facing the French clergy during this period was that its wealth was distributed very unevenly. Five-sixths of its revenues were concentrated in the hands of the wealthiest who lived in selfish luxury, while the poor village priests survived on 1% of the bishop's and archbishop's income. They had no say in the government of their diocese and their fixed incomes could not compete with the rise in the cost of living over the previous thirty years. The outcome was disciplinary problems, with some parish priests organizing themselves into delegations that came to Paris to complain about the way they were neglected by their indifferent bishops. A significant part of the Abbé de Périgord's time as Agent-General was spent reconciling bishops and their priests, entreating them to resolve their differences amicably. Assuming a stance of the most strict neutrality, he dealt with this matter in two ways: he appealed to the king to prevent the parish priests from holding meetings outside the existing arrangements and in September 1786 the monarchy accepted a salary increase of 28%, although by the time of the Revolution only a few local administrations had approved this measure. Three years later, during the Revolution, he awarded the village priests an adequate subsistence wage in his famous motion to nationalize the clergy.

At the end of his term in office in 1785, the Agent-General was required to present a report to the next general assembly summarizing the activities of the previous five years. Talleyrand read his huge report to the General Assembly on the "Inalienable Possessions of the Church". It provided a wealth of information on the plight of the village priests, the increase in taxes and the rise of inflation, receiving lavish praise from the committee responsible for examining the report, which expressed its recognition of his services. He was, therefore, the best-informed person in the country on the state of the clergy, its income and its possessions. Four years later in the early days of the Revolution, his detailed knowledge about the church's true financial situation would be employed to its detriment.

Charles-Maurice was a model Agent-General who respected the hierarchical system of authority and spared no effort in protecting the wealth and privileges of the clergy. Already he was displaying the qualities of statesmanship that would be the hallmark of his subsequent career—hard work, imagination, discretion, a splendid memory, inspired decisions and a keen judgement of men and situations. What gave the Abbé de Périgord particular satisfaction was that the delegates voted him a reward of 100,000 livres as compensation for his efforts. It was the first time such detailed information had been collected and made it clear to his superiors that he was more useful in administration than in conducting religious ceremonies. While defending the ancient privileges of the church against royal prerogatives, he took care to steer clear of participation in any religious duties.

Still benefiting from the living of two ecclesiastical properties and with his uncle as archbishop, in 1783 he actually found himself in Reims. Three young Englishmen came on study leave to the city and the Abbé de Périgord enjoyed their company so much that he offered to share with them the apartment that his uncle had made available to him. One of these guests, the son of Lord Chatham, was a keen and highly principled politician who fascinated the Abbé de Périgord with his ideas on political reform. The priest's dissipated life-style did not make a similar favourable impression on his upright English guest. Their paths would cross again ten years later when, as Prime Minister, William Pitt would expel Talleyrand from England.

When not carrying out his functions as Agent-General of the Clergy, the Abbé de Périgord liked to spend his spare time with government ministers and ex-ministers. In 1784, he made the acquaintance of Etienne François, the Duke de Choiseul (the uncle of his boyhood friend Auguste), who had been Louis XV's foreign minister for eleven years before being banished to his Château de Chanteloup in the French countryside near Amboise. Choiseul liked to share with his guests his ideas about how one should behave as a royal minister. His words could not have fallen on the ears of a more attentive listener. Choiseul told his devoted audience "you should have the manner, the behaviour and the bearing of a minister". He also stated that a minister of foreign affairs should not remain stuck in his office all day reading written reports but should get out and about in society, meeting ambassadors so as to learn what was going on. These conversations could be used to spread an idea or to defuse a problematic situation, as well as being a way to apprehend the latest intelligence. "In my ministry I always made others work harder than I did myself. You should not become buried under a pile of reports; you must employ men who can fend for themselves," explained Choiseul. One of the people Talleyrand met at Chanteloup who could "fend for themselves" was Alexandre Blanc d'Hauterive, a professor at the University of Tours who had attracted the attention of ex-minister

Choiseul. Upon being appointed ambassador to Constantinople in 1784, his old school friend Auguste de Choiseul-Gouffier gathered about him a semi-formal academy of gentlemen, one of whom was d'Hauterive, who was engaged in recording the antiquities and treasures of the city. Significantly, during one of his visits to Chanteloup, the Abbé de Périgord met d'Hauterive.

Some thirteen years later, the Abbé Desrenaudes and, after many adventures, d'Hauterive himself would become Talleyrand's closest collaborators at the Ministry of Foreign Affairs, the latter often standing in for the minister when he was travelling. Although they ultimately followed careers as respectable and competent civil servants, one is tempted to use the word "henchmen" when referring to Desrenaudes and d'Hauterive. Later, we shall meet the other members of Talleyrand's "gang"—Chamfort, Durand de Mareuil, Montrond, Radix de Sainte-Foy, Roux-Laborie, and Emmerich and Karl-Theodor von Dalberg.

Nicolas Chamfort had been born as Sébastien-Roch Nicolas at Clermont-Ferrand in 1741. While earning his living from writing, his good looks, ready wit and audacity brought him to the attention of the royal court, where the king gave him a pension and he met Mirabeau, Talleyrand and Sieyès. With the outbreak of the French Revolution some years later, Chamfort threw himself into the new movement with almost fanatical ardour, forgetting his old friends at court. He became a street orator and was among the first to enter the Bastille when it was stormed in July 1789. Threatened by Robespierre in 1794, he died some months later finally succumbing to injuries in an earlier suicide attempt.

In Paris, the great ladies who hosted salons were the arbiters of elegance, ethics, politics, fashion and the arts. Through these ladies, the young Talleyrand entered into the restricted world of the Orléans faction circulating around Philippe, Duke de Chartres, who would inherit the title of Duke d'Orléans in 1785 upon his father's death. After the members of the Bourbon family, the next-in-line to the throne was the Duke d'Orléans, effectively a distant cousin of the king whose royal line descended from the brother of Louis XIV. Since the end of the 1770s, the Orléans faction had been hostile to Marie-Antoinette, who could not fail to be aware of its sentiments towards her and also the names of those who belonged to it. The Duke d'Orléans was extremely rich, intelligent and welcoming and his home, the Palais Royal, became the meeting place for all those inclined to criticise the government in favour of more liberal and progressive politics—in other words, the "opposition".

One member of the Duke d'Orléans's circle was Pierre Choderlos de Laclos, the author of *Les Liaisons Dangéreuses,* who left an impressive picture of the corruption of the world in which he lived. In Talleyrand's gallant world, he assumed a position of leadership and the women he loved were the most beautiful, the most intelligent and the most influential. Talleyrand and the Duke d'Orléans shared many things in common: they were good at off-the-cuff wit, they shared business interests and both favoured closer trade relations with England. They also shared two mistresses: Talleyrand's neighbour Félicité de Genlis and the Countess de Buffon. Well-born women of this era had no scruples about sinning with a priest. It is believed that the Duke d'Orléans also introduced Talleyrand to Free Masonry and late-night card games of whist for heavy stakes in the company of his friends Narbonne, La Rochefoucauld, Mirabeau, Chamfort and Biron. The Duke de Biron would remain faithful to Orléans and die on the scaffold, whereas Charles-Maurice would renounce his allegiance in good time, flee and survive.

In the seventeenth century, there had been a confrontation between the King of France and the landed aristocracy with Louis XIV finally achieving absolute power over a subservient nobility. In England an exactly similar confrontation at the same time had resulted in the defeat of the king and the ascendency of the parliament. However, both the English king and the French nobility had been allowed to retain certain privileges, although no longer playing a leading role in the government of the country.

From the middle of the seventeenth century until the 1760s, the French monarchy had held absolute power, but this situation began to weaken as the aristocracy lost its respect for the sovereign. Among the reasons for this situation was King Louis XV's choice of mistresses: first a member of the middle class—Mme de Pompadour; and subsequently a lady of the streets—Mme du Barry. A feud between Mme du Barry and the popular Duke de Choiseul ended with the duke being dismissed as the king's minister. Following this incident, people deserted the Palais de

Versailles and flocked to pay homage to Choiseul at his residence at Chanteloup. With the death of Louis XV in 1774, his newly crowned grandson Louis XVI failed to recover the lost prestige. A devout Christian, the youthful new monarch was desperately anxious to do what was right for the nation but could not conceal the fact that he was not a handsome and charismatic leader but a clumsy, ugly, conservative, indecisive incompetent.

The Duke de Choiseul was not the only politician whose company the Abbé de Périgord sought. Charles Alexandre de Calonne had been appointed Controller-General of Finances by Louis XVI in November 1783. As well as being a skilled administrator, the suave, smiling Calonne was the embodiment of the urbane courtier, enjoying the favour of Marie-Antoinette and the Duke d'Artois, the king's youngest brother. It was his habit to reply to the queen: "Madame, if it is possible, it is already done; if it is impossible, it shall be done." Calonne belonged to the new generation of capable politicians who were attracted towards liberalism—a concern for involving the common people in their own government. Nevertheless, France's finances were in a pitiful state; a bad harvest in 1788 aggravated the situation. The price of bread doubled and even the middle class—doctors, businessmen, lawyers and teachers— began to have misgivings about the government.

Alongside his duties as Agent-General, Talleyrand had managed to sandwich in a regular post at the Ministry of Finance, where he served as a creative mind on tax reform. In 1786, a new commercial treaty had been concluded between France and England, which established something like free trade between the two countries. Initial feeling in France was that it was too favourable to England, but Talleyrand defended it on the grounds that France was an agricultural country and England a manufacturing one, so there was every reason to believe it served the interests of both of them. This was an example of policies that Talleyrand would pursue all his life.

If there was one place in Paris where one would be sure to encounter the Abbé de Périgord it was in the salon of the 22-year-old Comtesse de Flahaut. Born Adélaïde Filleul, she belonged to a family where no-one was actually the fruit of union between the father and mother but more the result of some fleeting sexual liaison on the part of their mother. Her sister Julie was one of the innumerable illegitimate children of Louis XV, while Adélaïde's biological father was a *Fermier Générale* (one of the king's hated surrogate tax collectors) and at that time her mother's "protector". Sister Julie had been married at the age of 16 to Abel Poisson who had a very celebrated sister: Mme de Pompadour, the official mistress of Louis XV from 1745 to 1751. Mme de Pompadour made sure that, thanks to her royal lover's patronage, her brother Abel became wealthy and acquired a noble title—Marquis de Marigny. When Adélaïde Filleul became an orphan at the age of 15 in 1776, her well-to-do sister the Marquess de Marigny took her in and made sure she received a good education. Adélaïde grew up to be intelligent and beautiful. At the age of 18 she married Charles-François, Count de Flahaut de La Billarderie, a respectable 54-year-old army officer from a noble family, whose even more respectable and honourable brother, the Count d'Angiviller, was manager of the king's buildings. This explains why the young Countess de Flahaut benefited from an apartment in the Louvre Palace. It was here that she opened her salon, which soon became one of the most fashionable places to be seen in Paris, where card games and gambling set the tone—Finance Minister Calonne was known to drop by. The Count de Flahaut was hardly ever present (Adélaïde declared that the marriage was never consummated), but her salon was the place to be entertained by the conversation of the charming Abbé de Périgord, who before long became her lover. Their relationship was to be one of the longest-lasting and most intimate love affairs of Talleyrand's life, since they lived together from 1783 to 1792—which is not to say that he was faithful to her during this period. With the Countess de Brionne, she was one of the rare mistresses who would not remain his devoted friend for life, although their paths would cross many times throughout the following decades. In his memoirs, Talleyrand makes a single spiteful reference to her.

Already in 1786, Calonne placed the facts before the king: it was not possible to govern a country where a multitude of inconsistencies existed between neighbouring administrations, where taxation was unequally distributed with some regions exempt and others not, where the richest people paid hardly any taxes at all, where commerce was handicapped by innumerable tolls, communications blocked, agriculture burdened with dues, and taxation itself sapped by the costs of actually collecting the revenue. Since there was no consistency in the rules, Calonne recommended introducing some standard procedures—a comprehensive attempt at fiscal reform to avoid national bankruptcy. Panchaud, Mirabeau and Talleyrand also suggested the formation of a national bank, based on the model of the Bank of England. Some three years after entering office, Calonne had been introduced to the Abbé de Périgord. Before receiving the long-desired bishop's mitre, Talleyrand was already employed by the king's financial minister in drafting laws on reform— taxation, the grain market, debt management—to be discussed by *une grande affaire:* the summoning of the Assembly of Notables. By March 1787, Mirabeau, Calonne and Talleyrand belonged to a mutual admiration society. Talleyrand acquired his political apprenticeship through Calonne, who dealt with affairs in a relaxed manner to which the Abbé de Périgord brought the quality of farsightedness. Calonne had disguised the bankruptcy of the French state, while in his personal life he juggled with the money market, making the most daring investments. The Abbé de Périgord too was passionately attracted to speculation on the stock exchange.

An Assembly of Notables (consisting of magistrates, mayors, nobles and clergy) was convened in February 1787 to adopt the enlightened financial measures proposed by Calonne. However, he had waited too long to call the meeting and opposition to his proposals had had time to organize itself. It was no surprise that the nobles wanted their privileges extended rather than curtailed. Then, the Prime Minister Vergennes, who supported Calonne, died suddenly days before the meeting and, furthermore, Marie-Antoinette had grown tired of her favourite. His proposals were rejected outright and, as a result, on 8 April 1787 Louis XVI dismissed Calonne and exiled him to Lorraine. His place was taken by Étienne Charles de Loménie de Brienne, the Archbishop of Toulouse. Brienne attempted to salvage Calonne's reforms but ultimately failed to convince the notables to approve them. A frustrated Louis XVI dissolved the assembly. The sequence of events resulting in the French Revolution had now been set in motion.

Brienne's reforms were then submitted to the *Parlement de Paris* in the hopes that they would approve them. This body refused Brienne's proposals and pronounced that the introduction of any new taxation would require calling the States-General (the nominal parliament of France, which had not met for 174 years!). Louis XVI and Brienne ignored these proposals and required the *Parlement de Paris* to ratify the desired reforms without further delay. This led to unrest in the provinces, where people revolted against the reforms. Similarly, the clergy also condemned Brienne's proposed tax reforms. Brienne conceded defeat in July 1788 and agreed to the States-General being called to meet in May of the following year. He resigned from his post and was replaced once again by the Genevan banker, Jacques Necker. At the same time, Panchaud and the Abbé de Périgord were released from their responsibilities as financial advisers. It is for this reason, no doubt, that Talleyrand began to hate Necker, although at the time he did not reveal his true feelings for he had just met Necker's 22-year-old daughter.

A great deal has been written about Germaine Necker, known to posterity as Mme de Staël. In spite of the Abbé de Périgord's opinion that Necker was a mediocre financial charlatan, the Swiss banker was on several occasions appointed Financial Controller for Louis XVI. Brought up in elegant Parisian luxury, his daughter Germaine met the cleverest men of her time at her mother's salon, joined in the discussions at these male-dominated occasions and acquired a reputation for precociousness and great intelligence—if not for beauty, for Germaine did not inherit her mother's good looks. Her father provided her with a considerable dowry but it would not be simple to find her a husband for no member of the French aristocracy would sue for her hand since she was a Calvinist. In 1786, at the age of 20, she married the Swedish ambassador to France, Baron Eric von Staël-Holstein. This marriage of convenience allied the rich and clever Mlle Necker to an easy-going, debt-ridden diplomat... with a title. Like her mother before her, Mme de Staël opened her own salon in the grand tradition of eighteenth-century French society. When the Revolution broke out in 1789, the Swedish embassy in Paris would provide her and her friends with an extremely valuable diplomatic sanctuary. An eccentric, dominating personality, with a rapid and penetrating intelligence, she is going to appear constantly in our story as Talleyrand's altruistic and zealous mentor. His behaviour towards her was not always so admirable.

In November, a second Assembly of Notables was convened by Necker to consider who would be eligible to sit in the future States-General. The *Parlement de Paris* recommended that this body should be formed in the same way as the last assembly in 1614, with the clergy and nobility combined having more seats than the Third Estate—or common people. Necker disregarded this viewpoint and convinced Louis XVI that the Third Estate should be awarded extra seats giving it an overall majority. Louis agreed to Necker's proposal on 27 December 1788, with the States-General required to meet five months later.

Those priests who had served the church well as Agent-General of the Clergy—and it was universally agreed that the Abbé de Périgord was one of them—would under normal circumstances have been rewarded with a bishopric upon completing their tour of duty, but this did not happen to him in 1785. The reasons were many but it was, of course, necessary for a suitable vacancy to arise and there was a waiting list, while many of these posts were passed on from uncle to nephew within the same family—the Rohan family had occupied the archbishopric of Strasbourg for over a century. In the last half of the eighteenth century, nearly one-quarter of the 130 bishoprics were controlled by just thirteen families. In order that these lucrative posts should not escape the family's control, regardless of their qualifications and sometimes against their will, many young men were forced into clerical service—Talleyrand among them. When a member of the Turgot family announced that he was unable to enter the priesthood through lack of faith, his colleagues urged him not to trouble himself with this "scruple". Furthermore, Talleyrand was keen to be appointed to a diocese that was well paid, not too far from Paris and offered the opportunity of being voted to a superior political or administrative post. Later, when he became Bishop of Autun, Talleyrand gave instructions to his Episcopal Council that no candidates should be admitted to the priesthood unless they showed evidence of a "proven vocation".

The vast majority of the members of the Church were pleased to display their faithfulness to the traditions of the Christian priesthood and were wary of those ambitious young men who did not respect its most sacred rituals. Before the Revolution the way "dissipated" priests conducted their lives was known only to a small circle of indulgent people in high society. The king and queen were aware of the Abbé de Périgord's less-than-perfect way of life and did not consider him to be the most rigorous and pious Christian. The fact that this brilliant conversationalist was all the rage in the Parisian salons did not count for much in the respectable corridors of Versailles. Despite his rather obvious shortcomings as a devout member of the clergy, he had a solid reputation as an administrator among the members of the religious hierarchy, who defended him as the financial wizard who had kept the church's money out of the hands of the royal tax collectors—so did it matter that he was an imperfect priest? The Papal Nuncio in Paris asked two serving bishops for their opinion of the Abbé de Périgord in the event that the king appointed him to head a diocese. They replied that he was "serious, prudent and competent" and that his behaviour was "far from giving rise to a scandal on faith, morality and doctrine". Nevertheless, for some years his name was passed over on the list of potential candidates to fill vacant bishoprics. During the period 1785-1788, only twelve new bishops were appointed in France and many of these were reserved for members of the families who habitually occupied these posts. There were two further obstacles in his path. The influence of his uncle, the Archbishop of Reims, had waned, while the Abbé de Périgord's association with the Orléans faction was viewed unfavourably in the court of Marie-Antoinette.

Finally, in May 1787 the Archbishop of Lyon died and Monsignor Yves-Alexandre de Marbeuf, Bishop of Autun, was nominated to take his place. Charles-Maurice's father had been an attendant at court for most of his adult life, sometimes forming part of Louis XV's hunting team. As he lay on his deathbed, he wrote to Louis XV's grandson asking him to make the 33-year-old Abbé de Périgord the next Bishop of Autun, having advised his son to be more discreet about the gambling, the financial speculation and the pursuit of women. Louis XVI, who had the highest esteem for Talleyrand's father, accepted. The Abbé de Périgord himself had been known to the king since 1775 having participated in state meetings at the court of Versailles. The religious hierarchy once again expressed its favourable opinion of its former Agent-General. Thus, on 2 November 1788, after a wait of three years, the circumstances were finally right for this priest with a multitude of mistresses, this recidivist stock-market speculator, this inveterate gambler who did not believe in God to be selected to fill the post. Louis XVI is supposed to have remarked: "This will correct him." The king's confidence was to prove unfounded.

The document announcing the Abbé de Périgord's nomination as the Bishop of Autun stated that the Abbé Desrenaudes would share the responsibility of administering the diocese. The new Bishop of Autun was only interested in the post for the income he would derive from it and the seat it would secure him at the forthcoming States-General. The consecration ceremony for the Bishop of Autun took place on 4 January 1789 in a humble Parisian chapel conducted by Bishop Grimaldi, a family friend. Once again, Charles-Maurice took one of his many vows to be a faithful and obedient servant of the Roman Catholic Church ... Of all the vows he took during his lifetime, it would be this one that would cause him the most anguish. Grimaldi had already ordained the Abbé de Périgord in 1779 and had a reputation as one of the more worldly members of the clergy. We now plunge into the fateful period of French history during which everything from the past would be swept away— except sacred oaths to serve the Roman Catholic Church.

In his diary, the one-legged American diplomat living in Paris, Gouverneur Morris, painted a vivid picture of life in the city during the Revolution, with almost daily references to Talleyrand since the two men often met in Adélaïde de Flahaut's apartment at the Louvre or crossed on the stairs. Morris was in love with Adélaïde, spending many hours waiting in vain for his opportunity. He noted details of the domestic arrangements in the household of Adélaïde and her partner. Despite their rivalry over Adélaïde, the two men seemed to have liked each other. Early in 1789, the Abbé de Périgord had just been appointed Bishop of Autun and Morris could scarcely believe his eyes as he observed him placing a hot-water bottle in Adélaïde's bed. "I watched," he wrote, "because it was fairly unusual to see a reverend father of the Church occupied with this pious operation." A son had been born to the couple in 1785 named Charles de Flahaut who would subsequently enjoy a distinguished career as one of Napoleon's generals. We shall meet him again. Although he carried the family name of Adélaïde's husband, whose absence seemed to be permanent, he shared his first name with Talleyrand. The only person who was dismayed by this situation was Adélaïde's brother-in-law M. d'Angiviller, who poured anger and scorn on his sister-in-law's relationships. In 1791 when Talleyrand received death threats, he wrote his will and gave it to Adélaïde, recognizing their son as his heir. Given his reputation, she could have had no illusions about the way their relationship would end. In January 1791 he transferred his attentions to Germaine de Staël while Adélaïde, in retribution, allowed herself to fall for a charming young Englishman, John Henry Petty, Lord Wycombe, much to the disappointment of Gouverneur Morris.

From his different sources, Charles-Maurice had an annual revenue of approximately 55,000 livres. He was never satisfied with the money he received for he spent it as soon as he received it. Alongside this, we must consider the fee he had to pay to the Vatican for the papal bull confirming his appointment as a bishop, for which purpose he was obliged to borrow 135,000 livres from his brother Archambaud and wife Sabine. In desperation, he sought other sources of revenue—financial speculation and gambling—which were more likely to ruin him than make him rich. Apart from the modest revenue that the new bishop would gain from his appointment, he believed that obtaining a seat in the future States-General could lead to the higher echelons of political power and wealth. However, his appointment as the Bishop of Autun did not necessarily guarantee this position since he would actually have to be elected by the local clergy. Talleyrand had never met the clerical community of Autun and they did not know him either, so they would have to be persuaded to vote for him.

It was obvious that to benefit from the support of the priests of Autun would require him to visit the town, however the new bishop was in no hurry to do so. What interested him most in the early months of 1789 was the political scenario developing in Paris. He was involved with the faction formed around the Duke d'Orléans who, despite being a member of the royal family, favoured transforming the actual absolute monarchy into a constitutional monarchy as in England. This is what attracted Talleyrand to his party. Orléans openly challenged the king by warning him that his measures on taxation were illegal unless approved by the chamber of nobles. The only concrete result was that Louis XVI banished Orléans to the provinces.

Since it was now approaching two years since the congregation of Autun had been without a bishop and they might ask themselves questions about the absence of the new incumbent, Talleyrand sent them a pastoral message to be read out in all the churches of the diocese. It was a masterpiece of unctuous ecclesiastical prose and appropriateness. It was elegantly written and dealt with all the matters that one might expect to find in an episcopal letter—it was also false. Working at Mme de Flahaut's desk, he wrote: "God is my witness that I never stop thinking about you." Since he spent his nights in the most dubious gambling dens accompanied by Narbonne and Mirabeau, it is difficult to see how he could pay any attention to the residents of Autun. What is particularly outrageous about this letter is the barefaced audacity of the new bishop in describing the purity of his faith. Some parts of his letter dealt with serious political issues that concerned everybody; for example, he was already thinking about reforming the education system. Other parts are pure melodrama; he gives a tear-jerking account of his vigil at his father's deathbed. No-one has ever testified that he was actually present but the population of Autun did not know this. He dwelt on the duties of a bishop weighed down with responsibility towards his flock. He begs God to send their bishop such human virtues as "pure intentions and piety" since he was "accountable for all his actions, at every moment... and for whom each new right that he acquires is in fact only a new duty". Rarely had a bishop expressed his devotion to his people with such fervour and opened his heart with such candour. The local priests waited with impatience to meet this wonderful bishop whose eloquent language imposed his authority.

When, some years later, the priests of Autun looked again at his episcopal letter with eyes that had been opened by Talleyrand's activities during the Revolution, they were horrified by what they now understood: a dreadful parody reeking with insincerity; an unspeakable attempt to deceive naïve citizens simply to obtain their votes. Towards the end of Talleyrand's life, the poet Lamartine also had an opportunity to reproach him for the dishonesty of this letter. He replied: "Your honesty is not mine." Rather than being "honest", he was obliged to say and do what was necessary—the unique objective was to be elected to the States-General by the clergy of Autun. The "honesty" of Monsignor de

Talleyrand was directed to achieving his ambitions, which were to serve the progress of society as a politician—as well as to line his own pockets.

In March 1789, he went to the town of Autun in order to conduct the election campaign. The first task was to set out a list of "grievances" that the diocese of Autun would like the forthcoming States-General to discuss and pass laws on. Talleyrand made a speech listing in the clearest terms the matters that the citizens of Autun—or rather their bishop—wished to see addressed. First, the States-General should meet in regular sessions, where all public laws would be discussed by the representatives of the people before adoption. Then, national institutions that, with the passage of time, had outlived their usefulness should be abolished. The holding of private property and individual liberty were guaranteed—all of which meant drafting new laws. Justice should be the same for all people and guaranteed by the presence of a jury and by the law of *habeas corpus*—no one could be arrested arbitrarily without being brought before a court. Importantly, it also implied that some form of democracy should be introduced into the existing absolute monarchy, for instance a constitutional monarchy as in the United Kingdom. These were revolutionary concepts and no doubt reflected the discussions that had been held with his friends over the breakfast table at the Rue de Bellechasse in Paris. We have already noted that the Bishop of Autun was very attracted to financial matters. Thus, his manifesto demanded that everyone should be taxed fairly and equally through the abolition of tax concessions, proposed the necessity of balancing the state's budget and the setting up of a national bank—as his friend Panchaud recommended. Reflecting the Abbé de Périgord's days as Agent-General of the Clergy, he requested that an inventory should be carried out of all the kingdom's possessions. There would inevitably be far-reaching consequences for the distribution of land and the imposition of taxes. The manifesto also called for intellectual and religious tolerance, free trade, freedom of the press, education for all and the inviolability of private correspondence. The government should also guarantee everybody's right to work since it was "the only possession of those who have no property". In short, the new bishop proposed reforming the voting system, the taxation system, the education system, the banking system, the economic system and introducing justice for all. The immediate conclusion to be drawn from these proposals was that the Bishop of Autun was one of the most far-sighted, enlightened and progressive politicians of the eighteenth century. What is new in all this was the unification of all these different themes into a single, coherent document suggesting that respect for the law was the act of a normal citizen. In contrast to the manifestos of other potential candidates, we may also note the absence of any emotional appeals to people's feelings or vague statements of political theory. Talleyrand restricts himself to what is practicable and offers no opinion with regard to the way the country would actually be governed in the future.

The religious community of Autun must have been overwhelmed by the range of their bishop's grasp of political issues and, perhaps, intimidated too. However, we must not forget that he needed their votes, so on another level he set out to charm them. Everyone was welcome in his residence where an open house provided an ongoing banquet. As it was the season of Lent no meat could be served but in the frosty weather fresh fish arrived daily from Dieppe. In the meantime, the bishop sent his senior rectors to all the parishes to drum up support from local priests. His community was so impressed by his generosity that, as a particular expression of their respect and gratitude, they asked him to celebrate mass in the cathedral on Palm Sunday, the Sunday before Easter. We have seen that, up to now, the Abbé de Périgord had steered clear of any religious ceremonies but as the Bishop of Autun he could not possibly refuse. It was a disaster. The new and inexperienced bishop got into a muddle and stumbled over the responses. His congregation realised with stupefaction that this superior being did not know how to conduct a religious service.

Nevertheless, this did not affect his triumphal election on 2 April to be Autun's representative to the States-General. The objective having been achieved, he envisaged only one course of action and that was to get back to Paris as soon as possible, but common courtesy required him to stay for at least a few days. As Easter approached, there was no doubt that his entourage would expect him to celebrate mass on this auspicious day—and make a fool of himself again. Early on the morning of Easter Sunday 1789, after thirty-three days of residence in Autun, he climbed into his coach and fled, leaving a quantity of his possessions behind him.

He would never return. Some 120 years later, in 1909, the then Bishop of Autun ordered one of the boxes left behind by Talleyrand to be unpacked and discovered a magnificent set of crystal beakers manufactured by Creusot, glassmakers to Marie-Antoinette. They were destroyed in a bombing raid during the Second World War.

Although not particularly wealthy, the diocese of Autun's fundamental importance was that, since its bishop held the presidency of the Burgundy region, he had the right to be elected as a representative of the clergy at the States-General—a point of capital importance for Charles-Maurice. Louis XVI had called the meeting of the States-General to redress the government's critical financial crisis. In reality, he was opening Pandora's Box.

CHAPTER III
THE REVOLUTION

In contrast with the events of the following years, the inauguration of the States-General took place amid scenes of calm dignity and applause from the crowd in fine weather on 4 May 1789. Among the dignitaries of the clergy in the opening procession, the figure of Monsignor de Talleyrand, Bishop of Autun, stood out in his black robes, worn in mourning for his father's death the previous year, his uncertain walk aided by a cane. The members of the three orders, ushered by the master of ceremonies Henri Evrard, Marquis de Dreux-Brézé, proceeded through the streets of Versailles, with the clergy numbering 308 representatives, the nobility 285 and the Third Estate or commoners 621. The power of the Third Estate is evident from these figures since, if they met as a single body, it could outvote the other two orders. At first, no instructions were given as to whether they should or should not meet as a single body or as separate entities. It had been ingenuously anticipated that the meeting of these eminent men from all walks of life would be the remedy that would regulate the financial problems besetting the country. The calling of the States-General coincided with a series of crises in the French economy, culminating in a bad harvest in 1788 followed by a difficult winter—the harvest of 1789 was also to be bad. Famine lurked and the urban poor and peasantry were desperate. The consequences were to be more far-reaching than anyone could have anticipated.

As regards the nobility or First Estate, it consisted of some 400,000 persons out of a population of 23 million (similar to the clergy, approximately 1.8%) who enjoyed considerable privileges including exemption from several taxes—but not as many as the well-organized clergy. Absolute monarchy, as practised by the Bourbons since the seventeenth century, had deprived them of their independence. They were forbidden from exercising a profession or trade and, since they often managed their wealth very badly, to survive the nobility depended on the income from their estates, on marrying rich heiresses, receiving court sinecures, or entering the army or the church. You could not become an officer in the army or a bishop without being a noble. However, if they received a government appointment, they were not necessarily as competent as dedicated managers. Once they took up a governmental or religious position, the nobles seized every opportunity to increase their income by exacting money from the peasantry in order to offset inflation.

After the formal opening speech by the king, the three orders met separately. This diminished the power of the numerically superior Third Estate because it could then be outvoted two-to-one by the clergy and the nobility. If they were to meet as a single body, the Third Estate, representing 95% of the population, would be able to impose its voting power. It was for this reason that the Third Estate refused to do any business until the clergy and the nobility consented to join it in a single body where each person would have one vote. Since the grievances of the minor priests were as numerous and as profound as those of the Third Estate, the clergy was strongly divided between those in favour of and hostile to the unification of the three houses. On 17 June, with talks over procedure stalled, the Third Estate met alone and formally adopted the temporary title of National Assembly; three days later, its members met in a nearby building—because carpenters were working on new benches in their meeting room—and took the so-called Tennis Court Oath (*Serment du Jeu de Paume*), vowing not to disperse until constitutional reform had been achieved. Dreux-Brézé was sent by the king to inform them for the first time that he wished for the three orders to continue meeting separately, which Mirabeau rejected, replying that the hall could not be cleared "except at the point of bayonets". Dreux-Brézé withdrew in the face of Mirabeau's aggressive stance by walking slowly backwards out of the room. He reported the defiance of the Third Estate to the king, who was awaiting developments in the nearby royal apartments. His response was: "Damn! Oh well, let them stay."

Under the leadership of the Abbé Sieyès, Jean-Joseph Mounier and Mirabeau, and after a series of confrontations, the three orders met as a single body on 27 June. The previous day, the Bishop of Autun and a number of his noble and clerical friends had already deserted the ranks of their orders and joined the Third Estate. The king had thus been defied and the French Revolution had effectively begun. Since their first objective was to write a new constitution, the new plenary body called itself the Constituent Assembly. Here, Mirabeau's spellbinding eloquence would hold an audience in breathless silence and made him the victor in any of the debates in which he participated.

It is astonishing that the government had not anticipated that the three orders would wish to meet as a single body and prepared measures to deal with this situation. No guidance was given by the king until it was too late and the States-General had found the solution by itself. Talleyrand was in favour of reform but not revolution and would have liked to set up a two-chamber legislative system based on the English model. Despite the extraordinary absence of any reference to Mirabeau in Talleyrand's memoirs, we learn from Gouverneur Morris's diary that during the second half of 1789 the two men, as both allies and rivals, were obliged by necessity to work together. In his notes about a future government, Mirabeau always reserves the Ministry of Finance for Talleyrand. When asked what would be the ideal qualities for the perfect minister, Mirabeau replied: "Wide-ranging knowledge; a great talent; friends and perhaps parents among the aristocracy; sympathetic towards the lower classes; a powerful speaker; clever with the written word." To which the Bishop of Autun added wickedly: "Should not be scarred by smallpox."

Talleyrand was neither a great theoretician like Sieyès nor a great orator like Mirabeau and, realising that he could do nothing to stop the process that had begun, simply "made himself available to events". When the States-General met as one body, the confused debates in the chamber over its voting procedures took place amidst uproar and abuse, often threatening to turn to violence. One of the members present, Adrien Duquesnoy, wrote in his diary: "We conduct frivolous affairs with great seriousness and deadly serious affairs with frivolity. We do not deliberate or discuss; we shout, we insult, we get carried away with emotion." The Bishop of Autun was quite a popular figure, his interventions taking the form of speeches often written in collaboration with his colleagues. In fact, not being a very good ad-lib speaker, he read his prepared speeches that expressed concise, clear and coherent notions. Although he lacked impromptu oratorical skill, when he addressed the assembly, he had an impressive manner and a singularly deep voice, never taking the floor unless he had something important to communicate. On 3 July he spoke from the tribune on a matter which advanced the cause of the Revolution considerably by suggesting that the members should be free to vote according to the dictates of their own consciences and not be restricted by their previously published electoral manifestos. In the early days, Talleyrand played a considerable role in the assembly's work, not so much through speeches but through conversations in the corridors, leaving the floor open to Mirabeau. He supported the reforms that were adopted, even the more radical ones, but wanted them to respect the rule of legality—not imposed but accepted through discussion and negotiation. The fact that the assembly consisted largely of lawyers made him uneasy—"the kind of people who, due to their mentality, are generally very dangerous"—added to which their speeches were often too long. He would have preferred that those who participated in the debates on a particular issue were knowledgeable specialists in their field, such as the former managers of various state bodies. For him, reform, of which his country stood in urgent need, should take place on the basis of familiarity and experience.

There was a group within the assembly that included those nobles who were attracted to more liberal policies—Alexandre de Lameth, General La Fayette, the Duke d'Aiguillon, the Viscount Noailles, the Count de Lally-Tollendal—including those who already belonged to Talleyrand's inner circle: Boniface de Castellane, Mirabeau, Sieyès and the Dukes de La Rochefoucauld and Biron. What distinguished the Bishop of Autun at this time was his ability to be everywhere at once. It helped that he worked long hours and needed little sleep. He was a member of several political clubs that influenced the decisions of the assembly, such as the very restricted Valois Club associated with the Orléans party and the 1789 Club whose intention was to promote a new constitution. The Girondins represented a moderate group that hoped to turn France into a republic. Another party, at first derisively called the Jacobin Club after a former convent where they met, was later to play a pivotal role. Talleyrand was also elected to participate in several committees which, at this stage of proceedings, by preparing the ground for decision-making, exercised considerable power.

No-one could predict exactly what direction affairs would take—even Mirabeau could not hold the Revolution in check. The monarchy did not come crashing down with the Storming of the Bastille on 14 July. In fact, the king survived in one way or another for another three-and-a half years. Up until this time, the ministers appointed by the king maintained a certain influence but, with the dismissal of Necker on 11 July, rioting broke out in Paris and regiments of soldiers began to surround the city. One of Talleyrand's closest friends, La Rochefoucauld, master of the king's wardrobe, is supposed to have gone to Versailles and told Louis XVI: "Sire, it is not a riot; it is a revolution." Even if this remark is fabricated, it sums up the situation exactly. A wave of radical fervour quickly swept the country. Reacting against years of exploitation, peasants looted and burned the homes of tax collectors, landlords and the nobility. The king was persuaded to address the assembly on 15 July and, according to several witnesses, it was Talleyrand who wrote his speech in which he undertook to withdraw his troops from the Parisian region.

In the meantime, Jacques Necker had been recalled as Minister of Finance but could neither improve the economic situation nor curb the unremitting luxury and privileges of the court. He was unable to conjure solvency out of financial ruin since Louis XVI was a conservative who only paid lip-service to the concept of reform. Necker finally withdrew from public life on 4 September 1790 and retired to his Château de Coppet in Switzerland. With his strong sense of public service, he did not merit the derision heaped upon him by men such as Talleyrand nor the unswerving hero-worship accorded upon him by his wife and daughter.

On 16 July, two days after the Bastille incident, Talleyrand met the king's younger brother, the Duke d'Artois (and future King Charles X), at night in the Parisian suburb of Marly. In a long conversation, Talleyrand convinced Artois that, following the events of 14 July, the king had no more authority in Paris and was faced with a very serious crisis because the mob was now armed. Although Artois was not the shrewdest of the king's brothers, Talleyrand used this channel of communication since they knew each other quite well. Artois duly spoke to the king, who neither now nor later had any skilled politicians to advise him, and reported their conversation back in a second meeting with

Talleyrand—the king would do nothing, particularly he would not spill a drop of French blood to redress the situation. Louis XVI may not have understood the gravity of the situation but Artois certainly did—he intended leaving France the next day. Talleyrand urged him to remain since it would set a very bad example in an already tense situation and would leave the king isolated. But Artois had made up his mind, so Talleyrand told him: "Well, Monsignor, there is nothing left but for each one of us to think about our best interests," to which Artois replied: "Indeed, that is what I advise you to do too," and added "You can always count upon my friendship." In politics, friendship is a very short-lived commodity, as we shall discover.

At this stage, while the first members of the aristocracy began to flee the country, some people still believed that France was entering a new and joyous era. The liberal upper classes continued their giddy round of dinner parties, dancing, gambling, political intrigue, gallantry and, particularly, money-making. Talleyrand speculated on public funds thanks to information garnered from his banking contacts. However, as the revolution pursued its course during 1789, he found it impossible to combine the role of bishop with that of revolutionary leader. Little by little, he abandoned his ecclesiastical costume, just keeping the pectoral cross, but this too could easily be tucked under the waistcoat. However, his colleagues continued to address him as "the bishop".

On 14 July 1789—that day of days—he was appointed as a member of the Constitutional Committee with the task of drafting the "Declaration of the Rights of Man and of the Citizen", the Revolution's founding document. Its inspiration was the American Declaration of 1776 and expressed the right of every citizen to liberty, equality, property and justice. The nation recognized no interest on Earth other than its own and accepted no law or authority other than its own. The monarchy continued to exist but with faint vestiges of its former power; for instance, the assembly now controlled the army. All aristocratic titles and privileges were abolished with everybody becoming a simple "citizen". From now on taxation would be applied equally to everybody, civil and military positions would be open to all classes, justice would be free of charge and tithes and clerical dues abolished. During the assembly's discussion of the declaration on 23 August, the matter of religious freedom was raised with one group wanting to adopt Catholicism as the country's "dominant religion". Both Talleyrand and Mirabeau opposed this notion on the grounds that it conflicted with freedom of conscience. Louis XVI exercised his power of veto and refused to sanction the declaration and the measures adopted. After a heated debate, the assembly decided that he would in future benefit from a "suspensive veto", which would enable him to delay new laws but not to block them. From now on nearly all of Louis XVI's actions hastened his and Marie-Antoinette's downfall. Five months later, on 28 January 1790, the Bishop of Autun requested that the Jews of France should benefit from the same civil and political rights as everyone else and, despite the assembly's reticence, this measure was adopted. Other utilitarian matters in which Talleyrand expressed his opinion were the introduction of a uniform system of weights and measures, the creation of a national bank and the standardization of exchange rates with foreign currencies.

As the salon set continued to believe in a joyous new era, the population of Paris was discontented, short of food... and armed. On 5 October the Revolution took a decisive turn when a mob led by market women set out for Versailles to petition the king for bread, followed by detachments of the national guard led by General La Fayette. That night an unruly crowd broke into the royal apartments and almost murdered Marie-Antoinette. The royal family were seized and obliged to return to Paris as hostages taking up residence in the Tuileries Palace. The Constituent Assembly was also transferred from Versailles to the royal riding school on the north side of the Tuileries' gardens. The capital now had both the executive and the legislature within its grasp.

At this time, Talleyrand moved from the Rue de Bellechasse to a house on the corner of Rue de l'Université and the Rue de Beaune between the Boulevard St-Germain and the River Seine. His old friends Choiseul, Narbonne, Mirabeau and Biron joined him at the supper table as the core of a new group of followers centred around Philippe, Duke d'Orléans. Those who associated with this political grouping included the most reformist and outspoken politicians in the Constituent Assembly: the Duke de La Rochefoucauld, the Abbé Sieyès, General La Fayette and the Viscount Noailles. In the assembly, the Bishop of Autun came into contact with people who would remain his colleagues over the next few years: Beaumetz, Moreau de St Méry, Barère de Vieuzac and the young Mathieu de Montmorency. Since this group's ambition intended to limit Louis XVI's power, they were labelled "candidates for the gallows". It was no secret that they wished to remove Louis XVI and his brothers from occupying a position of absolute monarchy in order to create a constitutional monarchy with Philippe d'Orléans as king, as had been outlined in the Autun manifesto. Louis XVI still believed that he possessed the throne by divine right, so he would be forced to abdicate and sent into exile. Philippe would then take the desacralized throne, grant France a liberal constitution prepared by his colleagues and govern the country through a parliament—it was all rather simple.

The Bishop of Autun found this programme attractive for he liked Philippe d'Orléans and was ready to assume a role in his government, but avoided committing himself. The king's middle brother, Louis Stanislas Xavier, the Count de Provence, was intelligent and sought to play a greater role in political affairs. He secretly aligned himself with Mirabeau—and consequently with Charles-Maurice—with the payment of sums of money so that the former would "support the king with his advice, his strength and his eloquence". This mysterious affair turned sour in December 1789 when the assembly, Louis XVI and Necker all suspected that some plot involving the Count de Provence was afoot. The king's brother was obliged to make a public retraction, written by Charles-Maurice, in which he declared his support for the Revolution.

While these progressive politicians were making their plans for a game of royal musical chairs, the true French Revolution would take a violent and unpredictable course, with all of these noble plotters eventually being exiled, imprisoned or guillotined, along with Louis XVI and most of his family. They would ultimately come face to face with the "Jacobins" who did not play games and followed no rules. When Talleyrand perceived the way events were unfolding, he abandoned Philippe d'Orléans, who would attempt to ride the storm, changing his name to Philippe Égalité.

Through its various committees, the Constituent Assembly extended its powers over financial, diplomatic, military and religious affairs but, unfortunately, had no more success than the royal ministers in balancing the budget. Local authorities were confused and offered passive resistance to the deluge of new laws, while the general population refused to pay taxes such that the revenue problems undermining the monarchy only worsened after the Revolution. In a situation accepted by both parties, a large number of commercial creditors had loaned money to the state in order that public services should continue to function. These creditors should have confidence that the state would continue to pay interest on their loans, while unsurprisingly it was the state's policy that these interest rates should be as low as possible. This arrangement seemed obvious to financiers—both creditors and state officials—but in the assembly the situation was very different. Many of the people's representatives were ignorant of financial affairs and, furthermore, were not opposed to bankrupting the government in the belief that this would either bring the Revolution to a halt or hasten its complete victory.

As we have seen, the Bishop of Autun was particularly interested in financial matters. A radical solution for the state's finances was necessary and the former Agent-General of the Clergy suggested one. On 10 October 1789 he stood at the tribune and proposed a remedy to save France from bankruptcy: "Ordinary measures have failed, the people are burdened to the limit, any more pressure would be intolerable for them." If the country had no money, it had to be taken from those places where money still existed. He was uniquely qualified to present the organization, administration and wealth of the Roman Catholic Church and proposed that they should be transferred to the state—in short, to nationalize the church. That a member of Talleyrand's family, and a bishop at that, should propose such a measure immediately gave rise to cries of outrage and "traitor". The right-wing Abbé Maury reminded the Abbé de Périgord that his proposals formed a strange contrast with the "sanctity and immutability" of the church's property that he had stoutly defended a few years earlier. He had, nevertheless, found the solution to the debt crisis. In simple terms, the state would benefit from an immediate revenue of up to 100 million livres, its creditors could regain their capital by being rewarded with church titles and property, while the state would take responsibility for social assistance and education, paying the priests' salaries and particularly increasing the revenues of the poorest. This event also marks a rupture in the venerable union between the monarchy and the church. Once the motion had been accepted for discussion, Mirabeau was designated to carry it through to adoption—it became law on 2 November. Talleyrand was subject to a flood of abuse: he was a Judas who had entered the church simply to undermine it; he and Mirabeau benefited from underhand dealings on the sale of church lands. There is no doubt that one of the people who speculated profitably on the seizure of the church's property was the Bishop of Autun himself, who had never wanted to be a member of an unpopular religion and would soon resign his post. Nevertheless, this was among the worthiest deeds that he ever carried out for the French nation, even though it raised suspicions because he had already acquired a reputation for venality.

Despite such accusations among the general public, his standing at the assembly flourished and, in the month of February 1790, he was elected president, defeating the Abbé Sieyès, who was the only other candidate, by a large majority. In his acceptance speech, he reviewed from a rather optimistic perspective what had been accomplished over the previous seven months. He was rewarded with a long ovation from the revolutionary benches but silence from the nobility and the clergy.

Among the most outspoken critics of the confiscation of church property were the clergy of Autun who saw their assets falling into the hands of speculators and investors with their bishop doing nothing to stop it; in fact, quite the opposite. Far from being ashamed of his proposals, Talleyrand believed that they were most timely and had saved both the clergy and the state from an almost impossible situation. Such was the enthusiasm in the assembly, there was the danger that its members would simply abolish religion altogether! Another clash with his diocese took place in April 1790 following the Assembly's decision that Roman Catholicism would no longer be the exclusive state religion, a measure enthusiastically endorsed by the Bishop of Autun. Bishops and clergy would be chosen by popular election and swear an oath of loyalty to the constitution rather than to the Pope. The priests of Autun protested passionately and begged their bishop to vote against this measure. He replied in the strongest terms that he would not change his opinion and that they were mistaken because "all means of constraint in religious matters are a breach of the first human right". The Assembly's newsletter, *Le Moniteur,* published his response with the remark: "It was the wisest and most honourable instruction that a citizen bishop had ever sent to his diocese." For all his faults, the enlightened Bishop of Autun was in favour of and would defend resolutely religious freedom, equality before the law, individual freedom, the right to a fair trial and freedom of the press. The concept of freedom of conscience and a secular state were unknown at that time and the idea that a bishop should express them... well! Before long, an anonymous letter arrived from Autun expressing outrage. From this moment on, we can date Charles-Maurice's reputation as the renegade priest and, ultimately, as Satan's representative on Earth. On the day Talleyrand died nearly fifty years later, Pozzo di Borgo, the Russian Ambassador to France, remarked: "Now that he has gone to Hell, I am certain that the Devil would say to him: 'My Friend, you have exceeded my instructions'."

Early in 1790, the Bishop of Autun expressed the idea of celebrating the first anniversary of the French Revolution at an event to be called the *Fête de la Fédération* held on 14 July—a propaganda exercise showing that the nation had accepted the new order peacefully and remained united. At this relatively calm stage of the Revolution, many people considered erroneously that the country's period of political upheaval had come to an end. This, the first national celebration, gave King Louis XVI a central role that would unite him with the people, the aristocracy and the clergy. For having proposed such a brilliant idea, Talleyrand became an instant celebrity. During June, on the Champ-de-Mars in Paris some thousands of people armed with shovels and wheelbarrows erected embankments for the spectators to stand on. The Duchess de Luynes had a wheelbarrow specially made of mahogany so that she could participate in the earth-moving activities. It was therefore a great disappointment that on the chosen day heavy rain fell on the procession as it set out from the Bastille at 7 o'clock in the morning. The pageant crossed the Seine on a bridge of boats amidst a sea of umbrellas and stopped in front of the École Militaire where a royal dais had been constructed in blue and gold, while 300,000 wet and muddy people gathered in front to view the spectacle.

Opposite the royal dais, an altar had been erected on the summit of a pyramid surrounded by incense burners and flags in front of a triumphal arch (not far from where the Eiffel Tower now stands) as the focus of attention where Talleyrand would conduct the ceremony. This time he had taken the trouble to rehearse the mass the previous day, with Mirabeau, of all people, telling him what to say. On the Champ-de-Mars, the programme was running late due to the rain, with Talleyrand bringing up the rear of the ecclesiastical procession. Upon reaching the pyramid, the 300 priests accompanied by 100 children arranged themselves on the sides while General La Fayette with a solemn expression on his face waited to receive him at the foot among massed ranks of soldiers and drummers. As he passed by, Talleyrand muttered: "Oh, please, don't make me laugh." Upon reaching the altar, the Bishop of Autun was flanked by the Abbé Desrenaudes and the Abbé Louis, both as irreligious as himself, who whispered the responses to him. At the end, he blessed the Royal Family, the members of the Constituent Assembly, those present, the departmental flags and banners, and 1,200 musicians before tackling the *Te Deum* in his gravelly voice. The first French Constitution would not be ready until September 1791, but those present already understood the sense of it. La Fayette led the president of the National Assembly and all the deputies in a solemn oath to the forthcoming Constitution. From the royal dais opposite the altar, Louis XVI and the Dauphin then took a similar vow: "I, King of the French, swear to use the power given to me by the constitutional act of the state, to maintain the Constitution as decreed by the National Assembly and accepted by myself." The title "King of the French", instead of "King of France" was an innovation intended to inaugurate a popular monarchy. Afterwards, the Bishop of Autun summed up his opinion to Adélaïde de Flahaut: "After all the pledges that we have made and broken, after having so often sworn faithfulness to the Constitution, to the law and to the king, things which exist in name only, what does this new pledge represent?" Despite his cynicism, the whole grandiose affair passed off rather well.

There was one weakness that Talleyrand shared with Radix de Sainte-Foy and that was gambling. When the *Fête de la Fédération* ended at 6 o'clock in the evening, Talleyrand removed his bishop's robes and had himself driven to a gambling house. Luck was with him; he broke the bank. He had been invited to the Duchess de Luynes's house for supper where he turned up to the astonishment of his friends with his pockets and hat filled with money. After the meal, he decided to go to another gambling house—with exactly the same result.

Following the nationalization of the church's property, the clergy's status remained vague. Amidst all the other serious matters requiring the assembly's attention, this item was perhaps not particularly urgent nor particularly important, but a turbulent minority insisted that it should be addressed. Talleyrand felt that a hasty decision on the priesthood's status might result in a serious error being made, but he did nothing—or not enough—to postpone the debates or even to participate in them. He sums up the epoch's mood: "The torrent composed of ignorance and violent passions was impossible to stop." His indifference and flexibility in the face of political dilemmas could be considered far greater faults than his pursuit of money and women. Finally, on 24 August 1790, the Assembly adopted a decree announcing that, as of November of that year, all members of the church were obliged to swear an oath of allegiance to the Revolutionary Constitution—this meant that those priests who did not take the oath would forfeit their position and income. The rupture with Rome and the clergy's nationalization would now be complete with the sincerest Catholic priests beginning to leave the country. Louis XVI, still nominally the king, managed to veto this decree until 26 December, after which the first batch of priests accepted the legislation. The following day the Bishop of Autun was among three bishops to do the same thing. We have already seen that oaths were not taken very seriously by this man who had already sworn so many. What exactly did the people who organized such ceremonies believe to be the significance of such verbal assurances?

It would be the last pledge he would take as a member of the Catholic clergy, for three days later he wrote a letter to the king resigning, with a great sense of relief, from the bishopric of Autun. According to the new Constitution, a bishop was required to live within his diocese. As he had just been elected as a representative of the Seine Department of Paris, Charles-Maurice could afford to abandon his ecclesiastical revenues. But were the revenues of Autun actually lost? He did not bother to let Rome know, although he did inform the See of Autun. In view of the many divergences with his former Catholic colleagues in the town, they did not regret his departure. He asked them to elect a new bishop in his place, although their choice would turn out to be a poor one—his successor would sell off many of the diocese's riches and die by the guillotine.

Strangely, the municipal authorities of Autun had retained the fondest memories of Talleyrand's passage there in the spring of 1789 and thanked him for his generosity towards the town's poor. In the letter they wrote to him, they magnanimously stated that, given a choice between Paris and Autun, they understood perfectly well that he would choose the former. Nevertheless, as far as the Papacy was concerned, the Bishop of Autun could never repudiate his allegiance to Rome.

Having decided nonchalantly to resign from the church, by a most ill-timed circumstance a month after his resignation he was obliged to ordain two new bishops. The investiture of bishops no longer depended on Pope Pius VI or the king but simply on the endorsement of three French bishops designated by the Constituent Assembly, which had no intention at this time of departing from Christianity. It could have been argued that, having resigned from his post as Bishop of Autun, he no longer had the authority to consecrate new bishops but this is not true, since—from Rome's viewpoint—he would never cease to be a bishop. Nearly all the senior churchmen present in Paris at this time, including his uncle, the Archbishop of Reims, had made themselves scarce. This illustrates the difficulty that the Revolution was experiencing in finding respectable and qualified people to do its work. Finally, three bishops, Monsignors Miroudot du Bourg, Gobel and Talleyrand, were designated to consecrate the new brethren, who were in any event not the most outstanding aspirants for this office. "Designated" is not the right word for the three prelates were threatened with death by the partisans of rupture with Rome if they did not conduct the ceremony. The situation became impossible for Talleyrand when Miroudot and Gobel barricaded themselves in their quarters.

Given the oft-repeated threat of vengeance by both the clergy and the Royalists, Charles-Maurice feared for his life. He wrote his will and took it to Adélaïde de Flahaut. Then, armed with a gun he went to see Monsignor Miroudot. Talleyrand told the frightened bishop, casually taking the mother-of-pearl-handled pistol out of his pocket, that if he did not help him, he intended to blow his own brains out there and then. The trick worked and Miroudot caved in, agreeing to participate in the consecration ceremony. Confronted with the same comedy, Monsignor Gobel quickly agreed to be the third celebrant. The ceremony took place in the Oratory Chapel under the protection of armed guards with bayonets drawn. Did this mean that the new bishops of Aisne and Finisterre were consecrated in a true and proper fashion? We may assume that Talleyrand could not care less about the ceremony, nor what happened to the two new bishops, whom he considered as good-for-nothing wretches. During the next month he would participate in ceremonies to consecrate fourteen other bishops, as well as the new Archbishop of Paris, the afore-mentioned Monsignor Jean-Baptiste Gobel. For contemptuously participating in these ceremonies, the Pope took a stand and excommunicated Charles-Maurice on 13 April 1791. Indifferent, he wrote to his friend Biron: "Guess what? Excommunicated! Come and console me by having dinner."

As could be anticipated, Pope Pius VI in Rome disapproved strongly of the Constituent Assembly's assumption of religious decision-making, as well as the many other events taking place in Paris that diminished the church's authority. In response, Talleyrand resorted to a rather predictable political ploy: if there were to be a change of attitude, it was from Rome that it had to take place. We are far from seeing the end of Talleyrand's confrontations with the Pope. Many thousands of priests were fleeing the country but, when those who had refused to swear allegiance to the Revolution began to be persecuted, Charles-Maurice did not hesitate, in the name of freedom of religion, to defend them. "Among a free people and proud of it, freedom of religion includes all opinions without distinction: those of Jews, of Protestants must be respected; and those of non-conformist Catholics must be as well, since it is not forbidden either by the Constitution or the law."

Apart from the religious scuffles, the assembly had more serious issues on its agenda; the education system had been in ruins since the outbreak of the Revolution. The draft law on education, or "public instruction" as it was entitled at the time, became Talleyrand's pet hobby. He proposed a reorganization that was structured, logical and visionary. Primary education would be obligatory and free; children would be able to choose for themselves their secondary studies; the arts would form an integral part of education; teachers would be elected to their posts; each *département* would benefit from a public library; there would be a permanent body of school inspectors. The preparation of such an enormous undertaking could not be the work of one man and, in his memoirs, Talleyrand lists all those eminent colleagues who participated. Apart from his immediate entourage—the Abbé Pierre Daunou, Du Pont de Nemours, Desrenaudes, Chamfort—one particular name stands out: the Marquis de Condorcet.

Nicolas de Condorcet, a writer, philosopher, mathematician and politician, had been thinking about reforming the education system for some time. He had realised that the mediocrity of education provided in the schools was attributable to the grip of the Roman Catholic clergy who were not so much interested in education as in indoctrination. Condorcet wrote that the transmission of knowledge of the greatest public utility to everyone was the school's most important task. For this reason, teachers should be recruited for their knowledge and skills and not simply because they were good Catholics. In 20 April 1792, Condorcet presented his report on an education system that was free, compulsory, non-religious and universal. Due to the heavy timetable, the proposal could not be dealt with before the assembly dispersed on 30 September and fell into oblivion, not becoming reality until Jules Ferry achieved it ninety years later. In the assembly, Condorcet had uttered the most scathing remarks about the Revolution's new high priests, including the vindictive Robespierre who branded him a traitor. Later, in March 1794, Condorcet was arrested and imprisoned but found dead two days later; it is believed that he took poison. He was buried in an unknown grave but 200 years later an empty coffin bearing his name was interred in the Panthéon in Paris.

The French Revolution had not ceased to evolve—far from it—for now, inevitably, it entered into a phase where the Constituent Assembly began to concern itself with its member's morals. Talleyrand's reputation as a gambler was particularly detrimental to his image, not particularly because he had been a member of the clergy but certainly as a former president of the assembly. The pamphleteers of Paris noted with disgust that three of the assembly's past presidents, whose conduct should have been irreproachable, were regularly seen in some of the 3,000 gaming halls that had proliferated in the capital since the beginning of the Revolution. Charles-Maurice was not only active in these sordid dives, but it was known that even in the private apartments of his friends he would play passionate card games for high stakes into the early hours of the morning. In 1791, Gouverneur Morris, the one-legged American envoy in Paris, remarked in his journal that: "His passion for gambling has become extreme." Talleyrand was reproached for his gambling and stock-market speculation far more than the other forms of pleasure in which he indulged. The secret of these midnight card games was never to show the slightest emotion however much one lost or gained: "It was impossible to ruin oneself and to ruin one's friends with more grace and disinterest." Throughout his life, he does not seem to have been troubled by what other people thought of his behaviour. In February 1791 he did admit publicly to having a weakness for gambling, although he had an ulterior motive for this admission. His name had been put forward for the post of Archbishop of Paris and he declared his faults so as to make his candidature for this unwanted position unacceptable. Since this admission only stirred up more virulent criticism, he soon learned not to react to derision.

Although Charles-Maurice was a gambler, this was hardly the way to wealth. His position as representative of the Seine *département* only brought in 4,000 livres per year. It was by speculating on the stock market that he survived, drawing information from his entourage, including the wealthy Maximilien Radix de Sainte-Foy, of whom Talleyrand said he was: "A man whom, thanks to the few qualities that he has and the insignificance of his faults, succeeds in captivating you." Radix and his nephew Antoine Omer Talon were responsible for managing the king's secret funds. Among the advantages of this post, they became acquainted with important people in positions of power, which would later save their lives. From the diary of Gouverneur Morris, we learn of Talleyrand speculating on the *assignats,* on the American debt, on exchange rates and other commodities. Alongside playing the stock market, the former Bishop of Autun did not honour his debts, leaving at least two of his Parisian properties unpaid for and never quite reimbursing Mme de Staël for money that she lent him. Adding insult to injury, after her death, he claimed never to have borrowed any money from her, yet pursued her former consort Benjamin Constant for thirty years for non-payment of debts.

Talleyrand would have readily accepted a post as minister, perhaps for finance, the ruins of which were still supervised at that moment by Jacques Necker, the father of Mme de Staël. Louis de Narbonne, one of Talleyrand's closest friends, was Mme de Staël's lover by whom she would eventually bear two children. Although up to this time Talleyrand had shown nothing but contempt for Necker, in order to get close to the father he attended the daughter's salon, the preferred meeting-place for ambitious politicians, earning her impetuous devotion. He courted Germaine de Staël in an affair so public that all Paris followed its progress. And yet, she did not correspond at all to Talleyrand's usual choice of aristocratic beauty. Physically, she was a strapping 25-year-old woman of little grace and bizarre tastes. She was, however, profoundly intelligent, energetic and indefatigable with a heart of gold. Given the enormous difference in their temperaments, one could doubt as to whether Germaine actually ever became Talleyrand's mistress. However, she did admit later that: "The three men I have loved most since I was 20 are Narbonne, Talleyrand and Montmorency." She would remain Talleyrand's generous and staunch ally through many of the crises and adversities of the forthcoming years, that is until he had to choose between her and Napoleon. His attempt to acquire the Minister of Finance's portfolio would turn into a curious fiasco. As we have seen, the Assembly began to place more importance on virtue in public officials with one member describing the former Bishop of Autun as: "This man known for a scandalous immorality, disgusting speculation, [and] limitless ambition." Marie-Antoinette, who otherwise thoroughly detested Talleyrand, made discreet inquiries about the possibility of appointing him to the post of Minister of Finance. Although the assembly admired his expertise and views on financial matters, rumours of Marie-Antoinette's interest in him were enough to quash his appointment. Finally, all hope of being appointed as a minister disappeared when the assembly itself decided that, henceforth, no government appointments would be made from among its own ranks.

On 2 April 1791, his friend Mirabeau died taking with him "the last fragments of the monarchy". The following day Talleyrand read a text before the assembly declaring that they had lost their most illustrious speaker. A short service conducted by the former Bishop of Autun followed at the church of Saint Eustache. Two days later, the Constituent

Assembly voted to transform the church Sainte-Geneviève into a "Panthéon", or national mausoleum containing the remains of distinguished French citizens. Mirabeau was the first person interred in the Panthéon—his remains were later removed and buried anonymously. They have never been located. Talleyrand admired Mirabeau who had the strength to stand up to people like Robespierre and the dictature that followed, whereas Talleyrand could not. Mirabeau had been working with Louis XVI to find a solution to the crisis believing that the French were not ready for democracy. Mirabeau's death was a huge blow to many of the ideas that Talleyrand stood for and left a vacuum that would unfortunately eventually be filled by Robespierre—and not by the former Bishop of Autun. For over a decade Talleyrand and Mirabeau had shared a strange friendship but, in his memoirs, Talleyrand never mentions him!

Now that Mirabeau had departed, Talleyrand observed: "The monarchy has certainly gone with him into the grave." The Royal Family's position was made even weaker by the departure of a large part of the nobility, who placed pressure on Austria and Prussia to intervene militarily in France, the threat of which was to further undermine Louis XVI's position. By this time Talleyrand's mother, brother Boson, cousins and uncle Alexandre-Angélique had left the country. The last to go would be his other brother Archambaud who left behind his wife and children, with calamitous consequences. The constitutional monarchists around the Duke d'Orléans, who had been in favour of a middle path between that of the Revolution and the Royalists, also began to lose their influence. Up until this time, they had often been in the forefront of moderate policy-making on such matters as emigration and freedom of conscience. However, Talleyrand was not the orator and leader that Mirabeau had been. He was aware that Mirabeau maintained secret relations with the court. Although Gouverneur Morris tells us that Talleyrand had "good relations" with Marie-Antoinette, we can be certain that the king and queen had nothing but contempt for him. The royal family was now imprisoned in the Tuileries Palace and exposed to the greatest possible danger from the mob. Did the king appreciate his position? Soon after Mirabeau's death, Talleyrand arranged for one of his friends to pass a note to Arnaud de La Porte, the king's steward, suggesting that he was prepared to carry out any task in his power that

Louis XVI desired. The king did not react but, significantly, placed the note in an iron cabinet where he kept his papers. When, in the following year, the revolutionary authorities forced the lock and uncovered this document amongst many others, Talleyrand was condemned for a compromising counter-revolutionary act punishable by death, but by this time he too had left the country.

In June 1791, the national finances called once again for Talleyrand's attention. The assembly had already decided to issue a new paper monetary unit called the *assignat*. Charles-Maurice had been opposed to this currency from the very beginning believing that it would only accelerate inflation and uncertainty, drive out the previous monetary system, burden the poorest people with an increase in the cost of living, disturb the exchange rates and worsen the debt crisis. He would have preferred to remove the bells from churches, melting them down into a coinage that would give the people confidence, since good currency gave the country stability. If the country was at peace and ruled by a moderate government, then the coinage would reinforce the national edifice. Unfortunately, the political situation in France was far from stable and about to receive a mortal blow.

Before he died, Mirabeau had advised the royal family to flee the capital and seek refuge in a north-westward direction towards Rouen, the capital of royalist Normandy, where the Duke de La Rochefoucauld commanding a military division could offer them sanctuary. However, on 20 June 1791, Louis XVI and Marie-Antoinette attempted to flee north-*eastward* towards the Rhine frontier with their children in order to link up with other royalist factions, but were intercepted when they reached the town of Varennes. The royal family's flight sent shock waves that echoed across the nation because everyone now understood that Louis XVI was not willing to be a "popular monarch". The doors were now wide open for a harsher form of republicanism. Many of the extremists fled the country, including the audacious Danton. Significantly, Talleyrand chose this moment to abandon the revolutionary minority of the Jacobin Party.

A new club, the Feuillants, came into existence representing moderate elements who sought to counterbalance the left-wing Jacobins. They were few in number but strong in talent. The assembly voted a new constitution that increased the power and prestige of the king. When the new constitution was adopted on 3 September, Charles-Maurice deplored the passion and intolerance that accompanied it, convinced that it had become an unworkable monster. He was not enthusiastic about constitutions in general, feeling that they should be short, flexible and obscure since they were often out-of-step with a rapidly evolving political situation. Thus, on 30 September 1791, having adopted the new constitution, the first Constituent Assembly reached the end of its work and dispersed. By a thoughtless and short-sighted measure, the members decreed that none of them could stand for the forthcoming Legislative Assembly, which meant that not one of those who voted for the Constitution was there to implement it. Talleyrand, however, took the decision to remain faithful to the Revolution and to serve France in some beneficial way. It was no longer advisable to be idle in Paris and Gouverneur Morris proposed to Talleyrand that he should apply for the post of ambassador to Vienna so as to be an intermediary between Marie-Antoinette and her brother, Francis II, the Holy Roman Emperor.

At this time, Narbonne, Auguste de Choiseul and the former Bishop of Autun were inseparable to the extent that Marie-Antoinette labelled them scornfully "the triumvirate". Gouverneur Morris described them to George Washington: "All three are close friends and have together run the course of ambition to restore their fortunes. On the score of morals, neither of them is exemplary. The Bishop is particularly blamed on that head; not so much for adultery, because that was common enough among the clergy of high rank, but for the variety and publicity of his amours, for gambling, and above all for stock jobbing during the ministry of M. de Calonne, with whom he was on the best of terms, and therefore had opportunities which his enemies say he made no small use of."

Despite the wonderful windfalls he had won at the gambling table and on the stock market, Talleyrand's spendthrift way of life was ruining him. He had received a large sum of money from the Spanish Government for facilitating the renewal of friendship treaties and he had also benefited enormously from the sale of church lands following the nationalization of the clergy. All those, like him, sitting on committees overseeing French policies were ready to sell their services and influence to the highest foreign bidder. Some had no influence and therefore no offers. On the other hand, foreign dignitaries flocked to Talleyrand's door and were ready, as Catherine the Great had ordered her ambassador in Paris, "to demonstrate generosity". Nevertheless, rich or poor he always lived like a prince and his addiction to gambling inevitably drained his resources, although he pretended glorious indifference. Even when he had no cash, he appeared to live with careless insouciance, buoyed by his charm and manners, not to mention his wit.

Throughout his life he was a patriotic Frenchman, but the idea of a political and commercial alliance with the United Kingdom would be a concept that Talleyrand would always favour, although it would not mature for a very considerable time. He believed that agricultural France and industrial England had every reason to reach a trading agreement to their mutual advantage. Due to Talleyrand's reputation as a negotiator, Valdec de Lessart, the interim Minister of Foreign Affairs, chose to send him to London in January 1792 to ascertain the British Government's position in the event of a European war. Talleyrand was disgusted with the disorder taking place in France and was pleased to get away, even on a mission that had little chance of success. His visit to England turned out to be another fiasco since he was snubbed nearly everywhere. There was no French ambassador in London at this time and it had been anticipated that he could fulfil his secret mission in the capacity of a private individual. Unfortunately, in Protestant England his reputation as a revolutionary leader, womaniser, gambler and unfrocked priest had preceded him. King George III was barely polite and Queen Charlotte turned her back on him. It did not help that London was full of upper-class French refugees who painted an alarming picture of events taking place across the Channel and the people behind them, particularly the former Bishop of Autun. The Prime Minister William Pitt had not forgotten their indifferent encounter in Reims nine years previously and received him stiffly, as only Pitt could. The neutrality that Talleyrand wished England to pursue corresponded exactly to British policy but Pitt was equally determined not to commit himself in any way to a country that was unlikely to play an important part in European affairs for some time to come—or so he believed. Pitt brought their interview to an end because another visitor was waiting to see him—Gouverneur Morris!

A further blow to the mission's success came from an unexpected quarter. His friend Biron had accompanied him to England with the intention of purchasing 4,000 horses for the French Revolutionary cavalry. He had inadvertently been palmed off with false banknotes and was arrested for non-payment of the merchandise. He had to be bailed out, which did not reflect positively on their partnership. However, on 12 January 1792 Talleyrand presented his letter of introduction from Valdec de Lessart to Lord Grenville, Minister of Foreign Affairs. After a second meeting Grenville informed him that, while motivated with the best of intentions, the British Government could not negotiate with an envoy who was not properly accredited. Although the mission was a failure, Talleyrand took advantage of the situation to make contact with numerous members of the British liberal opposition who sympathized with the French Revolution: Charles James Fox, George Canning, Joseph Priestley, Jeremy Bentham, the poet Richard Brinsley Sheridan and particularly Lord Shelburne.

From the journal of Gouverneur Morris, we learn that Louis XVI and Marie-Antoinette, and also perhaps Valdec de Lessart himself, paid little importance to Talleyrand's mission to London believing that it was unlikely that hostilities would break out between England and France at this time. Although, officially, his mission was to ascertain the intentions of the British Government, he was also conducting secret negotiations over a debt worth millions of livres on behalf of French and British investors concerning the sugar-producing island of Tobago. In Paris, Valdec de Lessart was facing arrest for not pursuing the Revolution's aims with sufficient vigour and stopped replying to Talleyrand's dispatches.

Talleyrand returned to Paris in early March to find the political situation had changed dramatically due to the influence of the moderate Girondin party. Narbonne had lost his job as Minister of War on 9 March, while the Minister of Foreign Affairs, Valdec de Lessart, had been arrested for treason and subsequently murdered. Louis XVI had been persuaded to declare war on the King of Bohemia and Hungary, so that French foreign policy depended even more not just on British neutrality but on an actual alliance with the United Kingdom. Charles Dumouriez, the new French foreign minister, was determined to strike a blow at Austria by attacking the Belgian provinces, an Austrian possession. The

British Government would be very keen to learn into whose hands the ports of Antwerp and Ostend would fall. It was, therefore, even more important than ever to obtain Britain's commitment to stay out of the war, so Dumouriez decided to send Talleyrand back to England at once.

It would have been far too simple to appoint Talleyrand as an official French emissary to the British Government, so the nomination of a pseudo-French deputy minister to the court of St James would be a façade for negotiations. Talleyrand himself selected a young man, the Marquis de Chauvelin, who had the advantage of belonging to a family well known to George III, to be the delegation's acting head. Other members of his team included his assistants Reinhard and Desrenaudes, Talleyrand's Man-Friday, who came along to carry messages between London and Paris. Armed with a letter he had composed himself, signed by Louis XVI, he presented himself at the Foreign Office in London, where the pretence deceived nobody. The letter includes a reference to the secret negotiations over Tobago. Nevertheless, this mission could easily have had the same outcome as the first one. With passionate mobs in Paris sweeping all before them, the British court and the French refugees were in a state of deep apprehension. It had been decided that Chauvelin would present Louis XVI's letter to George III, but the text had been leaked to the French press beforehand, which the British considered to be very bad manners. Negotiations were not going to be easy since the French Army had by now invaded the Low Countries, setting off alarm bells in Whitehall, and soon retreated, which may have satisfied the British but did not create a very good impression. When the French delegation walked in the London streets and parks, members of the public gave them a very wide berth as if they were infected with a contagious disease. Nevertheless, Talleyrand's perseverance paid off, not with an alliance but with a declaration of British neutrality dated 25 May 1792. Dumouriez conveyed his warm congratulations to Talleyrand and Chauvelin but, in fact, they were in no way responsible for Pitt's long-term determination for England to remain neutral. However, the increasingly dramatic situation in Paris put paid to any financial, political and commercial agreement between the United Kingdom and France.

One outcome of his time in London was that the former Bishop of Autun acquired the reputation of a skilful diplomat. Among his tactics, he could adapt himself to the language, customs and manners of the other party. Other useful strategies he employed were never to give a precise answer, to (pretend to) consult his government before proceeding and never to be in a hurry. The Prussian ambassador, David-Alphonse de Sandoz-Rollin, notes in one of his dispatches to Berlin: "It is not in M. de Talleyrand's character to be clear and decisive... He hopes to negotiate better and to obtain more by making himself less clear." It was equally important to consult a wide network of contacts, "at the court, at the stock exchange, among the dealers", so as to be perfectly informed of the evolution of public opinion in one's own country and also to use one's own coterie of journalists so as "to speak well of us in the newspapers".

At this stage, the aggressive Girondins were determined to go to war, not only because the country was threatened, but because it would solve numerous domestic problems by encouraging nationalistic emotions protecting the Revolution from internal dissent. Given the state of disorder within the country, Talleyrand, the pacifist, believed that the last thing the country needed was war. The economy presented an abominable situation, with the mass of the people completely overwhelmed by an avalanche of reforms. In January 1792, the Girondin's leader, Jacques Pierre Brissot, demanded that the Holy Roman Emperor, whose troops were stationed on the Rhine frontier, should give assurances that he was still an ally of France according to a treaty of 1756. The lack of an answer would be interpreted as a hostile act, with the result that on 20 April Louis XVI was obliged to declare war. In so doing, he launched a period of hostilities between France and the rest of Europe that would endure almost uninterruptedly for the next twenty-three years—at the same time as signing his own death warrant. Talleyrand's friend Narbonne, who had become Minister of War under the Feuillant Government, launched an unenthusiastic "phoney war" against the Elector of Trier. The Prussians glibly took the bait and invaded north-east France. By a most fortuitous chance, two rather disorientated French armies accidently met up behind the Prussian advance and cut them off from their supplies. After an inconsequential artillery duel, the Prussians beat a hasty retreat at the Battle of Valmy on 20 September, a huge psychological victory for the Revolution. This success, thoroughly unexpected, emboldened the politicians to declare the end of the monarchy in France and to establish the First French Republic on that same day.

The government demanded Charles-Maurice's return to Paris in July 1792, where the political situation had deteriorated further. A demonstration on 20 June had been the last peaceful attempt made by the people of Paris to persuade Louis XVI to enforce the assembly's rulings, to defend France against foreign invasion and to preserve the spirit of the Constitution of 1791—in short, to establish a constitutional monarchy. The best salons were closed and anarchy ruled the streets. Dumouriez had dismissed his Girondin ministers who now joined with the Jacobins in planning insurrection. Dumouriez, having made himself Minister of War, proceeded to command the French Army in the field. He attacked the regular Austrian Army with his greatly superior force of volunteers and achieved a costly victory at the Battle of Jemappes on 6 November 1792.

At the National Convention, a representative from the Pyrenees had denounced "the Duke d'Orléans and his accomplices", among whom Talleyrand featured prominently. But worse, the former Bishop of Autun was accused of continuing to receive the salary from his diocese despite having resigned as bishop over a year earlier. The puritanical Jacobins were beginning to show their teeth and Talleyrand's pretence of indifference was not likely to shield him from their attacks.

The ability of France to wage war was complicated by the fervour of the population wishing to instigate a global revolution and the weakness of its unreliable army. If the country were to win unwinnable wars, it required unprecedented and radical methods. A political group, the Sans-Culottes, fearing that the revolution might be defeated by foreign intervention, realized that it was necessary to mobilize the whole nation, thereby bringing about the social justice that they so desired. By necessity, the young French Republic resorted to or invented the methods of total war: widespread conscription of soldiers, food rationing, a rigidly controlled economy and the subjection of the population to the needs of the war.

The situation worsened. Aristocrats, priests and those insufficiently committed to the Revolution were hunted down and executed, while châteaux and abbeys were sacked, churches closed and young men forced into the army. The days of Louis XVI and Marie-Antoinette were now numbered as they were held as helpless and terrified captives at the mob's mercy. In a perfectly disastrous move, on 3 August 1792, the head of the Prussian Army issued a statement in *Le Moniteur* newspaper, called the "Brunswick Manifesto", in which he threatened to punish anyone in Paris who endangered the royal family's lives or who did not come to their aid. Written by a group of Royalist *émigrés*, this document achieved the exact opposite of its intended purpose since it triggered the events of 10 August. On this day, the Parisian mob invaded the Tuileries where the Royal Family was being held. The Swiss guards resisted until they ran out of ammunition, whereupon most of them were slaughtered and the palace looted; the survivors were killed four weeks later in the September Massacres. The Royal Family took refuge behind the locked doors of the Legislative Assembly, while the mob dictated its conditions to those inside. The following day the assembly voted to suspend the king, replacing him with a five-man executive council—France became a republic. It also convened democratic elections for a new national convention scheduled for the following month. This twenty-four-hour period produced more political change than any other day of the Revolution. Since the king did not play an active role in these events, he had been totally humiliated and his reputation was now nil. When the news reached the monarchical governments of Europe, the French Revolution's image became irretrievably damned. Talleyrand noted grimly that the Revolution had now taken a direction that no longer served its own interests and he became extremely alarmed. If he were not to follow Mirabeau into the grave, it was time to get out.

CHAPTER IV
THE TERROR

Talleyrand had returned to Paris from his second mission to London on 5 July 1792. Anything could happen in the coming weeks as the French Revolution accelerated into the void driven by the mob. The good men of 1789, who had prepared the Declaration of the Rights of Man, and those of 1792, who had written the report on public instruction, were swept aside in the maelstrom. Evidently, those participating in the riots arising from the working-class suburbs would not be impressed by fine speeches about education and the respect of human rights and property.

The monarchy had collapsed but Talleyrand would have liked to have saved the lives of the king and queen who were in a perilous situation. To protect them, it was very important for foreign governments not to interfere in the internal affairs of France. Foreign armies crossing the frontier in order to restore Louis XVI to the throne only fanned the flames of passionate nationalism and appeared likely to create the ideal conditions for the Royal Family to be murdered. At this stage, Charles-Maurice kept his mouth shut and distanced himself from the Revolution from which he had expected so much.

The three years since 1789 had been marked by a struggle for power between three groups: the nobility keen to bring back the former regime and restore their ancient privileges; the Jacobins who, led by demagogues, were ready to massacre anyone who stood in the way of achieving the aims of the Revolution; and the Constitutionals whose moderate ideals united the nation's intellectual and moral elite. The moderates had not wanted a revolution but rather an opportunity to introduce some major reforms: a constitutional monarchy; the prohibition of privileges; equality before the law; a uniform taxation system. People like Talleyrand, who had looked forward to an age of wisdom and reform, were now faced with a senseless nightmare. He was convinced, nevertheless, that one day the French nation would seek peace and order again.

Before making his own escape, he took his friends Narbonne and Beaumetz to Mme de Staël's embassy hiding in the luggage compartment of his open cabriolet. This was a dangerous thing to do as Adélaïde's husband M. de Flahaut would discover. Germaine sheltered Narbonne in the chapel of the Swedish Embassy even as the patriots of Paris searched for him on the premises. On 20 August 1792, Beaumetz and Narbonne managed to make their way to the frontier, one disguised as a peddler and the other in a female costume as a governess. Mathieu Montmorency, François de Jaucourt and Gérard de Lally-Tollendal had been arrested and imprisoned.

Fearful of the risks of living in Paris, Talleyrand asked to be sent to London on a third official mission to pursue the work he had already begun there. Since he had already successfully completed his diplomatic assignment during his second visit, this suggestion fell on deaf ears. Using his imagination, he asked if a passport could be issued stating that he would be responsible for a new mission to England concerning the adoption by both countries of a uniform system of weights and measures. If he left the country without a passport, he would never be able to return; it was important to give the impression that he was not abandoning or fleeing the country, rather he was simply travelling abroad on official business. A lot of people who owed him political favours had already fled and, as the days passed, passports became more and more difficult to obtain, with those people making such requests attracting profound suspicion from the authorities. He recalled his past services to the nation, pointing out that he did not merit to be treated with distrust.

Talleyrand fixed his hopes on Georges Danton, who had recently returned from England, and was now Minister of Justice and president of the provisional government. Danton, a somewhat amoral and Bohemian character, represented the broad-minded radicals at this time, soon to be eclipsed by the harsh puritanism of Robespierre. Charles-Maurice and Danton knew each other because they had sat together for a year on the directory of the Seine *département*. At 11 o'clock at night on 31 August, he established himself in the lobby of Danton's office in the hope of seizing the great man as he came by. His former colleague from the Constituent Assembly, Barère, saw him there and described the scene:

"In the lobby I found the Bishop of Autun in moleskin trousers and boots, a round hat, a short jacket and a pigtail [i.e. dressed as a workman]. I knew him well having spent three years together in the Assembly. He greeted me warmly. I was astonished to see him at this hour in the Ministry of Justice. 'It's like this,' he said, 'I must leave tomorrow morning for London on an official mission and I have come to obtain my papers that Danton is bringing back.'" He left the office empty-handed.

From 2 September, gangs of enraged insurgents broke down the doors of the state prisons and indiscriminately massacred everyone inside in the most horrifying carnage, including the last remaining survivors of the king's Swiss Guard. The playwright and general rogue Pierre-Augustin de Beaumarchais had spent a few days in prison during August 1792 for criticising the government and, miraculously, was released only three days before every person in the prison where he had been detained was slaughtered. François de Jaucourt, another of Talleyrand's long-term friends, had an even narrower escape since Germaine de Staël managed to obtain his release from prison the day before the massacres started. Germaine herself decided to flee Paris in her private carriage but was called before the tribunal chaired by Robespierre before being allowed to leave.

Following the intervention of Alexandre de Lameth and Radix de Sainte-Foy, on 7 September Talleyrand received his passport signed by Danton and five other ministers: "Let pass Maurice Talleyrand going to London on our orders." "I owe my life to Danton," he admitted. Together with Jaucourt and his valet Courtiade, they made the journey to England over eleven difficult days. The roads and hostels were crowded with thousands of priests fleeing to England having refused to swear an oath of allegiance to the new constitution. He had already sent his book collection to England during his first visit in January.

Talleyrand already knew that the British were fiercely opposed to the French Revolution. He found the population of London busy organizing collections of money to help the French refugees, particularly the Roman Catholic priests. He met his former colleague Chauvelin, who was still in charge of the French delegation to the Court of St James. From London, Talleyrand wrote a memoir addressed to Danton that was both a summary of his political career and a warning. From it, we can highlight the phrases: "We have learned that... the true aspiration of free and enlightened men is to be master in one's own house and not to entertain the absurd notion of being master in another's;" "Both for states and individuals, real wealth does not consist of seizing or invading other people's lands but of exploiting your own;" "We have learned that all extensions of territory, all usurpations, by force or fraud, which have long been connected by prejudice with the idea of 'rank', of 'hegemony', of 'political stability', of 'superiority' in the order of powers, are only the cruel jests of political lunacy, false estimates of power, and that their real effect is to increase the difficulty of administration and to diminish the happiness and security of those governed for the passing interest or for the vanity of those who govern." At about the same time, he wrote to his British friend Lord Lansdowne: "Clubs and pikes kill energy, making dissimulation and meanness commonplace, and if we allow the people to acquire this vile habit, they will see no other happiness than that of changing one tyrant for another;" "[France] must remain circumscribed by her own borders." These prophetic words explain why he abandoned the post of Napoleon's Minister of Foreign Affairs fifteen years later.

In the royal apartments, Louis XVI kept his papers in an iron cabinet. On 20 November 1792, the revolutionary authorities prised it open with crowbars revealing some interesting contents. They found proof that Louis XVI and Marie-Antoinette had been corresponding with Vienna, together with the two letters that Talleyrand had sent to the king in May 1791 offering to be of assistance to him in any way within his power. On 5 December 1792, the assembly adopted a decree of accusation against the former Bishop of Autun placing all his affairs under seals—it would not be the last time this happened. This was serious. The faithful Desrenaudes who had stayed behind in Paris had an article printed in *Le Moniteur* in defence of Talleyrand's role in the Revolution so far, suggesting that the assembly would discover with joy that it had made an awful mistake. Talleyrand wrote disingenuously from London that he had never had any kind of dealings with the king or his steward, La Porte, which, given the two letters in the Assembly's possession demonstrating the opposite, had little impact. On 23 August 1792, Arnaud de La Porte became the second political victim of that new humane execution device: the guillotine. Talleyrand's name, together with that of seventeen members of his family, including his mother, was placed on the feared list of *émigrés*, that is, those considered as enemies of the Revolution and liable to be executed without trial if they returned. Although he was safe in London, all his efforts to leave France on pseudo-official business had served no purpose.

He informed British Home Secretary Lord Grenville that he had not, in fact, come to London on any official mission but for "the forthcoming sale of [his] fairly large library". The British Government was not deceived and even Grenville, who was far from being his enemy, considered him to be "deep and dangerous". Charles-Maurice rented a small house in Kensington, not far from Hyde Park, which was managed by one of his former mistresses, Marie-Charlotte, Countess de La Châtre. An ardent democrat, she was separated from her aristocrat husband and now shared her life with the recently-released Jaucourt. Talleyrand soon gravitated to the French community that met at Juniper Hall, a house leased to a group of French *émigrés* in the village of Mickleham near Dorking in Surrey. There he was received with open arms by several of his old friends—the Princess d'Hénin, Lally-Tollendal, Narbonne, Beaumetz, Montmorency, Charles de Lameth, La Rochefoucauld, Mme de Genlis, the Duchess de Laval and the handsome General Alexandre d'Arblay, who had been aide-de-camp to La Fayette—all living in situations of "estimable frugality". These remarkable and charming people had all escaped at the risk of their lives from the dramatic events taking place in France. For some months, this quiet residence became the centre of a life of such gaiety and charisma that those English neighbours who were admitted to it felt that they were in the presence of people from a different world. Talleyrand was a born entertainer and, employing his exaggerated courtesies and wicked repartee, soon became the star of the group. Thanks to her lover, Lord Wycombe, Mme de Flahaut had received a British passport and had also reached London in October with her son Charles. In the summer, she lived at Lord Wycombe's country residence, Loakes House near High Wycombe, and to save money Charles-Maurice often spent time there, making himself welcome by his wit and charming conversation.

Then a whirlwind passed through Juniper Hall. It was the earnest, brilliant, garrulous, liberal personality of Germaine de Staël, but so delightful that no-one could resist her. She loved Talleyrand; she loved Narbonne; in her generous heart she loved everybody! Later, she wrote of these "four months of escape from the shipwreck of my life". Mme de Staël read to her friends her latest philosophical essay on: "The influence of passion on the contentment of men and nations." Talleyrand liked the ideas and the style and she was flattered by these compliments from someone in whose taste and judgement she had confidence. The reason she had fled to England was to be with the handsome, witty, intelligent Narbonne, but he had grown weary of her and had not been replying to her letters. His weariness, however, was not an obstacle to living off her wealth nor from making her pregnant. In May 1793, she discovered that her proximity to Narbonne was not going to restore his feelings for her and returned to her father's Château de Coppet in Switzerland with the separation causing both her and Charles-Maurice great sadness. She wrote torrents of letters to him and he replied with little notes, their mutual affection being adulterated by politics. He would have liked to join her in Switzerland but the Swiss authorities let it be known they would prefer that he did not. Given the hostility of the British public and that of the French *émigrés*, he then approached the governments in Florence and Naples, who asked him politely not to disturb their peace.

Two neighbours, Mrs Susanna Phillips and her 41-year-old sister Frances (Fanny) Burney, lost no time in calling on the community at Juniper Hall, sending enthusiastic and detailed accounts to their correspondents about this colony of "exquisite people" including the most exotic members of the French nobility. Fanny was initially prejudiced against Talleyrand having heard reports of his "wickedness". Within a few days, however, both she and her sister were captivated by his charm and teasing humour. All the ladies at Juniper Hall were living quite openly with their lovers and the naïve Fanny gave a very innocent interpretation to the expressions of tender affection between men and women whose names suggested that they were not married—particularly the very plain Mme de Staël's passion for the very good-looking Narbonne. When the truth finally dawned on her of a sexual liaison, Fanny's moral principles were shocked and her previously keen admiration underwent a sudden coolness that perplexed Mme de Staël. The penniless General d'Arblay was enrolled to be Fanny Burney's

French teacher and before long became her husband.

The French community in London consisted of two mutually suspicious camps. The Royalists and nobles who had fled during the Revolution's early days detested the "Constitutionals" who had arrived after the events in the summer of 1792, and particularly among them a certain former Bishop of Autun. His erstwhile acquaintance the Duke of Artois, with whom he had had secret meetings in July 1789—and who had sworn eternal friendship—kept a list of all those suspected of involvement in the Revolution who would be punished once the Bourbons were restored. Talleyrand was destined to be hung, drawn and quartered!

In good weather, Talleyrand went fishing at Adélaïde de Flahaut's residence in the countryside and, when it rained, he could be found at her apartment in London. She had become a novelist writing an autobiographical book entitled *Adèle de Sénange* for which he became the proof-reader. When published, the book was a success, thus diminishing his need to supply her with money. The library that he had transferred from Paris to London represented his savings so that when short of money he sold off some of his books, although the aristocratic and religious refugee communities were shocked at some of the titles included in this former bishop's collection. The sales did not always go well since the Royalist *émigrés* in the city made sure that the connoisseurs stayed away. Among the numerous projects in which he was involved was the idea of sending to Toulon by ship all the former members of the Constituent Assembly who were located in London in order to form a breakaway government to resist the power of the Royalists in this region. Fortunately, the British Government was not enthusiastic about sending these men to their doom.

Still believing in the idea of a liberal monarchy that had inspired him at the beginning of the Revolution, in company with his friends Bon-Albert Briois de Beaumetz and Claude Bigot de Sainte-Croix, Talleyrand wrote a book on the life of Philippe, Duke d'Orléans. He tried to recruit Mme de Staël into the Orléans camp, but at this time she remained a steadfast supporter of the existing monarchy. The months of October and November 1793 marked a period when his spirits were very low. The tone of his letters to Mme de Staël become professions of faith as he tried to persuade her to return to London: "I have to say and say it very loud what I wanted, what I have done, what I have prevented from happening and what I have regretted; I have to show to what extent I liked liberty, that I like it still and how much I hate the French." It was a question of surviving and of waiting. When Sieyès was asked what happened during the Terror, he replied: "I lived."

An invitation came from Lord Lansdowne, who, as British Prime Minister, had met Talleyrand in Paris during the signing of the Treaty of Versailles in 1783. Lansdowne was the father of Lord Wycombe, Adélaïde's lover, and received Talleyrand in grand style at his stately home at Bowood near Bath. This liberal politician came from the same aristocratic background as Talleyrand and had been sympathetic to the ideas of the early French Revolution. Lansdowne played no further role in British politics at this time but remained violently opposed to the Prime Minister William Pitt. He was also in contact with other Whig politicians in conflict with Pitt, such as Warren Hastings, Lord Charles Stanhope, Jeremy Bentham, Richard Brinsley Sheridan and Charles James Fox.

Due to these links with the British opposition and as a French refugee with a suspicious past, Talleyrand began to attract the attention of the British Government with his presence in London becoming a cause for alarm. It had not escaped Pitt's attention that this "deep and dangerous" foreigner not only counted the main British opposition politicians among his contacts but carried out correspondence with the Continent that was too intense to be innocent. The British Parliament had just passed the Aliens Act and it would have been difficult to find an individual who fitted the description of a dangerous alien more precisely than Talleyrand. Furthermore, if the French Government had wished to place a secret agent in London, they could hardly have chosen a more suitable person than the former Bishop of Autun. Of the entire Juniper Hall set, he was the only one to attract suspicion. One grim day in January 1794, Pitt sent two gentlemen dressed in black to Talleyrand's residence presenting him with an order to leave the country within five days. He informed the two officers that he would obey their instruction. It was a bitter blow. At the age of 39, with hardly any money, his career as a bishop compromised, his vocation as a politician now over, what were his options? His presence had already been refused by Italy and Switzerland, and he was likely to be arrested at once if he set foot in France. When he asked the British if there were any grounds to negotiate with the people who required his departure, he was informed that it was Francis II, the Holy Roman Emperor, and Frederick William II, the King of Prussia, who had requested it. He wrote to Mme de Staël: "Apparently, the Emperor and the King of Prussia are afraid of people who go fishing in the summer and correct the proofs of a novel during the winter." On 30 January he wrote very dignified letters to Pitt, to Foreign Secretary Lord Grenville and to Henry Dundas at the Ministry of War asking for an explanation and the cancellation of the expulsion order. He appealed that, in a country where the system of justice functioned, he should benefit from the provisions of the law. He asked Narbonne to seek an audience on his behalf with George III. While the British Government accused him of being a dangerous revolutionary, the French Government had branded him at the same time as a Royalist traitor. Pitt did not reply—the kind of answer that Talleyrand understood perfectly—and George III refused to receive Narbonne.

When William Pitt the Younger became Prime Minister of Great Britain in 1783 at the age of 24, the country had just lost its American colonies and both its prestige and its wealth had received a severe setback. He set as his objective to make his country one of the world's dominant powers. Within ten years, and thanks to a balanced budget, the beginnings of the industrial revolution and the all-powerful British fleet ruling the oceans, he was on the point of achieving his ambition. It was to be spoiled, however, by France declaring war on the United Kingdom on 1 February 1793, leading to more than two decades of almost continuous conflict. At first, the war did not go well for the British forces: Captain Napoleon Bonaparte threw them out of Toulon; military support for the insurrection in the Vendée was a failure; the Duke of York with his troops was forced to evacuate the Netherlands; and the campaign in the West Indies turned to disaster. Such was the deception of the British population that "Jacobin" clubs sprang up all over the country. Pitt reacted violently and suspended the law of *habeas corpus*. It was at this point in January 1794 that the decision had been taken to expel the former Bishop of Autun from the British Isles.

Talleyrand decided to go to the United States of America. He asked Pitt to extend the deadline for the expulsion order until 15 February since he had been unable to reserve places on a ship before that date for himself, his friend Briois de Beaumetz and his valet Courtiade. Beaumetz, a lawyer from Arras, had been elected to the States-General in 1789, but had left France in August 1792 for Germany then England. Talleyrand's damning verdict of him was that, at the age of 40, his oldest friends were people he had known for a few months.

Upon leaving, Talleyrand would carry with him over $8,000 lent by Narbonne and several letters of recommendation, while Mme de Flahaut agreed to be a post-box where letters addressed to him could be forwarded, even those from Germaine. He was granted a month's delay for departure, but the ship never seemed to be ready. Finally, on 1 March 1794 he wrote a farewell letter to Mme de Staël stating that he was beginning a new life and suggesting that he might be absent for one year. Over the next two decades relations would cool with Narbonne, Beaumetz, General d'Arblay and even Germaine de Staël, but when he returned to Paris in September 1796, she would be instrumental in launching him on the path that would become his true vocation.

CHAPTER V
AMERICAN INTERLUDE

No sooner had the American merchantman *William Penn* carrying Talleyrand, Beaumetz and Courtiade left the shelter of the Thames estuary on 2 March 1794 than it faced a storm in the English Channel. The ship suffered such strain that the captain considered putting into a French port to stop the leaks, much to Talleyrand's alarm who feared being arrested. Finally, the ship docked at Falmouth in Cornwall to have its hull made watertight. The passengers and crew then set off across the Atlantic for a thirty-seven-day voyage to Philadelphia. As they approached the American coast, they passed another ship heading for Calcutta and on the spur of the moment Talleyrand asked about the possibility of finding a berth on board, but there was none.

He would spend over two years in this new country with just 4 million inhabitants and limitless frontiers. They arrived in Philadelphia in the middle of April where the streets with their identical brick houses in a grid pattern failed to impress. Lord Shelburne had given Talleyrand a letter of introduction for President George Washington, which he gave to Alexander Hamilton, Secretary of the Treasury, to pass on. Talleyrand believed that it would be a formality for the President of the United States to invite him to his dinner table, but this did not happen since Washington wanted to keep his country free from entanglements with a man who was denounced by his own people as an enemy of France. Thanks to the letters of Gouverneur Morris, his reputation as an unfrocked priest, philanderer and heedless gambler had preceded him and George Washington did not like what he read about the former Bishop of Autun's way of life. In France, Talleyrand was pardoned for his mistresses, but condemned for his financial dealings; in the United States, the opposite was true—his investments and speculation were admired, but his private life met with disapproval. Washington's refusal must have been a rude shock but Talleyrand does not mention it in his memoirs. He wrote to

Lord Lansdowne that he understood perfectly that during a period disturbed by revolution a man of Washington's standing had to hold himself aloof from passing political storms. On the other hand, Talleyrand soon became firm friends with Hamilton, a man with a perfect understanding of the political and financial situation in the United States. Thanks to this association, Talleyrand became a primary source of information for his European correspondents. He was also full of ideas on ways to make money, such as purchasing goods in Europe and selling them for a commission in America or speculating on the sale of land in the virgin territories of the United States. The banker Alexander Baring immediately recognized Talleyrand as a smart businessman who intended to make money, "but I doubt his honesty". Twenty years later, the Duke de Richelieu, who succeeded Talleyrand as French Prime Minister, wrote: "There are six great powers in Europe: England, France, Russia, Austria, Prussia and the Baring Brothers."

The puritanical attitude of American society was not the only obstacle Talleyrand encountered. The French representative to the United States at this time, a convinced Jacobin named Joseph Fauchet, a friend of Robespierre, considered Talleyrand and Beaumetz to be enemies of the French Revolution and required President Washington to shun them. Considering Talleyrand's contribution in the early days of the Revolution, this amounted to a considerable distortion of the facts provoked by ignorance. From the letters he wrote back to the Ministry of Foreign Affairs in Paris, it becomes obvious that Fauchet was a paranoiac who saw enemies of France everywhere. He understood these inoffensive refugees as sinister conspirators in an international plot to turn the United States against France. The first French representative to the United States, Edmond-Charles Genêt, had tried desperately to persuade George Washington to attack Spanish and British possessions in continental America, but the American president was equally determined not to become involved in any European conflict. Congress had voted a law of neutrality on 5 June 1794. Genêt was recalled to France but, since as a Girondin he would certainly be executed upon his return, the United States granted him political asylum. He married the Governor of New York's daughter and spent the rest of his life as a farmer.

Martinique's one-time representative to the Constituent Assembly in

Paris, Médéric Moreau de Saint-Méry, had escaped from Le Havre with his wife and children in November 1793 shortly after a warrant had been issued for his arrest. Arriving in Norfolk, Virginia, he relocated to Philadelphia and bumped into Talleyrand and Beaumetz there. He opened a store where he sold books, prints, maps and music—there was also a printing press. His bookshop became the permanent meeting point for the many other refugees from France—the Marquis de Blacons, Noailles, La Rochefoucauld and the bankers Cazenove and Omer Talon, the nephew of Radix de Sainte-Foy—where noisy meetings took place almost every evening fuelled by Madeira wine with each man believing he still had a role to play in the future of France. They appreciated Talleyrand's company as an incomparable raconteur and wit, often using the conformity and puritanism of the Americans as the butt of his humour. Talleyrand and Moreau became firm friends, discussing schemes for making money far into the night. When Moreau returned to France in 1798 Talleyrand found him a position in the government. Beaumetz, Blacons and Talon would all die miserable deaths, while Moreau de Saint-Méry and La Rochefoucauld would prosper alongside the former Bishop of Autun under the Napoleonic regime.

The first priority was to earn some money, even better to become rich. During the 1780s, Gouverneur Morris had already spoken to Charles-Maurice and Adélaïde de Flahaut about speculating on land purchase in the United States, but they had no capital to invest at that time. Now, Talleyrand wrote to Mme de Staël warning her about the unreliability of American businessmen and proposing his services instead to her father, Jacques Necker, one of Europe's richest men. He also had contact with a number of important financiers in London and Philadelphia. Germaine did not wish to mix friendship and business, preferring to deal with Gouverneur Morris. Curiously, it is from the correspondence of Joseph Fauchet that we learn of Talleyrand's financial dealings. He entered into a partnership with the respectable Frenchman named Théophile Cazenove, the representative of a bank, the Holland Land Company. Talleyrand had confidence in Cazenove, an acquaintance of several years' standing when both had known Panchaud in Paris. Cazenove formed part of the international banking fraternity that linked Philadelphia and New York with Amsterdam, Geneva, Hamburg, London and Paris. With the beginnings of the Revolutionary Wars in Europe, bankers sought to place their capital in neutral, risk-free, long-term havens abroad. The American economy was developing rapidly under a prudent government and with stable finances, which meant that the property market in the United States became attractive to the European bankers.

After considering several different ways of making money, Talleyrand's fertile imagination finally opted to speculate on the purchase of land in the north of the United States. The system was simple: American capitalists purchased vast areas of unsettled land, sold them in "townships" at a considerable profit to European investors, who would divide the terrains into lots of 640 acres and sell them at one dollar per acre to local farmers or emigrants who were desperate to set up a new life in America, thereby making an even greater profit for themselves. The problem was that it took two months for a letter to cross the Atlantic, while British, Dutch, French, German and Swiss banks had lost confidence in American agents, who had acquired a reputation for unpaid debts, unpaid interest and frequent bankruptcies. Therefore, a European agency selling land to a European clientele might inspire confidence. Cazenove presented Talleyrand to a wealthy speculator named Robert Morris. Talleyrand and Beaumetz arrived on the property scene a little late, but there were still vast expanses of land for sale. In June 1794, Cazenove asked the two men to prepare a detailed report on the land owned by the American Secretary of State for War, Henry Knox, in the state of Maine. They set out together to investigate the potential farmland in the region, travelling by mail coach to Boston and from there to the Canadian border by boat.

Accompanied by his faithful manservant Courtiade, Beaumetz and an agent from the bank, this former powdered and perfumed night owl set out on a reconnaissance mission on horseback through the thickets, forests and marshes of New England, armed with an axe in search of agricultural land. Even he found it amusing that the former Bishop of Autun, the former acquaintance of Mme du Barry and the Duke d'Artois at the Court of Versailles, should be paddling a canoe or riding a pony through insect-infested swamps. Before selling these terrains to European purchasers, he wanted to make sure that they actually existed, were accessible and would indeed make good farmland—it was not unknown for potential buyers to be ripped-off. He foresaw virgin forest replaced by "cities, villages, hamlets, […] the hills covered in harvests and already the herds would come and graze on the meadows that lay before our eyes." He wrote to Germaine de Staël (who would inevitably inform her father) that anyone wishing to invest in these lands should deal with the bank of Maillard Seton & Company in London through the intermediary of a certain Abbé Desrenaudes in Paris! He later wrote in his *Memoirs*: "I found raw nature, wilderness, forests as ancient as the world; the remains of plants and trees dead from old age rotting on the ground from which they had grown naturally… creepers that often blocked our way; the river banks carpeted with a fresh and lush greenery; sometimes wide-open natural pastures. In other places, flowers I had never seen before." The houses they stayed in were remarkable for the complete lack of comfort provided by the rustic furniture, although there was a weakness for expensive and completely useless trinkets. For instance, in a modest log cabin, miles from anywhere, they found an unplayable piano decorated with gilded candlesticks. Throughout their long association, even lost in the backwoods, Courtiade would still address Talleyrand as if he were the Bishop of Autun: "Oui, Monsignor."

In September 1794, the four men were joined by a rich Englishman, Thomas Law, who was also looking to invest money in the purchase and sale of land. They all set off to carry out another survey in the region of Albany in the State of New York. They sailed up the Hudson River to Albany, where they met the sister of Alexander Hamilton, Mrs Elizabeth Rensselaër. She told Talleyrand that although her brother, the honest Hamilton, handled sums of money every day at the Treasury amounting to millions of dollars, he never diverted any of it for his own personal use. On his modest government salary, he could not afford to bring his children up as he wished, so he had decided to give up politics and return to earning his living as a lawyer. Talleyrand was astonished because, if ever appointed again to a position of political power, he intended to take full advantage of the situation to improve his finances from those governments or individuals willing to pay to see their projects fulfilled, as had already been the case during the Constituent Assembly. Governmental posts involved hard work and long hours, but they could also easily provide extra sources of finance that would fuel a way of life featuring gambling, town houses, carriages, women, expensive furniture, rare paintings and books.

On 12 October 1794, the five intrepid explorers set off from Albany to discover new agricultural land in the general direction of Niagara Falls. Their route led them through virgin territory populated by the Iroquois tribe and home to buffalo, wolves and bears. To survive, the pioneers hunted wild deer which they cut into thin slices of meat and cooked over a camp fire, extinguishing it at night so as not to attract the attention of the local tribes. The ownership of this region was disputed between the British and the Americans, with clashes from time to time because the British Government encouraged the Iroquois to resist the constant advance of American colonists. Although the treaty of 1783 had placed the border further north, Canadian fur hunters still frequented the region and a line of forts in the region of Albany was still in British hands.

On their way back south, not far from Albany, they had promised to visit a beautiful young woman in the village of Troy who Talleyrand had known as a child in the Château de Versailles—the Marquess de La Tour du Pin-Gouvernet, who had been born as Mlle Lucy Dillon. After having been caught up in the drama of the French Revolution, she, her military husband and their children emigrated to the United States where they adopted the farming life. Although familiar with the ways of the French royal court, bi-lingual Lucy Dillon quickly adapted to life in the American backwoods, so that when Talleyrand discovered her, she was hacking up a leg of lamb with an axe. Unseen, he tiptoed up behind her and said in French: "One could not chop up a leg of lamb with greater majesty." Having overcome her surprise, she invited them for supper the following day to eat the leg of lamb. The family La Tour du Pin had escaped France through the city of Bordeaux in 1793 where the young Jacobin leader Jean-Lambert Tallien, Commissioner of the National Convention, ruled pitilessly over the life and death of the local population. Lucy Dillon became friends with Tallien's stunning mistress, Thérésa Cabarrús, who persuaded Tallien to turn a blind eye while the family boarded a boat for America. We will return later to the story of Tallien and Cabarrús, two of the Revolutionary period's most melodramatic personalities.

Many years later the Marquess de La Tour du Pin wrote the story of her life for her grandchildren, including an unadorned sketch of Talleyrand whose charm was so profound: "One regretted inwardly that there were so many reasons not to admire him... You had to protect yourself from his immorality, his behaviour, his life, from everything that you held against him, yet he would charm you even so, like a bird that is transfixed by the eyes of the serpent." He was, however, incredibly kind to Lucy Dillon and her family throughout her long, eventful and tragic life. At this time, he gave her as a gift a lady's saddle with all the accessories and when she fell ill with a stubborn bronchitis he inquired continuously after her health, sending her quinine. She was highly regarded by the local people since, while obviously a French aristocrat, she adopted the farming life, spoke their language and was as good as she was beautiful. In contrast to his *Ancien Régime* life-style in which he frequented several mistresses, the former Bishop of Autun reported to Germaine de Staël in amazement that she "sleeps every night with her husband; they only have one bedroom!"

In the company of M. et Mme de La Tour du Pin, the travellers went to visit General Philip Schuyler, the hero of the Battle of Saratoga and a gentleman involved in their business affairs. As they approached his house, he stood on the steps frantically waving a newspaper and shouting: "Come! Come! There's great news from France!" The newspaper informed them that on the *9 Thermidor* (according to the Revolutionary calendar corresponding to 27 July 1794) a group led by Tallien, Paul Barras and Louis Fréron had overthrown Robespierre, who had been executed the following day—the Terror had ended. Talleyrand's first thought concerned the fate of his sister-in-law, Sabine de Sénozan. His brothers Archambaud and Boson had both fled to Germany leaving Sabine and their children in France to look after the family's property, where she had been arrested for "conspiracy". At first, it looked as if she had avoided death but, elsewhere in the newspaper, he fell upon the list of the last group of people who had been executed on the morning of *9 Thermidor*; there he found the Countess de Périgord's name. She had been advised to declare that she was pregnant in order to delay the execution date, but she had refused to lie. She had detested "the bishop", although subsequently he did everything in his power to care for her three young children.

In 1793 and 1794 France had passed through dramatic events on a horrific scale. On 23 January 1793, the French National Convention had voted for the death of Louis XVI, causing a furore throughout Europe. The horrified British public turned against anything French that could be associated with the Revolution. Although Talleyrand was dismayed at the king's execution, since he was still living in London at that moment, inevitably he had become the focus for abuse by the British press. In the spring of 1793, the French Government was controlled by the Girondins, whose support lay largely outside Paris. The French Army had suffered a series of defeats raising the possibility of invasion, while the population was suffering from poverty due to inflation. The French General Dumouriez deserted to the enemy in April 1793, accompanied by the 19-year-old Duke de Chartres, the future King Louis-Philippe.

Following the execution of Louis XVI, the country had disintegrated with three-quarters of the *départements* seceding, the state bankrupt and foreign armies advancing on all sides. These events had been accompanied by an unprecedented economic and financial crisis leading to food shortages and galloping inflation. With the murder of the radical Revolutionary journalist Jean Paul Marat on 13 July 1793, it was realized that resolute action was the only solution. Faced with this emergency, the National Convention had created the Revolutionary Tribunal and the soon-to-be-dreaded Committee of Public Safety. The group calling itself *La Montagne*, led by Robespierre, feared that any interruption of revolutionary zeal would lead to restoration of the monarchy. The energetic, passionate, incorruptible, courageous Maximilien Robespierre was nominated to the Committee of Public Safety. The Reign of Terror began on 5 September 1793 with a declaration by Robespierre that the Jacobins would take violence into their own hands as an instrument of government. The Parisian mob rose up against the Girondins who tried to flee, but the majority were arrested and guillotined. Aristocrats caught in hiding and political rivals were all executed, among them Philippe, Duke d'Orléans, and Danton. The Montagnards were now free to adopt extreme measures in order to tackle threats from both the interior and the exterior, with the result that for thirteen months the country endured a period of carnage during which some estimates suggest that as many as

40,000 people perished on guillotines in various towns and cities. All men between 18 and 25 years-of-age were conscripted into the national army, prices were blocked, food requisitioned and the administration purged. The Terror began with the execution of all dissidents producing instant acceptance of these austerity measures. With a disciplined army of 1 million men, by the summer of 1794 the military situation had been entirely reversed with the invaders expelled. The French army was about to enter a period of almost non-stop and effortless victories. With no official office other than that of a member of the Committee of Public Safety, but with control of diplomacy, the army, the economy, security and the police, Robespierre was the undisputed master of France. He also believed that he had a private monopoly on virtue, although he eventually lost all popular support, as well as that of the religious authorities. On *8 Thermidor Year II* (26 July 1794) he threatened his opponents without actually naming any of them—everyone felt in the greatest possible danger. The following day, amid tumultuous scenes in the assembly, Robespierre and his supporters were denied the right to speak, arrested and guillotined the next day.

The same guillotine that on *9 Thermidor* executed a group of forty-five anti-Robespierrists, including the Countess of Périgord, accounted for the deaths of 104 Robespierrists on the following three days, bringing the total deaths for that month in Paris alone to 935. The Jacobins, who for five years had been the people's champions, were rejected by the working class whose interests they claimed to represent. Throughout France, the Jacobins underwent a bloody purge with the outcome that both they and the Girondins ceased to exist as a political force. Unfortunately, this crisis did nothing to alleviate the shortage of food and money.

After his expedition to Albany, it was upon his return to Philadelphia that Talleyrand and Alexander Hamilton held long conversations about the economy and foreign trade. There did not seem to be a lot in common between the former Bishop of Autun, cold, cynical and reserved, and the ardent, impetuous American orator. Nevertheless, they were both aristocrats by breeding, both passionately interested in politics and both practical statesmen who scorned the revolutionary who espoused liberty and the slave owner who endorsed freedom. However, while Talleyrand had earned a reputation for lack of integrity, particularly when it came to the money passing through his hands, Hamilton would have died rather than gain financially from a political position. Talleyrand became good friends with both Hamilton and his political rival Colonel Aaron Burr. In 1804, Burr mortally wounded Hamilton in a duel. Many years later, Burr left his visiting card at Talleyrand's house in Paris. When he called back again, he was informed bluntly that a portrait of Alexander Hamilton hung over the owner's mantlelpiece.

When peace had been signed between the Americans revolutionaries and the British in 1783, the 26-year-old Hamilton had been elected to represent New York in the Congress. At this time, each state of the United States wanted to maintain its independence and there were even armed skirmishes between some of them, with the Federal Government having limited powers. Representatives of each state met in Philadelphia in 1787 under the chairmanship of Washington to establish the Constitution of the United States, signed on 17 September, which granted power to the federal authorities over taxes, customs, the monetary system and the colonization of new territories, while each state was responsible for its own internal administration. Hamilton became leader of the "federalists" in favour of a strong central government.

Talleyrand moved restlessly backwards and forwards between Philadelphia in the winter and New York in the summer—there was always the danger of yellow fever in Philadelphia in the hot months carried by mosquitoes arriving on ships from the tropics. While setting up his new homes, he learned that the contents of his house in Paris had been sold by two public auctions in March and July 1795. Another French resident of New York was Alexandre d'Hauterive who Talleyrand had last met at Choiseul's residence at Chanteloup before the Revolution. D'Hauterive now found himself in a most unfortunate situation because, although he had been appointed as French consul to New York in 1790 by the Revolutionary authorities in Paris, he had subsequently lost his job at the same time as Genêt, the former French representative to the United States. To make a living, he sold the fruit and vegetables from his garden in what is now the vicinity of Wall Street. D'Hauterive was eventually replaced as French consul in New York by Antoine de LaForêt. Both of these men would subsequently become Talleyrand's closest collaborators at the Ministry of Foreign Affairs when he returned to France.

Talleyrand observed the United States from the perspective of an economist and a financier. While the French had contributed to the American War of Independence through the provision of troops, ships and money, he noted sadly that, twelve years after victory, the Americans appeared to have forgotten this generous gesture. American independence, rather than hampering British interests, had only multiplied them. At this time there was not a great deal of industry in the United States, so the British were selling more of their manufactured goods in America after independence than during the colonial period. He noted that, even though England had recently been defeated in the American War of Independence and was thoroughly detested for its opposition to the French Revolution, it occupied a privileged place in commerce with the United States. The two countries had in common a language, a religion and a system of justice including trial by jury—all the books on the shelves of American lawyers had been printed in England. Talleyrand observed that the relationship between the United Kingdom and its former colonies had yet to be defined, but: "It requires more time and thought than that employed by a simple traveller to discover that... America... is entirely English... which means that England has every advantage over France to gain from the United States all the rewards that one nation can gain from another." When he returned to France, Talleyrand published a report on the commercial links between the United States and England, having gathered the material for this document during his stay in Philadelphia and New York. He repeated the idea that the wealth of countries depends on peace since it is during these periods that what is most beneficial for civilization proliferates—trade. Passion in politics is an extremely undesirable emotion; it leads to war which paralyses the economic activity of a nation and destroys its wealth. Commercial interest makes former enemies forgive and forget—another golden rule of diplomacy. In Europe, France had every interest to remain within its traditional borders, to abandon conquering its neighbours' territories and to establish firm treaties with them leading to a stable league of powers. From these observations followed his pacifism.

Talleyrand quickly came to appreciate the strengths and weaknesses of the nascent American way of life. Close to his own doctrines were personal freedom and freedom of religion, as well as the importance of trade: "Everybody's business, without exception, is to increase one's fortune." Even though Philadelphia was the largest city and federal capital of the country at that time, Charles-Maurice realised that it would soon be overtaken by New York and it was here that the major European banks should expect to install their headquarters. He also prophesied that before long the United States would become a colossal world power. His most damning verdict was reserved for American cuisine: "The United States is a country where there are thirty-two religions and a single dish—and it's not good."

If wealthy merchants from the Indian sub-continent could be persuaded to purchase land in the United States, profits of as much as 500% were obtainable. Despite dreaming of returning to their beloved France, Talleyrand and Beaumetz borrowed money from Dutch and British banks and chartered a ship destined for India. The news from France was that, after the events of *9 Thermidor Year II*, the Assembly adopted the Constitution of the Year III (1795) and the Government of France was now in the hands of a five-man Directory. While powerful, this committee governed through a system of checks and balances known as *bascule* [see-saw]: an upsurge in Royalism would be met by favouring Jacobism and vice-versa. Among its first decisions was the suppression of the *assignats*, the paper money that Talleyrand had disliked from the very beginning. Moreau de St Méry published a news-sheet for French refugees entitled *Le Courrier de la France et des Colonies*. In the issue dated 26 February 1796 there is an anonymous article which revels in the disappearance of the *assignats* and hopes that the Directory's members will bring peace and prosperity to France. Who but Talleyrand could possibly have written such an article? Whatever political regime followed Robespierre's demise, Talleyrand wanted it to be devoted to the long-term interests of the French people, even if he was himself still obliged to live abroad under the threat of arrest if he returned.

With the change of regime in France following Robespierre's fall, Talleyrand's thoughts began to turn seriously towards returning home. In one of his letters to Germaine de Staël he wrote: "If I stay here another year, I will die." She encouraged him to return as soon as possible. He also wrote to Mme de Genlis in Hamburg, who had the habit of reading his letters out loud to the members of her salon—another way of keeping his name in the limelight. In his mind, it was not Charles-Maurice de Talleyrand who sought to return to France, but rather the evolution of political events in Paris that rendered his presence necessary. On 16 June 1795, he sent a letter (in three copies carried by different ships) from Philadelphia to the French authorities requesting that he might be allowed to return to serve the Republic. The task was given to Desrenaudes to transmit this letter to the Assembly in a form and at a time that seemed the most appropriate. In August, a visitor from France arrived in New York with a copy of the new Constitution of the Year III, together with the speech by François-Antoine de Boissy d'Anglas to the Assembly in which he said that the death of Robespierre had "given back to the people the exercise of their rights and the Republic its independence". That someone could actually stand up and say these words from the tribune without the danger of arrest and to be applauded for saying them was proof that the Jacobins were finished. This speech only fanned the flames of Talleyrand's desire to return to Paris. He wrote to Germaine de Staël: "Get the Abbé Desrenaudes moving!"

And that is exactly what the faithful Desrenaudes did. Now a professor at the École Centrale in Paris, he could judge the political climate. He placed the former Bishop of Autun's petition—written in his own hand—directly on the Convention's table where it could not be missed. It was read out at the assembly's meeting on 3 September and was also published in *Le Moniteur*. Everyone became aware that Talleyrand wished to return, that he supported the Republic, that he had never actually "emigrated", that he had never stopped promoting French interests and he was ready to promote them again if he were back in Paris. He added that he had been forced to leave England because of his close links with the French Revolution. Anxious to point out that the accusations against him were "frivolous", he casually dismissed the two incriminating letters discovered in the king's iron cabinet. His sister-in-law had been guillotined for far less serious crimes, while Mme de Flahaut's husband had suffered the same fate simply for trying to protect his lawyer.

Meanwhile, back in Paris, Pierre-Louis Roederer published a

brochure in which he distinguished between the "bad" *émigrés* who had left immediately after the Revolution in 1789 and who represented Royalist resistance to the Revolution, and the "good" *fugitifs* who fled at the time of the massacres of September 1792. He particularly singled out Talleyrand and Beaumetz whose patriotic conduct in England and in the United States had been outstanding—as Desrenaudes had taken the trouble to remind him. The great Tallien, equally primed, spoke in his favour from the tribune: "[He] was put on the list of *émigrés* even though he left on a governmental mission." However, in order that he should have his name erased from this list and be authorized to return, someone had to propose a proper procedure.

Germaine de Staël found that person and told him what to say. Her choice fell on Joseph Chénier, a poet, dramatist and at that moment one of the finest speakers in the assembly. Chénier did not know Talleyrand and at first resisted the bountiful siren's pleas, but he had a weak spot called Eugénie de La Bouchardie, who ran a gambling house with Germaine, and was also a friend of Thérésa Cabarrús and Rose de Beauharnais (the future "Josephine"). Chénier was persuaded to plead Talleyrand's cause and did his job admirably. Other influential acquaintances supported his petition: the Freemasons belonging to his lodge, as well as moderates, such as Pierre Daunou, Sieyès, Du Pont and Paul Barras, the latter of whom Talleyrand had never actually met. Even Boissy d'Anglas spoke on his behalf: "It is not a matter of friendship, but of justice. Talleyrand is not an *émigré*." By a large majority, on 4 September the National Convention authorized Talleyrand-Périgord, former Bishop of Autun, to return to the territory of the French Republic. When he learned of this decision in Philadelphia on 2 November 1795, he rushed to Moreau's shop and they fell into each other's arms. Quickly, he wrote letters of gratitude to the Citizen Minister for Foreign Affairs, Charles Delacroix, to Daunou, Boissy d'Anglas and Desrenaudes. The incomparable Germaine also merited a thank-you letter in which he assured her of his life-long devotion and asked if he might stay at her residence in Paris. In the short term, Delacroix and Chénier and, in the long term, Germaine, would all live to regret bitterly the return of the "limping devil".

In writing to Lansdowne, Talleyrand states deceitfully that the authorization to return had been granted without him having to ask for it! "This petition is not my work; I learned about it from reading *The Times.*" In his memoirs, he cavalierly negates the enormous exertions of his friends, and particularly those of Germaine de Staël—"of all women, the one who likes most to be of service"—and suggests that the doors preventing his return just opened effortlessly. His treatment of Mme de Staël in the years to come would be simply disgraceful. He would, from his perspective, concentrate on the more important issue—his ambition and his fortune—but she would be deeply wounded by his unprincipled conduct.

At the last minute, the idea of leaving for Calcutta with Beaumetz proved to be too much of a step into the unknown. He had perhaps a sixth sense that this trip was not going to work out. He had decided to return to France from Philadelphia, but before he left New York he had to tell Beaumetz of his change of mind. The two men went for a walk along the waterfront at Battery Park and, watching the waves crashing against the wall below, Talleyrand told Beaumetz that he would not be going with him to India. Beaumetz, who had shared so much with him over the past year-and-a-half and was already in a state of nervous depression, felt betrayed realizing that Talleyrand was abandoning him to his fate. Beaumetz, seized with a terrible rage, almost cast his friend into the water below, but Talleyrand anticipated his intentions and called him to order. Beaumetz collapsed in tears for, in his frustration and anger, he had truly intended to push Talleyrand over the wall. Beaumetz sailed to India from Wilmington, Delaware, in May 1796 via the Cape of Good Hope, accompanied by his new wife, the sister-in-law of Henry Knox, and her three children. When he arrived in Calcutta, he found that Robert Morris had had the same idea to capitalize on Indian investors and already had an agent at work. The last known letter from Beaumetz in India was dated 1801.

During the winter of 1795–1796, Talleyrand set to work assembling a cargo of coffee, sugar and spices to bring back to the needy people of France. He obtained a new passport from Pierre Adet, the replacement Minister of France in New York, who was not a rabid Jacobin like his predecessor. Before his departure, Talleyrand visited the enormous building site that would be the future capital of the United States designed by a Frenchman, Pierre L'Enfant, and named after its founding president.

For all his faults, Talleyrand could be extremely thoughtful about his friends. When the moment came to leave Moreau and Beaumetz, he proposed to each of them to take one of their sons to Paris. He would look after their education, their welfare and would find them a place corresponding to their skills. While the fathers were tempted by the offer, the mothers declined, terrified of the risks involved. Talleyrand loved risks, but did not oppose their decision.

For someone who was impatient to return to France, it is noteworthy that seven months elapsed between receiving the news of his removal from the list of *émigrés* and Talleyrand's departure from Philadelphia. Among the reasons for this delay, the news from France was very disturbing, with rampant inflation and disorder, while his business affairs in the United States may have taken time to wind up. Furthermore, crossing the Atlantic during the winter had, of course, little to recommend it. England was now at war with France and the Royal Navy was known to seize neutral shipping. Talleyrand was, however, very keen not to spend a third summer in the United States and searched desperately for a ship going to Hamburg. On 13 June 1796 he embarked on a Danish ship, *Den Ny Proeve* [The New Test], leaving Philadelphia bound for Europe. The becalmed ship took five days to clear the estuary of the Delaware River but, on the last day of July, he wrote to Moreau announcing that he had landed in Hamburg and that the tricolour cockade was very popular with the French people living there; he immediately began wearing one himself. As soon as the boat tied up at the dockside, a messenger came aboard sent by Adélaïde de Flahaut, a resident in the city, begging him to depart at once. No longer a young woman, she had set her sights on marrying a M. de Souza-Boltelho, Portuguese ambassador to Denmark. She feared that the presence of her former lover might be an obstacle to this enterprise. Talleyrand took no notice of her message, although she did eventually marry her Portuguese diplomat and became the Marquess Adélaïde de Souza-Botelho Mourão e Vasconcelos. Talleyrand maintained his patronage of their son, Charles de Flahaut, until the end of his life—one might add, through thick and thin!

One of his oldest acquaintances, now 50 years old, lived in the Hamburg suburb of Altona, his former neighbour Mme de Genlis, a convinced "Orléanist" favouring a constitutional monarchy for France. This political faction went back to the Revolution's early days with the group of people who had the idea of placing Philippe, Duke d'Orléans, on the throne. During the Revolution, Orléans had changed his name to Philippe Égalité, but as a Girondin had perished on the guillotine during the Terror. His son Louis-Philippe inherited the title of Duke d'Orléans upon the death of his father and his name had been mentioned in Paris as a person whose assumption of power might provide a solution to the political struggle taking place there. As Talleyrand arrived in Hamburg, Louis-Philippe was just leaving for Philadelphia. Although some thirty-four years later his hour would come, at this stage Talleyrand's verdict upon him was that of a "poor instrument" controlled by some ambitious people. He met the leaders of the group that circulated around Mme de Genlis: Charles, the Duke d'Aiguillon and his brother Auguste de Lameth, and also General Dumouriez. Talleyrand wrote derisively to Mme de Staël that his new acquaintances failed to impress him.

Mme de Genlis asked Talleyrand what he intended to do once back in Europe, to which he replied that he had decided to give up politics forever—she was not fooled by this answer. She asked him if, upon returning to Paris, he would buy for her a copy of *Le Traité de la Sagesse* by Pierre Charron, a book on religious tolerance dating from 1601 which tackled human folly, fanaticism and tyranny. To her surprise, she received the book the next day, since Talleyrand always carried a copy with him wherever he went. He made a profound remark about her which could so easily apply to himself: "The steadiness of her imperturbable character was distinguished by its flexibility." During this period, Félicité de Genlis earned her living as a famous novelist and writer on education.

Talleyrand had arrived in Europe armed with letters of introduction to various bankers, who formed one of the most secure networks for financial and political transactions. Governments systematically intercepted and copied letters posted to and from important personalities by the regular mail service and, under Napoleon, Charles-Maurice would use this system to keep track of the activities of the Royalist refugees in England, but banks used their own special couriers for their confidential correspondence. Together with London and Amsterdam, Hamburg would become one of the discreet and dependable places where in future he could hoard his money. The former Bishop of Autun was issued with a new passport by the Hamburg authorities camouflaging his identity as a Swiss businessman with the Latin phrase: *honestus Talayran negociator helveticus.*

He asked Mme de Genlis if she knew of a young Swiss politician named Benjamin Constant who had just written a pamphlet on *De la Force du Gouvernement* [On the Government's Strength] in which Talleyrand discovered to his surprise some of the ideas of his old friend Narbonne. Little did he know that the dear Germaine could have told him all he wished to know about Benjamin Constant, since she was involved with him in a passionate love affair. Constant, red-headed, tall and neither handsome nor cheerful, was, however, very smart and troubling—the very model of a cosmopolitan European intellectual having been educated in the Netherlands, Germany, England and Scotland. He wore spectacles for his short-sightedness, talked through his nose with a lisp and closed his eyes when speaking. Despite a distaste for his undeniable ugliness, poor Germaine was captivated by the young man and experienced a tumultuous love affair that lasted until 1806. Since Narbonne was the father of two of Germaine's children, it is not surprising that Constant acquired ideas arising from his mistress's past lover. Abandoning Germaine, in June 1808 Constant married Charlotte von Hardenberg.

The time that the former Bishop of Autun spent in the United States was not entirely without profit. When he returned to Paris, he sent Cazenove the equivalent of $142,000 as a settlement of their business dealings on the sale of land. We do not know how much profit he made for himself. After depositing in a Hamburg bank the cash he had brought back from the United States, Talleyrand set off for Paris via Bremen, Amsterdam (at that time capital of the French-controlled Batavian Republic), Brussels (at that time the principal town of the French *département* of the Dyle), Amiens and Chantilly. The new designations of these cities resulted from the successful military campaign conducted in 1794 by the French Revolutionary Army led by General Jean-Charles Pichegru. In Bremen, he spent a long time with the French minister, his former colleague Charles Reinhard, who brought him up to date with what was happening in France. He took his time about reaching Paris since he was not entirely confident about the reception that awaited him there. Meanwhile, the country's government staggered from crisis to crisis as the Directory's survival increasingly depended on a powerful element that would decide all political issues for the next eighteen years—the army.

CHAPTER VI
THE DIRECTORATE

Upon his arrival in the capital in September 1796, Talleyrand met again several of his former acquaintances: Pierre Daunou, Antoine Destutt de Tracy, Pierre-Louis Roederer, Emmanuel-Joseph Sieyès, the Marquis de Sémonville. He immediately made contact with the Parisian banking fraternity, including one of Panchaud's colleagues, Jean-Frédéric Perregaux, who had survived the Revolution and the Terror practically unscathed. He was invited to dinner at Perregaux's sumptuous mansion where he met again Radix de Sainte-Foy and the elderly playwright Pierre-Augustin de Beaumarchais, who had also just returned to France after his narrow escape during the Terror. Thanks to Radix, he came into contact with armaments dealers, among them the financier Michel Simons, linked romantically to the beautiful actress Élise Lange. No doubt it was in the apartment of Mlle Lange that Talleyrand met Gabriel-Julien Ouvrard, an eminent businessman and future purveyor of armaments to the French Navy. In the coming years, Charles-Maurice would have abundant dealings with Ouvrard but, as with so many of his closest companions, he never mentions him in his memoirs. As an illustration of his involvement in this world of finance, three months later he was a witness at the marriage of Michel Simons and Élise Lange. Talleyrand's enigmatic relationship with Mme Simons would continue for several years.

Talleyrand had been absent from France for over three years and the Paris that he found upon his return was like a ruined city. Weeds grew on the down-at-heel streets and shattered windows swung in the wind from looted buildings. Street monuments had been vandalized and the churches and monasteries ransacked. People who still had a roof over their heads were prepared to do anything to survive—open a gambling casino, a dance hall, a café, a brothel. While the unhappy French were weighed down with work and taxes, conscripted for war and terrorized by bands of robbers, the politicians tried to distract them with fun-fairs, ice-cream, dancing and fireworks. There was a new calendar, new fashions and new jargon—*monsieur* and *madame* had been replaced by *citoyen* and *citoyenne*. Except for those who had profited from the collapse of society, such as the *nouveaux riches* and the *jeunesse dorée* [the gilded youth], the inhabitants of Paris were faced with galloping inflation and poverty, while famine threatened. The people felt completely deceived by the politicians who had brought the country to its knees. A strong leader was needed. When would he arrive?

In the previous year, the Royalists had taken advantage of this disorganized situation to land an armed force of *émigrés* volunteers transported by British ships at Quiberon Bay in Brittany. They were met and outmanoeuvred by a Republican Army led by General Lazare Hoche, who trapped them on the Quiberon peninsula in July 1795. The National Convention sent Tallien to judge the prisoners, all of whom were convicted and several hundred summarily executed. Public opinion was outraged and Tallien began to lose the support of the *jeunesse dorée* and the right-wing politicians.

In the flush of this military success, the Convention decided to introduce the Constitution of the Year III, creating a double chamber legislature and an executive that would not drift too close either to dictatorship or to democracy. The two legislative chambers were labelled the *anciens* and the *cinq cents* representing all parties in the country, from Royalists to *regicides*. Wisely, two-thirds of the new legislature would in future consist of its previous incumbents, although the ballot was restricted to the wealthier bourgeoisie. The introduction of these new political measures meant that from November 1795 to November 1799 the country was governed by a five-man Directory. The original members of this government were La Révellière-Lépeaux, Rewbell, Barras, and Carnot, with one of them being replaced each year. While they had all voted for the death of Louis XVI, the biggest fish of all was Paul Barras who remained in office from the beginning to the end of the Directory. Of all the outcomes of the Revolution, this government counted as being the worst. The executive, the legislature, the judiciary and the treasury were all independent of each other, which meant that, to remain in power, the government had to play one group off against another.

The policies of the little hunchback Director Louis Marie de La Révellière-Lépeaux were marked by a bitter antagonism towards the Christian religion, which he proposed to supplant as a civilizing agent by theophilanthropy, a new religion invented by the English deist David Williams. He asked Talleyrand, in his capacity as a former bishop, how to make this artificial religion assume a more authentic charisma. Talleyrand listened to La Révellière-Lépeaux's presentation and replied with great gravity: "To found his religion, Jesus Christ was crucified and rose from the dead. Try to do the same."

Aristocratic, intelligent and dishonest, Paul-François de Barras had used the Revolution to fill his pockets. As a committed Jacobin, he had contributed to sending cartloads of victims to the guillotine, but had also risen to prominence during the events of *9 Thermidor* (27 July 1794) when, with Fouché and Tallien, he had brought about Robespierre's overthrow. Handsome, tall, with green eyes and the manners of a gentleman, this former soldier, aged 42, was the only member of the Directory who had created his own little court. Although his official residence was at the Luxembourg Palace, he preferred his luxurious house at Suresnes on the River Seine, furnished with national treasures, or his imposing hunting lodge at Grosbois where he kept his dogs, his horses... and his mistresses. At his crowded receptions, former duchesses rubbed shoulders with fashionable prostitutes. Citizen Beauharnais, the future wife of Napoleon Bonaparte, and Citizen Tallien, the former Thérésa Cabarrús, counted among his most intimate lady friends. Everyone knew that Barras had limited skills as an administrator, but in exploiting intrigues, manipulation, prostitution or orgies he had no equal.

Even before the Directory had actually entered office, these new measures provoked another Royalist revolt on *13 Vendémiaire Year IV* (5 October 1795) on the streets of Paris where the Republican forces found themselves heavily outnumbered. However, the Republicans had cannons and the rioters did not. A young artillery general named Bonaparte suppressed the rioters by firing grapeshot directly into them. He commanded the troops throughout the two-hour engagement and survived unscathed despite having his horse shot from under him. This day was an important step in Bonaparte's rise to power for he became a national hero and soon after was selected as commander of the French army carrying out operations in Italy.

People found Talleyrand's presence in Paris disturbing, since he had a lot of contact with the Orléanists, even though he had scorned them in Hamburg. He wrote to Moreau, still living in the United States: "They do me the honour of considering me as the leader of this learned faction." It is for this reason that the police commissioner, who enjoyed the delightful name of Citizen Cochon [Pig], required his staff to keep an eye on him. Rewbell, one of the Directory's five members and well known for his crude language, considered Talleyrand as a relic of the *Ancien Régime*. Beating the table with his fist during a meeting, he prophesied that Talleyrand might even be capable of plotting the Directory's downfall, so his name should be put back on the blacklist of *émigrés*. Indeed, he was not wrong, for these treasonable intentions had been uttered by the former Bishop of Autun. Barras did not consider a few Orléanists as a threat and advised his colleagues to: "Let these fellows go about their business." Rewbell replied sarcastically—but once again prophetically: "Let Talleyrand stay in France...? Hopefully you do not want him as one of your principal civil servants. Why not a minister?" A month later, a new report by Citizen Cochon listed the continuing suspicious activities associated with Citizen Talleyrand, who protested loudly: "My well-chosen wishes have been directed and are always directed to the joy and glory of the French Republic"—a claim that caused some people to smile. In the meantime, he became involved with Simons and Radix de Sainte-Foy in the Directory's efforts to stimulate the economy. Between politics and finance, the former Bishop of Autun plunged into deep waters.

Thérésa Cabarrús, the very colourful symbol of her era, had been married at the age of 14 (in 1787) to a wealthy aristocrat but divorced him four years later. During the Revolution, she took refuge in Bordeaux, where she met Jean Lambert Tallien, the merciless local Jacobin leader, and began an affair with him. When he was summoned to Paris to be interrogated about his Royalist sympathies, she accompanied him, only to be arrested on Robespierre's orders and thrown into prison, where she met Rose de Beauharnais—known to history as "Josephine". Tallien saved Thérésa from the guillotine on the fateful *9 Thermidor* and soon after rescued Rose/Josephine as well. Thérésa felt obliged to become

Tallien's wife, bearing his child and soon imposing herself as one of the leaders of the Parisian social scene, helping to launch the classic Greek Revival style of women's fashion during the Directory period. In 1794 Tallien had been one of the most influential politicians in Paris but, once the Directory was set up in November 1795, his political influence and relevance began to wane. Soon divorcing Tallien, Thérésa slipped into her crowded life a brief and unsuccessful flirtation with Napoleon Bonaparte. She then moved in with Paul Barras, whose former mistress Rose/Josephine became Napoleon's first wife. Later, Thérésa lived with Talleyrand's banking friend Ouvrard (with whom she had four children). Finally, in 1805 she became the very wealthy and extremely respectable Princess de Chimay, wife to the Comte de Caraman (with whom she had three children) and spent the rest of her life living in considerable luxury first in Paris, then on the family estates at Chimay (now in Belgium). Tallien, on the other hand, was appointed French consul at Alicante through the intervention of Talleyrand, remaining there until he lost the sight of one eye from yellow fever. In his later years, all of his political and financial supporters deserted him and he had to sell his books in order to survive. In a great twist of irony, after the Bourbon Restoration, Tallien ended up receiving a pension from—of all people—Louis XVIII, but sided with Napoleon during the 100 Days and died of leprosy in poverty.

Josephine's first husband, Alexandre de Beauharnais, perished on the guillotine during the Reign of Terror having been accused of leading his army to defeat on the Rhine front. She had herself been imprisoned in the Carmes prison until Tallien managed to release her. She eventually recovered her husband's possessions and thereafter was able to resume her comfortable way of life with her two children. She was part of the social circle that included Barras and, together with Thérésa Cabarrús, soon rose to the position of leader of Parisian society. A naturally kind, generous and charming person, she was admired as a delightful—though not particularly intelligent—hostess. Having belonged to the old society as well as the new one, Josephine was able to give her penniless Corsican husband Napoleon Bonaparte the social background that he lacked.

Bonaparte had first come to the attention of Paul Barras during the siege of Toulon in 1793. As a military man at a loose end in Paris in 1795, he was made responsible for confronting the Royalist insurrection on *13 Vendémiaire*, which he put down ruthlessly—to the satisfaction of the directors. Rose de Beauharnais had been Barras's mistress but, tiring of her, he introduced her to Bonaparte during one of his dinners on 15 October 1795, hoping that the young general would bring a certain stability to her life. She told Bonaparte that she possessed a great fortune—this turned out to be not entirely true. Mme de La Tour du Pin had no illusions about her: "The good woman is basically a liar." They became passionate lovers and soon decided to get married, which took place on 8 March 1796 with Barras and Tallien as witnesses. It has been suggested that, wishing to mark a break with her tumultuous past, Bonaparte decided to call her "Josephine". It has also been proposed that, as a wedding present, Barras accorded him command of the army in Italy. Soon after his arrival in that country, Bonaparte's army would sweep all before it.

By 1797, Talleyrand was one of the most aristocratic people who still possessed his head on his shoulders. Detested in some quarters, he did the rounds of the salons lauded by his friends Choiseul, Narbonne and... Montrond. This is the first time we hear of Casimir, the Count of Montrond, a handsome, smooth-tongued rogue who will become Talleyrand's principal henchman. Due to a malformation of the little finger on his right hand, he always wore a glove, which was considered to be extremely chic. In 1794, Montrond had been imprisoned in the Prison Saint-Lazare, where he met the beautiful Aimée de Coigny. During the early days of the Revolution, Aimée had visited Rome and become attached to the British diplomat Lord Malmesbury, returning with him to London, where she gave birth to his child. In January 1793 she returned to France with Malmesbury to find out what had happened to her estates since the beginning of the Revolution. It was quite the wrong moment to reappear in France. Her lover was arrested but soon released and returned to London. She retired to her property near Paris and resumed her family name of Coigny. The fact that she had been absent from France during her pregnancy attracted the suspicion of the authorities who believed that she was an *émigré,* leading to her arrest on 4 March 1794 and her incarceration in the Prison Saint-Lazare. A young poet, André Chénier, saw her in there and, before he died on the guillotine the day prior to Robespierre's downfall, was inspired to write an elegy addressed to *La Jeune Captive* [The Young Prisoner] in which he described her graceful figure and her easy and careless manner. Montrond was also captivated by the young prisoner and, determined not to die, bought their freedom for 100 louis—which he didn't have. In gratitude, Aimée married her saviour and travelled to London with him, but neither of them was made for matrimony and they eventually divorced. In the world of fashionable society, Casimir de Montrond became infamous for his elegance, wit and successes with women. Fortunée de Hamelin, one of his most famous conquests, came from what is now Haiti and wore daring costumes that shocked even these shameless times. Also renowned for her repartee, at one of Talleyrand's receptions Fortunée met Montrond. Not beating about the bush, he made her a gallant proposition, to which she replied: "But you are married!" He replied: "Only a little." She answered: "And me, even less!" Montrond soon became Talleyrand's bosom friend, right-hand-man and unprincipled stock-market broker, always giving satisfaction.

The 45-year-old Talleyrand was now set in his pre-Revolutionary ways. Even though his financial resources were dwindling, he wore his hair powdered, his coat and stockings were of silk, his linen edged with lace and his shoes decorated with brass buckles. He travelled around the post-apocalyptic Parisian society in his carriage, visiting its salons, its ministerial lobbies, the assembly's corridors and the gambling halls of the Palais Royal where one met the most corrupt and best-informed people of the day. He avoided any preconceived ideas about what he heard and saw, relying on his unshakable political sense to comprehend it. He remained faithful to his ambitions, his impudent tongue and his spendthrift ways. He had no money so he borrowed 25,000 livres from Mme de Staël. Director Carnot accused Talleyrand of having no principles. Despite his many faults, Talleyrand was always faithful to peace, free trade and liberty. Furthermore, he stood for education and justice for all, the right to own property and freedom of the press. In comparison, the members of the Directory had few principles except sleaze and survival.

During their first year, the directors worked harmoniously together. However, differences of opinion soon led to a schism between, on the one side, Carnot and Letourneur, with the triumvirate of Barras, Rewbell and La Révellière-Lépeaux on the other. In 1797, the assembly swung away from Jacobism towards the Royalists, resulting in Letourneur being replaced by Barthélemy, a former French ambassador to Berne and an acquaintance of Charles-Maurice. The Royalist revival disturbed the balance of power, presenting a threat to the Directory that could only be solved by calling in the army.

The army's emergence as a decisive political force was the most important event during the period 1794–1799. The first volunteer army, stiffened by veterans and the existing royal artillery, had won the day at Valmy and Jemappes, but had been dissolved during the winter of 1792–1793. The Jacobin Government of 1793 decided to create a standing army with the compulsory conscription of all Frenchmen aged 18 to 25. These conscripts were blended with the remnants of the old army, with the result that the Republic soon benefited from a huge force of thirteen army corps totalling about 750,000 motivated men. Since much of the nobility had fled the country, the new army's officers were drawn from the ranks, which contributed to a high level of morale. Generals, however, were often chosen for their loyalty to the Republican regime and had been politicians before being placed in charge. The ranks were infiltrated by civilian spies who kept a close eye on events.

For the next twenty years, the French Army acquired an unprecedented military superiority. After the initial wave of conscription, those who had no inclination for soldiering deserted, leaving a large, dedicated force of professional fighters. Due to its revolutionary ethic, new recruits received their training from their seasoned comrades, developing heightened cohesion. The soldiers were treated as individuals and promotion was based on courage in battle. There was never a proper supply system, since the troops found what they needed to survive by living off the land—also known as pillaging—which was to prove fatal in the meagre wastes of Russia in the autumn of 1812. Typically, enemy armies crumbled before the French onslaught with the result that casualties were slight and the troops never required a large munitions industry to serve their victories. These were also the days long before proper care for the wounded and knowledge about hygiene. It is estimated that the vast majority of casualties were not killed on the battlefield but died of wounds, disease, exhaustion and cold. Generalship and staff work were generally poor, since senior officers counted upon the initiative of non-commissioned officers, who owed their positions to bravery and leadership—and not necessarily to intelligence.

Talleyrand became a member of the *Cercle Constitutionnel*, which promoted the Revolution's principles and opposed the Royalists, since he believed at this moment that it was inconceivable to restore the Bourbon monarchy. France needed a constitutional government based on some form of democracy. This idea corresponded to the situation at that time; if the situation changed, then the ideas should evolve. The *Cercle Constitutionnel* had been founded by Benjamin Constant, the lover-in-residence of Germaine de Staël, and counted among its members many important figures: Pierre Daunou, Philippe-Antoine Merlin, Dominique Joseph Garat, Pierre-Louis Roederer, Du Pont, the ex-Abbé Sieyès and the Generals Kléber and Jourdan. Another member was the poet Marie-Joseph Chénier, from whose eyes the blinkers had fallen and who now detested the awful "Abbé Maurice". Talleyrand soon found a place in the *Cercle's* organizing committee, where he reminded his colleagues of his impeccable credentials. In the not-too-distant past he had been a close acquaintance of Mirabeau, had been issued with an official passport by Danton, had been an admirer of Philippe d'Orléans and the Girondins— now all unfortunately dead.

Several months before he returned from the United States and in his absence, Talleyrand had already been elected as a member of the influential *Institut des Sciences Morales et Politiques* [The Institute of Moral and Political Sciences]. In its early days, he had participated in the founding of this society, so his election came in recognition of his past intellectual contribution to education, the economy and democracy. On two occasions in 1797 the institute invited Talleyrand to read a paper before his learned colleagues. As mentioned in the previous chapter, the first one on 4 April dealt with trade between the United States and England and we know about its content because he described it in a long letter to Lord Lansdowne. The diplomatic corps of Paris attended to hear this person who spoke with authority on political and economic matters. On 3 July, the second paper that he read was prophetic because, following the loss of numerous colonies in the West Indies, it recommended the need for France to expand, particularly in a new direction—Egypt!

The capital did not survive uniquely on gambling, fun-fairs, dancing, fireworks and ice-cream. Reports of a stunning series of victories by the French Army in Italy achieved by the 27-year-old General Bonaparte intoxicated the population and gave the Directory unprecedented prestige. Paris needed someone admirable, noble, handsome, destined for glory; the common people began to worship Napoleon Bonaparte. Acting quite independently of the civilian government, he sent back to Paris consignments of captured enemy flags, which thrilled the people, and indemnities in the form of cash, which pleased the government.

Due to its army's successes, the French regime benefited from profound reservations about its intentions on the part of foreign governments. The Directory member who was the first to retire, Étienne-François Letourneur, had been sent to Lille together with Hugues-Bernard Maret in an attempt to open peace talks with the British Government. Given his past experience in negotiations with the British, it was proposed to send Talleyrand along as an adviser. When Rewbell heard about it, he had the appointment cancelled at once. Hugues Maret was one of the *éminences grises* of the Revolution who had been behind many of the secret moves taking place in the National Assembly. He had become acquainted with the refugee Charles-Maurice in London in December 1792. As the Duke de Bassano, Maret would later become Napoleon's able, warlike and devoted aide-de-camp—Talleyrand could not stand him.

One of the Directory's difficulties was in finding talented individuals to fill ministerial posts. They were not allowed to appoint people who were members of the two chambers, nor those serving in the army, while a large number of the most competent people had fled abroad. What was most needed was experience and ability, the very qualities that Talleyrand had to offer. One of Talleyrand's principles was "in important situations, let the women do the work", while his own manipulative skills were not negligible. Upon learning of Rewbell's cancellation of his mission to Lille, Talleyrand went to Germaine de Staël's apartment at the Swedish Embassy, Rue de Grenelle, threw his purse on a table in front of her and declared: "My dear, I have nothing but twenty-five louis left; it's not enough to last a month. You know I can't walk and need a carriage. If you can't find a way of creating a suitable position, I will blow my brains out." The extraordinary harridan needed no further inducement to launch herself into a direct assault on the Directory for, between them, they would find a place for him as a government minister or perish in the process! How to become a minister in a government that treats one with contempt? The Directory's attitude to one of the most outstanding political personalities of the epoch was one of scorn. From July 1797, Talleyrand and Benjamin Constant met each other every morning to plan their activities for the day. There had been some talk of replacing Delacroix, the Minister of Foreign Affairs, because he lacked dignity and, furthermore, he suffered from poor health. Some people already saw him departed, among them the former Bishop of Autun.

It was said of Germaine de Staël that she received "the Jacobins in the morning, the *émigrés* in the afternoon, and everyone to dinner", with the result that she was familiar with all political intrigues, allowing her to promote some of her own. She was a very good friend of Barras and drew his attention to "the bishop's" Republican commitment and his diverse talents; she even mentioned what a virtuous person he was! Barras had not met Talleyrand so Germaine arranged a meeting one evening at the Luxembourg Palace. When Talleyrand entered his office, Barras, if we can believe his description of the scene written some fifteen years later, tells us that he thought it was Robespierre! It is from this time that the legend of Talleyrand "the sphinx" begins, with his cadaverous, blank face, the eyes unmoving, disturbing, his body stiff. Despite bearing a striking resemblance to Robespierre, Germaine told Barras that Talleyrand was worth far more than his deceased lookalike, that he had a heart of gold, that he would be the most ardent friend. She concluded: "He would throw himself in the fire for you." The next evening, she returned to Barras's office and sang Talleyrand's praises again. Brimming with enthusiasm, she even extolled Talleyrand's vices. To a man like Barras, this did not go unnoticed, but he did not pursue the matter. She tried a different tactic: "He has a foot in each camp; you will not meet a more useful agent." He remained unmoved. "You must make him a minister," she added, "at least a Minister of Foreign Affairs." Barras agreed to speak to the Directory about finding him a place for him in the government; Rewbell's reaction could easily be predicted.

Two days later she came back. Barras had spoken to the others and told her: "The person you proposed to me brought together the almost unanimous loathing and lack of esteem by the members of the Directory." Germaine, not easily daunted, replied: "So much the worse for you, Barras! It is because he does not get on well with your colleagues that he will be most useful to you." Barras had had enough and told her to drop the subject. While Germaine had been pestering Barras, Talleyrand had been spreading the word among his friends that his devotion to Barras was boundless. He made sure that in the lobbies, in the salons and even in the government offices themselves someone extolled the former Bishop of Autun's attachment to the Republic's cause. Even the *Cercle Constitutionnel* promoted Talleyrand, since Benjamin Constant told Barras that this institution lay at his feet.

A few days later, Germaine returned for the final assault. She sat on the divan next to Barras and took his hands in hers. With tears running down her face she told him: "I am counting only on you in this world; without you we are lost, completely lost. Do you know what he told me?... He told me that he was going to throw himself in the Seine if you do not make him Minister of Foreign Affairs. He has just ten louis left." Her words make a curious leap of logic: he has no money, therefore make him a minister! She started to collapse on the divan and Barras, from whose memoirs this scene is taken, hoped the 31-year-old matron would fall away from him rather than on him.

Germaine got to her feet and moved towards the door: "I am going to see him. What can I say to encourage him?" This time Barras actually gave a response: "Tell your friend not to drown himself for then it won't be possible to do anything for him." The reasoning behind this statement was undisputable. "We will attempt to use his talents for the Republic and his good intentions for ourselves." Germaine floated down to her carriage which had been parked in front of the building. Hidden inside, the former Bishop of Autun did not look like a man about to throw himself into Seine. But what had actually been achieved? Would Barras do something? The next day Germaine returned to the Luxembourg Palace. She got hold of Barras and plunged in: "Oh! When you have a minister like that!" Barras cut her off: "The matter of your friend is exhausted... Goodbye, Madam!" But this is only one side of the story!

It will come as a surprise to learn that already by the month of May 1797 Talleyrand and Barras were on perfectly familiar terms with each other. Charles-Maurice was useful to Barras because he knew the businessmen and bankers who mattered and had links with all political parties. We also know that Talleyrand could be devastatingly charming when he chose to. How Barras and Talleyrand actually became acquainted depends upon which one of them you believe—both equally unreliable. Denying their already established relationship earlier in the year, Talleyrand states deviously that he never sought to become a minister and had never met Barras before mid-summer 1797! It was all Mme de Staël's doing, which she accomplished without consulting him!

In his memoirs—notoriously unreliable—the picture that Talleyrand paints is entirely different from that of Barras! Writing nearly twenty years later, Talleyrand wished to give the impression that Barras had begged him to accept the post of Minister of Foreign Affairs! He says that in July 1797, without ever meeting Barras before (!), he received an invitation to have dinner at his house at Suresnes to the west of Paris on the River Seine. He arrived early and, with no-one about, started to read a book in the library. Before Barras appeared, a panic-stricken gardener burst into the room shouting: "M. Raymond has just drowned himself." Who was M. Raymond? It turned out to be a young secretary, brought up by Barras and of whom the Director was extremely fond. That summer's day, Raymond Valz had gone for a swim in the Seine and disappeared. When Barras learned the news, he cried out in anguish and shut himself in his bedroom. Barras told his guest to have dinner without him, then changed his mind and asked him to come up to his bedroom. What a scene! Barras heartbroken and tearful, took Talleyrand's hands and held them tight. Meanwhile, the former Abbé de Périgord's ecclesiastical training had come to the fore: "I said to him all the gentle things that came to my mind for the situation I saw him in and in which I found myself. He asked me to come back and see him in Paris. I had hardly known him two hours and I could have believed that I was the very thing that he liked the most!"

According to Talleyrand, they rode back to Paris together in a carriage and Barras promised to help him find a post in the government.

Since Raymond Valz was drowned on 15 July 1797, while we know that Talleyrand had been a close associate of Barras since early May, parts of this story are apocryphal. Nevertheless, Talleyrand received the promise from Barras that Delacroix would be dismissed and he would become the next Minister of Foreign Affairs. It just needed Barras to convince his four reluctant colleagues. What could be easier? Two years later, Barras would have good reason to regret his association with Talleyrand.

The Directory's debate took place on 17 July. To begin, Carnot accused Talleyrand of selling the priesthood, of selling his God, of selling the king. Since Carnot had signed Louis XVI's death warrant and Talleyrand had not, this last statement seemed somewhat excessive. Furthermore, Talleyrand had not sold his God since he never had one in the first place. After a passionate debate, the directors decided to take a vote—four of the five members present had to vote against Talleyrand's appointment for the motion to be defeated. To the astonishment of Barras, three votes were in favour of Talleyrand and two against.

Without knowing the meeting's outcome, Talleyrand had gone to the theatre with Boniface de Castellane that evening. In the middle of the performance, Benjamin Constant burst in out of breath and told them the news. During the Directory's debate that day, and at the request of Germaine, he had been present standing silently behind Barras's chair. Upon being told of the outcome, Germaine had immediately sent Constant to find Talleyrand at the theatre. Talleyrand did not usually betray his emotions, but this occasion was not usual. He hugged Constant. All three men left the theatre, jumped in a cab and rushed to thank Barras in person at the Luxembourg Palace. As a general rule, in this age of corruption, men who went into politics expected to be well rewarded for their pains. During the journey, he kept repeating the phrase: "We are going to make an immense fortune... *une fortune immense.*"

Less than a year after this aristocrat of the *Ancien Régime,* this unfrocked bishop had returned from exile, he was ready to swear allegiance as Minister of Foreign Affairs for a government and a Constitution he held in contempt. One can only admire the subtlety of Charles-Maurice's manoeuvres to satisfy his ambition to become a minister. He described his appointment disingenuously to one of his colleagues with a perfectly straight face: "I accepted the ministry because I was nominated. That was my only motive."

The following day he happened upon Mme de La Tour du Pin who had just arrived back from the United States. Talleyrand offered to find her husband some kind of suitable employment. She declined stating that they did not have enough money to live in Paris and intended to live quietly on their family estate. Talleyrand's reaction was: "Bah! There's always money when one wants it." Somewhat shocked, in her diary Mme de la Tour du Pin wrote: "That's just the way he is!" The conversation then casually revolved around the events of the day. With his nonchalant air, Talleyrand informed them that several new ministers had been appointed. When interrogated on the subject, he finally confessed that: "Oh! Foreign Affairs? Me, no doubt!" and, picking up his hat, left the room.

CHAPTER VII
NAPOLEON BONAPARTE

Upon being appointed Minister of Foreign Affairs to the Directory and as one of the last surviving nobles who had been brought up in the customs of the *Ancien Régime,* Talleyrand went to the Luxembourg Palace and prostrated himself before Barras. It was late at night on 17 July 1797, but before his master went to bed the new minister insisted on an improvised ceremony of participating in his pre-sleeping routine—as in the past with the king at Versailles—and Barras just let him do it. Barras would learn that his new employee was extremely skilled at negotiating treaties, in arranging victory celebrations or a banquet and, if the occasion required, in organizing a coup d'état. Talleyrand was invited to return the following day to be introduced to the Directory's five members and to receive his ministerial portfolio from Charles Delacroix. Foreign Minister Delacroix had been outmanoeuvred, being dispatched as French ambassador to The Hague. Within a year, Mme Delacroix would give birth to a child who would grow up to become the celebrated painter Eugène Delacroix. Little did Barras know that the show of respect he had received was the prelude to a sequence of events over the next two years that would be the Directory's downfall. Seventeen years later, even Germaine de Staël would lament: "I am accountable and guilty before the gods and men of having introduced Talleyrand into the government; it was a crime, a terrible crime."

The new minister would receive a salary of 100,000 francs per annum plus 7,000 for the upkeep of his household. In comparison, an ambassador received 10,000 francs per annum. The salary was a matter of little importance to Talleyrand because it would be small change alongside the "advantages" he expected to attract in his position as minister. Within three months he had spent more than half of his salary on office furniture and an elegant white carriage that was instantly remarkable on the streets of Paris. Regrettably, the coach-builder had not been paid, so this craftsman waited at the entrance to the Ministry of Foreign Affairs in the hope of catching the new minister and presenting his bill. When the opportunity arose, he seized the passing carriage door and explained the situation, to which Talleyrand immediately responded: "You must be paid!" The coach-builder had probably heard this before so clung on to the vehicle: "You will pay me Citizen Minister, but when?" "When?" replied Talleyrand. "You are extremely curious."

The Ministry of Foreign Affairs was housed in a magnificent private house called the Hôtel de Galliffet, constructed between 1776 and 1792 at the heart of a block between the Rue de Grenelle, the Rue de Varenne and the Rue du Bac in what is now the seventh *arrondissement* of Paris. The building still stands and for our purposes will be known as the Rue du Bac [Ferry Street]. The Galliffet family never lived there since they had fled during the Revolution and the new building had been confiscated by the government. In those days the ministry was a small administrative unit employing some fifty people for correspondence, translations, encryption and passports, as well as three political departments and an accounting section. It was on the ground floor of this building that Germaine de Staël would be famously snubbed by Napoleon. It would also be here a few weeks later that Talleyrand would present the Ottoman ambassador, Esseid Ali Effendi, with the most beautiful women of Paris and, when asked who he would most like to dine with, chose the 27-year-old Marquess de La Tour du Pin—who we first met chopping up a leg of lamb with an axe in the American backwoods. Talleyrand opened a new section for French consulates responsible for trade relations in foreign countries and he persuaded the government to acquire an adjacent building to store the ministry's archives and library.

Talleyrand's predecessor, Charles Delacroix, and Charles Reinhard who would follow him at the ministry, both lived frugally as model civil servants. In contrast, Talleyrand conducted an extravagant lifestyle that needed to be sustained by huge amounts of cash. He sent a series of requests to the Minister of Finance, Dominique-Vincent Ramel, expressing his difficulties over the modest budget with which he had to work. These protests helped to conceal the opportunities for gerrymandering—it is estimated that soon after entering office he had managed to multiply his salary by six or seven times. It was not unusual for government officials to expect generosity from the people they dealt with in expediting certain affairs such that, if the foreign ambassadors resident in Paris expected Talleyrand to take them seriously, large sums of money had to change hands. Concerning the Rue du Bac's new resident, the Prussian ambassador Sandoz-Rollin communicated to his superior in Berlin: "We could give him a gift of any amount of cash, but it should not be less than 300,000 francs."

As always with the former Bishop of Autun, there is the façade of appearances and a parallel reality going on behind the scenes. Almost as soon as he took up his post, there were rumours of secret funds of considerable proportions circulating at the Ministry of Foreign Affairs. The origin of the rumours is believed to be a certain Lewis Goldsmitz, alias Henri, alias George Levy, alias George Hamilton, etc., who became responsible for the press and propaganda service at the ministry. Two years later, Goldsmitz walked out of the job and returned to England, resentful about the amount he had been paid. In 1805 the bogus memoirs of Charles-Maurice de Talleyrand were published in London, *Mémoires d'un Homme d'État,* authored by a certain "Stewarton", containing information in minute detail about the numerous payments made to the minister particularly between July and December 1797 amounting to some 700,000 francs. Talleyrand displayed the shallowness of his probity by simply denying the whole affair.

Diplomats and politicians keep silent about the financial wheeling and dealing that may have influenced their decisions. It is only when something went seriously wrong and the press intervened that the general public became aware of the circumstances behind the rumours. In London, thirty-five years later he gave the explanation that his personal fortune was first founded during peace negotiations with Portugal soon after taking up his post. On 20 August 1797, a peace treaty was indeed signed between France and Portugal, but the French annulled it in October because the Queen of Portugal, Maria I, had not ratified the treaty within the allotted time span and had also allowed British troops to occupy some of the principal military positions in her country. These events led to the blockage of commissions and a row between directors Barras and Rewbell. The press got wind of the affair and began to publish details, not always accurate but enough to attract attention. The Portuguese negotiator, Antonio de Araujo de Azevedo, who was also responsible for handling the payment of commissions, was thrown into a Parisian prison in January 1798. From there he sent a dispatch to his government in Lisbon saying that Talleyrand had not passed all the secret payments to the directors but kept a part for himself: "Proof of his immorality, but since they are all the same animal, Talleyrand knows how to use it and, apart from this chicanery, was always faithful to me."

The frenzy of money passing through Talleyrand's hands became so blatant that before long there was a scandal. A dispute between the young United States of America and France occurred over the violation of a trade treaty with the result that the two countries were conducting a war at sea. Several hundred American merchantmen had been seized by French corsairs, crippling American trade. Three American plenipotentiaries arrived in Paris in October 1797 seeking indemnities that the Directory should pay the United States for the vessels and cargoes seized on the high seas by French privateers. Before negotiations could begin, they were kept waiting for several weeks, during which time they received visits from a mysterious lady, then a banker and finally three of Talleyrand's "agents": Casimir Montrond, Maximilien Radix de Sainte-Foy and André d'Arbelles (christened "X, Y and Z" by the American delegation). These intermediaries proposed certain "simple arrangements" that would need to be addressed if the negotiations were to take place in a constructive atmosphere. The Directory's price was 50,000 golden louis, equivalent to more than 1 million livres. In other words, the Directory would pay the indemnities if part of the money was returned to them as a "commission". This colossal sum wasn't all for Talleyrand; he intended sharing it with the Directory's five members. The three guileless Americans were also expected to "reward" the intermediaries who had proposed the arrangement. They were not used to such underhand dealings and for six months refused to play along. In this affair, Talleyrand proceeded with a certain clumsiness which led to the whole matter being aborted. Already, on 22 October, the three Americans wrote a report back to Washington describing the perfidious manner in which the French Minister of Foreign Affairs proposed conducting diplomatic affairs. On 3 April 1798, President John Adams made a speech before the United States Congress referring to this shameful business. The French press kept very quiet about the "XYZ Affair", but the British Government managed to distribute in France part of the American correspondence translated into French. Talleyrand appeared unruffled and dismissed the matter nonchalantly. In order to protect Barras, who was one of the beneficiaries, a short anonymous article appeared in *Le Moniteur* of 9 June 1798 explaining blandly that a minister could not be held accountable for irresponsible activities carried out by government agents. The three Americans, on the other hand, were definitely ruffled and returned home indignantly pouring scorn on this ex-bishop who had asked for "sweeteners". Talleyrand rather liked the word and used it in future transactions—of which there would be many. Given the hostility generated by this affair and the rumours circulating in Paris, Mme de Staël went to see "the bishop" in his office seeking some kind of explanation or justification. After she had stated the case for the prosecution, the first cracks appeared in their friendship, for Talleyrand simply got up and walked out of the room. One hopes that she was repaid for her earlier loan. As much as we may admire the principles he stood for on peace, education and personal freedom, from the modern perspective he can be reproached for his lack of integrity.

It was difficult to catch the former Bishop of Autun red-handed in these affairs because he always acted through a series of front-men and go-betweens whose morals had little to recommend them. Although he paid them well, the greatest danger was that one day they might blackmail him. Certainly, the most reliable, the most faithful and the most buccaneering of these rascals was Montrond, the adventurous Casimir. As a young man serving in the army, there was an incident that rather set the tone of his career. He was caught in *flagrant délit* with the wife of a young lieutenant, who challenged him to a duel. When, later, Montrond was asked if he knew the officer in question, he replied brazenly: "By God, did I know him! I killed him!"

Montrond was a polite, charming and elegant dandy famous for his wit, his trend-setting costumes and his gambling; in fact, his company was so delightful that people forgave him for his faults. Throughout their long friendship Talleyrand called him "The child Jesus from Hell". Montrond had access to Talleyrand's office night and day where his less-recommendable skills made him indispensable when dealing with thieves, informers and spies… and the stock market. He spoke good English, so the Minister of Foreign Affairs used him for the most clandestine, the most delicate missions to London. Apart from Fortunée de Hamelin, his innumerable mistresses included Laure, the Duchess d'Abrantès (Bonaparte's "little pest"), Napoleon's sister Pauline and Lady Yarmouth, by whom he had a son, Henry, Lord Seymour, who later in the nineteenth century became famous as the promoter of boxing and fencing, but above all horse-racing. He also tried but failed to seduce the unconquerable and virtuous Juliette Récamier. Talleyrand said he liked Montrond because he was not overburdened with scruples, to which Montrond replied that Talleyrand had no scruples at all. Fortunée de Hamelin once asked Montrond why he liked Talleyrand so much, to which he replied: "Good heavens, Madame, who would not like him? He is so depraved!" Talleyrand's verdict on Montrond was equally succinct: "He owns no property; he receives no salary; he spends 60,000 francs per year; and he has no debts." In fact, Montrond gained his income from card games and successful investments based on the confidential information he obtained from his governmental and banking contacts.

There were a number of other "agents" who frequented the Rue du Bac to do the dirty work. We have already met the elderly Maximilien Radix de Sainte-Foy during the episode of the three American plenipotentiaries. He was a long-term associate of Talleyrand who no doubt managed the ministry's secret funds together with the banker Jean-Frédéric Perregaux. Radix had made a fortune out of various fraudulent activities and investments in property. Arrested many times during the Revolution, he had a number of narrow escapes from the guillotine thanks to the timely intervention of his powerful friends. Yet another visitor at the Rue du Bac was Gabriel-Julien Ouvrard, the wealthy banker and most-recent lover of Thérésa Tallien. When Talleyrand had returned from the United States, Ouvrard had given him advice on financial speculation and in return he now benefited from inside information on the government's future policies provided by the new minister. Through such colleagues as these Talleyrand was able to cultivate "the art of doing nothing".

At the Ministry of Foreign Affairs, Talleyrand built around himself an entourage of faithful civil servants, the first of whom was Alexandre-Maurice Blanc d'Hauterive, who we last heard of selling fruit and vegetables on the streets of New York, from where Charles-Maurice had rescued him and brought him back to France. He was provisionally given a small post in the consulates section but soon graduated to become head of the "South" political section, was consulted on all important matters and even replaced the minister when he was travelling. An amusing anecdote concerns an incident one morning when d'Hauterive entered Talleyrand's bedroom with an urgent dispatch requiring an immediate response that had to be in Talleyrand's handwriting. Too drowsy to concoct a suitable reply, Talleyrand complained: "To write it and to compose it at the same time is too much. So, d'Hauterive, I will write while you dictate." Another "American" was Antoine René Charles Mathurin, Count de LaForêt, who was appointed as head of the accounting section and brought order into an insolvent ministry. The "North" was directed by Joseph Durand de Mareuil, who was already working at the ministry as the head of the political section and would later in his career become a French ambassador. Two other staff members, Gabriel-Antoine Perrey and Charles-Maxime de Villemarest, would eventually turn against Talleyrand: the former resorted to blackmail while the latter wrote a book that took the form of an accusation.

Most of his colleagues on the Ministry of Foreign Affairs' payroll remained faithful to him throughout their or his lifetime. Charles-Maurice also recruited, on an ad-hoc basis, young journalists who might nowadays be grouped under the title of "spin doctors". The most brilliant of these was Antoine-Athanase Roux-Laborie, a former priest, who was responsible for a newsletter addressed to foreign embassies in Paris providing them with quasi-confidential diplomatic information. He subsequently became the editor of several successful newspapers which drew their information "directly from the cabinet of M. de Talleyrand". From the beginning, he was recruited to massage ministerial information and subsequently became involved in many of Charles-Maurice's business affairs. Descriptions of Roux-Laborie dwell on this bold, fast-moving personality, seen everywhere and difficult to seize: "This man so complex and rapid, well known for the variety, the quantity and the brevity of what he wrote." He employed his own form of roundabout double-speak; in the time it took to read and digest it, he had already passed on to another subject.

We have already mentioned the ex-Abbé Borie Desrenaudes several times, who now became Talleyrand's personal assistant and drafted the minister's communiqués. Talleyrand would describe to him what he wanted to say and Desrenaudes would prepare a first draft which the minister would then polish. Talleyrand was well-known for re-working his texts so that they incorporated a certain ambiguity that was at the same time clear, colourless… and elusive—they needed to be read with concentration. Over the years, the collaboration between Desrenaudes and Talleyrand became so close that they understood each other perfectly with the minimum of guidance. The Baron de Vitrolles, who we will meet later, worked closely with Talleyrand in 1814 and had this to say about his drafting practices: "When the letter he had asked for was brought to him, he would read it carefully. If he was not entirely satisfied, he would fold the paper and give it back to the author: 'That's not it' or 'That's not it yet' or even 'That's not quite it' without further explanation. One had to begin again until the final masterpiece was achieved: 'That's it'."

His political colleague Étienne Pasquier described how he would take hold of an idea—one of his own or somebody else's—and examine it from all its facets. He had acquired a reputation both for rapid conversations and rapid work. When preparing a report for Bonaparte: "He makes his plan, gathers his ideas and writes them down, without any order in a confused way… he writes in an illegible way cramming everything onto a single page." His personal notes were then read by one of his team, a draft version prepared in correct diplomatic language, and corrections discussed or written down. What distinguished his messages was their personal tone: "What you end up with is entirely Talleyrand."

One day Talleyrand read a remarkable report by a young man, Jean-Baptiste de la Gouay, Count de La Besnardière, who he subsequently recruited as a secretary in the ministry. They would work together until Talleyrand's dying day. La Besnardière would rise within the ministry to become head of the "North" department serving all the French political regimes up until 1830. Courtiade, Talleyrand's manservant, who had followed him faithfully to Autun, London, Philadelphia, New York and the middle of nowhere, remained his constant guardian angel at the Rue du Bac.

Under the Directory, the minister may or may not have been consulted on French foreign policy but was, nevertheless, expected to carry out the decisions issued from the Luxembourg Palace without further comment. When he resigned from the ministry on 14 July 1799, Talleyrand took care to state unambiguously that he had had nothing to do with a series of catastrophic foreign policy blunders and the appointment of unqualified ambassadors. Many of the diplomats appointed by the Directory were revolutionaries who had signed King Louis XVI's death warrant and were now representing France to the crowned heads of Europe, some of whom were linked to the late French monarch by marriage. The gaucherie of their manners and the ordinariness of their costumes contrasted sharply with the dignified reserve and regalia usually associated with an ambassador's position. Furthermore, they enjoyed a certain independence allowing them at times to cause havoc in the courts of foreign countries. Talleyrand's disdain also extended to the members of the Directory, who prevented him from making the changes within the ministry that he desired. Director Jean-François Rewbell, who was mainly responsible for foreign affairs, was a bully whose attitude to delicate diplomatic negotiations was often irascible and crude.

In 1797 and 1798, the French Republic was at war with many European monarchies due to an irreconcilable confrontation between the Revolution and the ancient Royalist order. The outcome was that the powerful French armies had overrun a number of satellite republics in what are now Belgium, the Netherlands, Switzerland and Italy. Talleyrand disapproved because he believed the peoples of these territories, once they had recovered from the initial shock of being invaded, would conceive a deep hatred for the French, becoming clandestine enemies all the readier to enter into a coalition against France. In a repetition of his visionary advice to Danton in 1792, he warned the government that, rather than becoming territorial acquisitions, the invaded lands could easily become a burden.

In May 1797, elections had resulted in a majority of Royalists in the Assembly under the leadership of Jean-Charles Pichegru, while François

Barthélemy's appointment to the Directory was also viewed as favouring a Bourbon Restoration. Lazare Carnot, the most respectable member of the government, was also believed to support the Royalist cause. At first, Barras had been undecided as to where to place his support but finally aligned himself with Rewbell, La Révellière-Lépeaux and the Republicans against the Royalists. Then, a Royalist agent, the Count d'Antraigues, was arrested carrying documents plotting to overthrow the Directory. It was decided to take firm action and the coup d'état of *18 Fructidor Year V* (4 September 1797) was designed as an operation conducted by three of the five directors against the other two with the support of the army. This blow was designed to weaken both the Royalists and the Jacobins. At dawn that day, General Augereau, who had been sent by Bonaparte from Italy, carried out the military occupation of Paris. Barthélemy, Pichegru, 140 Royalist members of the Assembly, council presidents, generals, politicians, priests and journalists were arrested and dispatched by ship to French Guyana— where only the very fortunate avoided a miserable death. However, both Barthélémy and Pichegru managed to negotiate their escape and eventually made their way back to Europe. Carnot had been allowed to flee to Germany with his family. In this way, the Royalist threat was thwarted. As would become his habit when dramatic events were taking place, Talleyrand was playing cards the evening before at the Rue du Bac, but he had taken care to warn Maret, Du Pont and Roederer to seek a place of refuge. With great irony, Talleyrand prepared a press release describing what had happened for the benefit of foreign governments: "The Directory, by its courage, by the broadness of its vision and the impenetrable secret that ensured its success, has shown to the highest degree that it possesses the skill to govern in the most difficult circumstances." Rather like his episcopal letter to the priests of Autun, it was a masterpiece of propaganda.

From 1798 onwards, the European governments realized that Talleyrand was an advocate of peace, so it was financially worth their while to encourage him to promote such policies rather than to go to war. When, after the coup d'état of *18 Fructidor*, it was proposed to make Talleyrand one of the five directors, several foreign governments supported his candidature. The best way to express their backing was with large quantities of money; Spain and Portugal placed a fund of 1,500,000 livres at his service to purchase the support of the assembly members who might vote for him. The directors were often uncouth politicians with narrow perspectives and were all disposed to serve themselves by being "purchased"—Barras first among them. It is believed that during his first two years as minister Talleyrand received gifts of 13.5 million francs from fifteen different foreign governments. Later on, when both Barras and Mme de Staël were his bitter enemies, they would give precise information about the bribes he received, with Barras careful not to disclose any information that would incriminate himself since he had often shared in the bounty. During his four years in power, Director Paul Barras acquired such wealth that he was able to live the rest of his life in luxury.

Talleyrand saw his first role as trying to reinforce the confidence of foreign governments in the directorial regime. For this purpose, he issued a circular to his ambassadors providing them with useful ways of explaining to their contacts that they should not be alarmed about "a few differences of opinion among the French". At first view, the divisions in French politics appeared to weaken the country. The Jacobins were always ready to pursue the aims of the Revolution and the Royalists to bring back the monarchy. In reality, France was not so weak since its army was conducting victorious campaigns beyond the country's borders. From time to time, the army sent back to Paris captured booty and cash, while the politicians were very keen that the army should fight its battles abroad and not at home.

However, it was Mme de Staël who behaved as if she were the head of state, making plans to place her friends and allies in key positions. "Bonaparte must take advantage of this. I want him to be made a Director at once. I want him to be there with Barras who I would keep. Sieyès, Talleyrand, Constant and him. The Republic would be perfectly well governed." She wrote to Bonaparte to assure him of her good intentions and support in offering him this place. The last thing that Bonaparte wanted was the good intentions and support of a woman, least of all a "female idealist". When he desired a place in the government, he would take care of it himself. But what about the two seats left vacant in the Directory by the removal of Carnot and Barthélemy? Bonaparte and

Talleyrand would have been two ideal candidates, but they were to be disappointed because the places were eventually filled by two unknowns: Neufchâteau, a modest poet; and Merlin de Douai, an unexceptional lawyer. Bonaparte was now fully alert to the political consequences of his military victories in northern Italy, and was beginning to think less like a warrior and more like a statesman. Talleyrand sent the ex-Abbé Sieyès, the best lawyer of his time, to create a constitution for Bonaparte's newly conquered Cisalpine Republic.

No sooner had Talleyrand assumed his office than, on 26 July 1797, he wrote a letter to Bonaparte in a majestic style: "I have the honour to inform you, General, that the executive Directory has appointed me Minister of Foreign Affairs. Awed as I am by the functions of which I appreciate the perilous importance, I need to reassure myself by being cognizant of the measures and support that your glory will contribute to negotiations. The mere name of Bonaparte is an instrument that overcomes all obstacles." Bonaparte soon realized that he was dealing with a personality out of the ordinary, unlike the bickering members of the Directory. Josephine came to see him in Italy on 20 August and brought him all the latest gossip from Paris, where everyone was talking about the new minister's good/bad reputation. Bonaparte congratulated the Directory on its choice of minister and then thanked Talleyrand for his letter: "The government's choice of you for Minister of Foreign Affairs is a tribute to its judgement. It is proof of your great talents, your refined sense of citizenship, a person who has not been tempted by the aberrations that have dishonoured the Revolution." These last two phrases skilfully acknowledged that Talleyrand was neither a Royalist nor a Jacobin. This was the preliminary contact in an alliance that would see both of these men, as well as Europe in its entirety, plunged into turmoil over the next eighteen years.

Bonaparte was a brilliant general who made war for his own purposes. When he won a victory over the Italians or the Austrians, he took it upon himself to sign peace treaties with them without any attempt to consult the Directory. The directors did not object or impose their authority because Bonaparte financed the French Government with the enormous indemnities he was extracting from his defeated enemies. Before Talleyrand entered office, Bonaparte had already signed treaties with the Pope and the Emperor of Austria. Rather than call him to order, Talleyrand hinted that he recognized in this brilliant young man the person who would save France. The Directory issued its instructions to Talleyrand, who had no real power, passing them on like a model bureaucrat, but he knew that Bonaparte would interpret them or ignore them as he wished. For example, in September 1797 Talleyrand informed Bonaparte twice that the Directory did not want the Republic of Venice to fall into Austrian hands, but on 17 October at Campo-Formio Bonaparte ceded Venice to Austria. The signed treaty was brought from Italy to Paris and presented to the Directory by General Berthier and the scientist Gaspard Monge. Talleyrand might have expressed outrage at this insubordination, but made no reference at all to his previous instructions: "Here then is peace accorded and peace *à la Bonaparte*. Please receive my heartfelt congratulations for it, my General; words fail to tell you all that one would want at this time. The Directory is happy, the public ecstatic. Everything is good." Bonaparte realised that in Paris he had within the government a reliable ally. In the next few years, the two men understood each other's usefulness, with Talleyrand behaving like an impresario managing a great star.

While establishing close links with Bonaparte, Talleyrand remained loyal to Barras, who had brought them together. One could even say that the three men had a common interest. From August 1797, Barras made Talleyrand responsible for informing Bonaparte of what was happening in Paris, either directly or through Lavalette, the general's aide-de-camp. Very soon a double exchange was taking place, one through official correspondence and the other through more discreet letters delivered by special courier. Bonaparte revealed to Talleyrand his interest in politics. He was disgusted with the legislature which, since the Revolution, had been chopping and changing the law at regular intervals, leaving the country "without laws, only 300 drafts". What was needed was a strong executive.

The staircases of the Rue du Bac were always heaving with senior officers from the army in Italy. On 2 September, the Ministry of Foreign Affairs was host to a series of dinners attended by six generals whose titles would become household names over the coming decade and a half: Augereau, Berthier, Bernadotte, Junot, Kléber and Lannes. Charles-

Maurice's guests also included Radix de Sainte-Foy, Boniface de Castellane, Mme de Staël, Thérésa Tallien, but also for the first time we learn of the existence of a certain Mme Catherine Grand. Lavalette tells us of one evening after dinner when the minister showed them into a small office "to see a portrait of the hero" by Andrea Appiani, which drew expressions of admiration. There could be no doubt whatever that Bonaparte would hear an enthusiastic report about it in Italy.

The first meeting of the Directory that Talleyrand attended was typical of its calamitous procedures. Barras and Carnot quarrelled violently over a missing file. On another occasion, the two men tore off their jackets and prepared to come to blows. Everyone in the room rushed to intervene, including La Révellière-Lépeaux, a hunchback, who called out desperately for Talleyrand's help, whose withered foot we already know about. Talleyrand, who favoured politeness and subtlety, could hardly have been more unimpressed with the way the government actually conducted its business. He feared to be drawn into the disorderly conduct of these unruly meetings.

On another occasion, Talleyrand was summoned before the five directors and made to stand before them while they interrogated him. The Directory's secretary-general who wrote the minutes of its meetings was one Citizen Lagarde, whom Talleyrand had attempted to entice into his network of informants in order to find out what was happening at the Directory's meetings when he was not present. Barras cross-examined him: "Citizen, your close relationship with Lagarde, our secretary, worries us and we expect you to explain your motives." It would take more than the five directors to intimidate Talleyrand. He asked for a sheet of paper and wrote words that he dared not speak: "It is because when you say 'fuck' Lagarde writes 'good Lord'." Case dismissed!

The members of the Directory were also intrigued by his suddenly avowed fidelity to Jacobinism and his profound "patriotic faith" in the Republic. Barras remarked sarcastically: "Really, Monsignor? Without being obliged to do it?" Rewbell hated Talleyrand and took every opportunity to humiliate him. The Directory had learned that the United Kingdom, France's enemy, had signed a trade agreement with Spain's American colonies. Rewbell was furious at this "treason" and demanded an explanation from the Minister of Foreign Affairs, although it was none of France's business if England and the Spanish colonies wished to trade with each other. Talleyrand's first report on the subject was refused by Rewbell with the remark: "Very bad! More detail required." The storm passed upon submission of a second report.

There was another day when Rewbell threw all the papers coming from the Rue du Bac angrily into the air treating Talleyrand like a naughty delinquent. Worse was to come. Rewbell asked Talleyrand a point-blank question and Talleyrand was unable to answer on the spot. Foreseeing another violent outburst, Talleyrand excused himself sarcastically: "I do not believe myself strong enough to enter into a discussion with Citizen Rewbell, who everyone accepts as Europe's first expert on diplomacy and administration," and asked to be given time to think about his answer. Rewbell was not impressed. He locked Talleyrand in an empty office and told him: "If you need to be alone to stimulate your genius, I'll give you a way of avoiding distractions." Upon his release, he complained of a headache and was sent away. Talleyrand's position remained very precarious since four of the directors were always ready to dismiss him, but Barras continued to protect him. On occasions when Barras left the Luxembourg Palace disgusted with the passions aroused in the Directory's meetings, Talleyrand would wait for him outside and they would ride away together in his carriage.

With war on its frontiers, poverty haunting the countryside, the economy in ruins and robbers roaming the roads of France, the government gave the impression that the country was being run by a band of squabbling brigands. Talleyrand felt certain that the Directory could not last but the most important objective was to keep one's post. He proposed to Bonaparte that Rewbell should be dismissed, but the general was more interested in removing the whole panel of directors in one go. For the moment, the general's ambitions were still set in the direction of Egypt.

New elections were planned for the legislative assemblies in April 1798. On the previous occasion in May 1797, the unwelcome outcome for the Directory had been a majority of Royalists and it had required the coup-d'état of *18 Fructidor* by the directors to restore the balance in favour of the Republican government. Talleyrand searched for a way in which he might entice Rewbell with a proposition that was attractive and likely to succeed, even irresistible. He suggested that, in order for deputies to be elected who would support the existing government, money should be spent to purchase votes and to sway the election. The initial reaction was one of outrage. Corruption! Treachery! However, the directors soon earmarked some secret funds which they placed discreetly at Talleyrand's disposal so that the election outcome would correspond to their expectations.

The Prussian ambassador described Talleyrand once more when writing back to Berlin: "He is Minister of Foreign Affairs in name only and does not enjoy the least influence." In fact, the Directory took all the decisions, while the minister could leave to his subordinates the tasks of issuing passports and signing visas. As later, when appointed foreign minister for Napoleon, Talleyrand cultivated an air of idleness, taking longer than usual to complete tasks, realising that his superiors might appreciate having time to reconsider some of their hasty pronouncements. He slowed things down, introduced subtleties into their texts under the impression that waiting was not time lost. He restrained the excesses, softened the violence and anticipated the better times that would surely come after the disappearance of this transitory regime. While he was not necessarily informed of the background to the Directory's major decisions, on the contrary, his contacts with Bonaparte suggested that he would soon occupy a central position in the affairs of this great man.

The Directory was, in fact, a dictatorship. Priests, Royalists and *émigrés* were arrested and imprisoned, shot or deported to Guyana. Opposition newspapers were suppressed, local authorities overridden and the legislature reduced to impotence. But it was a dictatorship that could only exist as long as the people's attention was distracted by a successful war, thus guaranteeing the regime's survival. The army's victories were crowd-pleasers stimulating nationalism among the population, while a military career offered young people prospects of rapid advancement that could not be found in civilian life. On the other hand, peace was likely to confront people with the true economic situation. One day, in front of Rewbell, Talleyrand defended the idea that peace and respect for individuals and nations was in the interests of both France and Europe, and suggested opening negotiations with England.

Rewbell exploded: "What are you talking about, making peace with England? You are the only one who could put forward such a ridiculous suggestion. I see only one way to achieve peace and that is to humiliate it [England] and subjugate it." How could a leader of the regime seriously suggest that France, ruined, divided and with a tottering government, could conquer England? Already, the British Navy ruled the waves. At sea the British stranglehold of French ports allowed only short-distance coastal trade, while privateering had been brought to a halt through the convoy system. By this time, the French colonies in the West Indies had either been captured by the British Navy or were prevented from exporting sugar and coffee by the blockade.

During this first period as Minister of Foreign Affairs, Talleyrand was responsible in 1798 for negotiating the terms whereby France annexed the regions of Mulhouse and Geneva. As one who was only interested in peace and order, he was not enthusiastic about these imprudent moves. Rome too was occupied by the army of General Berthier. On this subject, he said prophetically: "I declare that the system which attempts to bring liberty to our neighbouring nations through the use of force is the best way to make it hated and to prevent its success." The powerful French Army, driven by revolutionary zeal, was so strong that it spread fear throughout Europe, and it was this anxiety that stimulated further wars. In order to live in peace with its neighbours, France needed to convey to them a feeling of confidence so that they became allies rather than foes.

However, another, more comprehensive plan was stirring within Bonaparte's mind in 1798, although Talleyrand was initially not enthusiastic about his far-fetched project. Using the troops of his Italian Army, he proposed to capture Corfu and the Ionian islands, chase the Turks out of Greece, take Constantinople, invade Turkey and Syria, and end up in possession of Egypt, thereby cutting the British off from the short route to their Indian possessions. If France's most successful general wanted to take a large part of the army to invade Egypt, would it not be interpreted by France's neighbours as a way of diminishing European tensions?

With the participation of a certain number of selected foreign ambassadors, Talleyrand created a little coterie who he would entertain around the whist table or simply invite to evenings of after-dinner conversation in his apartment. These ambassadors provided him with an incomparable network of informers—they adored to spy on each other and share their gossip with him. It was not only the ambassadors but his network of women friends that became a useful source of information. There were more traditional sources as well, such as letters intercepted by the Director of the Postal Services, particularly those of other ministries and foreign embassies.

On 5 December 1797, Napoleon Bonaparte arrived back from the Italian front to the house he shared with Josephine situated on Rue Chantereine in what is today the ninth *arrondissement* of Paris. Three weeks later the city authorities decided to rename the street Rue de la Victoire in honour of the successful general. That evening, Barras came to visit him at his house. In contrast, the following morning Bonaparte sent one of his officers to the Ministry of Foreign Affairs asking for an audience with Talleyrand, who he had never met. The reply was that he could come at any time. At 11 a.m. on 7 December he arrived at the Rue du Bac where several personalities were waiting to meet him, including Mme de Staël and the explorer Louis-Antoine de Bougainville. A small young man entered, very pale, thin, with long dark hair falling over his forehead and ears. His expression, however, was one of determination and power. Up until this time Talleyrand had three passions—women, gambling and serving France—here was a fourth one. Bonaparte seemed to be blessed with divine luck—whenever he entered the field of battle, the god of victory accompanied him. "At first glance, Bonaparte appeared to me to have a charming figure. Twenty battles won suit youth so well, with a splendid expression, with paleness, with a sort of exhaustion."

At the age of 44, Talleyrand represented the older generation; in contrast, the glorious hero, young, pale and exhausted was 28 years old. Bonaparte had every reason to be astonished by the citizen minister who came to greet him on the steps, who looked like no other member of the government—standing stiffly with powdered hair, dressed in an elegant black silk coat with crimson lapels and embroidered sleeves, a waistcoat, with a high white cravat under his chin, wearing buckled shoes and crimson silk stockings, a sheathed sword and feathered hat—in appearance and dress a relic of a bygone era. His Ruritanian ensemble, designed by the members of the Directory, marks the high-water mark of ludicrous regalia. Talleyrand himself represented the nobility whom Bonaparte may have heard about but had not yet met—and in whom he was secretly fascinated. During this meeting at the Rue de Bac, Bonaparte paid hardly any attention to Mme de Staël, much to her dismay, spending a long time talking to Bougainville. She had wanted to discuss with him the liberal political ideas dear to her father, but he wasn't interested.

The two ambitious men shut themselves in Talleyrand's office for a private conversation. "He spoke to me with great charm about my appointment as Minister of Foreign Affairs and stressed the pleasure it had given him to exchange letters with somebody who was not one of the directors." Since Bonaparte would have known about the humiliations he had received from Rewbell, this was an indirect form of flattery that acknowledged Talleyrand as a personality superior to the directors. Bonaparte was also keen to draw a parallel between Talleyrand's uncle, the Archbishop of Reims and peer of France, and his own uncle, arch-deacon Fesch, who lived in Corsica and had brought him up. The comparison, however appealing, was a little one-sided. What the two men certainly did have in common was that the Revolution and more particularly Paul Barras—the king of corruption—had brought them together.

Talleyrand and Bonaparte had yet other similarities. They both detested the Directory and they believed that the Reign of Terror had been a ruinous aberration. Talleyrand observed: "What lessons could mankind draw from these unplanned acts, carried out spontaneously by uncontrolled passions?" For Bonaparte, it had been the disorder, the haphazard nature of justice and the proceedings dominated by wayward ideologists. They both believed that France deserved better, certainly better than the state of decline that it had reached under the Directory. Talleyrand, however, did not want France to dominate other countries, to seize their territory or to interfere in their internal affairs. To him, France should be the standard bearer of civilization, the homeland of famous people, the source of the Declaration of the Rights of Man and the cradle of the French language. France should conduct its affairs not by invading its neighbours but by respecting their frontiers and their political regimes. There should not be economic and financial rivalry because it led to war, but rather trade serving the general interest on a European scale. Talleyrand believed that Bonaparte shared this vision of a peaceful France reborn.

He was wrong. Bonaparte did not subscribe to Talleyrand's viewpoint because the only principles he followed were his own. Talleyrand felt that with his maturity, his experience, his breeding, his skill and his knowledge of Europe, he could guide Bonaparte towards the economic and financial policies that would enrich France. He wrote: "The true conquests, the only ones that do not lead to any regret, are those made over ignorance. The most honourable and the most useful occupations for nations are to contribute to the spread of humanitarian ideas." These ideas did not interest Bonaparte in the slightest but Talleyrand allowed himself to be fooled into thinking otherwise. The historian Émile Dard wrote the following about Bonaparte and Talleyrand's relationship: "It is unwise to like someone before getting to know them." These two men already liked each other before they met, but Talleyrand would soon discover the immense gulf between the admirable young hero he met in his office and the conquering megalomaniac who believed he was called upon to fulfil some great military destiny on a European scale. Barras had already been side-lined.

The five directors decided that it was necessary to organize a ceremony to honour the young general's victories and to thank him for the captured booty sent back from Italy. Although they were wary of the recently returned general, they owed the stability of their regime to him. Barras therefore asked Charles-Maurice to organize some kind of festivity to be held in the Luxembourg Palace's courtyard on 10 December 1797. On this cold, grey morning, the ceremony began with an artillery salute and a band playing republican melodies that revelled in massacres and bloodshed. The directors and their ministers sat in their gaudy operetta costumes beside an altar behind which stood the three statues of Liberty, Equality and Peace. This last symbol stood incongruously among the innumerable enemy flags captured by the French forces. Amidst frantic cries of "Vive, Bonaparte!", the young hero entered alone dressed in a plain grey suit, without any distinguishing marks of rank or medals. It was a public relations masterpiece; he came forward as the hero of the Republic, simple, virtuous, steadfast and unassuming; the tiny figure of Citizen Bonaparte who had been charged with a mission by the people and had fulfilled it beyond their wildest dreams. He gave the impression that, away from the battlefield, he was a peace-loving individual; the real Bonaparte remained completely concealed. He was followed by a military escort and, at the end of it, the master of ceremonies, the limping Talleyrand himself who made a flattering speech from which one could conclude that the young general had no further ambitions other than to retire to his modest home and devote himself to the study of science and poetry! In a weird diversion, Talleyrand suggested that Bonaparte was just the man to carry out the Directory's latest ambition—the invasion of England! Bonaparte responded briefly to all these accolades, concluding with: "When the French people's happiness is based upon the best organic laws, the whole of Europe will be free," which seemed to call for continental order and liberty and drew a deafening acclamation from the crowd. He made no reference to invading England. Barras spoke last and at length—his speech no doubt written by Charles-Maurice—whereupon the five directors in turn threw themselves into Bonaparte's arms. The ceremony ended with a series of revolutionary hymns sung by a choir.

What had taken place had been dignified but somehow lacked the character of a true celebration. Thus, on 3 January 1798—known in the Republican calendar as *14 Nivôse Year VI*—Talleyrand organized a reception at the Rue de Bac worthy of the victorious general and the like of which Paris had not seen for years. For one who was an unpopular member of an unpopular government, it was a daring move. Bonaparte had no conversational gifts and did not enjoy social occasions, so Talleyrand took the precaution of dedicating the evening to Josephine rather than to the general, which was a tactful way of complimenting the lady in order to dazzle the husband. Bonaparte would never forget the way Talleyrand had arranged proceedings with such taste and pomp with Josephine treated like a queen. Under the guidance of the famous architect François-Joseph Bélanger, and with the aid of an army of carpenters, painters, plasterers, florists and carpet-layers, the Hôtel de Galliffet had been transformed into an enchanted palace where music, illuminations, garlands of artificial flowers and perfumes intermingled. The ball was preceded by a firework display designed by the famous Ruggieri Brothers. Some of the directors, and particularly their wives, were horrified at the expense.

To pay homage to the hero, Talleyrand had invited 500 guests, including the heads of government and the principal ministers of state, bankers, businessmen, the entire diplomatic corps and the most beautiful women of Paris. The general and his wife were accompanied by Josephine's attractive daughter, Hortense de Beauharnais, aged 15. Among the guests was Germaine de Staël who coveted political power and had learned nothing from Bonaparte's cool reception on 7 December. Her opinion of Josephine was that she was a delightful but unsuitable companion for the great warrior. She was still determined to demonstrate that her limitless admiration for the hero of the Republic deserved to be reciprocated. Bonaparte liked women to be pretty, modest, unassuming creatures rather than thrusting, politically ambitious and tactless idealists. Germaine buttonholed Bonaparte's aide-de-camp, who feared there would be a repetition of the previous taciturn aversion on the part of his master and tried desperately to dissuade her from intruding upon Bonaparte, but she had a permanent need for display and self-advertisement, considering herself irresistible. Finally, she stood face to face with her idol, standing at least a head taller than him and unleashed a torrent of unconditional, eager, excessive, embarrassing praise. She saw herself inevitably as the centre of attention and asked: "General, who is the woman that you admire the most?" From her perspective, he was supposed to answer "You", but her train of thought was thwarted when he replied "My wife." She persisted hoping that he would eventually be forced to admit that he was being addressed by the nation's first lady: "Who for you is the first among women?" However, his Mediterranean upbringing had given him clear ideas about women's place in society as slightly inferior beings and he had no gift for small talk with fearsome society hostesses. He had both a physical and moral repugnance of her and stated bluntly: "The one who makes the most babies." He turned on his heel and moved away, leaving her flabbergasted. She would continue to admire him for some years to come until she found herself more or less obliged to become his principal adversary. Talleyrand was deeply embarrassed by this incident, realizing at once the irremediable incompatibility between these two personalities. He made sure that Germaine was never again invited into the presence of Bonaparte whose insolent indifference had prevailed. Talleyrand did not like losers and this incident signalled the end of their friendship as he gradually abandoned his former mistress. Some years later, Napoleon inquired about Talleyrand's friendship with Germaine de Staël, to which he replied: "Friend? She would throw all her friends into the water for the pleasure of fishing them out again."

At another time, Napoleon remarked: "You are the king of conversation in Europe. What is your secret?" Where Talleyrand excelled as a minister was in the field of obtaining information. The Baron de Vitrolles describes how Talleyrand went about this: "His conversation was distinguished by its subtlety and its grace. He was aware of how to conceal his thoughts or his intent under a transparent veil of implied meaning, his words revealing a sense beyond those that he actually used." His words never dealt with the subject under discussion, which did not concern him, but they were the vehicle to achieve some personal aim, such as procuring confidential information or simple flattery. In company, he spoke very little, yet people were charmed by his almost monosyllabic conversation. It is believed to be Talleyrand who said: "Speech was given to man to help hide his thoughts." If he did not agree with someone's ideas, he would never contradict them believing that no-one has ever changed the mind of an adversary. Each person holds on to his/her opinions becoming more excited and inclined to exaggerate as the conversation goes along. In this way, he avoided arguments.

Back at the Rue du Bac, the 500 guests were called to the dinner table. There were only enough seats for the ladies, so the gentlemen stood behind their chairs and served themselves as best they could. Talleyrand placed himself behind Josephine, sovereign for an evening, acting as her chamberlain. For people who had lived through several years of penury, the meal resembled a cornucopia of abundance conveying the message that the nightmare was over and the good times had returned. Compared to the violence that had ruled the streets of Paris over the previous years, for the first time since the collapse of the monarchy this event celebrated good manners, luxury and the pleasure of being alive. It was Talleyrand's masterpiece for he had managed to create a connection between the France before and the France after the Revolution—the aristocratic world of prestige and formality had been blended with the post-Revolutionary world of liberty, reason and justice. While eating, the guests were entertained with songs, including one especially composed for the occasion by Jean-Étienne Despréaux and a patriotic melody popular at that moment *Le Chant du Départ* [The Leaving Song] by Talleyrand's erstwhile saviour Joseph Chénier. The words of this particular sentimental song were among Bonaparte's favourites. Years later, when banished to Saint Helena, Bonaparte still remembered the good time he had had during the banquet at the Rue du Bac on 3 January 1798. He had taken the arm of Esseid Ali, the Turkish ambassador, and spoken to him at great length, but did not mention that his next project was to remove from Turkish control its most precious asset. Esseid Ali could not speculate as to why he had been the focus of so much attention at the reception.

Despite Bonaparte's ambitions in the Middle East, France was now preparing for total war with an army massing on the coast at Boulogne to invade England. Talleyrand, meanwhile, was convinced that, given the British Navy's overwhelming control of the sea, it was inconceivable that this force could ever cross the Channel successfully. However, it was unwise to oppose the wave of military fervour sweeping the country promoted by the government. Despite alarm in London, the accumulation of forces on the French coast was not a threat to the British Government, since Bonaparte's ambitions were unambiguously pointed in another direction. It is believed that Bonaparte never seriously envisaged invading England, but the presence of a large French Army on the Channel coast meant that the British were obliged to maintain a similar force in southern England.

Two weeks after the reception at the Rue du Bac, a small crisis threatened to rock the French Republic. The moment had come for the annual celebration of Louis XVI's execution but Bonaparte refused to have anything to do with it. He had, however, been a friend of Robespierre at the time of the execution; he was also responsible for massacring the Royalists on *13 Vendémiaire* with grapeshot and had nothing but contempt for the late king. Bonaparte's absence from the ceremony would be perceived as a setback for the Directory's prestige because it would suggest that he had Royalist sympathies. Talleyrand was sent to Bonaparte's house, now on the renamed Rue de la Victoire, to persuade him to change his mind. In the honied words of the former Abbé de Périgord, he offered the obdurate general a place on the front row of seats reserved for the regime's dignitaries. Bonaparte was not interested. Talleyrand tried a different tactic; his persistence paid off. While General Bonaparte declined to participate as a principal state dignitary at the forefront in the uniform of a general, it might be politically acceptable for him to take a more modest place as a civilian member of the *Institut des Sciences Morales et Politiques* seated in the third row on the left amongst the other members of the institute. His presence would then satisfy the regime's leaders and the Jacobin factions, while his less-prominent position would not alarm the more moderate political factions. This was one of the extremely rare occasions when Bonaparte actually allowed himself to be swayed by Talleyrand. During his lifetime, Talleyrand would attend several similar ceremonies on 21 January that alternately either celebrated or mourned the death of Louis XVI. He could attend these events with a clear conscience since he had had nothing whatsoever to do with the king's execution.

The ceremony was held in the church of Saint Sulpice, where Charles-Maurice had been christened and where, as a young man, he had met Mlle Dorothée on the steps in a shower of rain. He had been present at the coronation of Louis XVI at Reims Cathedral in 1775 with his father and uncle participating as the king's principal attendants. And here he was celebrating the same man's death, a so-called traitor. Upon leaving the church, the crowd only had eyes for Bonaparte, cheering him as he passed. It pleased Talleyrand that the little general attracted the applause of the crowd rather than the five directors.

The second Congress of Rastatt, held near Karlsruhe, began its deliberations in November 1797 with the intention of negotiating a peace between France and the Holy Roman Empire (Austria), and to draw up a plan to compensate those princes whose lands on the Rhine's left bank had been seized by France. Upon Bonaparte's return from Italy, Talleyrand sent him to the congress to breathe life into the negotiations. The young Klemens von Metternich described it as: "a congress which from beginning to end was never more than a phantom" and the word he reserved for the members of the French delegation was "slovenly". Bonaparte's mind was already preoccupied with preparations for the Egyptian expedition and he abandoned his post at Rastatt after a few days, with the result that no peace agreement was reached and war soon broke out again. On his return journey to Paris, Bonaparte made a detour to visit the build-up of troops at Boulogne ready for the supposed invasion of England, which even he declared impossible at this time. Esseid Ali was troubled about rumours he had heard concerning a fleet amassing at Toulon destined for the Turkish possession of Egypt. Talleyrand informed him that its first objective was Malta; after that... we would see.

We may recall that Talleyrand had read a paper before the Institute on 3 July 1797 on the subject of French colonization, and particularly hinting that the conquest of Egypt could give France control of the Mediterranean to compensate for its losses in the West Indies. The original idea had come from his friend Choiseul, who in his turn had been inspired by a book written by Constantin-François Volney, *Voyage en Egypte et en Syrie* [A Journey through Egypt and Syria], that had enjoyed a wave of popularity ten years earlier. Bonaparte had read Talleyrand's report and, on the spur of the moment, decided to carry the project out. It is therefore clear that it was inspired by Talleyrand and the subject crops up frequently in his correspondence with Bonaparte. The French consul to Egypt, Charles Magallon, who had lived for thirty-five years in that country, happened to be in Paris at this moment.

Bonaparte had no faith in the Directory, nor did he believe that the absurd idea of invading England had the slightest chance of success. During the winter of 1796 a French expedition to invade Ireland had turned into a calamity mainly due to storms at sea. Both Talleyrand and Bonaparte had their eyes on seizing power for themselves, while the little general had already revealed his ambitions to Barras but did not believe that the time was ripe. The three partners proceeded cautiously so as to remove all suspicion of their motives from people's minds.

Bonaparte proposed to the Directory that invading Egypt would deal a mortal blow to the British because it would cut off the overland route to their interests in India. He had ordered maps of the Middle East, begun to read the Koran and, in dispatches to Paris, mentioned the idea of extending French influence in the Mediterranean. When Talleyrand congratulated Bonaparte for this brilliant idea, the latter observed: "Why don't we take the island of Malta [as well]... We could leave here with 25,000 men escorted by eight or ten men-of-war." Nevertheless, the Sultan might well be outraged at losing control of his most important possession, so it was necessary to placate the Ottoman Government by explaining the French way of thinking. This is why Bonaparte turned his attention to Esseid Ali and not to Mme de Staël at the reception on *14 Nivôse*. Three weeks later, Talleyrand presented a report on Egypt to the Directory. The Ottoman Empire's collapse seemed imminent (in fact, this did not take place until another 120 years later) and it was necessary to forestall any attempt by England or Russia to take possession of Egypt. In order to assure a safe passage for the French Army to Egypt and to guarantee the supply chain, it would be necessary to occupy several Mediterranean islands. The style of this document is that of Bonaparte. How could Talleyrand, the pacifist, present such a bellicose report? The Directory still wanted to invade England but the Egyptian expedition would remove the pugnacious conqueror from France where he might pose a threat to their power.

Talleyrand subsequently attempted to pass the responsibility for this report on to Delacroix by saying that he found the report already completed when he entered office in 1797. This was blatantly untrue and Delacroix had no trouble demonstrating that the author was Talleyrand. The second report bears Talleyrand's signature but the style suggests that it was written in collaboration with Bonaparte. It states that the French monarchy had been too weak to undertake the invasion of Egypt, but the Republic would astonish the world by carrying it out successfully. The actual purpose of the expedition remained imprecise. The Prussian ambassador, Sandoz-Rollin, who was Talleyrand's friend and confidant, explains two of the expedition's theoretical objectives: "The first was to assemble monuments that might serve to clarify the history of this part of the world and the other was to remove the focus and the government's army from the revolutionary zeal that could have disturbed Europe." For Talleyrand, diverting Bonaparte and his army into the deserts of Egypt gave European nations confidence in a reduction of France's aggressive intentions. It served his interests that the Prussian ambassador would advise his government of this attitude, which would then filter through to the other European capitals. Next, the document describes the invasion itself in military jargon as simplicity itself; it even proposed that, after the capture of Egypt, Bonaparte would march through Palestine, Syria and Asia Minor to capture Constantinople. More soldiers would be recruited from the newly liberated Greeks and Arabs previously living under Turkish domination. Another detachment of 15,000 men would be sent on to India to take possession of its riches! How could the prudent Talleyrand have associated himself with such a scatter-brained scheme? The report makes no mention of the difficulties: storms at sea; interference by the British Royal Navy; resistance by the inhabitants; sickness among the troops; shortages of supplies and water; the breakdown of communications; the need for reinforcements. Success is achieved effortlessly and costs next to nothing. Before long, it seemed, Bonaparte would be master of the Orient treading in the footsteps of Alexander the Great!

The Directory reluctantly gave its agreement to the Egypt expedition on 3 March 1798. It was content to see the back of an over-ambitious general who had stolen the limelight. Bonaparte had intended that, while he was travelling to Egypt, some highly placed personality would undertake a mission to Constantinople to soothe the Sultan. The idea was to present the invasion not as a hostile act directed by France against the Ottoman Empire but rather to deliver it from its enemies—the English and the Russians. A highly skilled negotiator should undertake this mission; why not Talleyrand himself? He was reluctantly obliged to mumble his acceptance of this duty, but there was no show of enthusiasm. Before leaving, Bonaparte insisted once again that it should be Talleyrand who would travel to Constantinople and explain the situation to the Sultan. When the young general had departed, Talleyrand washed his hands of the whole affair. How can one explain his peculiarly ambiguous attitude? The prospect of being imprisoned in Constantinople certainly weighed heavily in the balance and he saw no attraction either in removing himself from the centre of power in Paris.

When the moment came for Bonaparte to leave, it turned out that he was broke and Talleyrand, who was ill in bed, told him to help himself to 100,000 francs that he kept in his desk drawer. For this generosity he received a hug from the young general. A couple of years later, when repaying the debt, Bonaparte asked Talleyrand what had inspired this generous gesture. The latter replied that he was bed-ridden, that he might never see Bonaparte again and he wished to be of service to him without second thoughts. Bonaparte's reply betrays his singular way of thinking: "In that case, it was the act of a mug!"

A fleet of warships gathered at Toulon and set sail on 19 May 1798. Upon arrival in Malta, Bonaparte sent a warship back to Toulon to transport Talleyrand to Constantinople, but it was intercepted at sea by the Royal Navy leaving Talleyrand with no way to reach his destination. This did not matter since he had no intention of going and did not nominate anyone else in his place. Bonaparte sent several messages from Egypt reminding Talleyrand of his assignment and asking him how negotiations were proceeding. The chargé d'affaires in Constantinople, M. Boulouvard, eventually found himself in a very disagreeable position, faced with an angry Sultan who was in the habit of reserving cruel punishments for people who offended him. Talleyrand tried to reassure Boulouvard that he had nothing to fear; the presence of Esseid Ali in Paris was the guarantee. Fourteen years later Napoleon admitted to his aide-de-camp General Caulaincourt that the mission to Constantinople did not have the slightest chance of success since the invasion of Egypt would be perceived by the Sultan as an act of aggression by infidels.

Talleyrand never went to Constantinople. In his defence, it should be pointed out that he was the Directory's servant with very little power, certainly not enough to appoint himself as plenipotentiary to Turkey. The directors had no particular wish to facilitate the expedition to Egypt and, because Bonaparte had deserted his post at Rastatt, war was imminent once again in Europe, so Talleyrand's presence was required in Paris. Furthermore, there was a new confrontation brewing with the United States following the XYZ Affair and Talleyrand could be considered as an expert on relations with that country. In conclusion, it can be stated that Talleyrand did nothing to obtain permission to go to Constantinople on a mission that he considered a lost cause. Behind the scenes, he was working discreetly to establish a peace treaty with London or, as some of his adversaries might say, keeping England informed of France's intentions.

For the invasion of Egypt, Bonaparte had equipped an expeditionary force of just under 40,000 men, including scientists, engineers and veteran troops from the Army of Italy. His fleet managed to escape from Toulon without being observed by the British and seized Malta, plundering its considerable treasury. It then proceeded on towards Alexandria where the city fell to Bonaparte on 27 July 1798. Meanwhile the powerful British fleet, under Horatio Nelson, had spent several weeks scouring the Mediterranean for the enigmatic French fleet, often missing it by a few hours. The French took Cairo but the campaign's successes were annulled when Nelson finally found and destroyed the French ships at Aboukir Bay on 1 August. The disastrous defeat at Aboukir was followed by the breakdown of negotiations at Rastatt, the loss of the conquests in Italy, the formation of a new coalition against France and the threat of invasion of its frontiers.

Due to favourable changes in the military situation, Austria pulled out of the peace talks at the Congress of Rastatt in April 1799, so Talleyrand told his representatives to return home. Their carriage, leaving the town in the middle of the night, was refused an escort. Once they reached open country, they were attacked by what were believed to be Hungarian Hussars and two of the four plenipotentiaries were killed. The soldiers had been instructed to relieve them of their papers, but the situation got out of hand. Talleyrand was furious, saying that the lives of envoys present at negotiations were inviolable.

Bonaparte was trapped in Egypt and cut off from his supply lines and reinforcements. He attempted to march north with his army towards Syria, but suffered defeat at Acre during May 1799. Three months later, Bonaparte gave up his Middle-Eastern enterprise, sailing for France in a small craft, miraculously evading the British fleet once again and arriving in France in October 1799.

CHAPTER VIII
THE COUP-D'ETAT

While Bonaparte had been preparing for his expedition to the Middle East, Talleyrand had fallen in love.

During the early months of 1798, a police report reached the Directory that a certain woman called Grand living in Paris was maintaining a correspondence with England. From the cryptic language used in her letters there was reason to believe that she might be a spy working for the British, a crime punishable by death. She refers to an important person in the government who went under the pseudonym of *pié-court* [short-foot] who was frustrated in his attempts to occupy an important function by *l'Enchanteur* [The Magician = Merlin]. She knew about the imprisonment of the Portuguese diplomat Antonio de Araujo, while another letter refers to the "Egyptian affair... arranged for the benefit of our English friends." Mme Grand was arrested. On 23 March 1798, *pié-court*, in his most frank style, sent a letter to Barras: "Citizen Directeur, Mme Grand has just been arrested as a conspirator. She is the person in the world most remote from and most incapable of becoming involved in any plot; she is a very beautiful Indian, lazy, the idlest of all the women that I have ever met. I ask you to take an interest in her; I am certain that you will find every reason to put an end to this little affair." Knowing Talleyrand, we should be astonished at what comes next: "I love her and I declare to you, man to man, that in her life she has not been involved in and has not been capable of being involved in any plot."

Catherine-Noël Worlée had come far in the world. She had been born on 21 November 1761 in the small town of Tranquebar (modern Tharangambadi) on the south-east coast of India, a Danish trading post. During her life, she progressively advanced her birth date by a few years to make herself appear younger. Her father, an officer in the Rajah of Pondicherry's army, was French. At the age of 16 she married an Englishman, George Grand, who was an employee in the Indian civil service. She brought nothing to the marriage but herself, for she was tall with a good figure, blonde with blue eyes—a beauty. Born in England of parents of Swiss Huguenot extraction, Mr Grand was heavy and serious, having a preference for the company of his male colleagues at the club.

Grand took his wife to Calcutta and into the big city life. A distinguished Irishman there called Philip Francis, one of the five members of Calcutta's Supreme Council, took a liking to "Cathy" and showered her with gifts. On the night of 8 December 1778, he climbed over the garden wall of George Grand's bungalow with the aid of a ladder and gave her a fright by entering her bedroom. One of the servants discovered the ladder and, fearing a robbery, raised the alarm. When the gallant lover climbed out of her bedroom window, Grand's servants seized him and tied him to a chair. Cathy's husband, who was dining out, was advised, became distressed and passed by a friend's house to pick up a sword on his way home. Meanwhile, Francis had accomplices waiting for him outside the premises and called for help by whistling. There was a scuffle in the dark with Grand's servants during which Francis managed to escape but one of his accomplices was apprehended. The following day George Grand sent his wife to stay with her sister in Chandernagore and his witnesses to Sir Philip challenging him to a duel. Francis denied any wrongdoing and refused to fight a duel, explaining that he had merely taken pity on a young lady married to an "ugly, old and sordid Frenchman". The affair went to court and the accomplice who had been detained by the servants was eventually persuaded to reveal the whole story. The guilty lover was condemned to pay 50,000 rupees (equivalent to about £5,000 pounds at that time and therefore a large amount) to George Grand, who announced that he was satisfied with the outcome—but never forgave his wife for the ease with which her lover had entered her bedroom. It would not be the last time he discovered her to be a useful source of unexpected revenue.

Cathy came back to Calcutta and sailed on a ship for England. Although her mother-tongue was French, she quickly learned English. Five years later she was in Paris and it may be assumed making her living as a courtesan of the demi-monde. She lived in a house on the Rue du Sentier in the banking quarter of Paris, where the rent was paid by a wealthy financier, Valdec de Lessart who, some years later as Minister of

Foreign Affairs, would send Talleyrand on his first mission to London. It was Valdec's habit to give dinners and it is perfectly possible that Talleyrand, Narbonne and even Biron may have been invited there, but there is no record. Other gentlemen of the banking fraternity shared her favours, such as Jean-Frédéric Perregaux and perhaps even Radix de Sainte-Foy. Mme Grand lived comfortably spending considerable sums of money on jewellery, dinner services, silverware and fur coats from the most fashionable establishments. She moved to a new apartment with a garden on the Rue d'Artois and purchased a horse and carriage. The well-known portraitist, Élisabeth Vigée-Lebrun, painted a striking picture of her in 1783 aged 21, at about the same time that Talleyrand commissioned a portrait of himself from the same artist.

By August 1792 events were taking place on the streets of Paris that no-one could possibly ignore. The porter of Mme Grand's building was seized by the mob and lynched. Fearing that it would be her turn next, she fled to England with a little cash sewn into her dress. On the quayside in Dover, a young Englishman leaving the country, Nathaniel Belchier, asked the still trembling, beautiful, blue-eyed blonde if he might be of assistance to her. He then travelled to Paris and, at the risk of his life, recovered her gold dinner service, her jewels and her furs. Life in London did not suit her since her trade was not as socially acceptable as it was in Paris. However, it is noteworthy that she was in London at the same time as Talleyrand. Two years later, once the bloody episode of Robespierre and the Terror was over, she set out on the return journey to Paris via Hamburg with her lover, Cristoforo de Spinola, even though her name was still on the dreaded list of *émigrés* likely to be arrested on sight. Spinola was refused entry but she was allowed to pass—Catherine Grand held a Danish passport. She found accommodation on the Rue Saint-Nicaise in the centre of Paris (nowadays, the Rue de Richelieu) and lived modestly. Nevertheless, the police had their eye on her since she was, indeed, an agent of the British Government. Her letters were intercepted and she was arrested. It was at this moment that Talleyrand intervened, although he was not the only one—the Danish minister in Paris also protested on her behalf.

The early relationship between Talleyrand and Catherine Grand remains shrouded in mystery. She was completely unlike any of his other mistresses in that she was neither noble nor particularly intelligent nor highly educated; she was never his friend and never formed part of his social circle. Nevertheless, she would become his wife. How did they meet? It is perfectly possible that they had known about each other's existence for several years either in Paris or in London. Nevertheless, the story as told by Édouard Colmache, who at a much later date became Talleyrand's secretary, is as follows: Late one night in October or November 1797, Talleyrand returned to the Rue du Bac in order to go to bed, having been playing whist all evening. He was informed that a lady had been waiting to see him for some time and that she had a letter of introduction from Montrond. Without enthusiasm, he was taken into the room where the lady was waiting. She had fallen asleep in an armchair in front of the fire and all he could see was a well-dressed woman hidden by an ample cloak and hood. Hearing him enter, she woke up, the hood fell back, the cloak fell on the floor and before him stood a truly magnificent creature. Talleyrand was smitten.

Montrond had spun Catherine a yarn that Bonaparte was on the point of invading England, where the banks would be looted and she would lose her entire savings. However, if she went to see Minister Talleyrand and threw herself at his mercy, he would be able to arrange everything. If there was one thing that Catherine Grand was good at it was throwing herself at people's mercy. It was evidently impossible for her to leave the ministry in the middle of the night and she made no difficulty about staying in a spare bedroom. She would stay for a very long time.

Catherine Grand was now 35 years old and still presentable, but obviously approaching the end of her career as a courtesan. Talleyrand said of her that she had sweet skin, sweet breath and a sweet character. Paris was soon awash with jokes about her faux-pas, although many of them are believed to be invented and aimed at belittling Talleyrand or they were resurrected humorous anecdotes that had been doing the rounds for decades. He appeared to suffer these jibes with complete indifference: "You have to have been the lover of Mme de Staël," he explained, "to understand all the pleasure there is to be the lover of a silly woman."

When Talleyrand's letter about Catherine Grand was read out to the five members of the Directory there was disbelief. First, La Révellière-

Lépeaux, who favoured a new form of religion, bellowed that one could expect nothing less perverse from a bishop of the Catholic Church. Merlin reproached a minister of the Republic for finding it necessary to take a mistress who came from the other side of the Channel. If she were a spy, then it was an opportunity to see that justice was done for Talleyrand was guilty too and would die by firing squad. One could always count upon a crude remark from Rewbell, who seemed to be particularly well informed about Catherine Grand's profession: "Could he not then satisfy himself in France where there is no shortage of whores?" François de Neufchâteau dared to raise the point that a minister's private life was his own affair and no concern of the Directory. Finally, it was decided to pass the matter to the Minister of the Police and to give him complete freedom to resolve the situation. Talleyrand took advantage of this opportunity because, before long, "the idlest of all women" returned to the Rue du Bac. Inexplicably, like Mirabeau and the banker Ouvrard, she does not appear in his memoirs.

By the time news of Bonaparte's successful landing with his army in Alexandria reached Paris on 18 September 1798, two-and-a-half months after the event, Nelson had already destroyed the French fleet on 1 August. Joseph Chénier was writing a victory song when the news arrived from London that the British Navy had crushed Bonaparte's fleet at Aboukir with Nelson now master of the Mediterranean. The general public's initial enthusiasm quickly switched to anger at the perceived deception. The Directory was immediately accused of deliberately sending Bonaparte to the Middle East in order to get rid of him—which was not too far from the truth—but hatred focused mainly on Talleyrand. Apparently, it was he who had insisted on this fateful expedition in order to engineer Bonaparte's downfall! Bonaparte, who was the real driving force and who had wanted to create for himself a Middle-Eastern empire resembling that of Ancient Greece or Rome, appeared in the eyes of the public as the innocent victim of a devious plot. The people's hero, handsome, brilliant and modest, had been betrayed! In the absence of Bonaparte, the French military situation was deteriorating rapidly, with the armies retreating everywhere. Italy, Switzerland and the Netherlands were lost, while Alsace had been invaded. The aggressive policies of the Directory had made sure that France was detested in all the European capitals, as Talleyrand had predicted. Nevertheless, it was he who was considered personally responsible by the Jacobins for the Egyptian debacle!

In May 1799, Rewbell ceased to be a member of the Directory, leaving with a generous parting gift. It had been intended to replace him with a nonentity, but the Senate insisted on nominating the French ambassador to Berlin, Emmanuel-Joseph, the former Abbé Sieyès, Talleyrand's ally. Although Talleyrand supported Sieyès, he considered him an odd fellow, cold and conceited, but he was a master with words and, since the beginning of the Revolution, words had marked its major achievements. For his part, Sieyès detested the aristocracy, but was prepared to overlook his prejudices in the case of Talleyrand. In June, the three Directory members of Treilhard, La Révellière and Merlin were replaced by Louis Gohier, General Jean-François-Auguste Moulin and Pierre-Roger Ducos. In order to comprehend the events later in the year, it should be noted that the Directory now included Sieyès, Ducos and Barras. At the same time, elections for the assembly gave a victory to the Jacobins and it looked as if they might once again take control of Paris.

A fresh spate of newspapers and pamphlets began to attack the government. A favourite subject for abuse was the Minister of Foreign Affairs, whose public and private morals, reputation for corruption, involvement in the Egyptian affair and supposed lack of commitment to the Republican cause provided an easy target. Talleyrand's situation was becoming intolerable, so he decided to sink into the background. At this time, he had been made responsible for both Foreign Affairs and the Navy, because his good friend Admiral Bruix had been sent to the naval base at Brest in an attempt to restore communications with Bonaparte in Egypt. Upon becoming a Director, one of Sieyès's first actions was to cancel the rescue mission for Bonaparte. By a troubling coincidence, at almost the same moment Talleyrand's banker friend Ouvrard was awarded the huge contract for supplying the French and Spanish Navies for the next six years. Barras had also asked Ouvrard to lend money to the Treasury to ward off a crisis. One of the most vicious pamphleteers, Pierre-Antoine Antonelle, the mayor of Arles, published a series of furious and unsubstantiated accusations against Talleyrand beginning in July 1799. While there was no shortage of incontestable charges that could be levelled at Talleyrand, curiously his critics decided to accuse him of being a noble, of being a bishop, of being a traitor who sold himself to the British, of drinking the Emperor of Austria's wine with his friend William Pitt, of wishing to end the Republic and of sending Bonaparte to Egypt in order to weaken France. As was now his manner, the victim did not react. We know that Talleyrand had wanted to become a minister in order to become rich, but also to bring peace to Europe. Finally, his accusers became incensed about this former officer of the Catholic Church who lived in sin with a beautiful woman from India.

Then, two more affairs burst into the limelight. Public opinion rediscovered Talleyrand's two missions to London in 1792 and accused him of selling France to the British. The fact that the second mission was successful in obtaining British neutrality was brushed aside. Chauvelin, who as a young man had been nominally head of the second mission, said that no wrongdoing could possibly be attributed to himself because he had not participated in any of the negotiations when in London. If any fault had been committed, Talleyrand had to be the unique "guilty party". The affair blew over, only to be followed by another.

Sébastien-Louis-Gabriel Jorry enrolled in the army in 1790 and rose rapidly through the ranks. At the Battle of Jemappes, in November 1792, he was cited for courage and reached the position of adjutant-general. Two years later, he was suspended from his rank and in 1797 dismissed from the army for cowardice. In October of that year, Talleyrand received two petty criminals sent by the Minister of Police who asked him if he could find some kind of employment for them in the Italian Army of Occupation. One was the "general" Rossignol and the other "adjutant-general" Jorry. He received them politely offering each of them a post as a spy in Rome and suggested that they should think it over. Rossignol decided against it, while Jorry accepted. He received 2,400 livres for his mission to Rome and disappeared without receiving further instructions.

Five months later, Talleyrand was asked for a justification for this expenditure by Director Merlin. He could not remember the circumstances, but it was considered that he had not pursued the Jorry affair with sufficient vigour. At Merlin's insistence, an order for Jorry's arrest was issued and he was soon located. Before the judge, he admitted having received the money, which was still intact and ready to be returned. He had not left for Italy because he had not been issued with the necessary papers! Two observations can be made here: first, that one does not normally give written instructions to a person being sent on a spying mission; and second that, having received his salary, he made no attempt to contact the ministry to confirm his instructions or to leave on his mission. Nevertheless, if the judge did not have faith in Jorry's good character, he need only refer to Director... Barras! On 8 April 1798 the judge dismissed the charges against Jorry.

A newspaper, *Le Journal des Hommes Libres,* took up the case by printing slanderous articles and posters against Talleyrand, which he treated with glorious indifference. Who was paying for this campaign? However, Jorry now sued the minister for wrongful arrest and false accusations. There was no way that Talleyrand could avoid being summoned to court. He wrote an article that appeared in *Le Moniteur* relating the circumstances from the official point of view of the Ministry of Foreign Affairs. He felt that the case had been exaggerated out of all proportion.

It was now obvious that someone somewhere was paying to have Talleyrand harassed. Could it be Barras? Already, the Directory did not send its instructions to the Minister of Foreign Affairs, ambassadors were appointed without consulting him and the salaries of his staff were not being paid. He made sure that his passport was in order in preparation for flight abroad, having money distributed between banks in London and Hamburg. He tried to postpone the date when the affair would be dealt with in court but, on 11 July 1799, Jorry asked why the affair was being delayed and two days later he was declared the victim of a miscarriage of justice. The Minister of Foreign Affairs was accused of dishonourable conduct in pursuing an innocent man, even though it was Director Merlin who insisted on the warrant for the arrest of the amateur spy. The simple fact that Talleyrand had given cash to a man who lived by his wits without requiring him to account for it became lost in the turmoil.

The minister was condemned to pay Jorry 100,000 francs compensation, was threatened with prison and required to print 2,000 copies of an official apology for public distribution. On 13 July 1799, Talleyrand sent a letter of resignation to the Directory fearing that the outrageous accusations to which he was subject every day would be interpreted by the government as an obstacle in conducting its affairs. The Directory did not react—Sieyès did not want to lose him—so one week later he re-submitted his resignation and this time the directors accepted expressing at the same time thanks for his energy, his good citizenship and his guidance. Upon leaving the ministry, Talleyrand took the very unusual step of printing a brochure in which he explained that it was not him who had sent Bonaparte to oblivion in the Egyptian desert— it was, of course, Delacroix! Since it was the minister who had been condemned and not the former Bishop of Autun, it was the ministry that paid for this publication. This brochure, extolling Talleyrand's republican past in the early days of the Revolution and his allegiance to Jacobinism, was to prove very embarrassing when it was unearthed during the Bourbon Restoration in 1815. Henceforth, Talleyrand never reacted to personal attacks and never gave any justification for his actions.

Le Journal des Hommes Libres snorted in indignation at the compliments addressed by the Directory to a "traitor". The person appointed to succeed him as minister of Foreign Affairs was the same Charles Reinhard who had accompanied Talleyrand on his second mission to London in 1792. He was honest and conscientious, and suggested to Talleyrand that he might only be occupying this position on a temporary basis. Reinhard, who had been in post at Florence, was devoted to Talleyrand and the latter showed no bitterness, being glad to abandon a sinking ship in good time. It would turn out that three months later the Jorry affair placed him precisely in the position where he wanted to be. We shall come in the next chapter to the extraordinary twist of fate that eventually befell Jorry.

It was typical of Talleyrand not to burn his bridges. He told his friend David Sandoz-Rollin, the Prussian ambassador, that he was leaving office but not leaving politics—one should always give oneself a choice between two options. Bonaparte was cut off in Egypt and the Directory did not appreciate Talleyrand's services; maybe someone else would, perhaps Louis XVIII exiled in England? He was thoroughly detested by the Bourbon family but, nevertheless, established contact through an emissary. He asked if, in the event that Louis XVIII returned to the throne of France, the former Bishop of Autun could benefit from a noble title and be considered to have left the church definitively. Louis replied that he would grant him the Duchy of Périgord on condition that the church accepted his transfer from an ecclesiastical to lay status. In short, not without dreadful complications.

For some months prior to Talleyrand's resignation, a young revolutionary by the name of Joseph Fouché had been attached to the Ministry of Foreign Affairs as ambassador to The Hague. Although Talleyrand did not know Fouché very well and did not count him among his friends, he believed that Fouché was worthy of higher office, the Minister of Police for instance. During the early part of the Revolution, Fouché had become a merciless, anti-church radical. From late 1793 until spring 1794, he had sent "batch after batch of bankers, scholars, aristocrats, priests, nuns, and wealthy merchants and their wives, mistresses, and children... taken from the city jails to Brotteaux field in Lyon, tied to stakes, and dispatched by firing squads or mobs." This made Fouché infamous as "The Executioner of Lyon". He assisted in Robespierre's overthrow, culminating in the dramatic events of *9 Thermidor Year II*, illustrating the pitiless nature of French politics at this time.

On *30 Prairial Year VIII* (18 June 1799), Pierre-Roger Ducos was named as a member of the Directory, thanks to the influence of Paul Barras, who counted on his support. A month later, Director Sieyès wanted to curb the excesses of the Jacobins. Sieyès was intelligent, a skilful lawyer with an incontestable reputation as a founder of the Revolution, who rapidly became head of the Directory. Talleyrand gave him some advice: "At a time when the Jacobins appear so audacious and violent against us, there is only one Jacobin who can oppose them vigorously." It was in this way that Sieyès appointed Joseph Fouché as Prefect of Police for Paris. At first, the Jacobins rejoiced. His credentials were so irreproachable that when he closed the Jacobin Club there was no real resistance. He then hunted down those pamphleteers and editors, whether Jacobins or Royalists, who were influential critics of the government, such as those people who had caused Talleyrand's resignation. At the time of the return of Bonaparte from the Egyptian campaign, Fouché was one of the most powerful men in France. The careers of Talleyrand and Fouché would run in parallel over the coming years, sometimes working together and at other times not trusting each other.

If the usefulness of the Directory was at an end, people began to consider seriously what kind of regime could replace it. At this moment, six years after the execution of Louis XVI, people were still thinking that the reinstallation of a king was the most viable answer. There were three strong candidates: the late king's brother, Louis XVIII; the young Louis Philippe, Duke d'Orléans; or a Prussian prince of the Hohenzollern family. Talleyrand's preference would have been to choose the Orléans branch of the royal family, but the young Duke of Orléans did not wish to become involved in politics at this stage. However, like a lot of other people, such as Talleyrand and Bonaparte, Sieyès believed that another solution for the nation's dilemma was a coup d'état by a strong military personality. He was wary of Bonaparte because this general was indeed too strong. His choice fell on General Barthélemy Joubert, who was good natured and popular, but had the misfortune to be killed at the Battle of Novi in August 1799. Other potential candidates were Generals Bernadotte, Brune, Macdonald and Moreau. While in conversation with General Jean Victor Moreau, news arrived on 9 October 1799 that Bonaparte had returned from Egypt and landed at Fréjus. "There's your man!" exclaimed Moreau.

Never had a general who had been defeated and who was liable to be brought to justice for abandoning his army in the field been received with such acclaim by both the Jacobins and the Royalists! Individually, the five members of the Directory thought that he should be arrested, but none of them took any action. On the route towards Paris he received a hero's welcome for nobody really cared about what had happened in Egypt. Now that Bonaparte was back, the country believed in itself again. Fearing that he might hear reports of her unfaithfulness, Josephine rushed to greet him before her accusers could, but missed him. He reached Paris on 16 October to find the little house on Rue de la Victoire empty. When Josephine returned to Paris, there was a violent scene but she was soon forgiven. Bonaparte met Talleyrand the following morning. The subject of Constantinople did not seem to trouble them as they threw themselves into each other's arms.

The situation in Paris in October 1799 had evolved. The people who had purchased land after the Revolution wanted security of property; the clergy wanted recognition of Catholicism as the state religion and a reunion with the Papacy in Rome; the country folk wanted the restoration of the village priest, the mass and the sound of church bells; merchants, industrialists and shopkeepers wanted peace and social order; and the politicians wanted a new constitution that guaranteed stability while avoiding despotism and Jacobinism. With Gohier and Moulin as members of the Directory, there had been a tendency in the second half of 1799 towards a hard-line Jacobinism. Upon his return, Bonaparte considered being elected as a member of the Directory, but eventually came to the same conclusion that had already been aired many times by different people—the dilemma could be resolved by the prompt seizure of power by a military hero.

By the end of the first day of Bonaparte's return, he and Talleyrand had decided on a course of action that required audacity and courage. Talleyrand, the born conspirator, was made responsible for gathering intelligence. Among his unique qualities were a taste for secrecy, the ability to promote both true and false rumours, and the talent always to be the first to know what was going on. For this purpose, he relied upon his agents Desrenaudes and Montrond, as well as the journalist Roux-Laborie. They circulated in the ministries, in the embassies, in the salons, even in the Directory itself. When his friend Jaucourt asked him what he was up to, Talleyrand replied with affected indifference: "Me? I am doing nothing. I wait!"

There seemed to be a demand among the general public for a strong man who would sweep away the ephemeral Directory and replace it with a government that was respected. Never anxious to play a leading role in such a major change, Talleyrand selected Sieyès as his instrument for the destruction of the Directory. He was passionate about acts and constitutions, knew everything there was to know about the law and was rumoured to carry a draft constitution around with him in his pocket. Talleyrand said to Bonaparte: "You want power. Sieyès wants a new constitution. Unite your forces to destroy what there is, since it is an obstacle for both of you." It was therefore most inconvenient that Bonaparte and Sieyès could not stand the sight of each other. Consequently, the former Bishop of Autun and Pierre-Louis Roederer set to work to convince the two men to meet. They sold the Director the idea that Bonaparte was the only person capable of bringing about the ideal republic that Sieyès had been dreaming of for so many years, the incomparable constitution of which he had already drafted. However, as a sign of things to come, the general wanted their meeting to take place at the Rue de la Victoire and Sieyès at the Luxembourg Palace. It took much going backwards and forwards on the part of Talleyrand, Fouché and Roederer before the two adversaries agreed to meet on 23 October at the house of Lucien Bonaparte, president of the Assembly. They had in common the desire to carry out a successful change of regime. Sieyès explained his plan to Bonaparte: to employ the least amount of force, to neutralize the Directory and to persuade the *Conseil des Cinq-Cents* to vote a new constitution. The general agreed in principle to the plan and guaranteed the support of the army and of the financiers—Perregaux, Ouvrard, Simons, etc.—and finally the members of the Institute. Bonaparte's role was not entirely clear but, even though Sieyès had been inveigled into the plot, there would only be one victor.

Because Talleyrand went to bed at 4 a.m. and woke up at about midday, most of his activities concerning the downfall of the Directory took place at night. At this time, he had moved north of the River Seine, living in Rue Taitbout in what is now the ninth *arrondissement* of Paris. One night, at about 1 o'clock, Bonaparte, Talleyrand and their trusted followers were plotting their next move when they heard the clatter of wheels and horses' hooves as a troop of cavalry stopped in the street outside the apartment. Everyone went pale as they realized that they could have been betrayed and the police had come to arrest them. They blew out all the candles and waited for a knock at the door. Soon, the cavalcade moved on. The next day, they discovered that it was a carriage transporting the evening's take from a gambling house that had lost a wheel while escorted by mounted gendarmerie. They had had a nasty fright.

The plotters realized that it was essential to count on the support or the non-interference of one person: Barras. If he was going to be asked to step down, it was simply a question of "how much?" but Barras would not commit himself. Bonaparte wanted the affair to be dealt with discreetly and was ready to pay whatever Barras demanded. Talleyrand visited Barras and explained to the Director that Bonaparte envisaged a slight reshuffle of the Directory and that he was part of the plot. Later, Barras received a second visit from Talleyrand, Lucien Bonaparte and the disturbing Fouché. He was informed that the new government would consist of only one person, but unfortunately it was not him. He had been side-lined.

After a couple of postponements, Bonaparte's coup d'état was finally programmed for Saturday, 9 November 1799, known in the revolutionary calendar as *18 Brumaire Year VIII*. It had been decided not to arrest the five directors but simply to oblige them to leave quietly. Prior to the coup, troops were deployed around Paris. The plan was that, after the directors had "resigned", the *Anciens* and the *Conseil des Cinq-Cents* (the upper and lower houses of the legislature) would appoint a pliant commission to draw up a new constitution to the plotters' specifications. As was his habit on the eve of great occasions, Talleyrand, imperturbable, played whist with his friends. He fulfilled no definite function but, acquainted with everybody, held all the strings.

Under normal circumstances, a coup d'état takes place rapidly so that those likely to oppose it do not have time to react. This one took place over two days and at a critical moment Bonaparte lost his head. Paris was calm but troops were stationed everywhere, particularly around the Luxembourg Palace and the Tuileries. On the morning of *18 Brumaire*, Admiral Bruix accompanied Talleyrand to Barras's office where, to convince him that his political life was over, they asked him to look out of the window. A large body of troops was ready to obey the orders of General Bonaparte, the people's idol, who could in one gesture crush the Directory, the ministries, the assemblies, the clubs and the newspapers. Barras realized that his resignation was required. He went to his desk, signed the letter previously written by Roederer and gave it to Talleyrand, who kissed his hand and called him "France's first patriot". With the resignation letter in his hand, Talleyrand was supposed to have given Barras a letter of credit for 2 million livres—the price of his departure. According to eyewitnesses, this did not take place— Talleyrand kept the 2 million livres for himself, perhaps to compensate for the support that Barras had given the impudent Jorry, allowing him to humiliate the Minister of Foreign Affairs. Escorted by a detachment of dragoons, Barras left Paris for his country estate at Grosbois and played no further role in French politics. Later that morning, as foreseen, Sieyès and Ducos resigned thus preventing a quorum of directors from meeting. Pierre-Louis Roederer, a lawyer and politician, was a long-term friend of Talleyrand, prepared the text of some posters announcing Bonaparte's seizure of power, which were set in type by his son Antoine.

Early in the day, Lucien Bonaparte persuaded the two legislative Councils—the *Anciens* and the *Cinq Cents*—that a Jacobin coup was at hand in Paris and induced them to disperse and meet the next day at the suburban Château de Saint-Cloud, where the comparative isolation would protect them—and make it easier to deal with them. Napoleon was charged with the safety of these two Councils and given command of all available local troops. In contrast to the Directory, the two Councils continued meeting. By the following day, however, the deputies had, for the most part, realized that an attempted coup was afoot rather than the threat of a Jacobin rebellion.

When the two chambers met at 1.30 p.m. on 10 November, Talleyrand and his entourage were gathered nearby in an upstairs apartment. In the middle of the afternoon, Lagarde, the Directory's secretary, sent a message to the President of the Council of *Anciens* that another of the directors had resigned making four out of five—which was not true. Faced with the resistance of the two legislative bodies, Bonaparte stormed into the chambers. There was pandemonium with cries of "Outlaw" and the little general seemed to be intimidated by the uproar. Montrond, who stood near him whispered in his ear: "General Bonaparte, this will not do!" The noise in the room was soon drowned when Lucien Bonaparte called upon General Murat, who entered with a squad of drummers escorted by a small force of grenadiers with fixed bayonets. The members of the Assembly fled by every available door and window. As planned, the new Consulate was born consisting of three members: Bonaparte, Sieyès and Ducos.

On this day, all the leading republicans of the moment were in favour of the coup d'état: Mme de Staël, Benjamin Constant, General Moreau, and even Destutt de Tracy, the leader of the "ideologists". It had been deeply desired that the event would take place without bloodshed and this objective was achieved. In the aftermath, there were measures of leniency, the cancellation of prison sentences and the suspension of deportation orders. Bonaparte had triumphed, but so had Talleyrand. At the end of the day, he looked at his colleagues—Pierre-Louis Roederer and his son Antoine, Montrond, Desrenaudes, Radix de Sainte-Foy and Moreau de Saint-Méry. "My friends," he said, "let's go and have dinner."

CHAPTER IX
THE CONSULATE

After Bonaparte's coup d'état, Talleyrand invited his friends to dinner in the suburbs of Paris near Saint-Cloud at the house of Mme Simons, whose husband was the Belgian arms dealer and banker Jean-Michel Simons. As the actress Mlle Lange, she had become rich and famous in 1793 for playing the lead role in the play *Paméla ou La Vertu Récompensée* [Pamela or Virtue Rewarded] by Nicolas François de Neufchâteau (one of the former directors), as a result of which straw hats *à la Paméla* became very fashionable in Paris.

A few days later, Bonaparte received Talleyrand and Roederer in his office at the Luxembourg Palace. The new First Consul took Talleyrand to one side and promised that he would be Minister of Foreign Affairs again and not, as he would have wished, Minister of Finance. Bonaparte did not trust the former Bishop of Autun in such a responsible position. Thus, on 21 November Charles Reinhard, accompanied by his wife, went back to Berne as the French ambassador to Switzerland, while Talleyrand returned to the Rue du Bac with his Indian-born lady friend.

The public, and particularly the Jacobins, had not forgotten the Jorry affair. Thus, seeing Talleyrand back in office only four months after his resignation stimulated them to a new campaign of derision. However, elsewhere in the press he was acknowledged as the peacemaker whose ideas on European solidarity had been frustrated by the Directory's desire to promote revolutionary war. Even Bonaparte was ready to sing his praises as a minister: "He has much of what is necessary to conduct negotiations, an understanding of the world, knowledge about European courts, finesse... finally, a great name." Bonaparte had a weakness for the old aristocracy. When his informants told him about the amount of bribes Talleyrand received, his nights spent gambling, his intrigues, his lewd escapades, Bonaparte was furious, but then shrugged his shoulders and sent his informants away: "He comes from a good family; that's the most important thing." At this stage, he paid more attention to Talleyrand's opinion than those of any other member of his state council.

The government during this period of French history is known as the Consulate, the three leaders of which were initially Sieyès, Ducos and Bonaparte. The Constitution of the Year VIII, adopted on *22 Frimaire* (25 December 1799), was devised by Sieyès to provide a balance of power. However, by securing for himself the title of "First Consul" Bonaparte made sure that he had the last word on all policies and appointments. This annoyed Sieyès, who saw his wonderful constitution being refashioned in the sense of a dictatorship. Discussions between Sieyès and Bonaparte had become heated over the former's desire for a head of state who would be a neutral, powerless figurehead, whereas Bonaparte sought to establish a "stable and strong" regime with the executive power entirely in his hands for a period of at least ten years. On 12 December, Sieyès was replaced as Second Consul by Jean-Jacques de Cambacérès, a most able lawyer. At Roederer's suggestion, Ducos was replaced as Third Consul and Minister of Finance by Charles-François Lebrun. In a jocular mood, Talleyrand labelled the new regime with the Latin pronouns *Hic, Haec, Hoc:* the masculine *Hic* for Bonaparte; the feminine *Haec* for Cambacérès, whose sexual orientation was well known; and *Hoc,* the neutral for Lebrun. Public opinion, both Jacobin and Royalist, soon came to respect Bonaparte's government with its appeal to all parties, the new laws it adopted, its solution to the church problem and its military victories. The legislature consisted of three chambers: the *Tribunal* where laws were discussed; the *Corps legislative* which voted; and the *Sénat conservateur* whose purpose was to "protect the Constitution". Three years later, the Constitution of the Year X, adopted on *16 Thermidor* (4 August 1802), would give Napoleon power for life, allowing him to nominate members of the Senate, which became the regime's most powerful legislative body, since it was able to dissolve the other two chambers. Only those notables who Bonaparte considered suitable for election would be allowed to sit in the parliament.

However, neither Cambacérès nor Lebrun were to play an important role in Bonaparte's government, since the divergent tendencies in French politics were more embodied in Talleyrand and Fouché. Bourrienne, Bonaparte's secretary, describes Talleyrand as "the second person of the consular government"; Fouché came third. When Bonaparte and company had been plotting the Directory's overthrow, they had been joined by Fouché in his capacity as Prefect of Police for Paris. His activity in furthering the coup ensured him Bonaparte's favour, who kept him in office and this is where he met Talleyrand again.

The period between the coup d'état of *18 Brumaire* (9 November 1799) and the breakdown of the Treaty of Amiens (May 1803) is one of the most glorious in French history during which Napoleon Bonaparte met with the general public's approval. It was for Talleyrand and Bonaparte a honeymoon period and the happiest of Napoleon's life. He was only 30 years old, anxious to learn and not ashamed to be taught. Soon after taking up his functions, Talleyrand was received by the First Consul at the Luxembourg Palace where Bourrienne was taking notes. Talleyrand explained his position: "Citizen Consul, you have placed in my charge the Ministry of Foreign Affairs and I will justify your confidence, but I wish to tell you that I intend to work only with you." He explained that the rebirth of France required that there should be one person who exercised power and to whom the principal government sectors, namely the ministries of the interior, the police, foreign affairs, war and the navy, were answerable. The ministries of justice and finance could be supervised by the two other consuls: "That will keep them busy; that will give them something to do." This arrangement corresponded to Bonaparte's way of thinking but he had not been able to formulate it so precisely. After Talleyrand had gone, he turned to his assistant and said: "Do you realize, Bourrienne, that Talleyrand gives sound advice; he is a person of great common sense." "What do you mean?" asked Bourrienne. "He got inside me!" concluded Bonaparte.

It is one of the ironies of history that the First Consul was popular because it was thought that he would bring a permanent peace both at home and abroad. Given their complicity in the years prior to the coup d'état, it would also have seemed plausible that Talleyrand and Bonaparte would have remained close colleagues. At the beginning of the Consulate they did indeed spend a lot of time in each other's company but it soon became clear that their relationship was that of master and servant. Although he was a child of the French Revolution, Bonaparte also appreciated the style and manners of those who had survived from the

Ancien Régime. In the early days, Talleyrand accepted Bonaparte's position of supreme power and always addressed him with the greatest possible deference, tact and affection with the clear intention of making himself a trustworthy and indispensable subordinate, perhaps "the favourite" who would enjoy the ruler's complete confidence. He quickly understood that Bonaparte was a military genius and some of the minister's messages express emotions of adulation so profound that they read like love letters: "I would like to say that if your absence lasts much longer, I would not only have the desire to find myself in your presence but I would feel the need." He flirts with him: "I am therefore probably going to write some very silly things but it is not my fault; when I am far from you, I am lacking something." His words would take the form of flattery so unctuous, of devotion so unconditional that Bonaparte soon became addicted to this potion: "Since I became attached to your destiny, I am yours for life and for death." Napoleon enjoyed the finesse of such courtly flattery, even when he took no notice of Talleyrand's advice. After the Battle of Marengo, Talleyrand wrote to congratulate the glorious victor on his success and slips into his letter the following phrase: "There has never been an empire founded on such marvels; here, the marvels are reality." This is the first hint of a Napoleonic Empire. Talleyrand's adulation was richly rewarded. In the beginning, it is possible to believe that Talleyrand's flattery was quite sincere; later on, it is evident that he did not believe one word of what he said or wrote. Eventually, he was driven to the conclusion that he could do nothing to deflect his master's reckless determination to be master of Europe. Despite the breakdown of their relationship in 1807, in later years Talleyrand remarked: "I liked Napoleon; I became attached to him despite his faults."

The myth of Napoleon is that of the "little corporal", the common man, who rose to be greater and more powerful than any European monarch through sheer personal charisma. He was a product of the French Revolution, but also an enlightened, rational, inquisitive product of the eighteenth century. While his armies conquered abroad, at home he brought stability—at least to begin with—and established many of the French institutions as they stand today. Many of his ideas had already been anticipated by the Revolution, but he adopted them in a conservative, authoritarian and definitive manner. Even though he did not respect the ideals of equality, liberty and fraternity, he brought glory to the entire French population—except for the quarter-of-a-million Frenchmen who did not return from the wars.

Since 1789, the Revolution had enacted thousands of laws without any reference to past practices. The country could not function without a well-defined set of laws and, since there had been no attempt to codify them since Colbert in the seventeenth century, Bonaparte created a committee of lawyers under Cambacérès to draw up a civil, criminal and rural code. The civil laws, finally enacted in 1804 and known as the *Code Napoléon*, set the rules for marriage, divorce, inheritance and common law and were later adopted by much of the non-English-speaking world. The hierarchies of officials in the civil service, local government, the education system and the army also date from this time. From the outset, Bonaparte employed men of energy and ability in the administration, whatever their political past, and showed his trust by maintaining them in office over many years. Where Napoleon and Talleyrand differed strongly was on freedom of the press and civil liberties. However, the Minister of Foreign Affairs and, indeed, a large part of the nation were ready to make concessions if it resulted in a strong leader who brought respite after years of turmoil.

No sooner had Talleyrand taken up his functions again at the Rue du Bac, when he learned that the imprudent Jorry, along with thirty-seven other villains, had been arrested and was due to be deported to Guyana— where a miserable death was still the expected outcome. Talleyrand immediately wrote to Fouché requesting that Jorry should be pardoned: "Since, to my knowledge, Jorry has only offended me, I believe it is my singular duty to place before you these observations; having the greatest desire to see my injury erased from the face of the Earth, as it is with myself, I would look upon it as a personal favour [for you to let him go]." Talleyrand's letter had such an impact that not only was Jorry saved, but the entire shipload of convicts had their deportations cancelled. In forgiving the insults and scorn of which he had been the victim, in the extraordinary humanity of this gesture one has the evidence that his training for the priesthood had not gone to waste.

At the end of December 1799, two envoys made contact with Bonaparte on behalf of the Louis Stanislas Xavier, Count de Provence, the late Louis XVI's exiled brother. In the mistaken belief that the First Consul had seized power simply in order to restore the Bourbons to the throne, the envoys' proposition was that, if he stood down in favour of Louis XVIII, the rightful heir to the throne, Bonaparte would be rewarded with a grand title, a distinguished decoration and a solid pension for life. Not surprisingly, Jean-Guillaume Hyde de Neuville and General Louis d'Andigné left Bonaparte's office empty handed. Like the Directory before him, Bonaparte had to steer a course between the Royalists on the one hand and the Jacobins on the other. He had nothing but contempt for the Jacobins who had tarnished the Revolution's image during the Terror. While the Royalists represented the more serious threat to his power, he was more sympathetic to them and his only objection was that they wanted to restore the Bourbons to the throne!

Talleyrand delivered the two envoys to the Luxembourg Palace in his carriage and picked them up afterwards, their conversation acknowledging the similarity of their personal backgrounds dating from before the Revolution. He had known "Monsieur", the form of address used for the future Louis XVIII, before the Revolution. He told the two envoys that, but for his physical infirmity, his family would have directed him towards a military career and, if this had been the case, he might have been forced into exile with Louis and could well have been sitting in their places. They asked if Bonaparte's regime was likely to last. Talleyrand was already aware and would remain deeply concerned for the next decade and a half that the regime's survival depended uniquely on Bonaparte himself. He told the king's envoys: "If he survives the first year, he will go far."

The attitude of Talleyrand and the First Consul to the monarchy was the exact opposite to that of the Bourbons. Their preference was that, if the Count de Provence and the other members of his family gave up all their claims to the throne of France, they would receive comfortable annuities as long as they resided in a place remote from France—Warsaw was not quite far enough; perhaps Moscow. Talleyrand tried desperately to persuade the British Government to send the Duke d'Artois and all his retinue away from Edinburgh, where they had been living, to join Louis XVIII who at this time was residing in Latvia and Warsaw. Louis XVIII was to lead a nomadic life until he was finally granted asylum by the British Prince Regent at Hartwell House, Buckinghamshire, in 1808. Louis sincerely believed that he was the true, unique and God-given inheritor of the French throne and was not ready to negotiate his position, certainly not for a pension.

On 15 December 1799, Bonaparte declared without ambiguity that the Revolution was over. In February 1800, he moved out of the Luxembourg Palace and into the Tuileries, the former royal residence in the Louvre gardens, so as to vacate a building where the Senate might meet. On most matters he had an extremely firm opinion and one of these matters was that a country could not exist without a hierarchy. The leader needed to be surrounded and supported by some kind of entourage consisting of an intelligentsia and military leaders who would be loyal to him through his largesse. Before creating his own nobility, Bonaparte considered it expedient to bring into his orbit those members of the former aristocracy who had survived the guillotine. He was not opposed to the idea of the exiled nobility returning—but not the royal family itself. He had no appetite for balls and receptions but, nevertheless, asked Talleyrand to organize such an event on 25 February 1800 where he could meet the *Ancien Regime's* survivors. Talleyrand invited a bevy of his noble female friends who had attended the royal court before the Revolution—even Mme de Flahaut, but not Mme de Staël! These ladies ran salons where Talleyrand would participate and listen. No head of state had ever benefited from so prestigious a minister of information.

Apart from Mme de Staël, there were also other friends who might overshadow the Minister of Foreign Affairs. He took care to keep the names of Calonne and Narbonne out of Napoleon's purview. Yet, he was able to render a great service to many other members of the aristocracy by having their names removed from the list of *émigrés* before the general amnesty. Bonaparte believed that he was doing Talleyrand a favour by taking his two brothers off the list, at the same time as restoring their property to them. Prior to returning, they had both been officers in the British Army but managed to leave England without receiving their final salaries. Talleyrand informed his British counterpart, Lord Addington, of this oversight, whereupon the two brothers received their outstanding payments and returned to Paris in style. Younger brother Boson boasted that his salary had been boosted by the personal intervention of Prime Minister Pitt and since, up to this point, he had been fighting against the French Revolutionary Army, this statement was considered to be so politically inept that Bonaparte banned the two brothers from Paris. Talleyrand decided that he had done as much as he could for them, so refused to intervene again to ask forgiveness on their behalf for this faux-pas. Bonaparte too had brothers and sisters who caused him strife, but he never failed to bail them out.

Both Talleyrand and Bonaparte's family began to consider the question of the regime's continuity—for the stability of France, it was necessary to have a dynasty. Since Josephine did not have any children by Bonaparte, a situation unlikely to change, Talleyrand and Bonaparte's brothers, sisters and mother began to think that sooner or later she was going to be an obstacle to their long-term plans. Lucien, Napoleon's brother, published a brochure in which he plunged straight into the heredity question concerning the Bonaparte family. This was so politically ill-timed that it could easily have drawn a strong negative reaction from the Republican politicians. Bonaparte was furious with Lucien, whose publication risked simply stirring up opposition, banishing his brother to Madrid. Talleyrand recommended a rather different approach. He began by gently drawing the public's attention to the idea that, in the presence of such a great man, in the unhappy event that he were to die, it would be very expedient if he had a son ready to assume the heritage of his title and to pursue his policies drawing inspiration from the Revolution. Together with Roederer, Talleyrand moderately explored the idea of a hereditary regime and encouraged the newspapers to spread this idea. Joseph and Lucien Bonaparte were perfectly aware that Napoleon's death would result in their instant removal from power. One person who was directly concerned by this matter, but whose opinion was not sought, was the 37-year-old Josephine. As her little general husband rose in stature, she felt her position weaken. She knew that the issue of heredity would be her undoing and was aware that Lucien Bonaparte and Roederer were pressing for action on this issue. Talleyrand kept his cards close to his chest, so she had no idea where his sympathies lay.

At the beginning of the Consulate, Talleyrand's policy was to keep Russia, Austria and Britain isolated from each other. During the early months of the Consulate, Talleyrand extended his control over the French diplomatic service. In two reports to Bonaparte in 1800 he recommended a return to former ways of working and a fixed system of grades and promotion for his ministerial staff. In general, the names he proposed for ambassadorial posts abroad were accepted by Bonaparte, such that he was able to place his most faithful colleagues in key positions. One of Louis XVIII's principal agents in Paris was the Abbé de Montesquiou, who had taken over from Charles-Maurice as Agent-General for the Clergy in 1785 and, for the time being, remained a close acquaintance. In important negotiations, Talleyrand also resorted to Bonaparte's brothers, Joseph and Lucien, although they were all expected to follow such strict daily instructions that their freedom of manoeuvre was very limited.

This period was notorious for a multitude of information networks using agents financed by Bonaparte's cabinet, the Ministry of Foreign Affairs, the police, etc., not to mention those functioning for foreign governments. Some informants were double agents employed by several different patrons. Talleyrand used these people who, while paid by the British Government or by the Duke d'Artois, kept him informed as well. The whole purpose was to be the first to find out what was happening in the Jacobin and Royalist camps hostile to the regime, and who was conducting secret negotiations with whom. As Bonaparte's Minister of Foreign Affairs, Talleyrand used his secret funds to finance his informants as he had done previously under the Directory, but now he came into competition with the network set up by Joseph Fouché, the Minister of Police. Fouché spied on everybody, his friends as much as his enemies—he saw everything and knew everything. He was a master, as Étienne de Pasquier observed, "of making everyone look a fool". In May 1800, Fouché arrested a certain Dupérou at Calais who, from his prison cell, accused the Minister of Foreign Affairs of providing the British Government with important information about French policies. Talleyrand quickly wrote to Bonaparte in Italy complaining that he had just been deprived of one of his best agents providing false information to the British minister responsible for intelligence, William Wickham. Even the French agent Louis Guillaume Otto in London complained of leaks of information arising from the ministry on the Rue du Bac. On behalf of the Minister of Foreign Affairs, Roux-Laborie issued an official bulletin, as well as an unofficial hand-written newsletter full of revelations and covert notes provided by ambassadors abroad or informants in Paris. This also meant that Talleyrand, like a minister of propaganda, was able to control the distribution of information—true or false—giving his own version of his role in certain controversial affairs for the benefit of foreign governments.

Following the Battle of Marengo, Talleyrand and Fouché, while far from being friends, discovered that they were in fact both concerned about the same issue: "And if—God forbid—Bonaparte did not return from Italy." He was, after all, involved in pitched battles and it was a very common occurrence for senior officers to be mortally wounded by stray cannon balls. If, with the aid of a telescope, the opposing general could be identified on the battlefield, artillery was deliberately aimed at him. And what about assassination attempts? What would happen then to Bonaparte's ministers if one of them were successful? As soon as he returned to Paris after the battle, Bonaparte was informed that his two ministers had met and discussed his succession. A third person who had been present at their meeting was Clément de Ris, who on 23 September 1800 was the victim of an extraordinary abduction in broad daylight that inspired much conjecture and even a few novels. He was seized by Fouché's agents and incarcerated in a cellar for nineteen days. It had not been Fouché's intention to kidnap him but rather to burgle his house to recover some compromising documents. Things had gone calamitously wrong. Did these documents concern the meeting between Talleyrand and Fouché? It is believed nowadays that Fouché was concerned by some other business involving dissidents. Bonaparte required Fouché to arrest and punish the perpetrators severely—who were, of course, his own agents. Instead, Fouché arrested three Royalists who were on his list of suspicious dissidents and, despite their watertight alibis, were executed by firing squad about a year later. One of the judges protested about the circumstances of their trial and was promptly retired from his functions. Clément de Ris returned to politics and lived to be an old man, but mystery continues to surround this affair.

An assassination attempt was carried out against Bonaparte on 24 December 1800 in the Rue Saint-Nicaise in Paris. As Bonaparte's carriage entered the street, a bomb in a horse-drawn vehicle exploded killing twenty-two people and injuring even more. Bonaparte was not hurt but his step-daughter Hortense travelling in a separate carriage was slightly injured. Talleyrand believed that the Jacobins associated with Fouché were responsible, while Fouché favoured the Royalist camp. For good measure, more than 100 Jacobins and Royalists were imprisoned, executed or deported. Questions were raised about Fouché's ability to protect the First Consul's life. For instance, all those informants and spies working in France against the First Consul were financed by the British Government. Given that both Talleyrand and Fouché had excellent networks of informants, it is possible that they both knew who was really behind the assassination attempt but kept quiet about it. Eventually, about eighteen months later, with the support of Joseph and Lucien Bonaparte, Talleyrand managed to engineer Fouché's retirement from his functions because he opposed Napoleon's bid for lifelong tenure. Fouché became a senator, although Bonaparte later came to regret losing his efficient Minister of Police. While Talleyrand was happy to see the back of Fouché, the latter would have been equally keen to see the former Bishop of Autun relieved of his functions. The first round went to Talleyrand, although this was far from the end of the long and complicated relationship between these two politicians. Bonaparte took care to promote their rivalry, but the subtler of the two was Talleyrand. While Fouché sought to preserve the First Consul's government respecting the republican tradition, Talleyrand realised that Bonaparte was only concerned about pursuing his own form of government. Another of Talleyrand's advantages was that he had managed to place one of his henchmen, LaForêt, as head of the postal service, who could then intercept and pass to the minister the most interesting letters, which may or may not have been tampered with before being brought to the attention of the First Consul. In this case, Fouché had found out exactly what was going on and reported it to Bonaparte. Of course, Charles-Maurice declared that he knew nothing about it! Roux-Laborie, who must have played an important role in this network, fled Paris in the direction of Hamburg with Bonaparte's police on his heels, while LaForêt was replaced in the postal service by one of the First Consul's most faithful aides-de-camp, Lavalette. Now that Roux-Laborie had been unmasked, it would soon be the turn of Montrond. However, Talleyrand's network of informants, consisting of men and women of the underworld and former *émigrés*, was so sophisticated that Bonaparte would never get to the bottom of it.

On 26 December 1799, Bonaparte had written to the British and Austrian Governments offering them peace terms. The British Government refused the offer and the Austrians did not reply. Austria paid the price of its silence when its army, thanks to the last-minute intervention of General Louis Desaix, was defeated at Marengo in Italy on 24 June 1800. When the Austrian minister Cobenzl came to Paris to sign the Treaty of Lunéville, Talleyrand would have liked to believe that the epoch of European peace and prosperity had at last arrived. By the terms of the treaty, France took possession of the left bank of the Rhine, including what are now Belgium and Luxembourg, as well as the Italian territories of Piedmont, the Cisalpine Republic and Liguria on the Mediterranean coast. In Talleyrand's opinion, it would have been better to appease Austria so as to make it an ally, whereas the severe terms of Bonaparte's treaty were likely to provoke the humiliated Holy Roman Emperor, Francis II, to seek revenge. After the Battle of Marengo, none of Bonaparte's crushing victories over the next decade actually served the interests of France.

Alongside the Treaty of Lunéville and thanks in part to Talleyrand, the very early years of the nineteenth century witnessed a remarkable series of treaties that brought peace, alliances or reconciliation to France with the United States, the Two Sicilies, Portugal (the Treaty of Madrid), Russia, Algiers, the United Kingdom (the Treaty of Amiens) and Turkey. An anonymous publication of 1800, describing in wide-ranging and forward-looking terms a liberal economic system for Europe with few customs barriers, bears all the hallmarks of having been written by Talleyrand and d'Hauterive. Particularly, it states that European peace depends upon respect for "maxims, principles and laws" based on each country's political, administrative and economic system. One definition of peace states that friendship should take the place of hatred, although clearly for many of these treaties this was not always the case. Since the middle of the eighteenth century the balance of power among European nations had been upset by the actions of Russia, Prussia, Austria and

England. The French Revolutionary Wars had only aggravated an already unstable situation. Since the 1770s, Russia had invaded the Crimea, Bessarabia (modern Moldova), Wallachia (part of Romania), Poland, Georgia and Persia, and had adopted an aggressive stance in the Mediterranean and in Afghanistan. It was also important to maintain a balance between the ambitions of the two Germanic powers: Prussia to the north and Austria to the south. Finally, the British domination of the oceans ought to give way to a more just distribution of commercial maritime traffic.

The Battles of Marengo and Hohenlinden had led to Austria signing the Peace of Lunéville (9 February 1801). Following an agreement between Russia, Prussia and the Scandinavian countries, the ports of northern Europe and the Baltic had been closed to British shipping. With Prime Minister Pitt resigning over domestic issues, the appointment of the more accommodating Henry Addington was regarded as an opportunity for peace talks. When the Russian Tsar Paul I was assassinated in March 1801, followed by the departure of William Pitt and Nelson's victory at the Battle of Copenhagen in April, the international situation underwent a radical change in favour of the British. Talleyrand asked Montrond to go to London for preliminary contacts with a view to making peace with England. It was at this same juncture that Bonaparte, profoundly suspicious of Talleyrand's role in money-making affairs, had sent Louis-Guillaume Otto to London to open peace negotiations. Talleyrand heard the canons at Les Invalides firing a salute and found out, to his stupefaction, that it was to mark the beginning of diplomatic contact with the British, for Bonaparte had established preliminary communications with British Foreign Secretary, Lord Hawkesbury, without informing him! Upon learning that his role as foreign minister had been completely usurped, Talleyrand did not resign but wrote fawning letters of adulation to his master, perfectly aware that he was suddenly no longer in favour.

Since the adoption of the 1791 law requiring priests to swear an oath of loyalty to the Republican Constitution, the Catholic Church had been split between the "constitutional" priests and bishops who had accepted the oath, and the "refractory" elements consisting of exiled bishops and those priests who refused to conform. Bonaparte was determined to enlist the church's support for his regime and, as of 29 December 1799, invited the members of the clergy who had fled abroad to return. In June 1800, he made proposals to the new Pope Pius VII for a long-term reconciliation. Following difficult negotiations, agreement was reached with the adoption of the Concordat of 1801. Unknown to the Pope, less than a year after the Concordat was signed, Bonaparte appended to the Law of Religion of 1802 articles which confirmed the primacy of the French Republic over the authority of the Pope, thus strengthening the state's hold over the church. Bishops would be chosen by Bonaparte but invested by the Pope. The borders of *départements* would now coincide with the borders of dioceses, while the sermons of bishops and priests were expected to speak in favour of the regime. The Concordat gave Bonaparte the support of the clergy and their congregations, at the same time robbing the Royalists of their chief ally against his regime.

Nevertheless, the situation of a government minister, an excommunicated bishop, who had not only contributed to the Revolution's break with Rome but illegally consecrated several bishops and was now living in concubinage with a courtesan, could no longer be tolerated. Talleyrand saw nothing wrong about sharing his household with Mme Grand and allowing her to preside at his dinner table, but Bonaparte did. He could not accept that one of his ministers lived with a "whore". The prudish Mathieu Molé described the relationship between Catherine Grand and Talleyrand as follows: "The power that she had over him was so loathsome that it could only be attributed to the most carnal origin." Catherine Grand was aware of people's attitude about her reputation, particularly the wives of foreign ambassadors who were reluctant to meet her, and was starting to make a fuss about it—even the very middle-class Mme Fouché hesitated to visit her. The First Consul's rather radical solution was to promote the former bishop to the rank of cardinal, since it had not been unusual for some of the church's senior officials to be key members of the government and to have a taste for high living and fast women. All that was needed was a large dose of hypocrisy but Talleyrand, who had never wanted to become a priest in the first place, was not at all tempted by this scenario. He was not opposed to seeing France return to the Catholic religion, as long as he did not have a hand in the process. For him, the Declaration of the Rights of Man and the Revolution's acquisitions in the field of liberty were far more important than religion, which he summed up in the phrase: "It is necessary that those who have been pardoned by the Revolution [i.e. priests] should also pardon the Revolution." In his opinion, there was no question of Roman Catholicism being labelled as the "dominant religion" or the "state religion" of France, but perhaps more modestly "the religion of the majority of its citizens".

While defending the principle of liberty, Charles-Maurice did not forget his own interests. His most ardent desire was that, somewhere in the Concordat's small print, there would be an unambiguous clause where the Pope would permanently and completely relieve him of every one of his functions as a bishop or, if this was not going to happen, he would attempt to make negotiations as difficult as possible. The Papal Nuncio Caselli wrote to the Pope: "We have many enemies and, above all, an implacable and very powerful one in Autun." There was such a clause in the Concordat concerning priests who had given up the church, married and had children, but a bishop was altogether a different matter. Bonaparte supported Talleyrand by writing a letter to the Pope describing his situation as "an object of doubt and controversy" and including a list of all high church dignitaries who had married or given up the church, requesting that Talleyrand should be granted lay status, having abandoned the idea of making him a cardinal.

The Pope did not have any problem in allowing Talleyrand to wear ordinary secular clothes and to fulfil his responsibilities as a government minister but he found no precedent for allowing a bishop, particularly a self-designated former bishop, to marry. The stumbling block was "The Mme Grand Clause". Talleyrand sent a letter to Rome by special courier asking to be relieved of his episcopal functions without further delay or ambiguity. The messenger was kept waiting for a month before returning with the Pope's reply in August 1801. As was his custom, Talleyrand was taking the waters at Bourbon-l'Archambault when he was advised ominously by both Bonaparte and the Pope's negotiator Cardinal Caprara that the reply had been received. Talleyrand asked that the letter should be passed to him and found in it the Pope's half-refusal. He returned to Paris and made no declaration, which Caprara took as evidence that he had accepted the decision. This conclusion was premature.

In examining the wording of the Pope's letter, one of its key phrases reads as follows: "The citizen Maurice Talleyrand, Minister of Foreign Affairs, is returned to secular and lay life." This sentence was registered with the state council and made known to the public. Less attention was paid to a second phrase in the letter which confirmed the irrevocable nature of a bishop's vows: "No bishop has ever been allowed to marry." The Concordat was signed on 15 July 1801 leaving the Bishop of Autun's marital status unresolved—but not as far as Talleyrand was concerned. To the annoyance of Pius VII and Cardinal Consalvi—the Pope's Secretary of State—he found a way of misrepresenting the Pope's letter by having it registered with the state council in a form so vague that it seemed the Church had indeed liberated him of any responsibilities. Subsequently, Rome always considered his marriage as sacrilege. When, some years later, Catherine Grand wrote a very nice letter to Consalvi, in his reply he carefully avoided addressing her by name and asked someone else to send it to her in a plain envelope not bearing his insignia.

François-René Chateaubriand had written a book entitled *The Genius of Christianity* which supported Bonaparte's reconciliation with the church and had a great deal of success. It was a few days after the signing of the Concordat that the First Consul congratulated him on his book, removed him from the list of *émigrés* and appointed him as secretary to Cardinal Joseph Fesch in Rome, the French minister to the Holy See. It was clear that Chateaubriand had no idea who Fesch was since he soon wrote letters addressed to the First Consul mocking the cardinal's abilities. The French minister in Rome was none other than Bonaparte's uncle. Who was it who dared to insult a member of his Corsican family? An order was given to arrest the author of the letters, who, after multiple interventions in his favour by Talleyrand, was banished to Switzerland. Chateaubriand would eventually become a major French political and literary figure.

To mark the Concordat's signature and the new era for Catholicism in France, a religious service was held for all the Consulate's senior officials at Notre Dame in Paris on Easter Sunday, 1802. In accordance with protocol, the former Bishop of Autun and the former Abbé Fouché sat side by side. Since it was at least ten years since a religious ceremony had been held in Latin in the country, we can be sure that these two at least were able to follow what was going on. Bonaparte insisted that some regular soldiers should also be present in the congregation, but General Augereau asked if they could be excused since they viewed the ceremony as a denial of the Revolution. Bonaparte reminded him that it was their simple duty to obey. The dissident General Moreau also refused to attend and, under the influence of his young wife, began to assemble around him all who were discontented by Napoleon's regime.

Through mutual exhaustion, the United Kingdom and France agreed to end a war that had lasted ten years. The Treaty of Amiens was signed by Joseph Bonaparte for France and the Marquess Cornwallis for the United Kingdom on 25 March 1802. Cornwallis was unhappy with the agreement, but he was equally concerned about "the ruinous consequences of [...] renewing a bloody and hopeless war." In the aftermath of the signing, the British Government felt it could not trust the French, while the shifting positions of Napoleon and Joseph Bonaparte only confirmed their misgivings. It was to be a very short-lived agreement since it represented for Bonaparte the point of departure of what he wanted to achieve and for the British the limit beyond which they were not prepared to go. Nevertheless, in the second half of 1802 British visitors flocked to Paris, while French visitors travelled to London.

On the day the Treaty of Amiens was signed, Bonaparte had been waiting for it to arrive with nervous anxiety. Talleyrand had already received the treaty and hid it in his documents folder. After all the other matters of the day had been dealt with at the council of ministers that morning, Talleyrand casually pulled the treaty out and laid it before the First Consul, who exclaimed: "Why didn't you tell me straightaway?" The former Bishop of Autun was not to be intimidated: "Ah! Because you would not have listened to a word I said about other matters. When you are happy, you are not easily accessible!"

Talleyrand declared to Mme de Rémusat that, in his position of Minister of Foreign Affairs, it was primarily with Bonaparte that he was obliged to negotiate. Mme de Rémusat was a member of the aristocracy who was content to act as a lady-in-waiting to Josephine. Rather like Mme de La Tour du Pin, Aimée de Coigny and Fanny Burney, Mme de Rémusat was prejudiced against Talleyrand from the outset, but found it impossible to resist his charm. She noted that, apart from treating views he did not agree with in silent contempt, he also had a playful way of poking fun at serious subjects and particularly at herself.

As the years passed, Bonaparte began to betray the trust that people had placed in him as the saviour of the nation. He took more and more personal responsibility for foreign affairs, bypassing Talleyrand, using Roederer and Michel Regnaud to prepare the ground and always resorting to annexation, military occupation and warfare to execute his policies. He paid no heed to calls by other nations and other politicians for moderation and for the respect of laws, people's rights and frontiers, which meant that, if he continued in this vein, his rule could only end one way—in a cataclysmic defeat. Where Bonaparte was quick and decisive, never negotiated and never waited, Talleyrand's method was "never do today what you can be put off until tomorrow". Bourrienne was surprised by the way they worked together: "When M. de Talleyrand managed to suspend the execution of an order, Bonaparte never showed the least impatience, and I must say in his favour that never were such delays the cause of the slightest reproach." If Bonaparte had issued an order in a peremptory manner and it turned out that Talleyrand had done nothing more about it than prepare a draft, the First Consul often concluded with: "On second thoughts, don't send it." Raising inactivity and lack of haste to an artform would become a trait of Talleyrand's diplomacy.

In total contrast, there are numerous stories about heated relations between the former aristocratic bishop and the upstart emperor. Elsewhere, Bourrienne describes dreadful scenes between the calm and collected minister and the agitated and irate master long before their major ruptures of 1807 and 1809. It was not government policy that lay behind these storms but reproaches about Charles-Maurice's doubtful financial dealings, in which it was difficult to know if Bonaparte was really angry or just acting the part of the outraged superior. For instance, much later Talleyrand described an incident in which Napoleon shouted at the Russian *chargé d'affaires*, beating the desk with his fist and, when the diplomat had gone, turned to Talleyrand saying: "Feel my pulse. I am perfectly calm." As a man who knew exactly how to manipulate others, Bonaparte was aware of the risks of dealing with someone as complex and impenetrable as Talleyrand. Even so, the First Consul continued to turn to him on the choice of men for state councillors and prefects, and on the most sensitive negotiations.

If, at this moment, Bonaparte had renounced war, the history of the world would have been quite different. Since he came to power, France's position had been transformed from one of humiliation to that of supremacy. France could once again find its proper place among the European nations as long as it cooled the passions of the Revolution, respected traditional frontiers and stopped conquering territories by "the diplomacy of the sword". The problem was to convince not only the European powers of the wisdom of these words but, more importantly, Napoleon Bonaparte himself. During the earlier negotiations in Italy prior to the Treaty of Campo-Formio, Bonaparte had already declared to the Austrian representative Cobenzl that he considered himself equal to any king and he regarded the Mediterranean Sea as a French possession. Was it possible for a wolf to become a shepherd? There was, during the second half of 1802, an uninterrupted series of provocative acts by the First Consul which further alarmed the European monarchies. The Prussian minister Haugwitz declared: "The English domination of the seas is a major inconvenience, but the continental domination is infinitely more dangerous."

Talleyrand wanted to give conquered territories back to their former owners, such as returning Piedmont and Turin to the Kingdom of Sardinia. However, in August and September 1802, without warning anybody about what he intended to do, Bonaparte annexed Elba and Piedmont to France. He then extended his control over Switzerland, the Netherlands and Tuscany. There was a strong reaction from all the European powers, particularly the British, since it violated the Treaty of Lunéville by which Bonaparte had agreed to guarantee the Italian Republic's independence. In January 1802, Napoleon had travelled to Lyon to "accept" the presidency of the Italian Republic, a nominally-independent French client republic in northern Italy established in 1797. British newspaper readers who were following events were shocked at this "gross breach of faith". Despite Talleyrand's efforts to stop him, Bonaparte was little by little extending his hegemony over Europe.

Up until 1805, the relationship between Bonaparte and Talleyrand remained in a delicate state of balance since one of them was good at making war and the other at avoiding it. Talleyrand did not cease repeating to Bonaparte the need for moderation and to take the interests, pride and traditions of other nations into account. Talleyrand could be accused of betraying Bonaparte by not insisting that he should respect such ideals such as wisdom, humanity and justice. But what would have happened if he had? He would have been dismissed in a tirade of invective. Unfortunately, it was not in Talleyrand's manner to force his master to confront alternative policies and eventually Napoleon would not tolerate anybody contradicting his opinion. Then, Napoleon's police discovered that confidential information was being leaked to Russian spies and suspicions pointed to the involvement of the minister's office on the Rue du Bac. Bonaparte was tempted to lay a trap so that the guilty party would be caught red-handed, but at the last minute decided against it. The explanation of this situation will be given in the next chapter.

Following the signing of the Treaty of Amiens in 1802, the British blockade of French ports had been relaxed, so Bonaparte had taken advantage of this opportunity to dispatch a naval expedition to regain control of Haiti following a slave revolt and to occupy French Louisiana. It was in October that General Charles Leclerc, the expedition's leader, succumbed to yellow fever in Haiti, leaving the very pretty 20-year-old Pauline Bonaparte a widow. A period of mourning was declared. Talleyrand arranged for the entire diplomatic corps in the capital to present their condolences to the First Consul during a ten-day period of mourning, making it clear that Leclerc was a bona fide member of the head-of-state's family. This display of sorrow was all the more remarkable in that Leclerc was not a noble but, like so many of Bonaparte's generals, a revolutionary soldier who had risen through the ranks. Bonaparte was impressed by Talleyrand's adroitness. No more was said about the leaked information.

In another important sequel to the Treaty of Amiens, in 1802 "the great and magnificent" Charles Whitworth was chosen to fill the post of British ambassador to Paris. In November, he and his retinue were officially received at Calais with enthusiasm, for it had been a considerable period of time since a British ambassador had been seen in France. He was presented to Bonaparte and Josephine on 7 December. Whitworth's wife, Arabella Diana, Duchess of Dorset, whose aristocratic lineage was remarkably blue-blooded, had reservations about calling upon Mme Grand. Although Whitworth was anti-French and anti-Talleyrand, he soon came to realise that the French Minister of Foreign Affairs was the strongest defender of peace in Bonaparte's government.

In order to reward them for their military service, Bonaparte appointed his generals to important functions within the government. Without informing Talleyrand, he decided to send General Antoine-François Andréossy, an artillery officer, as the new ambassador to London. Talleyrand already knew about this vital appointment but pretended ignorance by suggesting several other names, including his friend General Horace Sebastiani. Finally, Bonaparte said: "I've made up my mind. I'll send Andréossy" [In French: *André as well*]. "You want to send André... as well? Who is this André?" Bonaparte started to fume: "I am not talking to you about an André. I'm talking about Andréossy. Good Lord! Andréossy! An artillery general." Talleyrand allowed the penny to drop as slowly as possible expressing reservations: "Andréossy! Ah! Yes, it's true. I hadn't thought of him. I was looking for someone in the diplomatic corps and I didn't find him. It's true, yes, yes, it's true! He's in the artillery!" During his time in London, Andréossy repeatedly informed Napoleon that the British Government was ready to reach a long-term peace agreement if treated with respect. His advice was disregarded.

Very soon, Whitworth mentions in a despatch to London two rumours: the First Consul was meditating a divorce from his wife; and he was also considering assuming the title of Emperor of France. However, during his first two months' sojourn in Paris there seemed an unspoken agreement to avoid disagreeable subjects. Napoleon ignored the English press's attacks, the British retention of Malta and the long-drawn-out evacuation of British troops from Egypt, while England kept silent about the recent French military incursions in the Netherlands, Piedmont, Elba, Parma and Switzerland.

After the initial fervour, objections to the Treaty of Amiens quickly took root in the United Kingdom for it seemed that the British were making all the concessions. If Bonaparte broke agreements, so could the British. One of the treaty's most significant measures was that the British forces would evacuate the island of Malta. This proved to be the stumbling block leading to the treaty's breakdown. After the British Government had digested Bonaparte's illegal moves over northern Italy, it refused to evacuate the island and hand its government over to the Knights of St John, fearing that the French would quickly move in. Talleyrand would have chosen the path of justice and wisdom in the belief that Malta was not worth another declaration of hostilities. Bonaparte, however, decided that war was the only way to make one's position clearly understood. He started to assemble a huge invasion force around Boulogne on the Channel coast.

The Addington ministry instructed Whitworth, through the foreign minister Hawkesbury, to resist any demand for the prompt evacuation of Malta. Whitworth hesitated to contact Talleyrand, while the latter did not wish to be seen in the vicinity of the British embassy in case he was accused of collusion. The whole situation took a change for the worse on 18 February 1803 when, after a stormy outburst with Whitworth, Napoleon concluded with the remark, "Malta or war!" When Whitworth reminded the First Consul about the Netherlands, Piedmont, etc., he replied: *"Ce sont des bagatelles"* [They are trifles]. There was another violent scene on 13 March when, during a reception for the diplomatic corps hosted by Josephine, Bonaparte summoned the British ambassador and, in front of 200 diplomats, exclaimed: "Woe to those who do not respect treaties!"

Upon returning to the embassy, the agitated Whitworth packed his bags ready to leave instantly for London. They were already on board his carriage in the courtyard when Talleyrand drove up in haste. The former Bishop of Autun succeeded in pouring oil on troubled waters; the ambassador agreed to stay. Even Josephine reproved Bonaparte for his behaviour at the reception: "You scare everyone; they will take you for a nasty person!" He replied: "It's true. I was wrong." Apparently, in a meeting immediately prior to Josephine's reception, Talleyrand had warned Bonaparte about losing his temper. He could not tolerate anyone making reproaches to him—except Josephine herself. Rather than improving his temper, Talleyrand's remarks only triggered it.

During April 1803 relations between Napoleon and Whitworth had been calmer. However, the British Government sent an ultimatum to Paris: the British would continue to occupy Malta until Piedmont was returned to the King of Sardinia. It was Talleyrand who placed this document on Bonaparte's desk and received another outburst of invective, although he was merely the messenger. A meeting was called to prepare a response. Whitworth informed London that Talleyrand and brother Joseph Bonaparte were the only ones who supported moderation and peaceful overtures, but they were silenced. Bonaparte gave Talleyrand the most detailed written instructions about how he was to conduct himself in the presence of Whitworth—the minister preserved this sheet of paper; it was to come in very useful some years later! On 12 May 1803, Whitworth demanded his passports, and six days later Britain declared war against France—a personal blow for Talleyrand. Whitworth reached London on 20 May, having encountered Andréossy three days earlier on the quayside at Dover. A cartoon by Gillray appeared in the British press showing Talleyrand desperately trying to restrain his master: "The butcher of Europe." The Minister of Foreign Affairs now realised that the Emperor of France had lost his way. The country would be involved in hostilities until the final collapse of Napoleon's regime twelve years hence.

Although it took some time for the state of war to declare itself on the battlefield, there was a very remarkable event that had already taken place on 2 May 1803. Under the Louisiana Purchase, the United States doubled its size by extending its territory beyond the limits of the Mississippi River across the western plains. The city of New Orleans had been founded around 1700 and its huge hinterland west of the Mississippi had been named Louisiana. With little idea of its extent or its resources, the French had casually ceded it to Spain a half-century later. When, in late 1800, Napoleon had the Bourbon monarchy in Spain at his mercy, he requested Talleyrand to negotiate a secret agreement whereby France took possession of it again. With the death of General Leclerc and the failure of the campaign to recapture Haiti in 1802 (more than two-thirds of his troops died of disease), Napoleon realized that New Orleans would soon be seized by the British as a naval base. To prevent this, Bonaparte proposed to sell Louisiana to the United States. The asking price was originally set at $80 million but soon fell to $60 million. Finally, France received the sum of $54 million because $6 million was attributed as compensation for the losses of American shipping to French corsairs.

Gradually, over the five years of the Consulate Bonaparte extended his power and curtailed freedom of speech. Benjamin Constant was one of those who thought that parliamentary privileges would be maintained and one could speak one's mind from the tribune of the assemblies. The first time that he drew attention to the autocratic tendencies of Bonaparte, his faithful consort Mme de Staël threw a dinner party so that her friends could congratulate Constant on his courageous stand. By an extraordinary coincidence, all the guests invited that evening were unable to attend due to a last-minute engagement. It was therefore not a surprise that Mme de Staël's published writings began to champion unpopular causes and draw attention to inconvenient principles. She pointed out that Bonaparte was becoming a despot who was an enemy of humanity and enlightenment. Her fame as a social conscience began to spread throughout Europe.

Talleyrand no longer lived on the Rue du Bac, nor on the Rue Taitbout, but in a magnificent residence called the Hôtel de Créqui on the Rue d'Anjou where he was able to offer dinners for 100 guests. There were also residences in the suburbs at Auteuil and Neuilly, and he had purchased the former home of Mlle Lange/Mme Simons at Saint-Cloud. As if this were not enough, for several years in the summer months he rented the Château de Bry-sur-Marne to the east of Paris built earlier in the eighteenth century by General Silhouette. The way he acquired the money to pay for this extravagant life-style draws our wonder because, by today's standards, it was often criminally fraudulent.

For example, Bonaparte told Talleyrand one day that the monthly subsidy of 5 million francs paid by Spain to France would be suspended. Talleyrand observed that it would be better if, in the first instance, it was reduced by half before being halted altogether. The Ministry of Finance was therefore instructed that it would henceforth receive 2.5 million francs monthly from Spain, but the Ministry of Foreign Affairs somehow forgot to inform Charles IV of Spain about this change, who continued to pay 5 million. What happened to the other 2.5 million? It was split between Talleyrand and Manuel Godoy, the chief minister in the Spanish court. This lucrative affair lasted for two-and-a-half years before Bonaparte put an end to it and required Spain to be repaid for the entire sum.

Another "scam" took place during the signing of the Treaty of Lunéville. Talleyrand knew that a clause in the treaty obliged Austria to continue paying interest on the state loans it had taken out in what is now the Netherlands and Belgium. However, someone—who?—let it be known that the interest would no longer be paid when this territory came under French control. Before the treaty was signed, those who had loaned money to the state tried to sell off their bonds, which they believed to be worthless pieces of paper but were snapped up by an anonymous purchaser. When the treaty was signed and the terms concerning the interest payments known, the bonds regained their full value and were now in the possession of the former Bishop of Autun.

Those ambassadors, bankers and businessmen wishing to know where the government's money was going might obtain this information from the Minister of Foreign Affairs, whose lady-friend Mme Grand was very partial to jewellery. She benefited from a magnificent necklace made of Siberian sapphires from the ambassador in Saint Petersburg; six rows of pearls from a minister in Vienna; diamonds from Prussia; a diadem from Rome.

General Jean Lannes had been appointed to the post of French ambassador to Lisbon, but there were conflicts between him, British diplomats and the Portuguese Ministry of Foreign Affairs, so the Portuguese Government asked to be relieved of their brave and dashing soldier. Talleyrand met the Portuguese minister in Paris, M. de Souza (the husband of Adélaïde de Flahaut) and informed him that he shared their opinion about General Lannes—for a price. The Portuguese were soon relieved of Lannes's presence and 4 million livres, which went into the pocket of Talleyrand. The Portuguese complained about the size of this sum, which is why we know about it.

With Bonaparte, treaties, wars, plunder, the redistribution of frontiers and annexations had become a daily occurrence and these events often involved the movement of huge sums of cash. The money circulating around Talleyrand was impressive but, since he maintained the extravagant *Ancien Régime* life-style, no sooner did he obtain it than he spent it. In order to guarantee the supply of cash to sustain his life-style, Talleyrand was obliged to put up with Bonaparte's humours. Mme de Cazenove d'Arlens, a visitor from Switzerland who was Benjamin

Constant's cousin, noted in her diary in 1803: "M. de Talleyrand has no influence over the First Consul. It requires tremendous flexibility and skill on his part to remain in place exposed to the caprices and whims of his boss." She adds: "M. de Périgord is the victim of this little Corsican's brutal and vulgar outbursts." Indeed, throughout his period in power Bonaparte would address his ministers in general, and Talleyrand in particular, in the uncouth language of a drill sergeant reprimanding a raw recruit on the parade ground. Why did Talleyrand put up with it? "A liking for his place which makes him really vulnerable whenever he is afraid of not giving satisfaction."

Why did Talleyrand marry Catherine Grand? Among a whole host of reasons more or less plausible, including the feeble ones that Talleyrand put forward himself, there is not one that clearly explains this unexpected event. Bourrienne stated that the principal reason was to resolve the protocol problem of Catherine's status when hosting dinners for foreign dignitaries. Bonaparte had a passion for marrying people off, particularly his generals with his sisters. Did he require Talleyrand either to discard or to marry his mistress in order to become a respectable member of his government and avoid an on-going scandal? In examining the different documents that the couple signed together, one has the impression that she has the upper hand and is dictating the conditions— no doubt, with the help of some histrionic scenes. If she were familiar with some of his political secrets, perhaps he could not face the risk of a breakdown in their relationship. Catherine had become an excellent businesswoman and was perfectly familiar with turning influence and intrigue into hard cash. She made sure that her very valuable collection of jewellery was her property and would not fall into the hands of Talleyrand's family. We learn from the diaries of Mme de Rémusat that several ambassadors' wives complained to the First Consul that they had been received by Mme Grand at the Rue du Bac, while fully aware of her reputation and relationship with Talleyrand. Since they did not intend issuing a return invitation, Bonaparte was angry with his minister because his regime craved respectability. He gave Talleyrand an ultimatum that Catherine Grand must leave Rue du Bac and all his other residences. It had often been said that she was not very intelligent but she always seemed to react adeptly to threatening situations, for what she did next was brilliant. Who could understand her position better than Josephine Bonaparte? Pretty women who loved luxury, extravagance and adventures should stand together. She went to see the First Consul's wife one evening, who took the staircase to her husband's office and asked if he would come to her apartment to meet the visitor. Bonaparte's new aide-de-camp, Claude François de Méneval, described what happened. When the First Consul arrived, Catherine collapsed, crying, stammering, pleading her cause and wringing her hands. The First Consul could not resist the tears of a woman and cut to the quick: "I see only one way. Talleyrand marries you and everything will be alright. You will bear his name but you will no longer appear in his office." Mme Grand had obtained what she wanted. Bonaparte continued to treat her with contempt believing it was legitimate and normal to insult a woman with such a reputation—as well as Talleyrand for having married her. Nevertheless, Bonaparte knew that his talented foreign minister could easily have escaped from his grasp and into the Royalist camp. But a bishop who married a divorced woman and a notorious courtesan could never be forgiven by the church and would certainly never be employed by the respectable House of Bourbon—or at least, not yet.

Catherine Worlée had married George Grand in two ceremonies, one Catholic and the other Protestant. When she obtained her divorce from Grand in 1798 it cancelled the Protestant ceremony; she never asked for an annulment from Rome. She had, however, paid her respects to the Papal Nuncio Caselli and to the Pope's negotiator Cardinal Caprara. While the Pope, Bonaparte and Talleyrand were wrestling with the "Mme Grand Clause" in the Concordat, by a curious coincidence three other protagonists from Mlle Worlée's early life happened to be in Paris during the peace brought about by the Treaty of Amiens. The first was Sir Philip Francis who had come to Paris hoping to renew his relationship with his "Dear Cathy". To avoid a scandal, she fled to the countryside. The second was the judge who had condemned Sir Philip to pay 50,000 rupees to Cathy's wronged husband. And the third was George Grand himself, who arrived in July 1802 hoping for a second windfall, taking up residence in the Rue de Richelieu not far from the Louvre.

Charles-Maurice de Talleyrand married Catherine Grand on 9 September 1802 at Neuilly. The marriage contract bore the signatures of Napoleon and Josephine Bonaparte, the two other Consuls Cambacérès and Lebrun, Hugues Maret, Secretary of State, as well as Talleyrand's two brothers Archambaud and Boson. On the following day, a modest civil ceremony took place in the tenth *arrondissement* of Paris officiated by Adrien Duquesnoy, an old friend from his days as one of Mirabeau's colleagues, and the witnesses included Talleyrand's closest political, military, diplomatic and banking companions: Roederer and Admiral Bruix for the groom, Beurnonville and Radix de Sainte-Foy for the bride, as well as the Prince Nassau-Siegen—a sort of high-born mercenary, courtier and adventurer. In the contract, Talleyrand showed himself to be of magnanimous generosity, conferring on his wife ownership of the Hôtel de Créqui, a property at Port-de-Sains in northern France and a part of his wealth. Considering that she had turned up at his office in financial difficulties, the new Mme de Talleyrand had done rather well for herself. In the event of her dying before him, these items would revert to him. In the marriage document, Talleyrand declares his mother to be dead, although she was still alive and well but living in Germany. No-one knew why he made this statement or even why he decided to get married in the first place. Catherine outdid him by stating that she was a widow and several years younger than her 41 years.

The wives of ambassadors who had been reluctant to visit the former Mme Grand now flocked to Mme de Talleyrand-Périgord's door and no-one mentioned her colourful past. Nevertheless, Talleyrand's passion had cooled into boredom. He soon ceased to love her. Her vanity, her silliness and her indiscretions kept pace with the size of her waist. There was, however, a shadow from her past that risked spoiling her new happiness—George Grand. Any evening, he might turn up at one of her receptions and try to cash in on her new-found glory. What was needed was a prestigious post for him with a comfortable salary... as far away from France as possible! Talleyrand contacted his counterpart in The Hague, Van der Goes, and asked if he could find a job for George Grand that corresponded to these specifications. One was identified at the Cape of Good Hope and was judged to be very suitable indeed. At the end of September 1802, Mme de Talleyrand wrote to Van der Goes to thank him personally for his suggestion, but five months later George Grand was still stuck on the quayside in Amsterdam, while the forthcoming war with

England was likely to bring all navigation to a standstill. An urgent message was sent to Van der Goes such that, finally, in 1803 George Grand, his pockets filled with £10,000 of Talleyrand's money, sailed into the harbour at Cape Town and out of our story.

Talleyrand's friends, who were his true family, were flabbergasted by his marriage. The Duchess de Luynes, the Viscountess de Laval, Aimée de Coigny and even Montrond couldn't quite believe it. His best friend, Choiseul, tried desperately to extract some kind of explanation— in vain. The person whose censure was the most damning was his manservant Courtiade, who is supposed to have said: "Who could have believed that we did something so stupid? We who have had all the beautiful ladies of the court? We who have had that charming Countess de Brionne, to end up billeted like this, it's incredible!"

Immediately following the marriage of Talleyrand with Catherine Grand, Mme Constance de Cazenove d'Arlens left a detailed account of life at the Rue du Bac: "The courtyard […] was so full of carriages that we could not enter; we had to wait for one to come out. I arrived, I went up the grand staircase, well lit, full of flowers." The Hôtel de Galliffet had become the Versailles of post-Revolutionary society. The visitor had never met Talleyrand before and had the surprise of her life when he appeared: "A figure like death wearing a red velvet costume embroidered with broad gold bands. Large coat, sword, wide sleeves, powdered hair. This was the minister; this was M. de Talleyrand. Ah! What an expression!" Talleyrand was 50 years old and this is another reference to a death mask that would become his hallmark. The ministry's salons were thronging with ambassadors, bankers, travelling royalty and state officials who had all come to pay homage to Mme de Talleyrand, despite Bonaparte requesting that she would no longer reside at Rue du Bac. "She is tall, beautiful, stately but her secret can be read on her face: silly and vain… lots of diamonds." Finally, Mme d'Arlens was underwhelmed: "The pleasure of bearing a great name and of occupying an important position has turned her head. She fears that she is being too polite and spares herself from this discomfiture by being not at all."

Bonaparte could not stand Catherine de Talleyrand and continued to humiliate her until his fall from power. The first time she attended a reception at the Tuileries after her marriage, he told her with characteristic bluntness how she should now behave so as to obscure her past life. It was unforgivable conduct towards a woman and insulting for her husband. She was, however, equal to the task: "All I have to do, Citizen First Consul, is to base myself on Citizenne Bonaparte [i.e. Josephine]!" He eventually forbade her access to his court because, as he claimed later on in Saint Helena, he discovered that both she and her husband brought an air of scandal and venality to his entourage that was contrary to the morality he wished to see respected.

How did Talleyrand acquire his expressionless death mask? In the Tuileries Palace, at diplomatic receptions, round the card tables he wore the same impenetrable straight face upon which no emotion could be read. Was it because he was a creature of the night, often having supper at 2 a.m. and not to be seen in daylight before midday? He frequented the Duchess de Luynes's salon where he formed part of a closed circle with his lady friends of twenty years earlier who gossiped into the early hours: the Viscountess de Laval, the Princess de Vaudémont, the Countess de Montesson. There was a remarkable absentee in all this: Mme de Staël. A similar nocturnal event would take place at the Hôtel de Créqui, but this time with his male friends: Narbonne, Choiseul, Montrond, Radix de Sainte-Foy and the newcomer, Prince Nassau-Siegen. The relationship between Talleyrand and Desrenaudes came to an end when he abandoned his former henchman without second thoughts in 1802. As a member of the *Tribunal,* Desrenaudes had become too liberal in his views and therefore was a potential opponent of Napoleon's regime. On one occasion, Desrenaudes did not vote as he had been instructed to since, he explained, he had followed the dictates of his own conscience. Talleyrand put him straight: "The conscience is certainly yours, but we did not place you in the *Tribunal* for that reason but for your vote."

At about the same time and for the same reasons, there was a rupture with Benjamin Constant and, since Mme de Staël remained faithful to her most recent lover, Talleyrand and Germaine parted company too. Almost imperceptibly her position had changed from besotted fan of Bonaparte to that of leader of the opposition, speaking her mind on subjects that were so painfully pertinent that Talleyrand preferred not to know about them. As an expression of her frustration, she wrote a novel entitled *Delphine* where she figures in the guise of a beautiful, good-natured creature. Talleyrand also appears masquerading as a malevolent old woman called Mme de Vernon: "false to the point of treachery. At the bottom of her heart, she did not like anything, did not believe in anything, was not troubled by anything." Somebody gave him a copy of the book and people waited expectantly for his reaction. There was none, so finally one evening around the dinner table he was asked pointedly what he thought about Mme de Staël's book. Given the author's superficially masculine, opinionated and overbearing traits, Talleyrand's verdict was: "I hear that Mme de Staël has disguised both of us as women." Germaine's independent political views and criticism of the consular regime annoyed Bonaparte to the extent that he banished her to her father's residence at the Château de Coppet near Geneva, which soon became a gathering place for the European intelligentsia. The Juniper Hall group reformed and she became leader of the *Groupe de Coppet*, a cosmopolitan society ahead of its time that was a harbinger of modern international organizations. Although these people had limited power, they taunted Napoleon and seemed to threaten his hegemony. In this way, she never sacrificed her integrity as Talleyrand, Narbonne and Constant would for the sake of their political ambitions.

For thirty years, Talleyrand would spend the month of August taking the waters, usually at Bourbon-l'Archambault in Burgundy, for he believed that the baths and treatments were good for his feet and legs. He was the small town's most illustrious visitor with his own private pool. In 1803 he took the new Mme de Talleyrand with him, walking around the town with his personal retinue, including his doctor. Other members of his entourage were a priest, who entertained him with songs, and his personal barber. In this relaxed mode, he would play whist for hours, while granting audiences to the local nobility, who might take advantage of the opportunity to place before him some personal petition. In contrast with the minister of the Rue du Bac who was almost monosyllabic, at Bourbon-l'Archambault he let his tongue loose with the telling of stories. One of his secretaries recalled these delightful days: "One would say a big child abandoning himself to the joys of play."

One day, a little girl about 4 years old, called Charlotte, made her appearance walking between M. and Mme de Talleyrand, neither of whom ever gave any satisfactory explanation for her presence. If she was about 4 years old in 1803, then she would have been born in 1799. Amidst a raft of possible explanations, including that she was a foundling, it was suggested that she could indeed have been the daughter of M. and Mme de Talleyrand, although this seemed highly improbable. The couple lavished care and attention on the child. When she grew up, Talleyrand married her off to one of his cousins, conferring on her a comfortable dowry. In fact, he behaved towards her exactly as a doting father would towards his own child.

The historian Daniel Chartre has provided an explanation for the appearance of Charlotte. Since 1780, one of the ladies-in-waiting to Marie-Antoinette at the royal court was Mme Cathérine Beaugeard, particularly serving in the household of the beautiful and charismatic Duchess de Polignac, the queen's favourite. When the Polignac's emigrated to Switzerland at the outbreak of the Revolution, Mme Beaugeard went with them. By 1796, she was in London where she became acquainted with a certain Mme Catherine Grand. On 4 October 1799, Mme Beaugeard, who had not seen her husband for nine years, gave birth to a baby girl, who was baptized Elisa Alix Sara at the French Chapel on Conway Street. Talleyrand agreed for his wife to adopt a child provided it came from a "good family". So, this is the girl who became a member of Talleyrand's household.

Towards the end of his stay at Bourbon-l'Archambault in 1803 and before returning to Paris, Talleyrand asked Bonaparte for permission to make a detour to visit the Château de Valençay of which he had recently become the proprietor. His honours already included being a minister, a diplomat, a financier and a leading politician, why not the owner of a vast country estate? The building manager of the Tuileries Palace was M. de Luçay who owned this enormous château in the Indre *département* and was no longer able to support its maintenance. He wished to sell it and the property's description pleased both the First Consul and Talleyrand, but the price was too steep for "his modest means". One day Bonaparte told Talleyrand: "I want you to purchase a grand estate where you can impress the diplomatic corps and foreign dignitaries, who would look forward to going to your place and for whom such an invitation is a reward for the ambassadors and sovereigns who have pleased me." Since the First Consul had said "I *want* you to purchase a grand estate...", he was obviously prepared to participate financially in the acquisition of Valençay. While he often treated Talleyrand with contempt, Bonaparte knew what a wonderful minister he had, unlike any other and who brought to his government the dignity and prestige he sought. Rather than punish Talleyrand for his taste in extravagant luxury, he would exploit the situation to make him the steward of imperial festivities. Talleyrand liked the idea and, until it became his permanent summer residence, he would return to Valençay every September with one or two privileged guests.

The domain was very impressive: 19,000 hectares incorporating twenty-three parishes, one of the three largest estates in France, a relic of bygone times, permitting Talleyrand to live the life of a lord until his death. The château sits on a crest dominating a valley and is surrounded by extensive forests. The main building, constructed in the sixteenth century, consisted of an enormous keep and two large towers connected by galleries. During their first visit, M. and Mme de Talleyrand were unable to complete their tour of all the château's different facilities because, after three days, Bonaparte recalled his minister to Paris.

CHAPTER X
THE EMPIRE

By the end of 1803, Talleyrand was the second most important political figure in France, having become rich and powerful during the Consulate. Bonaparte's tenure as First Consul had at first been extended for a period of ten years and then, on 2 August 1802, for life. What worried Talleyrand was that, having first-hand knowledge of Napoleon's temperament, could he be controlled? Behind a mask of deference and flattery, he set himself the task of restraining Napoleon by continually reminding him to act with moderation. Despite his courage, he failed miserably for Europe was about to enter an age of conquest that it had not experienced for 1,000 years. Furthermore, Napoleon held the French Revolution in contempt, for his idea of social order was more akin to military discipline.

From August 1802 to February 1803 there were meetings in Regensburg, Germany (known in French as Ratisbonne), and in Paris to decide the fate of the territories on the left bank of the Rhine, which had become French following the Treaty of Lunéville. They had previously formed part of the ancient Holy Roman Empire and consisted of a multitude of principalities, bishoprics, electorates, free towns and villages. The wheeling and dealing resulted in a population of over 3 million people falling under the influence of the French Republic and prepared the ground for the creation of the Confederation of the Rhine three years later. What took place in Regensburg and Paris was one of the most financially fruitful events of Talleyrand's career, a huge auction where his assistants LaForêt, Durand de Mareuil and Radix de Sainte-Foy explained what was required of the plaintiffs before presenting them to the all-powerful minister. It is estimated that the former Bishop of Autun obtained 10 million francs for "mediating" the affairs of these principalities, a windfall that he shared with his acolytes. During a visit to Aachen and Mainz in September 1804, Napoleon was disturbed to learn how Talleyrand had been turning his ministerial post to his personal profit. Here, the King of Prussia reported to Napoleon that part of a subsidy payable by the French to Willem V, the Prince Orange-Nassau, his brother-in-law, was missing. The transaction had passed through Talleyrand's hands and a letter from Durand de Mareuil was discovered mentioning the distribution "of the difference". Bonaparte interrogated Talleyrand who, as was his habit, denied any knowledge of the affair. Bonaparte was less concerned about the theft than the fact that he knew Talleyrand was lying to him. Finally, he dismissed Talleyrand angrily and sent him back to Paris in disgrace. He was prepared to relieve the minister of his functions but asked himself who would then occupy this important post on the Rue du Bac. Even if he was unhappy with his minister's avarice, Bonaparte valued Talleyrand's skill in the field of foreign affairs. Talleyrand, meanwhile, felt that Bonaparte did not reward those who served him best, so it was up to each person to look after their own interests. The First Consul did not lose confidence in his abilities as a minister but—as with others—continued to treat him with contempt.

It was perfectly normal during these times for political and military figures to amass colossal fortunes in relatively short periods of time through venal practices, even the members of Bonaparte's own family would succumb to this practice. Nevertheless, Bonaparte's attention was drawn to the wealth Talleyrand had been able to accumulate very rapidly since becoming a minister and asked him to his face how he had achieved it. Talleyrand answered smugly: "Oh, it's very simple. I made some investments on *17 Brumaire* and sold them three days later." Five years after this conversation, Bonaparte was still lost in admiration for his nerve in eluding a direct question at the same time as paying his interrogator a backhand compliment, for Bonaparte's assumption of power was followed by a surge in the national economy that anticipated a period of peace and prosperity.

Talleyrand's greatest happiness was to obtain huge sums of money and to spend them. During the early years of the Consulate, he preferred to live in rented properties rather than houses he had purchased. Lucien Bonaparte, Napoleon's brother, was impressed by the sumptuous dinners provided at his hired residence at Auteuil: "We were served in the Greek tradition by nymphs with mythological names who served the coffee in golden urns; incense burned in silver trays." At the dining table, Mme de Talleyrand was served by two coloured waiters in splendid livery and afterwards in the salon there were two vestal virgins in white dresses whose sole purpose was to supervise the incense-burners. However, not all his money went up in smoke. Behind the image of rich and liberal hosts, Charles-Maurice and Catherine de Talleyrand began to invest in property. At this time, they purchased the château and forests at Pont-de-Sains in the north of France, the Château de Haut-Brion in the village of Pessac just outside Bordeaux and, as mentioned in the previous chapter, the enormous Château de Valençay and its extensive grounds in the Berry region.

Having made peace with the religious authorities, Bonaparte was aware that the population of France had a certain nostalgia for the former monarchy. Should the First Consul's position be converted into something grander and more permanent? If Bonaparte did become a sovereign, there were a large number of highly placed people who would be very nervous about their involvement in the execution of Louis XVI and how vulnerable their position would be when faced with an all-powerful ruler. Their misgivings could be alleviated if, for instance, Bonaparte was guilty of a similar act of bloodshed concerning the House of Bourbon. Who would have thought of such an idea? Since he had been sent back to Paris in disgrace, the former Bishop of Autun sought some way of ingratiating himself with Napoleon. He proposed to kidnap and assassinate the Duke d'Enghien.

A great deal of the history connected with the Duke d'Enghien's assassination is conjecture because all the relevant state papers were destroyed by Talleyrand when the Bourbons returned to power in 1814. Reports to Bonaparte about how it was intended to kidnap the young prince must have existed. One letter from Talleyrand (dated 8 March 1804) did survive, however, and was subsequently read by two people: Claude François Méneval, Bonaparte's personal secretary, and François-René de Chateaubriand. Méneval sums up the content of the letter as follows: Talleyrand reminds Bonaparte of their conversation of the previous day and repeats the arguments he used to convince the First Consul of the need to carry out some significant deed to show the French (and particularly the Jacobins) that he would never restore the Bourbons to the throne. He suggested that a recent Royalist plot to kill Bonaparte—the Cadoudal/Pichegru Affair—was Enghien's work and that therefore he merited punishment.

Georges Cadoudal had been sent from London to assassinate Bonaparte, landing secretly on the Normandy coast on 31 August 1803. He took up residence in Paris where he had contacts with the army through General Pichegru. Furthermore, the dissident General Moreau was aware of what was going on and awaited the outcome. In October Fouché's police learned of Cadoudal's mission and in February 1804 all those connected with the plot were arrested with the conspirators mentioning a prince of the House of Bourbon who would assume Bonaparte's place. A Bourbon prince who lived not far from the French border was Louis-Antoine de Bourbon, the Duke d'Enghien, the last of the Condé branch of the Bourbon family. The young, handsome and chivalrous duke was the most admirable of the Bourbon princes, having fought for the rights of his family and had nothing whatsoever to do with either Cadoudal or Pichegru.

There had been an attempt by the French police to capture the Duke d'Artois, Louis XVI's brother, but he had been alerted and had escaped the trap. Savary, the chief of Napoleon's police at this time, waited on the cliff of Biville in Normandy, where the plotters were in the habit of landing at night, and sought, by trying to imitate the Royalist signals, to tempt the Duke d'Artois to land. In this he was unsuccessful. Following this failure, Talleyrand suggested to Bonaparte that another suitable target was the Duke d'Enghien, a prince of the blood who was known to reside at Ettenheim in Baden. The First Consul later declared that this was the first time he learned of his existence. Talleyrand hinted that his location close to the French frontier made it easier for him to direct Royalist plots against the First Consul—and also facilitated his capture and execution. Bonaparte became annoyed when he heard that the Duke d'Enghien had been seen in the company of General Dumouriez, the victor at Jemappes and once the foreign minister of the Republic who had deserted to the Royalist camp. Much later, it was discovered that this was a silly mistake. The duke had been visited by an innocuous General de Thuméry; the German pronunciation of this name resulted in it being understood as "Dumouriez". Both de Thuméry and Enghien were harmlessly going about their own affairs. However, the duke had previously been condemned in absentia for having fought in the Royalist armies against the French Republic.

On 10 March 1804, Bonaparte held a meeting with Fouché, Talleyrand, Cambacérès and Lebrun, where he informed them that he had decided to capture the Duke d'Enghien for the security and the honour of the French people. Cambacérès expressed some reservations but was rapidly silenced by Bonaparte who reminded him that he had voted for the death of Louis XVI. In his will, written during his exile on Saint Helena, Napoleon accepted full responsibility for this incident, but he had previously explained elsewhere that he would never have considered the idea had not Talleyrand suggested it to him. After the subsequent rupture with Napoleon in 1807, Talleyrand claimed his innocence, which caused the emperor to exclaim in front of Roederer, Caulaincourt and even Talleyrand himself: "I find it pleasant that he twists the truth at my expense. Did I know him, the Duke d'Enghien? Did I want to kill him?"

On 10 and 11 March 1804, Talleyrand sent two notes to Baron von Edelsheim, Baden's representative in Paris, informing him that the Duke d'Enghien, living in Baden, would be arrested together with the "General Dumouriez" and abducted by a detachment of French soldiers. This was an incursion by the French military on the territory of Baden and General Caulaincourt was given a letter to present to the local authorities to explain what was otherwise an invasion. Enghien was arrested during the night of 14/15 March by a detachment of soldiers headed by General Ordener, taken to Strasbourg, then to Paris, and finally to the Château de Vincennes. On 21 March, he was tried by a kangaroo court and found guilty of bearing arms against France—the verdict had been decided some days earlier. He was immediately taken out into the fort's moat at 2.30 a.m., a lantern tied to his shoulder indicating the position of his heart and executed by firing squad commanded by General Savary, near a grave that had already been dug. The only person to come out of this incident with any dignity was the helpless victim. At the same time, Pichegru was strangled to death in prison and Cadoudal guillotined. General Moreau was also arrested but allowed to flee to the United States. Enghien's death was a clear warning to all the surviving members of the House of Bourbon about their safety.

In the centuries since this incident, historians have attempted to throw light on the sequence of events. Following the angry scene when Napoleon misunderstood that the General Dumouriez, rather than the General de Thuméry, had held a meeting with Enghien, Talleyrand's informant in Baden, Nicolas Massias, could report nothing suspicious about the duke's acquaintances and activities. However, the previously established timetable would be respected. Talleyrand, who was playing dice, looked at the clock early that morning on 21 March and observed to his bewildered friends: "The last of the Condés has ceased to exist." In fact, the Duke d'Enghien's grandfather and father survived him, but died without producing further heirs. In his capacity as the faithful minister, Talleyrand was already thinking about a bland communiqué addressed to foreign governments that explained and justified the whole affair. Upon reading the news in *Le Moniteur* at his office on Rue du Bac, d'Hauterive was flabbergasted. "What's the matter with you, with your eyes sticking out of your head?" asked Talleyrand. "What's up?" exclaimed d'Hauterive, "You would feel the same if you had read *Le Moniteur*. It's awful! We cannot continue to serve that man." On the contrary, Talleyrand found nothing awful or extraordinary about it. With diplomatic politeness, the foreign capitals seemed to accept his explanation without fuss, except the government in St Petersburg, which demanded further clarifications about the French Army entering the territory of Baden. Talleyrand's pen was equal to the situation; he responded with a letter from the First Consul stating that the French Government had not felt it had a duty to intervene concerning the recent assassination of the mentally deranged Tsar Paul I, whose murderers had not been punished. Paul's son, the new Tsar Alexander I, was not amused by this insulting reply.

Aimée de Coigny wrote that "M. de Talleyrand was the key to this affair." Even if Bonaparte took full responsibility, his Minister of Foreign Affairs advised and hastened the arrest of the Duke d'Enghien. Here we come face to face with the artful escape artist. Many of those involved, particularly Generals Caulaincourt and Savary, would ultimately suffer disgrace for their role in this affair, but Talleyrand was far too crafty. The more an event threatened him, the more he resorted to false alibis, false accusations and false witnesses. For instance, the shadowy Count d'Antraigues—a spy working for the Russians—soon passed on to his masters in St Petersburg a letter written by his Parisian informant "The Friend", who appears to have been a close collaborator of Charles-Maurice (possibly Emmerich von Dalberg). This letter, written on 19 April almost a month after the assassination, reports an entirely fictitious scenario that is supposed to have taken place on 11 March. It suggested that the former Bishop of Autun had just been made aware of the order to arrest the Duke d'Enghien and entered Durand de Mareuil's office "pale and troubled"—we know, of course, that he had already been deeply involved in the plot for several days before this! Immediately, he is supposed to have sent the Duke d'Enghien a hastily-scribbled message: "Leave at once!" It was most unusual for Talleyrand to commit himself to a secret message in his own handwriting and he would certainly never sign it. According to "The Friend", the message arrived but the duke took no notice. General Caulaincourt is named as being principally responsible for the duke's death—this is a most appalling accusation for the honourable Caulaincourt was actually mortified about the minor role he had been duped into playing. Due to this false information, Tsar Alexander became convinced that Talleyrand was an innocent victim and not the perpetrator of the assassination, treating him like a trusted friend at Erfurt in 1808 and in Paris in 1814. This was not the only time that Talleyrand would resort to this ploy.

There were not only false letters, but real letters that disappeared. In 1814, just before Napoleon's abdication, Talleyrand sent his secretary Gabriel Perrey to the state archives in the Louvre to sort through Napoleon's correspondence and to remove any documents that might compromise him in dealings with the Pope, Enghien's fate and the war in Spain. Many letters were destroyed, but not all—Perrey decided to keep the most incriminating ones for his personal use, particularly the one dated 8 March 1804 mentioned above. Much later, Perrey fell out with his master and started to blackmail him. Talleyrand sent money and Perrey promised to burn the letters—but did not. In 1831, Talleyrand sent his agent M. Rihouet and his son to make proposals to Perrey that would bring the affair to an end. The incriminating letter was supposedly burned in front of them—but perhaps it was only a copy since Perrey could imitate Talleyrand's handwriting. Forty years after this incident, in 1844,

M. Rihouet's son had been reading the memoirs of Claude François Méneval, Napoleon's former aide-de-camp, where the author describes having recently been shown the letter which he had last seen on Napoleon's desk on 8 March 1804! By this time, Talleyrand was dead, but his inheritors made it be known that—despite all the evidence to the contrary—this letter could only be false.

Talleyrand was not a cruel or violent person and the idea that he suggested to Bonaparte the capture and assassination of the Duke d'Enghien seems quite out of character. One plausible motive was the desire to restore his standing with the First Consul following the suspicion of financial scandals raised in Aachen and Mainz. Another argument states that he wished to protect the person who had restored order to the nation and make it impossible for the Bourbons to ever return to the throne of France. The fact that he wrote the incriminating letter to Napoleon, did not protest about the incident, performed his duties in connection with it without question and subsequently defended this action suggests that he was part of the plot. However, like many of the others involved, from this moment on he tried to provide himself with an alibi—such as the false letter passed on to the Russians by the Count d'Antraigues. In this affair, Talleyrand convinced Bonaparte that the assassination was a positive move and he was even capable of making those who carried it out ignore the enormity of their crime. Then he stood back out of danger and observed. Nevertheless, the political aims that Talleyrand had pursued during his life so far—freedom, justice, respect of the law—had been forfeited. This affair would continue to haunt those involved for the next thirty years and Talleyrand would be obliged to employ increasingly desperate measures in an attempt to minimize or obscure his role. What we can be certain of is that Bonaparte and Talleyrand now knew what each was capable of. The complicity between them turned to wariness, but the rupture did not take place immediately. Fouché is claimed to have commented upon this event: *C'est plus qu'un crime; c'est une faute* [It's worse than a crime; it's a blunder].

Two months later, on 18 May 1804, a salute of cannons announced the publication of an official document, or *Sénatus-consulte,* confirming that the First Consul was henceforth to be known as Emperor Napoleon I. Talleyrand had already sent a carefully written circular to France's representatives abroad providing them with arguments to be presented to foreign governments justifying the legitimacy of this operation: "It is a wish that has formed in our hearts since the end of our troubles." He sold the illusion to the people that the country needed a single head of state, although he did not mention the word "empire". Talleyrand was not enthusiastic about the title of "emperor", preferring that of "king". For him, an emperor implied a military context, coming to power through invasions and conquests of neighbouring lands—in a word, through "war". Napoleon needed little encouragement on this score. The title "King of France" suggested a more noble, wise, legitimate power that existed in a world ruled by peace and benevolence. Bonaparte did not share Talleyrand's opinion about the role of king since it was already occupied by Louis XVIII and might imply that he followed in the wake of the Bourbons. Henceforth, in France, Jacobinism, republicanism and royalism were outlawed and driven underground.

Outside France, declaring himself emperor was understood as the act of a megalomaniac. Talleyrand had few doubts himself, having told Mme de Rémusat that "this combination of Roman Republic and Charlemagne" had taken possession of Bonaparte's mind and was beginning to lose its lustre. As time passed, his illusions about Napoleon evaporated. During Napoleon's visit to Aachen, the capital city of Charlemagne's Empire, he had been presented with the iron sceptre of his predecessor—it turned out to be a copy purchased from the local flea market. Talleyrand continued to smother the emperor with boot-licking flattery encouraging him to believe that he had become the worthy inheritor of an ancient and illustrious throne. This was a way of ensuring for himself the position of court favourite resulting in significant "favours". Napoleon did not always fall for this adulation. If their relationship had been conducted with more confidence, Talleyrand would have received the rewards for which he craved and Napoleon would have benefited from the guidance of a counsellor who he could trust.

On 11 July 1804, Talleyrand received his first title under the new regime: Grand Chamberlain to the Imperial Court. This post meant that he formed part of the emperor's close retinue and was responsible for his wardrobe and the organization of festivals, ceremonies, receptions and entertainments. He had unrestricted access to Napoleon's private apartments and stood near him when he was at table. Napoleon could gloat over this aristocrat of the *Ancien Régime* whose job was to wait on his master at mealtimes fitted out with an elaborate official costume—but not quite as gaudy as the one designed by the five directors. It was Cambacérès who was granted the superior post of Archchancellor, which Talleyrand had coveted for himself. One of his friends, the gossip Mme de Vaines, tells us why: "His wife is the reason he is not archi. They did not want her to bear the title Serene Highness and, given the rank of her husband, find herself alongside the emperor's sisters… What do you expect? Sooner or later, you have to pay for your mistakes." Mme de Talleyrand, somewhat chastened, explained to whoever wanted to listen that her husband was pleased with the way the honours had been distributed. She gave this version of events to the diarist Mme de Rémusat who wrote: "She told me with such pretence that her husband was very happy, very content, very delighted, very satisfied with the emperor that I was almost tempted not to believe her." Six months later Talleyrand received the great chain of the *Légion d'honneur*, the highest French order of merit. As Napoleon famously remarked (or is supposed to have remarked): "It is with such baubles that men are led."

To inaugurate the Napoleonic Empire, an awe-inspiring ceremony was required in the capital. When Napoleon announced that he would be crowned at Notre Dame by Pope Pius VII himself, there was a moment of disbelief among his retinue. Since Napoleon's troops were occupying the Papal States around Rome by force, how was His Holiness to be persuaded to make the journey from Rome to Paris? Napoleon's invitation was part of his policy to reconcile Catholics to the regime, but also to mark his power over the Pope. The task of twisting the Pope's arm to come to Paris was given to Talleyrand and Cardinal Fesch, Napoleon's uncle. The first overtures were rejected by the Holy See but Napoleon was inexorable in his demands. "His Majesty," Talleyrand then replied to the Pope, "observes with distress that He has not done all that He could do in order for the Reigning Pontificate to reply to his invitation." What might have appeared to be an invitation was in fact a summons for his presence. To force the Pope's hand, Talleyrand listed all the many marks of favour that the First Consul had bestowed on the

Church of Rome, including the return of two former pontifical principalities: Pontecorvo and Benevento—of which we have not heard the last! When the Pope realized that he had no choice, he reluctantly made the journey, being accommodated at the Château de Fontainebleau where he was greeted by His Majesty's Grand Chamberlain. It would have been interesting to know what words passed between the married former bishop and the Pope, but there is no record. Mme de Talleyrand wanted to be received by the Pope, but he refused, much to Talleyrand's annoyance.

Napoleon had unearthed a symbol of the Merovingian kings of France going back to the Dark Ages. When Talleyrand went to the imperial apartments to accompany Napoleon to Notre Dame for the ceremony, he found the emperor barefoot, wearing white satin trousers and a crimson tunic both embroidered with a swarm of bees. Fortunately, someone had warned Talleyrand of what to expect and he managed to restrain his mirth.

The consecration of Napoleon I took place at Notre Dame on 2 December 1804. The governments of Western Europe watched with unadulterated horror as a new emperor was created in their midst. Preparations for the ceremony had involved the participation of all the city's craftspeople, dressmakers, embroiderers and jewellers, and even those of Lyon. The cathedral's interior had been dressed with painted cardboard pillars representing a Greco-Egyptian temple, embellished with trophies and flags adorned with eagles. The regime's dignitaries wore ostentatious costumes, while Napoleon and Josephine's carriage, constructed especially for the ceremony, was covered in gold leaf and fitted with velvet upholstery embroidered with the initial "N" under three gilt eagles holding aloft a golden crown.

That morning, the Pope and the other officials had been shivering in the freezing building waiting for the ceremony to begin since the doors stood wide open. The service went on for three hours, so guests had to put up with the discomfort as best they could. The Imperial couple entered the cathedral near the high altar slightly before midday. Following the agreed order of service, Napoleon placed the crown upon his own head. He then proceeded to crown Josephine, a moment that the painter Jacques Louis David chose to depict in his impressive representation of the scene, illustrating the political but also spiritual power that Napoleon aimed to wield over Pius VII. Standing in the right foreground of David's picture, wearing a vivid red cloak, was a figure who had been present at the coronation of Louis XVI at Reims in 1775, at the opening of the States-General at Versailles in 1789 and at the *Fête de la Fédération* in Paris in 1790—the Grand Chamberlain, as usual, wore an expression of amused indifference.

Faithful to the ideas of 1789, Talleyrand attempted to introduce into the new imperial constitution "the independence of the principal authorities, freedom and enlightened voting on taxation, the security of ownership, individual liberty, freedom of the press, of elections, ministerial responsibility and the protection of constitutional laws." However, France was now governed by an autocratic regime and Napoleon's ambitions would not accept any form of legitimate opposition or interference in his affairs. Anybody who did not agree with the emperor's policies would be obliged to keep their opinions to themselves. The time would soon come—if it had not already arrived—when the interests of Napoleon and those of France would cease to be the same.

On 26 March 1805, Talleyrand was present when Napoleon crowned himself King of Italy in Milan. This time, Talleyrand was convinced that it was a mistake. In a conversation with Josephine some weeks earlier, he stated that the emperor should attempt a reconciliation with his brother Lucien and the best way of doing it was to make him King of Italy. When Lucien learned about the concessions his brother required him to make, he declined the offer. Joseph Bonaparte too would not accept the position—so Napoleon kept it for himself. A few days later, he annexed Liguria to France adding it to Piedmont which had been a French possession since 1802. A violent reaction could be expected from Austria, which saw the French frontier edging closer to the Tyrol, Venice and Trieste. Despite his own deep misgivings that these events would inevitably lead to war, Talleyrand acquiesced to Napoleon's ambitions. He was obliged to convince the Senate of Napoleon's "restraint" in taking possession of these territories. At the same time, he attempted to warn Napoleon once again of the need to make peace rather than war.

While Napoleon and his retinue toured the Italian cities in triumph, and Mme de Talleyrand remained in Paris, a rumour began to reach the capital that Talleyrand had died in Milan. This news was confirmed by some correspondents who must have based themselves on some very untrustworthy informants, for during this time Talleyrand was taking the waters in the company of Mme Simons/Mlle Lange, who had been his hostess at dinner after the events of the *18 Brumaire* in 1799.

The early part of 1805 marked the high point of the relationship between Talleyrand and Napoleon during which almost every day the Grand Chamberlain held long conversations with the emperor. Talleyrand would then submit written reports on certain points of their meetings—its author destroyed all of this documentation in 1814. Meanwhile, trouble was brewing across Europe with England soon being provided with the allies it lacked. Relations with Russia were tense following a rift between Talleyrand and Markoff, the Russian ambassador to Paris. The British were still holding on to Malta in retaliation for the French take-over in northern Italy. To Talleyrand's profound despair, the elderly Austrian ambassador to Paris, Philipp von Cobenzl, had presented an ultimatum from Emperor François II requiring Napoleon to evacuate Lombardy. Talleyrand and Cobenzl were old acquaintances having known each other at the Collège Harcourt in Paris. This friendly and unconventional ambassador was also a frequent visitor at Talleyrand's various residences and was on familiar terms with Mme de Talleyrand's dogs.

Napoleon's reaction was swift. Since May 1803, the Grand Army had been camped on the Channel coast waiting for an opportunity—that would never come—to invade Great Britain. In London, William Pitt signed an agreement with the Tsar's representative and then with Austria creating a Third Coalition against France. The arrangement was relatively simple: British gold in exchange for Russian and Austrian soldiers. After making himself King of Italy, Napoleon had given himself little room for manoeuvre with the British and Austrians. If he were to survive, he was obliged to make war... and win. He was tired of gazing impotently at the white cliffs of Dover and now ordered the Grand Army to abandon the French coast and move rapidly in the direction of Germany with every unit having a precise itinerary and its destination for each day mapped out. To Girolamo Lucchesini, the Prussian representative in Paris, Talleyrand the Pacifist appeared ready to prevent the outbreak of hostilities, to bring them to a halt, to negotiate, to recommend moderation, to make concessions, in fact, to do anything to avoid war—but secretly knew that it was all to no avail confronted with Napoleon's resolve to seize the initiative. The Minister of Foreign Affairs was obliged to write a new circular which threw all the responsibility for the outbreak of war on the wrongdoings of Austria. Furthermore, he had to give up the pleasures of the Rue du Bac, the Hôtel de Créqui, Mme Simons and the elegant company of the Duchess de Luynes's salons as he was dragged across Europe in Napoleon's wake seeking confrontation with the Austrian Army, whose movements were being reported by Talleyrand's network of spies. The Ministry of Foreign Affairs was now on the move, its chests full of false passports. Talleyrand's assistant, La Besnardière, used to the comfort of his office, became acquainted with conducting affairs without the basics—bread, coffee, chairs, tables, horses—encountering dead and wounded soldiers on the roads with the Austrian rear-guard taking pot-shots at them. At every stage, Charles-Maurice paid particular attention to what was on offer on his dining room table: "Good dinners lead to good dispatches."

On 1 October 1805 in Strasbourg, Talleyrand had dinner with Napoleon and his assistant August de Rémusat, husband of the diarist Mme de Rémusat. After the meal, Napoleon visited Josephine and then the three men retired to Napoleon's bedroom to continue their discussions. They were alone when there followed a scene that left its mark on all of them. Napoleon just had time to tell Talleyrand to close the door when he fell on the floor foaming at the mouth and seized with convulsions. They loosened his cravat, bathed his face in eau-de-Cologne and after about fifteen minutes he recovered, sat in a chair and straightened his clothes. He made the two witnesses promise complete secrecy to what they had just seen—an epileptic fit. Before they could catch their breath, the emperor had left to join his army. This raised, once again, the thought that had already haunted Talleyrand and Fouché in 1800—what would happen if Bonaparte were to die? The minister was very nervous about seeing Napoleon depart, fearing for his safety and the regime's survival. When writing to Napoleon, Talleyrand mentions ominously that he had received news of Nelson and the mighty British fleet sailing from Portsmouth for Cadiz.

At the Battle of Ulm, taking place over 16–19 October 1805, Napoleon brought the Austrians into combat with the French Army before they could meet up with the Russians. He managed to trap the entire Austrian Army under General Mack and caused it to surrender with 30,000 officers and men, all their artillery and equipment. "The unfortunate General Mack" presented himself to Napoleon and offered his sword. Bonaparte gave the unfortunate general his sword and his freedom back, as well as that of his officers, requesting them to give his regards to the Austrian Emperor. Mack's soldiers were marched off to captivity. Francis II had Mack court-martialled and sentenced to two years' imprisonment.

The extraordinary rapidity of Napoleon's military successes caused Talleyrand great alarm. He did not like miraculous victories and the French Army's campaign in the autumn of 1805 brought a sequence of them. Evidently, Napoleon and his generals were carried away with enthusiasm to pursue and eliminate the last vestiges of opposition. Talleyrand was stuck in Strasbourg and then Vienna with Hugues Maret, Napoleon's Secretary of State, studying peace plans with the two Austrian plenipotentiaries Friedrich von Gentz and Johann Philipp Stadion, as well as their Prussian counterpart Christian von Haugwitz. Talleyrand believed that Maret's job was to keep an eye on him and report his activities to Napoleon, which he resented.

Hugues-Bernard Maret had been a lawyer from Dijon who, when the Revolution broke out, became a journalist and helped found *Le Moniteur* newspaper, which gained a wide reputation for correctness and impartiality. Upon Napoleon's return from Egypt, he joined the general's party in time for the coup d'état of *18 Brumaire* and was appointed as one of Napoleon's secretaries, soon becoming head of the cabinet. An experienced, hard-working and devoted politician, he rendered services of major value to the emperor who made him Duke de Bassano. He accompanied Napoleon throughout Europe on his military campaigns, remaining faithful to him until the very end, assuming major responsibilities. He always encouraged Napoleon in his warlike initiatives and was therefore viewed as one of the principal obstacles to peace. For this reason, Talleyrand said of him: "There is only one person more stupid than M. Maret and that is the Duke de Bassano."

On 17 October 1805, after the Austrian capitulation at Ulm, Talleyrand wrote a very important memorandum to Napoleon proposing a means of achieving order out of chaos. With Austria at his mercy, he should not exploit his victories but, on the contrary, propose a restrained peace treaty that would tempt Francis II to become his ally. If there were two large powers who were on good terms with each other, it would make the outbreak of any other European war almost unthinkable. The existence of Austria as a European power was a guarantee of stability, whereas humiliating it or breaking it up was likely to stimulate further wars. It is a mark of his courage that, with an emperor marching from victory to victory, he recommended peace and moderation.

If France and Austria were to become allies, it was important that there should be no point of friction between them, such as a common border. Talleyrand was aware that Russia coveted the territory of the Ottoman Empire, where there was a risk of a confrontation with Austria over Moldavia, Wallachia, Bessarabia and part of Bulgaria. He proposed to consolidate France's domination by giving independence to Austria's last Italian possessions—Venice and Trieste—making the Tyrol independent and compensating Frances II with territory in the Danube basin so as to frustrate the Russians. French territory would be limited by its natural frontiers of the Rhine and the Alps, and its two Italian possessions of Genoa and Piedmont—Talleyrand did not dare to suggest to the emperor abandoning them. He observed that the moment France took possession of territories beyond its natural frontiers, violent opposition arose in Europe provoking countries to turn towards England as an ally. The ten-page letter written in Strasbourg and addressed to the emperor somewhere on campaign with his army, is a model of tact, political common sense, moderation and far-sightedness.

Beyond containing advice, the letter was a very strong warning to the Napoleon that he had every interest in seeking a long-term, peaceful settlement, because the alternative was being condemned to make war ceaselessly against a growing number of enemies until, through exhaustion, in the long term he would be defeated—which is precisely what happened. In Europe at this moment there were four major powers: Austria, France, Russia and the United Kingdom, with France locked in a war against various alliances of the other three. In the short term, Talleyrand's objective was not to humiliate Austria—and, if possible, to satisfy Napoleon in the process. The true drama of this moment in history was that Napoleon had the political and military means to apply Talleyrand's peace plan, but would never accept anyone telling him what to do. On 26 October, a meeting was held to examine Talleyrand's report of 17 October but he soon learned that his plan was doomed: "The outcome of the meeting is the very opposite of my opinion." Napoleon could only think of issuing new decrees from the Schönbrunn Palace in Vienna and of keeping Talleyrand out of his affairs. From now until 1814 Talleyrand would not cease to recommend to Napoleon an alliance with Austria.

On 13 November 1805, Generals Murat and Lannes had entered Vienna without a shot being fired. Meanwhile, Napoleon had begun to think about creating the Confederation of the Rhine as a buffer state between France, Austria and Prussia, dictating his thoughts to Talleyrand, whose job it was simply to write them down. The Confederation would take concrete form after the Battle of Austerlitz.

Two days after the Battle of Ulm, Nelson crushed the combined French and Spanish fleets at Trafalgar. Three weeks later the news reached Talleyrand. He informed Napoleon: "It gives me great pain in sending to Your Majesty the sad news that I have received from Cadiz on the situation of the combined fleet... The genius and the good fortune were in Germany." He wrote to d'Hauterive, who was manning the ministry in Paris, in a different tone accepting that it was a calamity that would have an adverse impact on the morale of the remainder of the French fleet.

After Ulm, it was necessary to tackle the remnants of the Austrian and Russian Armies, which were overcome at Austerlitz on 2 December 1805, known as "The Battle of the Three Emperors", since Napoleon, Tsar Alexander I of Russia and Emperor Francis II of the Holy Roman Empire were present on the battlefield. Of the countries involved in the Third Coalition, only the British Army remained undefeated. On 5 December, Talleyrand made one last effort to convince Napoleon that magnanimity towards Austria and reaching an alliance had a number of political advantages that would seal his reputation as a glorious leader.

He implored him to consider again his memorandum sent from Strasburg on 17 October but began to understand that Napoleon was intoxicated by his headlong desire to crush everybody. While rising to absolute power, the causes of his downfall were already apparent: he was at war with England but could never hope to defeat her; he seemed determined to make as many enemies as possible; he had entered into an uneasy alliance with the Papacy which would end in a bitter feud; and he had created an imperial court where the fawning formalities gradually removed from him all self-restraint. Talleyrand could already see that Napoleon would soon be required to rush from one end of Europe to the other in the fruitless attempt to overcome an escalating series of crises. Talleyrand's report of 17 October was an ultimatum to Napoleon that the emperor chose to ignore.

The Treaty of Pressburg (today's Bratislava) was signed on 26 December 1805, as a consequence of the French victories over the Austrians at Ulm and Austerlitz. Despite Talleyrand's wishes, Napoleon gave him instructions that paid no heed to his minister's advice. Within months of the treaty and after a new entity, the Confederation of the Rhine, had been created by Napoleon, Francis II renounced his title as Holy Roman Emperor and became Emperor Francis I of Austria instead. A humiliating indemnity of 8 million gold francs in France's favour was also provided for in the treaty. Even so, Napoleon accused Talleyrand of having negotiated a treaty that was too favourable to the Austrians.

Ignoring the advice of his Minister of Foreign Affairs, Napoleon then established an alliance with Prussia. Talleyrand did not have a very high opinion of Prussia, while the wavering attitude of King Frederick-William during the preceding military campaign only reinforced this view. However, Napoleon insisted on signing a treaty which included granting possession of Hanover—which actually belonged to George III of the United Kingdom—to Prussia. In a few months, Prussia, Russia and England would all be at war with France.

A week after the battle, Talleyrand visited Austerlitz and described the scene in a letter to d'Hauterive in Paris, with complete indifference for its tens of thousands of dead soldiers and slaughtered horses—once more, d'Hauterive was shocked by his indifference. The figures on the loss of life during the battle cannot overlook the fate of the host of soldiers who suffered and died during the weeks after the battle, since nearly all wounds became infected and even a minor injury could be fatal. Over 11,000 wounded and sick Russian officers and men were treated in Austrian and French hospitals after the battle. The French did not expect the Russians to flee towards Vienna, yet, after the battle, thousands of Russian soldiers drifted to the Austrian capital, where they were sheltered for days by local citizens or begged on the streets. The recuperating and convalescent soldiers were eventually organized into groups and marched back to Russia accompanied by Austrian officers, who moved ahead of them to prepare shelter and provide food for them each day.

Napoleon thought of everything, decided everything and controlled everything and everybody. In the middle of this military campaign, he decided to marry Josephine's son Eugène de Beauharnais to Augusta-Amélie, the daughter of Maximilien, the Elector of Bavaria. The envoys sent to negotiate with Maximilien presented him with a document which contained the insolent phrase: "Napoleon's will and personality cannot accept a refusal." In return, Napoleon raised Bavaria from a state to a kingdom. Two months later, on 16 January 1806, Eugène and Augusta-Amélie were married. Even though it was a marriage arranged for political convenience, the couple were very happy together and had seven children.

We may recall the noble and extremely beautiful Countess de Brionne who had the premature ambition of making the young and handsome Abbé de Périgord into a cardinal in 1787. This lady was now about 70 years old, still good looking, still considered by the French Government as an unforgiven *émigré* living in the Austrian town of Linz. After her initial appreciation of his good qualities, she had never pardoned Talleyrand for his activities in the early days of the Revolution. He found himself in Linz and wrote asking if he could visit her. When he turned up on her doorstep, he was informed that she had most unfortunately just left town but had addressed an envelope to him. She had written his name on the envelope and underlined furiously all the grand titles he had acquired since Napoleon came to power. All the envelope contained was the letter he had originally sent to her.

While in Vienna, Talleyrand met Charles Joseph, the Prince de

Ligne, for the first time. He had once been appointed a field marshal by Catherine the Great of Russia, more recently become a prolific writer, but above all an intellectual, a Bohemian and wonderful wit. Apart from Catherine the Great, his acquaintances and correspondents included Giacomo Casanova, Germaine de Staël, Jean-Jacques Rousseau, Voltaire, Goethe and Frederick the Great. As a member of a princely family, he had inherited his father's vast estates in what is now Belgium, living in great splendour and luxury. He had travelled all over Europe—Austria, England, France, Germany, Italy and Switzerland—attending impartially the courts, the military camps, the salons and the learned assemblies of philosophers and scientists in each country. His estates had been overrun by the French Army in 1792/1793, since when he had lived modestly in Vienna. Meeting this charming elderly statesman compensated Talleyrand for his rejection by the Countess de Brionne. We shall meet the Prince de Ligne again at the Congress of Vienna eight years later.

Once more, during his long absence it was announced in Paris, to the joy of the working classes, that Talleyrand was dead. His brother Archambaud, now pardoned, went to his sister-in-law, Mme de Talleyrand, in Paris to present his condolences on the death of her husband. The imaginary widow put on a splendid performance of wailing, dishevelled hair and final collapse. Soon, her husband's next letter announced that he was alive and well. In the Parisian salons it was very much the fashion to announce each evening that so-and-so had died. Talleyrand's verdict was: "The gossips of the Faubourg Saint-Germain have killed more generals than the Austrian cannons."

Reports reached Napoleon's headquarters that members of the French aristocracy in Paris were scornful of his "pretended" victory at Austerlitz. He was terribly susceptible to the jeers of the nobility and these remarks drove him into an uncontrolled frenzy involving his hat being stamped on. Talleyrand, imperturbable, noted how the victorious military genius of Austerlitz became transformed into a puerile tyrant when a few members of the *Ancien Régime* made sarcastic remarks about him. Napoleon believed he had gained a satisfactory revenge when some of the attendants of the former royal court accepted positions as ladies-in-waiting to Josephine.

Metternich, the Austrian ambassador to Paris, noted significantly that at Pressburg Napoleon's foreign minister took the decision to oppose "the emperor's destructive projects" with all his might. However, as the two men drifted apart, Talleyrand would continue to flatter his master with terms of superficial devotion and admiration, while Napoleon awarded him state honours—as if to delay as long as possible the moment of their final rupture. Talleyrand had no wish to cut himself off from a position of power and a source of wealth, whereas Napoleon believed that he could keep an eye on his minister's activities if he were kept close at hand—in this he failed. Whatever image he presented of himself to Napoleon, Talleyrand had understood that the fabulous victory at Austerlitz and the devastating defeat at Trafalgar would only generate further conflict. For all his military genius, Napoleon was now committed to a path that could only end with his downfall. After a period of working together with a good understanding, the two men now entered a period of hostility with Napoleon resorting to temper tantrums and Talleyrand to betrayal.

CHAPTER XI
THE TYRANT

The ratification of the Treaty of Pressburg between France and the Holy Roman Empire took place on 1 January 1806. This was an auspicious day for another reason for it was decided to abandon the French Revolutionary calendar, with its months of *Pluviôses, Ventôses, Vendémiaires* and *Fructidors*, and return to the Gregorian calendar employed by the rest of Europe. It is believed that Talleyrand was some 5 million francs richer due to the manoeuvring that took place around the meeting rooms in Pressburg. Another significant outcome of Napoleon's victorious military campaign against the Austrians was that, in March 1806, Joseph Bonaparte became King of Naples, ousting the previous Bourbon incumbent Ferdinand IV. Napoleon's younger brother Louis assumed the throne of Holland with his wife Hortense de Beauharnais, Josephine's daughter. Talleyrand noted that, in granting these kingdoms to members of his family, Napoleon anticipated unswerving loyalty from them. However, the new sovereigns enjoyed their new-found power so much that they resisted their brother's authority with more or less audacity.

Among a series of other appointments for his entourage, Napoleon conferred upon Talleyrand the Pope's former Principality of Benevento in Italy, thus granting him the title of Prince who should henceforth be addressed as "Your Serene Highness"—and the same applied to the former Mme Grand. We may recall that, when trying to persuade the Pope to come to Paris for the consecration of Emperor Napoleon in 1804, Talleyrand reminded His Holiness that the principalities of Pontecorvo and Benevento had recently been restored to him. This situation did not last for, not long afterwards, they became annexed to France by imperial decree, which is just another way of saying upon a caprice of Napoleon. The letter that Talleyrand sent to the Pope justifying this annexation contained the implausible argument that the French Government wished to "relieve" the Reigning Pontificate of the difficulties he faced in administering these two enclaves lying within the territory of the Kingdom of Naples. Furthermore: "Under a new government and in such a flammable country, all points of friction should be avoided." It is difficult to imagine two small, obscure, isolated territories in southern Italy setting Europe alight. Pontecorvo was awarded to General Jean-Baptiste Bernadotte.

Foreign governments were astonished by these measures for, under Napoleon's rules, he could apparently do whatever he liked and no-one could stop him. However, in all these political shuffles it would eventually become clear that decisions based on the will of one person are not eternal. Talleyrand instructed Charles-Jean-Marie Alquier, who had replaced Cardinal Fesch as the French representative to the Holy See (Fesch having been transferred to Frankfurt), to advise the Vatican that it was expected to give up its rights to Benevento and Pontecorvo without protest. Nevertheless, the Pope did point out that these two principalities had been the undisputed property of the Catholic Church since time immemorial.

In Paris, high society flocked to pay homage to the new Prince de Benevento at the Rue du Bac, but he quickly diverted these people to the presence of his wife because "women are always enchanted to be princesses". Mme de Talleyrand was in seventh heaven, receiving visitors seated in a large armchair with her feet resting on a cushion. She began to sign her name "Sovereign Princess de Benevento" or, when pressed for time, "Reigning Princess". The diarist Mme d'Abrantès commented: "She visited me regularly twice a week, coming in the morning to see me personally and coming in the evening, as she said, for the sake of decency, and always annoying me, which I could not tell her and she could not see. I would go and hide near M. de Talleyrand where I was sure she wouldn't find me because she was scared of him and did not love him anymore." As for Talleyrand himself, the title was a trinket that did not lead to any particular expressions of vanity. During the forthcoming voyage to Poland, his German friend the Baron von Gagern frequently addressed him in public as "Your Highness". Talleyrand scolded him: "Don't call me Highness. I am perhaps less and perhaps more than that. Call me simply Monsieur de Talleyrand."

It was, nevertheless, necessary to persuade the Pope's troops that they were no longer welcome in the Principality of Benevento. Talleyrand requested that this should be accomplished peacefully and with as much dignity as possible. Unfortunately, these instructions arrived after a French general had marched boldly into the town with a detachment of soldiers and drummers throwing the Pope's men out. Talleyrand was distressed to learn this news, so sent his own representative, Louis de Beer, whose first task was to eject the French general and his men leaving no trace of their occupation. De Beer's verdict on the town was: "We are still in the Middle Ages here." De Beer had a difficult job since he was viewed by the local population as a usurper, while French troops continued to make incursions into the territory.

The new ruler of Benevento turned the duchy into a mini experiment for his liberal ideas on social life. Even though he never set foot in the town, his wish was that the inhabitants should be happy and well governed. He reinvested the principality's revenues in its infrastructure such as roads, the water supply, a botanical garden, a public library and free primary education for all boys and girls. He declared: "The care that we give to women's education is one of the surest methods to polish and purify people's manners." He introduced civil and criminal law and made vaccination obligatory. The coal industry in the vicinity was encouraged. In total contrast to his reputation as the crafty and venal politician, every time Charles-Maurice was involved with the government of human beings, he behaved as a modern, enlightened and liberal ruler.

At the Congress of Vienna following the Napoleonic Wars, the Pope recovered his two properties, while the former Bishop of Autun relinquished his part with such good grace that he was awarded a small pension drawn on Benevento's revenues. Before we become too impressed with Talleyrand's good graces, his final intervention took place in June 1814 when he sent a secretary from the French embassy in Rome to take possession of all the money to be found in the state coffers of Benevento and send it to him in Paris.

When the British Prime Minister William Pitt died suddenly on 23 January 1806, Talleyrand's old Whig friend Charles James Fox was offered the post of Foreign Secretary. The British police in London had just foiled a plot to assassinate Napoleon and this gave Fox an opportunity to write an official letter to Talleyrand about it, accompanied by a more personal letter expressing the desire for a lasting peace. With the British Navy dominating the oceans and the French Army ruling the Continent of Europe, were there not grounds for reaching an understanding? This was a golden opportunity to make peace, since both Talleyrand and Fox sincerely desired it. Talks were speedily entered into but, despite their good intentions, the difficulties were insurmountable. The British king's legacy of Hanover had been annexed by Napoleon and swiftly awarded to Prussia; the British were still holding on to Malta in retaliation for the French grip over northern Italy. Furthermore, what was to be done about the Kingdom of Naples ruled at this particular moment by Bonaparte's elder brother Joseph, while the former King of Naples— a Bourbon—had fled to Sicily, under British control? By July the mood had completely changed and Fox was forced to admit that his assessment of Napoleon's peaceful intentions had been premature. Fox died in September of that year.

Initially, Lord Yarmouth, held as a prisoner in Paris since the renewal of hostilities following the collapse of the Treaty of Amiens, had been appointed to conduct peace negotiations on behalf of the government in London. He was a hard drinker, a committed night owl and pursuer of women. A good friend of Montrond, he could drink him under the table. Lady Yarmouth was apparently an even more intimate friend of Montrond. In August, the British Government sent Lord Lauderdale to join Yarmouth and he reported "the complete system of terror which prevails here", with a climate of fear preventing French friends from calling on him. Despite Talleyrand's attempts to oblige Napoleon to accept a peace agreement, the negotiations petered out following a number of sudden reversals and double-dealings on the emperor's part, who was not prepared to make a reasonable peace with anybody. He did not trust Talleyrand and humiliated his minister by appointing new plenipotentiaries to conduct the negotiations in his place, exercising complete control over their activities. At the same time, it finally dawned on the Prussians that after all Napoleon was not going to give them Hanover as he had promised.

The talks broke down when the United Kingdom realized that

Napoleon had no wish to make peace. Based on what had happened previously, England had no influence over Napoleon during peacetime; the only way to make an impact was through the threat of warfare and by making alliances with other European powers. Upon the breakdown of the talks, Lauderdale offered his French counterpart, Jean-Baptiste de Champagny, the present of a ceremonial sword, which he refused. Talleyrand was not happy about this breach of etiquette and reminded Champagny that he was required both to accept the gift and to give one in exchange. Napoleon had not anticipated any satisfactory result from these negotiations for, even if a solution had been found, it would have been rendered null and void by his forthcoming project to create the Confederation of the Rhine. Another of his far-fetched ideas would make all further peace talks futile: a continental blockade cutting the United Kingdom off from all trade with Europe.

Before the French Revolution took place, the realm of the Holy Roman Emperor included a large part of what is now Germany and pockets on the Rhine's left bank stretching from Switzerland to the sea, including some isolated ones within French territory. Under the Holy Roman Emperor's authority, a multitude of kings, dukes, princes, barons, margraves, bishops and electors ruled over larger and smaller principalities. By 1806, Napoleon had seized most of these lands and proposed to reorganize them into the Confederation of the Rhine under his protection. The German princes flocked to Paris to find out what fate awaited them. The Prince de Benevento received them at his office on Rue du Bac either with charm or with intimidation depending on the decisions that had already been taken about their territories. Talleyrand profited largely from the negotiations taking place, since the princes who thought their lands were in peril paid Talleyrand handsomely to ensure that they retained them or were granted comparable territories on the right bank of the Rhine. Although he greeted the future rulers of the Confederation of the Rhine with his legendary charm and politeness, the more desperate the prince, the higher the price. Those princes who turned up at his office empty handed were likely to lose their territories in favour of those who came better prepared. It served no purpose either to propose a bejewelled snuff-box or a purse of diamonds; only cash was acceptable, with the result that there is very little trace of these transactions. Once they had paid up, Talleyrand in Paris—or his agents in Germany—decided who were the winners and who the losers. It is estimated that Talleyrand gained between 10 and 15 million livres from this commerce. He tried to reassure his clients that, under the protection of the invincible French Army led by Emperor Napoleon, they had nothing to fear from the Holy Roman Empire, in whose realm they had been located up to this point. After he had spoken to them individually, he brought all sixteen of them together on 12 July 1806 to read the terms of the Confederation of the Rhine's Constitution. There was no discussion; those present were simply required to sign it. The document was ratified at Munich on 26 July, in front of General Berthier, and carried to Paris by Talleyrand's favourite nephew Louis de Périgord, the eldest son of his brother Archambaud. On 1 August, the members of the confederation formally seceded from the Holy Roman Empire and, on 6 August, following an ultimatum from Napoleon, Francis II declared the Holy Roman Empire dissolved.

Talleyrand found himself walking an increasingly thin line between the respect of his principles and the tempting financial benefit he derived from Napoleon's munificence. At the same time, the emperor became increasingly suspicious of his foreign minister, requiring him to report every day on the correspondence he received from ambassadors and what the foreign press was saying. Talleyrand was also told to treat the Austrian and Prussian ambassadors with distrust, both of whom were his friends. Napoleon also hinted that his private mail was being intercepted and read, so Talleyrand warned his correspondents that they might not be the first to read his words. Even as the relationship between Napoleon and Talleyrand turned sour, ministers, princes and ambassadors flocked to the Ministry of Foreign Affairs to find out what was going on. In Paris, Mainz, Berlin or Warsaw one had to wait for hours to obtain an audience with the great man. His reputation as the most able diplomat in Europe grew day by day. One of Goethe's friends described a meeting with His Serene Highness the Prince de Benevento, French Minister of Foreign Affairs: "After five hours of deadly waiting and nervous tension, at last the door opened to allow through an elderly gentleman, fairly large, of middle height, dressed in an embroidered coat *à la Française,* with powdered hair and a pronounced limp. His pale face, expressionless and unremarkable, seemed to me like an impenetrable veil concealing his soul. His small grey eyes did not display the slightest expression, but his lips bore a light smile, half-serious, half-amused."

Talleyrand hated being alone. When he travelled in the wake of Napoleon's army, he was accompanied by La Besnardière, Durand de Mareuil, Roux-Laborie, his new friend the Prince Nassau-Siegen and, of course, Montrond, as well as translators, secretaries, three or four servants, including Courtiade and his cook Chevalier. When he arrived in a city with his entourage, he would seek accommodation in the most prestigious buildings. While some of his faithful collaborators were actual staff members from the Rue du Bac, others belonged to a secret "ministry of the shadows". Among the latter were two members of the German noble Dalberg family, but particularly the young Emmerich, who had become and would remain Talleyrand's faithful companion and shrewd business partner during the Napoleonic Empire and the early days of the Restoration. He was small, fragile and cunning. Pasquier describes him as: "A schemer ready to conspire at any time, unprincipled on any matter, liberal, both proud and crafty, deeply corrupt as are jaded layabouts, without moral standards through boredom and satiety." Talleyrand did not entirely trust him, but without Emmerich von Dalberg he could not have manipulated the German princes or later betrayed Napoleon with such skill in the corridors of power.

Coming from a wealthy family, Emmerich's even more distinguished and noble uncle Karl Theodor von Dalberg had held a range of important religious positions in Regensburg, Worms and Frankfurt. Before 1789, Karl Theodor had been an ecclesiastic rather like the Bishop of Autun, an enlightened and worldly host inviting to his sumptuous palace at Erfurt the chief intellectuals of the day. Karl Theodor von Dalberg and Charles Maurice de Talleyrand had very similar origins, manners and tastes—particularly for pretty women. Both Dalbergs had been invited to Paris in the winter of 1804 to be present at Napoleon's consecration, where the Pope and Cardinal Consalvi received Karl Theodor coldly. In contrast, he swore undying loyalty to Napoleon and was received by both the emperor and Josephine with enthusiastic expressions of friendship.

The Dalbergs presented to the world a remarkable duplicity so that, while detesting France, the Revolution and particularly Napoleon, they took pains to convey the facade of obedient and faithful subjects. Karl Theodor offered the same obsequious flattery to Napoleon as Talleyrand, while his true allegiance was to reach an effective unified government for Germany. Both the uncle and nephew had turned to the rising star of Napoleon, believing that he represented the only force strong enough to save Germany from further disintegration. At the same time, they were organizing resistance to his empire and even planning his death! In much the same manner as Talleyrand, at one stage Karl Theodor wrote to Napoleon pointing out that in peaceful times all countries were connected by prolific commercial, political and intellectual ties, and that it was the emperor's duty to maintain these links in everybody's interests.

We may recall that Talleyrand had not appreciated the Russian ambassador to Paris, Markoff, because Napoleon's police had discovered that his embassy was the hub of a spy ring circulating around the infamous Russian agent, the Count d'Antraigues, located in Dresden. Markoff was recalled and not replaced, while the Russian embassy in Paris continued with its espionage activities. According to the Count de Vitrolles, the task of communicating the secret information from Paris to Saint Petersburg was henceforth delegated to... Emmerich von Dalberg. He was therefore in contact with Tsar Alexander, who passed the information he received on to London. Earlier, First Consul Bonaparte had been suspicious of secret information being leaked from the Rue du Bac, and particularly from the office of the Minister of Foreign Affairs, whose constant companion was... Emmerich von Dalberg. Talleyrand himself may have remained completely ignorant of Dalberg's role in espionage. However, one item of information leaked to d'Antraigues turned out to be of capital importance. Early in 1805, Napoleon gave orders to Admirals Villeneuve and Ganteaume for the French fleet to leave its harbours of Brest, La Rochelle and Toulon, join up with the Spanish fleet under Admiral Gravina and sail to the West Indies, hopefully with the British fleet in hot pursuit. This would leave the English coast unprotected, giving Napoleon an opportunity to cross the Channel with his army and invade the country. The combined French/Spanish fleet would avoid the British, turn tail immediately and head back across the Atlantic giving them the liberty to attack the undefended British ports. However, Admiral Nelson seems to have been aware of what was afoot and eventually caught up with Admiral Villeneuve at Trafalgar. We know that Talleyrand used Dalberg to execute his affairs and in return Dalberg was allowed to use the confidential courier services of the Rue du Bac for his private correspondence. His letters addressed to his Uncle Karl Theodor in Frankfurt were therefore not intercepted by Napoleon's police and eventually ended up in the hands of Tsar Alexander, who passed them on to London.

Remarkably, it is obvious that Napoleon knew nothing about this correspondence for Emmerich von Dalberg was rewarded with French citizenship, appointed as an ambassador and even elevated to the nobility during the Napoleonic era, with a comfortable remuneration. After the Bourbon Restoration, he ended his career as French ambassador to Turin. Following the dissolution of the Holy Roman Empire in 1806, his uncle Karl Theodor formally resigned in a letter to Emperor Francis II and, together with other princes, joined Napoleon's Confederation of the Rhine as Prince Primate of Frankfurt. It was at this time that Karl Theodor appointed Napoleon's uncle, Cardinal Fesch, as coadjutor in his archdiocese. It is remarkable that Karl Theodor von Dalberg, through his writings and his activities, is considered a true German patriot, while his nephew Emmerich, despite his long-term opposition to Napoleon, is not.

In 1803, the British territory of Hanover had been conquered jointly by the French and Prussian armies. In August 1806, Frederick-William III, King of Prussia was deeply concerned by Napoleon's reorganization of the German states into the Confederation of the Rhine. Europe gave the impression of being calm but to him France appeared to be dictating terms to states that were under his protection. Prussian concerns led to the War of the Fourth Coalition. Even though Prussia had paid France upon receiving the "present" of the British possession of Hanover, Napoleon, with typical callousness and cynicism, intended taking it back again with the possibility of returning it to England. Prussia, supported financially by England and Russia, decided to mobilize its army against France.

On 8 August, Napoleon received an ultimatum from King Frederick-William requiring him to remove all his troops from the right bank of the

Rhine. The French emperor immediately set out towards Prussia with his army, while the Ministry of Foreign Affairs was obliged to follow. Talleyrand and his staff had to endure once again the hardships of temporary bivouacs, long hours of work day and night, and the disagreeable company of Napoleon's officers. When they reached Mainz, Talleyrand could no longer conceal from his close associates—the Dalbergs and Metternich—his disapproval of the war. He vowed that, when the time was right, he would resign as Napoleon's foreign minister. He had no particular sympathy for Prussia but he found it inexplicable that in 1805 Napoleon would favour Prussia over Austria, and one year later set out to destroy it. Within a week of declaring war, the Prussian armies were overcome at the joint Battles of Jena and Auerstedt (14 October 1806). Prussian resistance collapsed and Napoleon marched into Berlin on 25 October.

It had been Talleyrand's habit to visit the waters of Bourbon-l'Archambault at the end of each summer for the sake of his legs. Since he had been obliged to follow Napoleon's Army, he attended the spa at Wiesbaden instead where he met the beautiful Queen of Holland, Josephine's young daughter Hortense. For years, she had known Talleyrand in her mother's residence at Malmaison as a dour figure who limped, barely acknowledged other people's presence and propped himself up silently against the nearest chair. In Wiesbaden, she discovered a completely different person. "I was surprised, even flattered, for the attention of a man who usually shows none always affects you more." Hortense observed that he listened but never entered into a discussion; he would not contradict people; if he didn't agree with them, his smile would indicate his dissent. She adds that he was "very tolerant about vices". For decades he had lived through evolving situations where the definition of morality had changed like the leaves torn off a calendar. Nevertheless, he could not stand vulgarity. Despite giving birth to three sons, her marriage to Louis Bonaparte was not a success, but if there was one member of Talleyrand's family for whom Hortense had a weakness, it was his son Charles de Flahaut.

During the course of 1806, Talleyrand's conviction that Napoleon had become a megalomaniac received confirmation. By a decree dated 12 November, Napoleon required all healthy Frenchmen between the ages of 20 and 60 to be available for military service, while any dissent would be dealt with by long-term imprisonment without trial. His police were authorized to place under surveillance anybody they considered worthy of suspicion. Even d'Hauterive, manning the ministry back in Paris, realized that for every king he deposed Napoleon was making another enemy. Nevertheless, Talleyrand continued to flatter Napoleon with apparently unconditional praise. After the victories of Jena and Auerstedt over the Prussian Armies, Talleyrand tried once again to persuade Napoleon to reach a reasonable peace agreement that would persuade the Prussians to become an ally. Despite ignoring his suggestions, Bonaparte continued to consult Talleyrand, who by now had completely abandoned any attempt to make the emperor confront such ideals as wisdom, humanity, peace and justice. In his determination to make enemies of all countries, Napoleon seemed to think that moderation simply exposed him to needless annoyance. It did not help that Talleyrand had a very poor opinion of Prussia, believing it to be a backward country compared to the mainstream of civilization to be found in London, Paris and Vienna.

At the very height of his power, on 21 November 1806, Napoleon signed the decree creating the "gigantic and disastrous" Continental System in Berlin. This was an embargo forbidding trade between the United Kingdom and the European mainland. The fundamental idea was to make the Napoleonic Empire the reserve of French commerce. If he could bring about Britain's economic collapse, Napoleon believed that he would be able to conquer that country without difficulty. However, Portugal openly refused to join the Continental System and the British rapidly increased their trade with the rest of the world. In order to enforce his decision throughout Europe, Napoleon would now be obliged to turn his attention to overcoming one point of resistance after another, during which time his embargo was hurting his own economy far more than that of the United Kingdom, as coffee, tea and sugar were no longer to be found in Parisian shops.

On this day, Talleyrand called a staff meeting in his office. He explained that, under normal circumstances, an imperial decree was based on a report submitted by a minister. In the case of the Continental System, however, the decree had already been signed when Talleyrand was made responsible for writing the historical and legal arguments justifying it. Talleyrand had a very high opinion of the British political system and feared that, if ever it was severely damaged, global civilization itself would be in danger of collapse.

Very soon, the first cracks began to appear in the emperor's foolish enterprise as European countries realized that they were condemning themselves to economic ruin. While still in Berlin, Napoleon received a letter from Manuel Godoy, the Spanish Prime Minister, announcing that his country did not wish to participate in the Continental System because it would harm its trade with England and bring with it ruin, hunger and social instability. Since this secession would weaken the whole edifice, Napoleon immediately decided that his next great mission was to invade that country in order to teach the Spanish a lesson and destroy their monarchy. This move is often considered as the beginning of the end. In his memoirs, Talleyrand writes that it was at this point that: "I swore to myself that I would cease to be his minister as soon as we were back in France." However, these words were written ten years later and, with him, decisions were not acted upon hastily, nor without preliminaries, nor without intrigue. For the next year, Talleyrand wore the mask of Napoleon's devoted minister while attempting to appease the impact of his master's wild schemes. He had not given up on his plan to make peace with Austria and to award it the provinces in the Danube Basin as a rampart against Russia.

In the town of Poznan, Talleyrand met the King of Saxony, Frederick-August I, who signed the Confederation document on 11 December 1806 and thereby became Napoleon's ally. Frederick-August was a courteous gentleman of the old school who sought Talleyrand's friendship. Members of Napoleon's entourage, however, had noted his collection of paintings in the splendid gallery in Dresden and had expressed the idea that they would look better in a Parisian setting. The king could not hide his distress at this proposed looting, since he considered the paintings as national treasures and would not even allow himself to hang them in his own residence. Talleyrand understood the king's anguish and intervened personally with the emperor, who accepted that the gallery in Dresden should not be ransacked. Upon leaving Poznan, Talleyrand found himself a million francs richer.

The journey from Poznan to Warsaw in the middle of winter was a nightmare. Talleyrand's carriage sunk up to its axles in the mud and a dozen soldiers were required to heave it out. Since 1772, Poland had been a phantom country divided into three zones occupied by Prussia, Russia and Austria. Talleyrand felt that the division of Poland into three geographical zones of influence thirty-four years previously had been a great mistake that had upset the traditional balance of European power to France's detriment. It had not benefited from this division and there was the added threat of the Russian border creeping closer to Western Europe. He believed that a strong and independent Poland would contribute to European peace and stability. Metternich shared his opinion precisely. Talleyrand also warned Austria that having a common border with Russia presented a potentially dangerous point of friction that could have easily been avoided by creating a buffer state between them, i.e. an independent part of Poland. French Ambassador Andréossy, now located in Vienna, was charged with explaining Talleyrand's point of view to the Austrian Government suggesting that, if it would give up part of its territory in Poland, it would receive another piece of land elsewhere in Europe as compensation. Dalberg informed the Polish authorities of this proposed manoeuvre, with the result that Talleyrand received 4 million florins for his pains.

Having defeated Prussia, the French were well received in Warsaw. Not long after arriving in the city, Charles-Maurice made the acquaintance of Marie-Thérèse Poniatowska, the Countess Tyszkiewicz, who had been separated from her husband for many years. Mme Tyszkiewicz was neither young (she was over 40), nor especially beautiful (she hid her glass eye under wide-brimmed hats), but she was rich, intelligent and elegant, knew everybody and was widely appreciated. She was the hostess of the most stylish soirées at the Blacha Palace, which she shared with her brother and his mistress. Charles-Maurice quickly became the grand passion of her life and she his greatest confidante. When she eventually joined him in Paris, she became the most faithful and devoted member of his "harem", almost ruining herself in showering him with gifts. She had her own apartment at the Château de Valençay and for many years accompanied him wherever he went. In the winter of 1806/1807 Mme Tyszkiewicz became a primary agent in keeping Talleyrand informed of what was going on in Warsaw. Through her, he was introduced to Alexander Batowski who dined nearly every evening at Talleyrand's mansion and passed on the minister's orders and dispatches in Polish. An extremely handsome man, he had been the lover of the Duchess von Courland with whom we will soon become familiar.

Since the Polish winter did not lend itself to conducting military operations, Napoleon decided that it was time for a season of balls. Talleyrand, who had had considerable success in organizing festivities in the past, was put in charge. The Poles saw the arrival of the French Army as a step towards independence so were very ready to co-operate. Talleyrand rounded up all the beautiful women of the Polish aristocracy to present them to the emperor. Although Napoleon had been welcomed in Warsaw as a liberator, he did not, in fact, have any policy to implement concerning that country. The diarist Mme Potocka was very interested to meet Napoleon's Grand Chamberlain because her aunt, Countess Tyszkiewicz, had become one of his close friends. She had heard that Talleyrand was the most intelligent, the most courteous, the most amusing, the friendliest, etc. Her first impressions, therefore, will come as a surprise: "I would say that he appeared indifferent and bored with everything, only interested in making money, keen to earn the favour of a master whom he detested, without character and without principles, in a phrase, unhealthy in mind and body."

In the ballroom at the Radziwill Palace, Napoleon had seated himself on a chair in a prominent position while Talleyrand, in the role of flunky, had to "walk with difficulty to the middle of the room, a folded serviette over his arm, an enamelled tray in his hand having come to offer a glass of lemonade to this monarch who he considered as an upstart". Talleyrand not only served refreshments, but presented to Napoleon the tiny 20-year-old Countess Maria Walewska, because it was the done thing for the emperor to have a mistress—perhaps it would make this tedious workaholic more human. Napoleon had already noticed Mme Walewska dressed as a peasant on the road leading to Warsaw and Talleyrand had been put in charge of locating her. Although she was a devout Catholic, sometime later Napoleon's reported: "Mme Walewska did not put up a fight." In 1810, she bore Napoleon's son who grew up to be Count Alexander Walewski, an important nineteenth-century

French political figure and diplomat. Otherwise, the emperor made Talleyrand's life wretched, working until 5 o'clock in the morning, waking him up in the early hours for him to read a story because he couldn't sleep. The book in question was *Corinne,* Mme de Staël's second best-seller. This time, the Prince de Benevento appeared in the book lightly disguised as "M. de Maltigues" who says: "There is nothing good in this life but fortune and power, or both of them." And again: "Friendships are means that one should accept or drop according to circumstances." Napoleon was soon irritated by the book's anti-imperial plot, while as usual Talleyrand kept his opinion to himself.

Napoleon's Great Chamberlain spent December 1806 to May 1807 as the very active Governor of the newly created Duchy of Warsaw, where he was responsible for a large number of administrative tasks that did not necessarily fall under the title of foreign affairs. For instance, he was charged with supplying the 150,000 French troops stationed along the Vistula River. It was necessary to build boats, find flour mills, ensure warm clothing and provide brandy and beer in order to keep the army functioning. Talleyrand brought in supplies from areas to the south and west of Warsaw. He was hoping that, if he gave satisfactory service to Napoleon in this position, it would soften the emperor's resistance to his peace plans. The government in Vienna sent Baron Nicholas-Charles de Vincent to Warsaw to negotiate with Napoleon but also as a special envoy attached to Talleyrand. Vincent and Talleyrand had known each other for a long time and, with the assistance of Emmerich Dalberg, held secret conversations about how to promote Austria's interests and what would happen if Napoleon were killed on the battlefield. Napoleon suspected that he was not being kept fully informed about the conversations with Vincent, while his minister pretended otherwise. Vincent soon realized that Talleyrand was a friend whose ambition of a grand alliance between France and Austria would have guaranteed long-term peace in Europe. The Austrian Foreign Minister, Johann Philipp Stadion, proposed an armistice allowing time for a congress to be held in Vienna bringing together all the belligerents, including England.

Once again, Talleyrand asked himself the same question: "What would we do if Napoleon were killed?" The most obvious solution would be to place Napoleon's elder brother Joseph, with whom Talleyrand had a very good relationship, on the throne of France. Joseph would be provided with a solid government, preferably one under the control of Talleyrand. France would withdraw to its traditional frontiers of the Alps and the Rhine while a general European peace would be declared. Talleyrand went so far as to ask Dalberg to share this idea with Metternich, the Austrian minister to the French court. At this stage, Talleyrand and Metternich did not know each other very well but were both masters in the art of circumlocution, intrigue and dissimulation, and understood each other very well. During negotiations with Talleyrand, Metternich found him forever placing obstacles in the path of positive actions; however, in private he was "as trustworthy as he was agreeable."

Without Napoleon realizing it, the Austrian Government became aware that the French Foreign Minister was an ally. While Talleyrand sought an alliance with Austria, Napoleon was more interested in signing a treaty with Russia. The Tsar of Russia, Alexander I, had once dreamt of recreating Poland but of one thing he was determined: if he did not succeed in restoring Polish independence, no-one else would. Napoleon succeeded in creating a limited, independent Polish state—the Duchy of Warsaw—in the middle of the country. He may have upset the Russians, but he secured for himself a valuable ally in the Polish people.

Despite the difficulties of conducting military operations during the Polish winter, on 8 February 1807 the Battle of Eylau took place between Napoleon's Army and the Imperial Russian Army in a snowstorm with terrible slaughter on both sides and an indecisive result. Even Napoleon's marshals looked for a conclusion to the conflicts taking place throughout Europe that might easily bring the regime to an abrupt end. After the Battle of Eylau, Talleyrand kept a letter ready addressed to Joseph Bonaparte in Naples requesting him to go immediately to Lyon in the event of his brother's death on the battlefield. If this took place, Talleyrand would immediately propose an alliance with Austria and a peace treaty with the British, before meeting up with Joseph. As usual, Talleyrand benefited from a first-class information network. In Warsaw in the spring of 1807, his informants included his nephews Louis and Edmond de Périgord and their cousin Alfred de Noailles, all of whom were young aides-de-camp in Napoleon's Army. At the same time, Talleyrand was attempting to introduce his son Charles de Flahaut into

Murat's entourage. These family members were able to transmit news and provide him with important details about what was happening to the army. Talleyrand suggested once again to Vincent that Austria should give up its part of Poland in exchange for another piece of territory elsewhere. Vincent was almost ready to accept this arrangement when, following the French success at the Battle of Friedland (14 June 1807), Napoleon lost all interest in negotiating with anybody except the Russians. He seized several states and principalities in north-western Germany, including some Prussian territory and the much-disputed former British possession of Hanover, moulding them into a new Kingdom of Westphalia ruled by his youngest brother Jérôme.

Talleyrand had gradually concluded that, because of internal squabbles, Polish reunification was never going to succeed and that Napoleon should fall back on Western Europe. He even gave back the 4 million florins he had received from the Poles because he no longer wished to be involved in their affairs: "One can do nothing with these people; you can only organize disorder with these people." At this time, Napoleon was preparing to cross the Niemen River, with Talleyrand deeply alarmed about the idea of the French Army plunging into the wastes of Russia. Finally, talks were held with Tsar Alexander on a raft in the middle of the river where he and Napoleon agreed on the terms of the Treaty of Tilsit (7 July 1807). The dreams of General Murat, who wanted to become King of Poland, had been upset because he had favoured an attack on Russia. This would, nevertheless, take place five years later.

In mid-June, Napoleon let his Foreign Minister know that he would deal directly with the Russian Tsar Alexander and, furthermore, his presence was not required for negotiations with the Ottoman representative Seïb-Wahib, which would take place under the authority of General Caulaincourt. Thus, at Tilsit Talleyrand was once again kept out of the discussions, his only role being to sign the treaty document with the Russian representative, General Kourakin. The French forces had occupied the city of Danzig at the end of May 1807, where Talleyrand took up residence to supervise the supply situation. A couple of weeks later, somewhat at a loose end, he wrote a letter to Napoleon couched in the most elegant language but which carried a clear warning:

"I have at last gleaned some information about the Battle of Friedland; and I have now learned enough to know that it will figure among the most renowned recorded in history. But it is not simply for its glory that it gives me pleasure to regard it; I like to consider it as a sign of things to come, as a guarantee of peace; thus giving to Your Majesty the repose that, at the cost of so much effort, privations and danger, will give his people confidence. I like to look upon it as the last one that you will be obliged to win; it is for this reason that it is dear to me for, as wonderful as it is, I must confess that in my view it would lose more than I could express if Your Majesty felt obliged to march towards new combats and to run the risk of new hazards for which my devotion is so easily alarmed knowing how much Your Majesty disdains them." He was telling the emperor to stop, but it was useless—Napoleon's mind was already elsewhere.

During the discussions leading up to the Treaty of Tilsit, the Prussians, the Austrians and even Talleyrand himself were kept in the dark. Count von Goltz, the Prussian Minister Plenipotentiary, who feared that his country was going to be sacrificed in the Franco/Russian agreement, looked to Talleyrand to save his country. Even Caulaincourt felt that the Minister of Foreign Affairs was entitled to call himself the European Minister of Peace. By the Treaty of Tilsit (7 and 9 July 1807), some of the central Polish provinces were formed into the independent Grand Duchy of Warsaw under the sovereignty of the King of Saxony. It had been promised—but not included in the treaty—that Russia would seize the territories of Moldova and Wallachia (nowadays southern Romania) from the Ottoman Empire. Talleyrand was frustrated by this move since these were exactly the territories he had wanted to construct as a buffer zone between Austria and Russia. Ultimately, the Russian border would creep even further westward.

The terms of the Treaty of Tilsit were conveyed to London with extraordinary rapidity arriving on the night of 21/22 July. Despite a large majority of the Russian aristocracy being pro-British, at Tilsit Alexander I had agreed to join Napoleon's Continental System. The British Foreign Secretary, George Canning, realised that, with almost the entire continent of Europe against the United Kingdom, Napoleon might oblige the fleets of northern Europe to unite against Britain. Indeed,

Napoleon had proposed to the Tsar a great naval combination, of which Denmark and Portugal would also be members. Canning quickly sent a naval squadron to Copenhagen, which captured the entire Danish fleet.

Apart from French soldiers, the camps on the banks of the River Nieman were swarming with French, Prussian and Russian diplomats. This life-style did not suit Talleyrand at all who liked white tablecloths, silverware, skilled chefs, music and carafes full of wine in comfortable surroundings. Another visitor to the camp on 6 July was the unfortunate Queen Louise of Prussia who came to plead for clemency. The beautiful, intelligent and dignified first lady was received harshly by Napoleon, despite Talleyrand's attempts to intervene on her behalf. The meeting with the Queen of Prussia upset him: "I was indignant at everything I saw, everything I heard, but I was obliged to conceal my indignation." As he conducted Queen Louise in tears to her carriage, she turned to him and said: "There are only two people who regret that I came here: it is you and myself." He was no longer able to conceal the fact that his views were not those of the emperor. Even though Napoleon could be considered at the height of his glory, Talleyrand disapproved of the emperor's policies, while his repeated expression of misgivings about the military campaigns had been ignored.

Aged 53, Talleyrand now resigned his position as foreign minister and abandoned Napoleon to his fate. Secretly, he hoped that Napoleon could not survive without him. He was annoyed that Napoleon had kept him in the dark during all the negotiations in Berlin and Tilsit, and yet it was to him that all the diplomats, the Queen of Prussia and even Napoleon's generals referred asking him what was going on and that he should intervene with the emperor to cease his warlike activities. Furthermore, Talleyrand considered that he was not sufficiently rewarded for his efforts and had been humiliated in 1804 by not receiving the most prestigious positions in the French political hierarchy, which had gone to the former consuls Cambacérès and Lebrun.

The only country that had protested strongly about the murder of the Duke d'Enghien in 1804 had been Russia. After Tilsit, Napoleon appointed General Savary as the French ambassador to St Petersburg, the commander of the firing squad at the Château de Vincennes on the night of 21 March 1804. The repugnance of the Russian dowager empress for

Savary is said to have been one of the reasons for his prompt recall, but Napoleon's cynicism is remarkable. Savary was soon replaced by General Caulaincourt, the officer who had unwittingly organized the arrest of the Duke d'Enghien.

Talleyrand was thoroughly fed up with Poland, Russia, Napoleon and living in a bivouac. He was keen to get back to Paris where the rupture between himself and the emperor remained to be consummated. On the return journey, Talleyrand stopped in Dresden to see the amiable Frederick-August, King of Saxony. He stayed in the French ambassador's residence where he was inundated with visitors. The king gave him another million florins.

The principal impression that he brought back from this trip to Eastern Europe was not reassuring. He could see that, if the French Revolution was going to have any long-term impact, France should remain confined within its proper frontiers. From 1807 onwards, Talleyrand worked to thwart Napoleon's ambitions and to hasten his downfall, while at the same time continuing to receive financial benefits from the emperor. While Talleyrand was aware of his own limits, Napoleon running amok with his army conquering territories further and further away was evidently beyond these limits. On 9 August 1807, Talleyrand informed Napoleon of his decision to resign declaring that he was tired and his health was not good, but asked if he might be rewarded with an honorary position in return for his services. Napoleon accepted and made him Vice-Grand Elector in accordance with his policy that the principal state dignitaries could not at the same time be government ministers. Fouché had the last word: "It's the only vice he lacked."

Uncertainty often surrounds the key changes in Talleyrand's life and, in this case, there is contradictory evidence about whether he resigned or whether he was fired. While Talleyrand states that he left the ministry on his own terms, Napoleon tried to seize the initiative. In his memoirs, he wrote that he had heard so many reports of his minister's venality that he withdrew the minister's portfolio. However, at the time of this resignation, there is no official mention of Napoleon's version of events and he continued to consult Talleyrand as often as before. There had already been numerous very good opportunities for Napoleon to dismiss Talleyrand, but he had never done so since he found him irreplaceable and regretted their parting. In private, in talking to Caulaincourt and others, he accused Talleyrand of lying, of political intrigue and money-grabbing, and he detested the company he kept, but he appreciated his charm, his farsightedness, his patriotism and his network of informers. Savary reports that Napoleon was annoyed by Talleyrand's resignation, while during the sleigh ride back to Paris after the Russian debacle in 1812, Caulaincourt wrote that Napoleon remarked: "Why did he want to quit the ministry? He would still be there today if he had wanted." It should also be borne in mind that Talleyrand knew a great deal about Napoleon's money affairs, state secrets, his relationship with Josephine and his epilepsy.

In his memoirs, Talleyrand declares that he served Napoleon "with faithfulness and zeal". It is true that he often undertook tasks that were contrary to his own principles in order to satisfy his master. However, when he claims that he contained "the sovereign's authority within just limits", this is an exaggeration because he was rarely able to halt his master's overpowering will. He was unable to stop Napoleon's intention to annex or invade a territory or his desire to redistribute the map of Europe. While Talleyrand possessed the wisdom, he never succeeded in correcting Napoleon's faults. His place at the Rue du Bac was taken by Jean-Baptiste de Nompère, Count de Champagny, who had earlier carried out fruitless peace negotiations with the British Government. It was probably because of his pliability that Napoleon chose him for the job. In introducing his former staff to the new minister, Talleyrand emphasized the advantages of not acting too hastily: "When you will have conducted the emperor's European affairs for a little while, you will see how important it is never to hurry when sealing or dispatching his orders." He paid an oblique compliment to his staff by describing them as: "faithful, skilful, precise, but, thanks to my care, not at all zealous". Even Napoleon was amused by this accurate observation. He himself said: "You must keep my letters three or four days by your bed before sending them."

In signing his last letters to Napoleon's as his minister on 10 August 1807, Talleyrand promised his eternal gratitude and devotion. We have already had occasion to note that eternity is a very short-lived commodity in politics. As regards Napoleon's comment that he was dismissed for venality, we may note that Talleyrand's salary as Vice-Grand Elector now amounted to 330,000 francs per annum compared to his post as Foreign Minister of 100,000 francs. He received other revenues as Grand Chamberlain, as Prince de Benevento and as a member of the *Legion d'Honneur*. Thus, his income amounted to perhaps half-a-million francs per year but he would lose access to the "sweeteners" on which he depended. Was this sum adequate to support his extravagant way of life?

Uncle Alexandre-Angélique
believed that nepotism was
not a sin

Mme de Staël: Talleyrand's
altruistic friend

Catherine Grand: Talleyrand
was smitten

Dorothea, Duchess of Dino:
a fascinating and elegant
adventuress

Louis XVI: a clumsy, ugly, conservative, indecisive incompetent

Louis XVIII: a clever, hard-hearted man, shackled by no principle

Marie-Antoinette thoroughly detested Talleyrand

Pope Pius VII: imprisoned… to satisfy some "puerile vanity"

Napoleon: the "little corporal"
…more powerful than any
European monarch

Tsar Alexander played against
Talleyrand in Vienna and lost

The Duke of Wellington: "He is
an admirable man."

Lord Castlereagh: as a statesman
and a gentleman, he had no equal

CHAPTER XII
TSAR ALEXANDER

Talleyrand had no further wish to be associated with his master's policies in the belief that they were a curse on the nation. As was his custom, Talleyrand's letter to Napoleon resigning as Minister of Foreign Affairs contained lavish expressions of deference, gratitude and devotion. Meanwhile, in the salons of Paris he could be heard to mutter: "What we are doing on the other side of the Rhine will only last as long as the great man in charge." There was no actual need to betray Napoleon for, evidently, he was set on a path of self-destruction with his empire destined to die with him. Having resigned his post as minister, Charles-Maurice found himself in semi-disgrace and, not enjoying this situation, sought to maintain his contacts with Napoleon in one way or another. An opportunity for reconciliation occurred in September 1807 when Talleyrand was invited to the wedding of Napoleon's youngest brother Jérôme Bonaparte (the King of Westphalia) with Princess Catharina von Württemberg at the Château de Fontainebleau. Despite numerous infidelities, the marriage of Catharina and Jérôme was a happy one, and they remained firmly attached to each other for the remainder of their lives. During the evenings at Fontainebleau Napoleon held long discussions with Talleyrand about how to deal with the Spanish and Portuguese, whose governments had refused to participate in the continental embargo against England. Such consultations must have given the ex-minister great satisfaction, although the emperor's intentions did not. Napoleon was contemplating crossing the Pyrenees with his army to teach the Iberians a lesson: "He is blinded by ambition, anger, pride and the advice of some fools that he listens to," commented Talleyrand, no doubt referring to Hugues Maret, Napoleon's Secretary of State. It was certain that he would not receive any impartial advice from Joachim Murat either who now had his sights set on becoming the next King of Spain—once again, he was to be disappointed. The fact that these discussions took place over several weeks during September and October 1807 suggests that Napoleon could not make up his mind about Spain and Portugal and hesitated between several options.

The Spanish Government had had the greatest difficulty accepting Napoleon's policy requiring all commercial ties with England to be cut. Napoleon still believed that, if he could stop its trade with Spain and Portugal, the United Kingdom would be forced to the negotiating table. The first act was to convince the Spanish Prime Minister Godoy that there already existed a close relationship between France and Spain. In the autumn of 1807, Godoy had entered into secret negotiations with London. Nevertheless, a worried Godoy had sent his envoy Eugenio Izquierdo to France where Talleyrand met him at Fontainebleau to discuss support for Napoleon's plans for seizing Portugal, a country which relied even more heavily upon trade with England. Talleyrand later denied any involvement in establishing a treaty with Spain, saying that negotiations were conducted by General Duroc and signed by Champagny. Then why did he spend so much time with Napoleon at Fontainebleau and why did he later destroy all the documentation? As a result of the discussions with Izquierdo, on 27 October the French Army was given permission to cross Spain on its way to Lisbon and a licence to occupy as much of northern Spain as it desired—Napoleon's secret instruction was to take over the whole Iberian Peninsula. His plan was to be frustrated since, as the French forces approached the city of Lisbon, the Regent of Portugal, his government and the royal court of 15,000 people boarded a fleet of ships and sailed to Brazil. Rio de Janeiro became the capital of the Kingdom of Portugal until 1820 and Brazilian ports were opened to world (principally British) trade. One unforeseen outcome of the French invasion was to persuade the British to send a military expedition to Portugal commanded by the junior general Arthur Wellesley, later known as the Duke of Wellington.

In his memoirs written in 1816, Talleyrand stated that he opposed Napoleon's intervention in Spain "with all my energy", although there is no evidence at the time to suggest that he did anything of the kind. The doubt concerning his role can be attributed to the fact that he had all the correspondence concerning the invasion of Spain along with that concerning the fate of the Duke d'Enghien destroyed in 1814.

Furthermore, Talleyrand was involved in several lucrative financial affairs involving the Spanish Government and its colonies. Contrary to his declared opposition, he is reported by the politician Étienne Pasquier as saying at a dinner at the time that the crown of Spain formed part of the French heritage and Napoleon was the logical inheritor of Louis XIV, who had placed the Bourbons on the Spanish throne. Talleyrand's statement was probably made for public consumption or at least for the benefit of Napoleon's police. Talleyrand, who had recommended moderation after the Battles of Ulm, Austerlitz and Jena, had no faith in Napoleon's plans.

At the beginning of 1808 Napoleon could still be said to be at the summit of his power. Three of his brothers sat upon various European thrones, the Tsar of Russia and the Emperor of Austria were his reluctant allies, while his armies controlled much of the European continent. By crossing the Pyrenees with his army, he now took the fatal step that would ultimately lead to his downfall. The consequences of the Peninsular War, which at first sight appeared to be a minor military skirmish, were to prove terminal.

Another person who did not wish to participate in the Continental System was Pope Pius VII, who had enthroned the emperor in 1804. In the spring of 1799, his predecessor, the aged and frail Pius VI, had been insulted, made prisoner and brought to France, dying in captivity at Valence the following August. He had already been forced to sign away some 100 priceless works of art which were seized and transferred to Paris—Josephine hung some of them on the walls of her house at Malmaison. The new Pope lived in Rome until 1809 when he too had his lands seized by Napoleon who declared the territories of the Papal State were to be annexed to the French Empire. The Pope was imprisoned in the city of Savona in Italy. The only purpose of these actions seemed to be to satisfy some "puerile vanity", as Napoleon's ludicrous justification was that Charlemagne had only transferred these lands temporarily to the Papacy in the Dark Ages. Pius VII retaliated by excommunicating Napoleon.

The troubled country of Spain was ruled by the Bourbon King Charles IV who had married his cousin, María Luisa of Parma. His strong-willed and estimable wife governed the country behind the scenes in company with the thoroughly detested Prime Minister Manuel de Godoy, while the king busied himself with hunting and his hobbies. Economic troubles, rumours about a sexual relationship between the queen and Godoy, and the king's ineptitude caused the monarchy's prestige to collapse. Events began to move quickly in March 1808 when Godoy persuaded the king and queen that they should flee the country, as the Portuguese royal family had already done. On their way to the coast Godoy was captured by a mob. To save Godoy's life, Charles IV abdicated in favour of his 23-year-old son, the Prince de Asturias, the title used for the Spanish heir-apparent. The prince assumed the throne as Ferdinand VII on 19 March, being received as the country's saviour when he rode into Madrid. By this time, Napoleon already had an expeditionary force of 100,000 soldiers in Spain on their way to Portugal and a few days later General Murat entered the city—which lay on the road to Lisbon—releasing Godoy. Charles IV subsequently retracted his abdication saying that it had been obtained under duress and appealed to Napoleon for help. During the discussions held with Talleyrand at Fontainebleau the previous September, Napoleon seemed to favour the idea that France might support the Prince de Asturias/Ferdinand VII rather than Charles IV—but then changed his mind. Through a series of threats and ruses, in May 1808 the emperor lured Charles IV, María Luisa and Ferdinand VII to a "conference" at Bayonne in France—Godoy, rescued from captivity, was also there. With all the contenders in his presence, Napoleon revealed to them that he required the rival kings to abdicate in favour of his elder brother, Joseph Bonaparte, still at that time King of Naples. On 8 May, the throne was formally signed over to Napoleon in exchange for generous pensions for the royal family and guarantees of Spain's territorial and religious integrity. Joseph's reign on the throne of Spain would last two weeks.

Talleyrand was not at Bayonne because, having expressed his reservations to Napoleon about the Spanish enterprise and no longer a member of the government, he had been kept at a distance. Charles IV, María Luisa and Godoy were subsequently held captive at various places in France before moving in 1812 to Rome. Ferdinand, his younger brother Charles and uncle Antonio were confined for several years at Talleyrand's château at Valençay. Napoleon appeared to have achieved his every objective, while the Prince de Benevento was even overheard by Pasquier declaring his joy at being selected as the chosen jailer for the Spanish princes. Once again, these expressions can only have been for the benefit of the emperor's informers, since it was widely believed that Napoleon's choice of Valençay was one of his pranks repaying Talleyrand for his lack of enthusiasm for the Spanish adventure. The more Talleyrand was humiliated, the more he publicly congratulated Napoleon for "the happy outcome" of successfully springing a monstrous trap on the Spanish royal family. It is impossible that one of the authors of the Declaration of the Rights of Man should be sincere when expressing such sentiments. To his inner circle, he described the trap at Bayonne as "as vile, cheating trickery"—the work of a Corsican bandit rather than a head of state. His obsequious letter to Napoleon, nevertheless, included a veiled warning: "Your Majesty would allow me to hope that everything will be arranged in Bayonne and he will not be obliged to go beyond the frontiers of France, which I desire with all my heart." Both Talleyrand and the French ambassador to Madrid, François de Beauharnais, favoured a marriage between a Spanish Bourbon prince and a princess of the Bonaparte family as a way out of the situation confronting Franco/Spanish relations.

A successful battle conducted by General Bessières ensued at Medina de Rioseco. However, the news from Spain was not all good, with growing opposition among the population and the capitulation of the French General Dupont at the Battle of Bailén in July 1808. When he next met Napoleon at Nantes in the following month, Talleyrand tells us in his memoirs that there was a violent scene because he stated his opposition to the morality and legality of the Spanish enterprise. Once again, other eye-witnesses do not corroborate this version stating that he appeared to be enthusiastically in favour of continuing the occupation. What was the point of presenting this façade of unqualified support for the emperor? Since he was in secret contact with the governments of Austria, Russia and Prussia, it was necessary to dispel any suspicion of disloyalty. It worked marvellously! The blinkers fell from Napoleon's eyes only during the voyage to captivity in Saint Helena in 1815.

However, Talleyrand did inform Napoleon that he had lost more prestige than he had gained by the seizure of the Spanish Royal family at

Bayonne. When Napoleon asked him to explain himself, he is supposed to have made the following statement: "If a gentleman makes mistakes, keeps mistresses, treats his wife and his friends badly, he will be blamed no doubt, but if he is rich, powerful and intelligent, society will forgive him. But if that same man cheats at cards, he will immediately be banished from decent society and never forgiven." At Bayonne, Napoleon had deceived the Spanish royal family and although the crumbling façade of his regime would endure for another six years, his fate was sealed. He had treated the Spanish Bourbons with complete contempt and no-one could be in any doubt about the fate he reserved for the other rulers of Europe, be they Austrian, Prussian, Russian or English.

It can be recalled that Napoleon had participated financially in the purchase of the Château de Valençay, so Talleyrand could not seriously object if the emperor wished him to accommodate the three Spanish princes and their retinue. Napoleon gave precise instructions about the manner of their reception and how they were to be entertained during their enforced stay. He thought of everything: "If the Prince des Asturias takes an interest in any pretty woman, one we are sure of, this does not present a problem because we would have an extra way of keeping an eye on him." Then, as an afterthought: "You could bring Mme de Talleyrand with four or five women." There can be little doubt that in assigning the three Spanish prisoners to Valençay, Napoleon's intention was to belittle Talleyrand for his lack of enthusiasm for the Spanish adventure. Not betraying his true state of mind, Talleyrand thanked Napoleon profusely for the great honour of being chosen to guard the three Spanish royals. He wrote from Paris that Mme de Talleyrand had already left to make preparations: "The château is plentifully supplied with cooks, linen, and every kind of tableware. The princes will enjoy there every pleasure according to the season [...] I will give them mass every day, a park for walking, a forest with alleyways, but there is very little game, horses, abundant meals and music. There is no theatre and it would be difficult to find actors. There will, however, be enough young people enabling the princes to dance." A troop of mounted police would be stationed at various key points to carry out discreet supervision of the château's grounds.

Everything went well. At last, Mme de Talleyrand had an absorbing occupation and assumed her functions with enthusiasm. The three prisoners arrived at Valençay on 18 May 1808 in their ancient carriage plated with gold leaf, together with several dozen chamberlains, chaplains and servants. The Spanish princes were also accompanied by their equerry, José Miguel de Carvajal Vargas y Manrique de Lara, the Duke de San Carlos. Since their marriage, Talleyrand had lost all interest in his wife and very soon a passion developed between the Princess de Benevento and San Carlos. The prisoners seemed to have no interest in anything except looking after a few pot plants within their chambers and regular religious services. Talleyrand encouraged all the staff working at the château to participate in these ceremonies, including the guards and local policemen. Since Napoleon had given no further orders, during the summer of 1808, the prison custodian and his captives languished in exile lost in the Berry countryside.

While suffering this isolation in frustration, Talleyrand received some dreadful news. His favourite nephew, Louis de Périgord, died of typhoid fever in Berlin on his way back from the Battle of Friedland. He had placed in Louis all his hopes for the future of the family and had named him as his heir. Those who knew Louis had agreed on his qualities: a loyal, brave officer, a gentleman, a flawless friend. This news was particularly sad since his younger brother Edmond did not share the same qualities, although he will play a significant role in Talleyrand's story. Upon the Prince's return to Paris, his friends were struck by the evident grief of their impassive friend.

Finally, in mid-August 1808, Talleyrand was summoned to a meeting with the emperor in Nantes. Fourteen months had elapsed since Tsar Alexander I and Napoleon had met each other on a raft in the middle of the River Nieman at Tilsit. The two emperors had decided to meet again at an international congress in the Principality of Erfurt, one of Napoleon's domains in Germany. Given their disagreement over the invasion of Spain, Talleyrand was surprised when the emperor invited him to Erfurt. His three Spanish captives were so disappointed to see him leave that they presented him with their most precious possessions—their Spanish prayer books. After the nasty surprise that Napoleon had sprung on them in Bayonne, the prisoners were grateful for their luxurious accommodation under the friendly protection of their aristocratic host.

They may have been deprived of their liberty but certainly not of their dignity. During their six-year stay at Valençay, the château was enlarged with the construction of a theatre and extensive stables. In 1814, Ferdinand VII would reign once more over the Kingdom of Spain, although his mother and father lived until 1818.

Talleyrand reached Erfurt first in order to prepare for Napoleon's arrival, finding a comfortable mansion for himself only a stone's throw from the tsar's residence. The events of Erfurt were so far-reaching that he would not return to Valençay until 1816—eight years later—by which time his prisoners had returned to Madrid. The affair between San Carlos and the Princess de Benevento would continue through various vicissitudes until the former's death twenty years hence. Even the Prince de Benevento came to appreciate the many fine qualities of San Carlos.

The Erfurt Conference brought together Alexander I of Russia and Napoleon I of France; the grand absentee was the Emperor of Austria, Francis I, who had no doubt that, once Napoleon had finished his military manoeuvres in Spain, he would turn his attention to dismembering Austria. Metternich, the Austrian ambassador to France, concluded that Austria should not hesitate to rearm with haste and Talleyrand encouraged him in this belief. Despite Talleyrand's long-term policy of an alliance with Austria, Napoleon was now more interested in a treaty with Russia. Talleyrand kept Metternich up to date with any information that concerned his country but was disappointed that there was no representative of Austria present at the conference table in Erfurt. Talleyrand's latest idea in the art of conciliation was that Napoleon and Francis I should each award their opposite number and senior dignitaries the highest national awards—for France, the *Légion d'Honneur*; for Austria, the Golden Fleece. This made Metternich smile because candidates for the Golden Fleece had to prove that they had at least 500 years of nobility: "You are therefore the only suitable candidate," he informed Talleyrand. The subject was quietly dropped.

Napoleon urged Talleyrand to see the tsar as often as possible and gave him *carte blanche* to explain that an alliance between France and Russia would be providential for Europe as a whole. Once again, Napoleon did not know that Talleyrand had been in secret correspondence with the tsar since 1801, having received a portrait framed in diamonds and a charming personal letter from him. Furthermore, Caulaincourt, Napoleon's ambassador to St Petersburg, was devoted to both the tsar and Talleyrand, telling each of them how wonderful the other was. Because of this, the tsar was also aware of the evolution in Talleyrand's thinking since 1804 when he had begun to distance himself from the emperor's belligerent policies. When Napoleon spoke directly to Alexander, there was a danger that he would overwhelm him for the tsar was weak and impulsive, while the emperor was forceful, cunning and charming when necessary. Before tackling the small print of the treaty, Napoleon intended to spend a few days impressing the tsar by surrounding himself with ruling German princes who came to pay him homage: "Before beginning, I want the tsar to be blinded by the display of my power; there is no negotiation where this does not make matters easier." However, once Talleyrand entered the equation, Napoleon's powers of persuasion were contaminated. The Prince de Benevento was in secret correspondence with Caulaincourt, on friendly terms with the tsar and enjoyed the confidence of Metternich.

In 1792, Armand de Caulaincourt, from an ancient noble family, had been serving as a captain in the French Army when the revolutionary authorities became suspicious of his noble lineage. He volunteered to serve in the *Garde Nationale* in Paris as a common soldier. While on his way to join his regiment, he was denounced and thrown into prison but escaped, returned to serve the army and, in three years, regained his previous officer rank. As an honourable, modest and respectful army officer, he was eternally ashamed about the role he had played in the arrest and execution of the Duke d'Enghien. In 1808, Caulaincourt exchanged letters with the tsar explaining that he had unwittingly played only a minor role in the arrest of the duke; the tsar accepted his innocence. He lost his idealism for Napoleon and, thereafter, questioned the emperor's policies, telling him precisely what he felt at every opportunity—Napoleon tolerated his extraordinary integrity and frankness. Fluent in Russian, after he was appointed ambassador to St Petersburg in 1807, he lived a life of considerable luxury in the Volkonsky Palace in Saint Petersburg. Nevertheless, despite everything, he was a loyal equerry to the emperor and would remain responsible for his security until the end of his regime. Caulaincourt's situation has been described as that of an upright soldier thrown, against his wishes, into the world of diplomacy, where he was taken advantage of by Talleyrand, Napoleon and the tsar. His own verdict on Napoleon was: "The emperor paid no heed to the conscience and honour of those he employed."

Caulaincourt and Talleyrand became firm friends, both wishing for peace. Caulaincourt's devotion to Talleyrand was all the greater because his mistress was the tall, graceful and intelligent Mme Adrienne de Canisy. Her mother, father and brothers had all died on the guillotine and she had been married to her father's brother at the age of 13, subsequently bearing two children by him. Later, she divorced her uncle but Napoleon, who loved to torment and humiliate those around him, opposed her marriage to Caulaincourt because he still craved respectability at his court, thus guaranteeing the enmity of the divorced Mme de Canisy. Talleyrand was familiar with her because they both frequented the salon of Mme de Laval on the Faubourg Saint-Germain, the principal source of slanderous epigrams against the emperor. The ex-minister promised to support Caulaincourt's marriage petition with Napoleon and, when writing to Caulaincourt in Russia, always included news about the doings of Mme de Canisy. His letters, full of flattery for Caulaincourt, never failed to express gushing admiration and commitment to Napoleon— they were probably intercepted and read by the police. Furthermore, Caulaincourt found employment at his embassy for Talleyrand's nephew, Edmond de Périgord. Thus, in dealing with the tsar and his ambassador to Paris, Count Tolstoy, Talleyrand could always count upon the good offices of Caulaincourt. The estimable Caulaincourt would eventually marry Mme de Canisy in May 1814, immediately after the fall of Napoleon. Despite everything that took place at Erfurt, it is remarkable to note that the Caulaincourt remained completely faithful to Napoleon's person until the very end.

Napoleon's main long-term objective at Erfurt was the destruction of the United Kingdom, which, in his mind, would be achieved by forcing Spain and Portugal to sever their commercial links with the British. After the battles of Ulm, Austerlitz and Jena, Talleyrand had told Napoleon to be magnanimous towards Austria and Prussia in order to encourage them to be his allies. He had not listened and now found himself, with his best troops tied up in the Iberian Peninsula, fearing that these two central European countries might seize the opportunity to turn against him. The purpose of the Erfurt meeting was therefore, in the event of Austria declaring war on France, that Russia would cover Napoleon's rear by fighting on France's side. Talleyrand, meanwhile, was determined that the Russians would give no such assurance. Only Talleyrand had an overall view of affairs. Caulaincourt, as ambassador to St. Petersburg, endeavoured to maintain the terms of the Treaty of Tilsit. Although he was and would remain one of Napoleon's most trusted aides, Caulaincourt's friendship with Talleyrand meant that he kept nothing from him, particularly the conversations between Napoleon and the tsar during which he was present. Napoleon did not know this.

While keeping Austria away from the conference table, Napoleon was aware that his confidence in his supposed future ally, the 31-year-old tsar, was not total. His policy, therefore, was to keep Austria and Russia separated and to "con" the tsar into signing a treaty of friendship whereby France took all while Russia was fobbed off with a series of empty promises concerning Turkish territory. Napoleon could then concentrate all of his attention and forces on subduing Spain and Portugal in order that they would cease trading with England. Alexander's weak point was that he was determined to get his hands on some of the most tempting parts of the Ottoman Empire, for instance, the Bosporus and the Dardanelles. Meanwhile, it was already clear that Napoleon's Continental System was doing terrible damage to the European economies, Russia among them.

In taking Talleyrand with him to Erfurt, Napoleon made a great mistake. He believed that his former minister was the man he needed more than the actual Minister of Foreign Affairs. Although Champagny was present at Erfurt, he did not play a significant role in proceedings. Napoleon knew that Talleyrand was also opposed to an alliance with Russia but he believed that he was himself the mastermind at the conference table and Talleyrand was a compliant tool—on this point he was seriously mistaken. Metternich wrote in September 1808: "Men like M. de Talleyrand are like sharp instruments with which it is dangerous to play."

Napoleon asked Talleyrand to draft a discussion document for an alliance with Russia. He explained roughly what he wanted: take everything, give nothing. Napoleon was pleased with Talleyrand's draft which set out "principles" rather than "concessions": "Principles are good, they commit nothing." However, "commit nothing" applied to both sides. Once again, Alexander was promised Moldova and Wallachia, which would pose a threat to Austria. Napoleon liked to threaten nations and people: "They only obey when they are worried." Nevertheless, Talleyrand's draft treaty lacked the requirement that would oblige Russia to be France's ally against Austria in any future war, an article that had not been included because Talleyrand did not like it. "How can you have forgotten that?" asked Napoleon. "Are you still pro-Austrian?" Indeed, he was more sympathetic to Austria than to Russia.

When Talleyrand arrived in Erfurt on 24 September 1808, the first person he met was Caulaincourt, who was to play a major role in the "Erfurt Affair". Talleyrand did not admire a large number of people, but Caulaincourt was definitely one of them. They both agreed that Napoleon's tyranny had become harmful for Europe and that a way must be found for containing it. While Napoleon wanted Russia to be his ally against Austria, Talleyrand was telling both of these countries that, if they were to survive, they must form an alliance.

The handsome Klemens von Metternich, appointed Austrian minister to France in 1806, would remain at the centre of European diplomacy for more than four decades—until 1848. In a memorable event at Napoleon's thirty-ninth birthday celebrations in August 1808, he had argued with Napoleon over the increasingly obvious preparations for war against Austria, with the result that Napoleon refused to invite him to the Congress of Erfurt. Nonetheless, Talleyrand kept Metternich informed of events and, particularly, the fact that Alexander had rejected Napoleon's request to place his troops along the Austrian border. Metternich was also allowed to view certain confidential documents, while Talleyrand advised the government in Vienna about how Austria could defend itself. Despite his successful marriage to Countess Eleanore von Kaunitz, Metternich was renowned for his love affairs with numerous beautiful, intelligent and aristocratic women, including Caroline Murat, Dorothea Liéven, the Princess Bagration and Wilhelmine von Sagan.

There were, in fact, two matters that had to be discussed between the

French and the Russians at the Congress of Erfurt: a treaty of alliance and a matrimonial affair. Because she was unlikely to bear any more children, the emperor intended to repudiate Josephine, so Talleyrand and Caulaincourt were charged with approaching the tsar to see whether he would accept for Napoleon to marry one of his young sisters. The successful signing of an alliance with the Russians would seriously upset Talleyrand's peace plans, so he undertook his own personal negotiations to undermine those of Napoleon. This was the outcome of the numerous discussions that Talleyrand held with the tsar—in conformity with Napoleon's instructions but not corresponding to his intentions. Talleyrand did everything in his power to gain the tsar's confidence and to fan his suspicions about Napoleon's motives. The tsar's mother was already apprehensive that Napoleon would kidnap her son, as had happened to the Spanish Royal Family at Bayonne. While Napoleon would have viewed the content of these discussions as treason, was it really treason to promote the national well-being above that of a tyrant whose cause was no longer that of France?

When Napoleon arrived at Erfurt on 27 September, the German princes waiting to see him were in a state of fawning apprehension. One evening, at the stylish salon hosted by the Princess von Thurn und Taxis, the sister of the Prussian Queen, Talleyrand was present surrounded by a circle of countesses and duchesses when the tsar walked in unannounced and asked for a cup of tea. They had previously met briefly at Tilsit but the tsar did not know beforehand that Talleyrand would be present at Erfurt. He murmured in Talleyrand's ear: "We will meet again"—which is exactly what Napoleon wanted. Looking fixedly at Talleyrand, he told the Princess that he would come to her apartment every evening at the same hour. The days were devoted to negotiations, festivals, military displays, receptions and the evenings to the theatre, but at two-thirty each morning Talleyrand and the tsar (often accompanied by Caulaincourt) sat down together to talk. Talleyrand explained to the tsar: "It is up to you to save Europe and you will only do so by standing up to Napoleon." Believing that he represented the true feelings of the French population, Talleyrand told him: "The Rhine, the Alps and the Pyrenees are the conquests of France; the remainder is the conquest of the emperor and France doesn't care about it." Alexander's eyes were opened to the fact that he had every interest in making overtures to Austria, as indeed Austria had to reciprocate. Metternich concluded: "Finally, Europe can only be saved by the closest union between Austria and Russia."

Talleyrand would meet Napoleon every morning, where the emperor would explain to him what he intended to do about the Ottoman Empire, the conduct of the campaign in Spain and what he was going to say to Tsar Alexander. Every night, Talleyrand would meet the tsar at the salon of the Princess von Thurn und Taxis and repeat to him the most interesting parts of his conversations with Napoleon. Talleyrand, Caulaincourt and the tsar would then discuss together the attitude that the latter should adopt in the following day's discussions with Napoleon. Talleyrand said about these late-night discussions: "As soon as I opened my mouth, he understood me and he understood me exactly as I wanted to be understood." If Alexander had difficulty remembering the most important points, the princess would write them down and the tsar would leave with her notes. The two men had such confidence in each other that one evening Alexander took the draft of the final treaty proposed by Napoleon out of his pocket and showed it to Talleyrand. Napoleon had copied Talleyrand's draft treaty in his own handwriting with two added paragraphs: one described under what circumstances Russia would declare war against Austria; and the other required the Russians to move their army up to the Austrian border immediately. The former Bishop of Autun indicated to Alexander the text's deliberate ambiguities, then persuaded him to dilute certain phrases to render them meaningless. Talleyrand explained exactly how to proceed so that the proposed treaty would lose all of its significance and he observed with satisfaction that the tsar wrote down what he was saying. The next day, Alexander showed Talleyrand the arguments he intended to adopt and said: "You will recognize yourself at certain points." Of the two emperors at Erfurt, Talleyrand had made one his dupe and the other his agent.

Although there was no place for Austria at the discussion table, Napoleon accepted that a representative, Baron de Vincent, should attend from Vienna as an observer. Talleyrand asked Dalberg to keep Vincent informed of everything that was going on, to the point that the Austrian position was better defended by Talleyrand than by the Austrians themselves. Caulaincourt, Tolstoy, Talleyrand and the Princess von

Thurn und Taxis all informed the tsar that Francis I was not his enemy and was ready to stand with him against Napoleon. Vincent himself confirmed this position. Napoleon, believing he had already manoeuvred the tsar into just the position he wanted, was flabbergasted to discover the unyielding attitude of his adversary. The tsar was now clearly aware of the weakness of Napoleon's position with his forces being frittered away in Spain and his regime in Paris no more than a hollow façade. After the congress, Napoleon said to Talleyrand: "I made no progress at all!" for he failed to obtain from Alexander the alliance he sought against Austria. Talleyrand knew just what to say: "I believe that Your Majesty has achieved a great deal since he arrived, because the Emperor Alexander is completely under your spell." "If you believe that," replied Napoleon, "he has fooled you. If he likes me, why has he not signed?" Talleyrand was ready with more excuses: "He feels more committed to you by his words and his esteem than by treaties." "These are just futile remarks," concluded Napoleon impatiently. Talleyrand promised to redouble his efforts on the noble task of persuading the tsar that an alliance with Napoleon was in his best interests. The next time they met, Alexander told Talleyrand that he had decided to write to Francis I of Austria with a view to establishing further contact. At Erfurt, Napoleon failed to reach his objectives but then proceeded to act as if he had indeed achieved them.

In Napoleon's mind the culminating point of the negotiations would be obtaining the hand of the tsar's sister, the Grand Duchess Catherine, in marriage. When Caulaincourt first raised the subject with Alexander, the tsar did not seem opposed to the suggestion but explained that his sisters were entirely under the control of their mother, Dowager Empress Maria Feodorovna. Talleyrand, on the other hand, thought it was a very bad idea for there to be a further and long-term connection between France and Russia, almost certainly to be exploited in France's favour. He spoke to the tsar on this subject, who very soon accepted Talleyrand's point of view. In order that Napoleon should not lose face, Caulaincourt was instructed that there would never be a refusal to his proposal but there would never be a positive answer either. Since the lady in question was only 14 years old, the tsar made vague but obliging noises and asked Napoleon to wait. Less than a year later, she married her cousin Duke

George von Oldenburg, whose homeland lay on the North Sea coast of Germany. On 22 January 1811, Oldenburg was annexed by Napoleon—a great insult to the Russians.

At Erfurt, the two emperors separated on 14 October 1808 with warm embraces. They signed a document which was not really a treaty and did not bind anybody to do anything in particular. Russia was promised possession of Moldova and Wallachia as soon as negotiations were opened with England—the possession and the negotiations were both equally unlikely. All the hopes that Napoleon had placed on this congress had been rendered inoperable by Talleyrand, but he was not alone, for several others were working for peace, such as the Dalbergs and Caulaincourt. Alexander's ambassador in Paris, Count Tolstoy, had also discovered that two of Napoleon's generals, Berthier and Lannes, were ready to abandon their beloved master's policies. It is remarkable that a man so suspicious of betrayal and who in other circumstances was aware of every nuance of what was going on behind his back, should have been completely deceived, so completely that...

...four years later, Napoleon was hurrying back to Paris in an enclosed sleigh following his catastrophic retreat from Moscow. Wrapped in furs and blankets, he tried to explain to himself what had gone wrong at Erfurt. His travelling companion was none other than Armand de Caulaincourt, who wrote down his words at the end of each stage of the journey. Napoleon bitterly regretted not listening to Talleyrand's advice, but did not suspect him of betrayal. Suddenly, Napoleon found the culprit for the "treason" at Erfurt; he was convinced that it was General Jean Lannes, who had been sent on ahead to escort the tsar to the rendez-vous. This was not really fair to Lannes who, despite his outspoken opinions and wavering loyalty, had served the emperor with great courage up to this point. Caulaincourt made no attempt to enlighten Napoleon of the wrongdoer's true identity. By this time, Lannes had died of wounds received in battle but Talleyrand was still up to his usual tricks.

If the former Bishop of Autun had sabotaged the meeting in Erfurt, he did not overlook his own interests. Since the death of his favourite nephew Louis, Talleyrand had begun to think about the future of his surviving nephew Edmond de Périgord, the youngest son of his brother

Archambaud. Assuming the role of head of the family, the Prince de Benevento sought a profitable marriage for Edmond. In France, Napoleon controlled who should marry wealthy heiresses, often reserving them as a reward for his most loyal officers. The prefects of departments were required to inform the emperor about girls of marriageable age who possessed large fortunes. Edmond was not one of Napoleon's aides-de-camp and Talleyrand was no longer Napoleon's minister, so it was unlikely that they would benefit from this largesse. Accordingly, Talleyrand prospected Europe in the search for a foreign heiress of marriageable age.

Nearly thirty years earlier, the 55-year-old Duke von Courland, Peter von Biron, had married the 18-year-old Anna Dorothea von Medem. The Duchess von Courland gave birth to four daughters who each grew up to be beautiful, marrying into European aristocracy and detesting Napoleon. In 1795, the region of Courland in Latvia had fallen under Russian stewardship, with the tsar compensating the duke and duchess handsomely for the loss of their independence. The duchess eventually possessed one of the greatest fortunes in Europe, being the owner of estates in Courland, the Duchy of Sagan (Poland) and Bohemia, as well as the Courland Palace on the Unter den Linden in Berlin. The family estate was at the Château of Sagan, but the duchess preferred to live at her own private residence of Löbichau in what is now Thuringia, Germany, where she invited poets, philosophers, relatives and friends to stay.

The Duchess von Courland did not devote a great deal of attention to her daughters' upbringing. Her youngest daughter Dorothea, born in 1793, had been educated by a conscientious German governess, Regina Hoffmann, and an excellent Italian priest called Scipione Piattoli, the nearest thing to a father figure she ever had. Piattoli was great friends with Prince Adam Czartorisky, a nobleman profoundly involved in the intricacies of Polish politics. Even though the handsome prince was 40 years old and she had never met him, the teenage Dorothea had decided that she was going to marry him. As for Hoffman and Piattoli, Dorothea said of them: "They had nothing in common except a passionate affection for me." As young people, both of her teachers had taken an interest in religion and had subsequently abandoned it, with the result that Dorothea received no religious education at all.

In his memoirs, Talleyrand gives the impression that discovering the 15-year-old Dorothea von Biron was a remarkable stroke of luck but, in reality, Emmerich Dalberg and the Polish nobleman Alexander Batowski had been instructed to help him identify a suitable heiress. During the winter of 1807, which he spent in Warsaw, Talleyrand had employed Batowski and had learned to trust him. The sullen Batowski had once been the Duchess von Courland's lover and was, indeed, the biological father of her youngest daughter Dorothea, sometimes called Mlle Batowska. Although officially recognized as the Duke of Courland's daughter, the serious Dorothea actually lived with her real father Batowski at Tannenfeld Castle, situated in the middle of a forest near Löbichau. In 1804, the court of the itinerant French King Louis XVIII had been located at Mittau in Latvia and both the 11-year-old Dorothea and Mlle Hoffmann were often invited to the royal residence, where the child would sometimes sit on the future monarch's knee. It was even contemplated that she would one day make a suitable wife for the king's nephew, the Duke de Berry, but fortuitously the royal court moved to Sweden before the matter could be pursued. Another person who she met during her childhood was the young Baron de Vitrolles, who we will encounter again during the events of 1814.

The 21-year-old Edmond de Périgord, meanwhile, was a captain in the French Army. While appreciated by his colleagues, he had a weakness for women, horses and gambling, where he lost huge amounts of money. Of his mother's immense fortune, there remained very little. His father, the obscure Archambaud, was also a keen gambler and had been definitively side-lined by Napoleon. In fact, there was not a lot to be said in favour of either Archambaud or his son Edmond.

During the meeting in Erfurt and as part of the sensitive negotiations concerning the possible marriage of Napoleon with the tsar's sister Catherine, Talleyrand slipped in a second request that his nephew Edmond should be allowed to marry Dorothea von Biron, one of the tsar's subjects. This proposition had far greater success than Napoleon's and the grateful tsar quickly rewarded Talleyrand with his assent. Once he had the tsar's approval, Talleyrand spoke to Napoleon about it, who would be flattered about this link to one of Europe's noblest families and saw no reason to object to Alexander's decision. Two days after the Erfurt conference terminated, on the evening of 16 October 1808, the Duchess von Courland received four visitors at her residence in Löbichau: Tsar Alexander, Prince Alexander Troubetzkoy, General Caulaincourt and Captain Edmond de Périgord. The Duchess von Courland was attended that evening by her two eldest daughters Wilhelmine and Pauline, and she had also managed to extract Dorothea from her father's residence in the forest. A meal took place in a reserved silence during which Dorothea did not appear to notice the young French officer sitting at the end of the table until Caulaincourt started to describe his virtues. The tsar and the Duchess von Courland withdrew to another room in order that he could advise her of what had already been decided at Erfurt. She was perfectly happy, even enthusiastic, that her daughter would marry Talleyrand's nephew and reside in Paris. She was anxious to get her youngest daughter off her hands and had ambitions herself to live in the French capital.

All that remained was to obtain the consent of Dorothea. The Duchess made it clear to the tsar that she had very little influence with her strong-willed daughter, who was consumed with anti-French sentiments. Dorothea considered herself to be a Prussian and hated the humiliation that her country had suffered at Napoleon's hands. Dorothea was intelligent, self-confident and solitary, waiflike, with black hair and dark violet-coloured eyes. Alexander swept aside any objections, saying that he had given his word that Dorothea would marry Edmond de Périgord and that he could not suffer a refusal. The Duchess curtseyed and shortly afterwards the tsar and his retinue departed. Dorothea left immediately for a stay of several weeks in Berlin not expressing the slightest interest in her French husband-to-be. Talleyrand recruited his brother Archambaud, Batowski and even his own mother to keep the marriage prospects alive—to no avail. By late-December 1808 there was no progress, so Talleyrand, having little confidence in his nephew's chances of success, asked if the tsar might intervene once more by making his wishes quite plain. Alexander wrote to the Duchess von Courland on 12 January 1809 stating that he wished Dorothea von Biron to marry Edmond de Périgord. On 3 February, Dorothea came to Löbichau for her mother's birthday. On the way she visited her old teacher Piattoli, a dying man, who had been instructed by Batowski to tell her to forget all about Prince Czartorisky. Later, in the presence of

Batowski, Dorothea was shown the tsar's letter and understood that she had no choice. There was also a charming letter from Talleyrand, carefully written and employing the most flattering terms for both Edmond and Dorothea. Edmond was a handsome and agreeable young man, but with neither a strong personality nor great intelligence. Finally, the Duchess brought the two young people face to face and left them alone. Dorothea spoke first: "I must tell you myself what you probably know already, it's that I give way to my mother's wishes, not with actual repugnance, but with complete indifference towards you." Edmond's thoughts were not very different: "Good Lord! I find that perfectly natural. In any case, me too, I am marrying only because my uncle wishes it, for at my age one likes to be free." The only point they had in common was that they had no desire to get married to each other.

The Périgord family would now benefit from one of the most colossal fortunes in Europe. Talleyrand assured the mother that her daughter would be surrounded by love and attention, while congratulating the tsar on his successful intervention. Talleyrand's letter to Alexander might be intercepted by Napoleon's police, so it contained wide-ranging compliments and declarations of fidelity to Napoleon— you cannot be too careful—but said nothing about a political alliance between France and Russia. When Dorothea came to Paris after the wedding, her mother accompanied her; would the Duchess von Courland not make an ideal and inconspicuous channel for communicating with the tsar? From the moment the Duchess arrived, an almost daily correspondence was initiated between her and Talleyrand: at first, friendly, then affectionate and finally extremely tender.

The marriage between Edmond de Périgord and Dorothea von Biron took place in Frankfurt on 21 and 22 April 1809, with Talleyrand's friend Prince-Primate Karl Theodor von Dalberg officiating according to the Catholic rites. The very Protestant Prussian Royal Family and Berlin society were outraged, so that none of Dorothea's elder sisters attended the wedding. The young couple came to live with the Prince de Benevento at his residence in Paris where Edmond could now begin his second career as a gambler and rake. This is how the astute Dorothea entered Talleyrand's existence. Although he had never met the Duchess von Courland or her daughter Dorothea before the wedding, they will both play a central role in the last decades of his life.

CHAPTER XIII
TREASON

In 1808, French prisons were crammed with political detainees and hostages, while the countryside was populated with widows and orphans. Even those fathers and husbands who had completed their military service were re-conscripted by law back into the army. It is estimated that a further 300,000 young men were hiding in the forests of France in order to avoid doing military service, for public opinion accepted that draft-dodging was a legitimate way of expressing a lack of confidence in Napoleon's regime. Flying columns scoured the countryside in search of these fugitives, persecuting members of their families and even demolishing their homes if they did not cooperate. Aimée de Coigny tells us that it was a calamity to see the fields of ripe wheat with no-one to harvest them but old men and children. Village dances consisted uniquely of women, since there were no craftsmen or labourers. The rural population was taxed into a state of poverty and foreign trade paralyzed. At the same time, the armies of foreign powers counted a large number of French soldiers.

Napoleon had reached the conclusion that the notorious Germaine de Staël was a meddlesome nuisance whom he could well do without. He considered her as the most dangerous obstacle to his ambitions and was prepared to brush aside anyone who stood in his way. He sent her friend Joseph Bonaparte to let her know that the emperor would have no objection if she left her home in Switzerland for foreign parts, providing her with letters of recommendation. She wrote in desperation: "I was condemned to leave two countries, Switzerland and France, as a criminal on the orders of a man who is less French than me... The whole Earth is subject to him." By exiling her, Napoleon had inadvertently bestowed on her fame on a European scale. Contrary to his expectations, "that blasted woman" was received in Germany and Austria with great honours like a head of state. For years afterwards, the Viennese would refer to 1808 as the year of Mme de Staël's visit. Although she was banished, exile became a powerful weapon for she became "the conscience of Europe", more celebrated than any other European personality and continued to goad Napoleon, humiliating him with her writings. Talleyrand and Mme de Staël had nothing to do with each other anymore, but he must have been aware of her internationally accepted star status. She represented a relentless threat to Napoleon since the books she wrote demonstrated the fragility of military conquest.

As Emperor of the French, Napoleon should have asked the Senate—the people's representatives—to vote on taxation, to examine how the revenue was spent and to ensure that the people benefited from freedom of conscience. On the contrary, he had taxed the people simply to satisfy his own whims and the population was oppressed in both its thoughts and its deeds. The national industry had become war, to the detriment of business, society and education. The country was equipped with an army so powerful that the national resources were exhausted, the dead bodies of its soldiers could be found scattered across European battlefields and France was surrounded by enemies seeking revenge. Therefore, according to the right-wing intelligentsia, the emperor had broken the terms of the contract on which his authority was founded and he should be declared an outlaw. The proposed solution was to pronounce the country a constitutional monarchy with the adoption of a document stating clearly the rights of the people and those of the ruler, and to invite the brother of Louis XVI to assume the throne.

Talleyrand was aware that his personal sentiments about Napoleon, evolving since 1804, were now paralleled by public opinion. As one who believed that the people's happiness depended upon wealth generated by trade during peacetime, how could he not be disturbed by the reckless invasions and annexations of Napoleon's imperial rule? He saw France as bounded by the Atlantic Ocean, the Channel, the Rhine, the Alps, the Jura, the Mediterranean and the Pyrenees, a country that was the birthplace of some of the greatest names in science, art and industry, a country governed by tradition, wisdom and respect for the law. He felt called upon to assume the dangerous duty of starting to dismantle the regime that was leading France to chaos—a vocation also known as treason.

In 1809, Talleyrand was 55 years old. He sold the Hôtel Créqui on the Rue d'Anjou and purchased the Hôtel de Monaco on the Rue de Varenne—nowadays this building is known as the Hôtel Matignon, the French Prime Minister's residence. Napoleon had ordered his Vice-Grand Elector to entertain on a grand scale by holding a dinner four times a week for thirty-six guests chosen by himself from the ranks of members of parliament, state councillors and ministers. It was not entirely clear if Talleyrand was supposed to be spying on his guests or if these faithful servants were expected to keep an eye on him. If Napoleon could have read the secret of Talleyrand's soul, there was the risk that he would teach them lessons in conspiracy and betrayal, but Talleyrand was too cautious to venture into such waters in public. He did, however, remark to Napoleon that the state's legislative body was deprived of any say in the nation's affairs and this was certainly a source of frustration to its members.

Meanwhile, hardly had he returned from Erfurt than Napoleon left for Spain, probably thinking that his mere presence would terrify the Spanish people into submission. Talleyrand continued to send letters to Napoleon gushing with admiration and encouraging him to reach the final victory which could not be far away. He was perfectly aware, of course, that the Spanish affair was running into trouble and the people were ferociously resisting the French troops stationed in their country. Napoleon had transferred the bulk of his troops and his best generals from Germany to Spain, leaving Austria to rearm unhindered. Back in Paris and speaking an entirely different language, Talleyrand was conspiring with Metternich, the latter dutifully passing the content of their conversations on to Vienna. It was accepted in the Austrian capital that Talleyrand's information had to be paid for on a regular basis. With the modifications to the Hôtel de Monaco, the dinners for thirty-six guests and looking after the Spanish prisoners at Valençay, Talleyrand's enterprise required millions of francs to function. In contrast, the Russians did not seem to have the same understanding of the urgent need to oil the wheels of diplomacy.

Without his government post, it could have been believed that Talleyrand was idle. During the winter of 1809, could the dinners, salons and whist evenings pose a threat to Napoleon? He was aware that things were not going well for Napoleon in Spain so that in Mme de Rémusat's salon he predicted the Empire's collapse. "To declare oneself an enemy of the people is an irreparable error." How was it that the imperial police did not take an interest in what he was saying? Were his words ignored? And if the emperor did learn about them, why did he not react? However, one man by himself, particularly one who thinks but does not act, is not going to topple a regime. What he needed was an ally.

There was a man who shared Talleyrand's fears about the consequences of the emperor's constant warfare and what would happen to the government if he were killed in battle—his name was Joseph Fouché, the newly re-appointed Minister of Police. Fouché brought out the epithets in Talleyrand: "A Minister of Police is a man who becomes involved in matters that concern him and then in matters that don't concern him"; "The Minister of Police has a total contempt for mankind because he has examined himself very closely." The trouble was that Talleyrand and Fouché were so very different in their origins, their upbringing, their acquaintances and their habits. Talleyrand was the wealthy aristocrat, well-dressed, well-connected, corrupt, witty, a libertine, a gambler, while Fouché was a foul-mouthed Jacobin, a joyless, hardworking, ugly, red-headed, sinister organizer of massacres and street-corner murders—altogether an unattractive person who was unlikely to be forgiven by the Bourbons for his role as a *regicide*. Talleyrand lived with a beautiful mistress and discussed affairs of state with the emperor, ministers and ambassadors amidst sumptuous surroundings. Fouché was a model husband and lived with his ill-favoured wife in perfect harmony, with the couple devoted to the upbringing of their bevy of children. He did not spend the money he earned or stole on extravagance, so he was taken for an honest man. Apart from his unpardonable crimes against humanity, he was entirely faultless.

The divergence between them seemed insurmountable until a common interest brought them together. Talleyrand's former chief assistant d'Hauterive was on good terms with Fouché and could not understand why these two conspirators whose ideas were so similar did not pool their talents. He convinced the two men with a common purpose to meet at his house where they agreed to work together against Napoleon. Then they were seen together at the salon of Talleyrand's former mistress Louise de Montmorency, the Princess de Vaudémont. Aimée de Coigny describes what made this salon so suitable: "One could plot there in complete security and life was so agreeable and simple that the spies fell asleep." However, one onlooker who was wide awake was Napoleon's mother, Letizia Buonaparte, who attended one of these social evenings and was astonished to find the two men deep in conversation. She wrote to her son on campaign in Spain about this abnormal event. Metternich also knew the purpose of their meeting and reported back to Vienna: "M. de Talleyrand and M. Fouché, once with opposite views and interests, have been brought together by circumstances over which they have no control." He also had a clear understanding that the French people were no longer interested in war: "France has not been at war since the Peace of Lunéville [1801]. It is Napoleon who has been at war using French resources."

How was the overthrow of Napoleon to be accomplished? Fouché mentioned the word "assassination" followed by a new government created by Talleyrand and himself. Who would be the head of government? They quickly dismissed a member of the Bourbon family and any of Napoleon's brothers. Their choice fell on Napoleon's brother-in-law Joachim Murat; he was well-known, courageous, ambitious, easy to manipulate and would rally the Bonapartist clan. With unbelievable daring, the two plotters sent him a letter in his Kingdom of Naples asking him to be ready in the event that he received news of Napoleon's death. Why did the usually cautious Talleyrand take such a risk?

On 20 December 1808, members of the diplomatic corps, government ministers and notables were invited to one of the many dinners at the Hôtel de Monaco. At one moment during the course of the evening, the name of the Minister of Police was announced and Fouché made a theatrical entry into Talleyrand's salon as if it were visiting an old friend. Talleyrand limped over to greet him and they performed a tour of the rooms arm in arm smiling with the pleasure of a renewed acquaintance. By the next morning dispatches were flying across Europe to all the various capitals.

It is not clear why the subtle and cautious Talleyrand should have made a public exhibition of his association with Fouché. Their collaboration was a threat and, if it attracted a sufficient number of the discontented population, Napoleon might feel compelled to moderate his aggressive policies. Metternich—dragging himself from the arms of Caroline Murat—evaluated the situation very carefully and left for consultations in Vienna. According to him, there were two parties in France: one consisted of those military personnel whose fortunes were tied to the emperor's continued success on the battlefield; while the other—the great mass of the population—believed that the country was being driven headlong towards total disaster. Two representatives of this second point of view were the former Minister of Foreign Affairs and the newly restored Minister of the Police. Metternich is quite categorical: "M. de Talleyrand has, since the 1805 campaign, conceived a plan to oppose Napoleon's destructive projects with all his might." In a coded message to Vienna he stated that Talleyrand would not become involved in an attempt to assassinate Napoleon but was ready to take action if he were killed in battle.

Things were not going well in the Spanish War, while both official and public opinion in France had clearly turned against Napoleon. At his headquarters in Valladolid, Napoleon received at the same time the letter from his mother, Murat's reply to Fouché that had been intercepted by Eugène de Beauharnais in Italy and the news of the "conspiracy" in Paris sent by his secretary Lavalette. He was stunned and left for Paris immediately, where he arrived five days later on 23 January 1809 at 8 o'clock in the morning. He spent a few days catching up on business, receiving ambassadors and checking with his own informants exactly what had happened. Then, four days after his arrival Talleyrand received a letter signalling his removal from the post of Grand Chamberlain and requiring him to return the symbolic key of office that granted him access to the emperor's private apartments. He sent the key back accompanied by a humble letter attempting to defuse the situation: "My consolation is to be devoted to Your Majesty by two feelings that pain could neither overcome nor weaken, through a recognition and devotion that will only end with my life." The following day, Napoleon called a meeting of a restricted group of councillors: Cambacérès, Lebrun and the ministers Decrès and Fouché—and the Prince de Benevento. Talleyrand's place as Grand Chamberlain would be taken over by his colleague Montesquiou, who was also present.

Napoleon's explosion of Sunday, 28 January 1809 was neither the first nor the last aimed at Talleyrand, nor over the years had he been particularly singled out for the emperor's wrath. His fury often vented itself on objects; his hat was stamped on a number of times. In the past, he had labelled Talleyrand as "the man who has stolen the most", although in this practice he was simply more successful than Napoleon's brothers, sisters and marshals. He had also been accused, with good reason, of being a liar, although once again he was not alone since Napoleon had himself lied callously to the Pope, to the Spanish Royal Family and had even tried to bluff Tsar Alexander I. What distinguished the scene that followed was that several people present wrote down Napoleon's words.

To enter into the subject, Napoleon paced backwards and forwards in front of the fireplace at the Tuileries Palace, to the window, past his desk, his hands behind his back, thoughtful, agitated. Talleyrand, who could not sit down in front of the emperor nor stand unaided, propped himself up on a corner of the mantelpiece facing the other people present. Napoleon then began by recalling the disappointing events that had taken place in Paris during his absence: the legislative body had opposed some of his measures; the stock exchange had lost value; finally, *somebody* had anticipated his death, *somebody* had doubted him, *somebody* had even envisaged a world without him. "Those who become state dignitaries or ministers are not at liberty to think and speak as they wish. They can only be my instruments." Napoleon confronted Talleyrand: "For these people, treason has already begun when they allow themselves to doubt; it becomes complete when, from doubt, it becomes dissent." With the pronouncement of the word "treason", Talleyrand must have felt that his hours were numbered. Certainly, those present in the room envisaged no other issue than the firing squad. Without betraying any expression, Talleyrand looked down at the ill-looking 40-year-old, already getting podgy, losing his hair and no longer the young god of victory. Without naming the guilty party, the more Napoleon stared at Talleyrand, the more Talleyrand wore the expression of an unconcerned spectator. The emperor turned his wrath on him: "Thief! Thief! You are nothing but a thief!" He showed a fist to Talleyrand: "You are a coward, a feckless person, you do not believe in God! All your life you have failed in your duties, you have tricked, betrayed everybody. Nothing is sacred for you. You would sell your father! I have gratified you with rewards and yet there is nothing that you would not be capable of doing against me! For the last ten months you have had the cheek, because you think mistakenly that my affairs in Spain are going badly, to say to anybody who wants to hear that you have always had misgivings about my affairs in this kingdom, while it was you who first gave me the idea, and who continuously encouraged me."

Evidently, Napoleon was so angry that he was grasping at every nonsensical piece of mud to sling at Talleyrand. To say that Talleyrand pushed him into invading Spain was, of course, wrong, since Napoleon took the decision himself and, in recent years, nobody had ever been able to influence his choices in any way. Talleyrand had advised him against the invasion of Spain and had been recommending peace and appeasement for a number of years without effect. Next, like a scorned woman, Napoleon brought up the Enghien Affair: "This man, this wretch, by whom was I told where he was living? Who encouraged me to deal severely with him?" Then, Talleyrand's house was described as a lair of crooks and whores. Inflamed by the lack of reaction, he lost all control in incoherent threats: "I should smash you like a glass; you deserve it. I have the power but I have too much contempt to take the trouble. Why have I not had you strung up from the Tuileries' railings? There is still plenty of time!" And finished with a flourish: "Ah, what's more, you are just shit in silk stockings!" Those present were horrified by such a display of invective and ashamed to see the emperor lose his dignity, while Talleyrand's silence signified a certain superiority and courage.

Throughout, the former Bishop of Autun continued to show no sign of acknowledgement, his eyes dead pan, his face imperturbable. Rather than the wrath of the Gods, he had witnessed the vulgar strutting of a parade-ground corporal. Losing all self-control, Napoleon searched for some further insult: "And your wife? You didn't tell me that San Carlos was your wife's lover." Talleyrand responded in the terms of the perfect courtier: "Indeed, Sire, I did not think that such reports could interest the glory of Your Majesty... nor mine." Having lost face, Napoleon was required to conclude with a smart parting shot to both Talleyrand and

Fouché: "Take note that if there were to be a revolution, whatever role you played in it, you will both be destroyed by it." Exit.

The storm of abuse could be heard throughout the apartments of the Tuileries. The fact that Fouché had not been singled out for attention during the same outburst was obviously designed to create a breach between the two conspirators. According to some reports, Fouché had already been upbraided beforehand in the privacy of Napoleon's office. It is also possible that the emperor was more inclined to trust Fouché since, as a remorseless Jacobin and regicide, he was never likely to be forgiven if the Bourbons returned to the throne of France—or so it seemed at the time.

Talleyrand limped towards the door in front of his terrified colleagues and, passing through, was heard to remark: "What a pity that such a great man should be so badly brought up." There was no more question of being strung up on the gates of the Tuileries, it was all a question of good manners. A concise quotation comes to mind: "Insults are the argument of those who are in the wrong." He hurried off to recount the day's events to his friends at Mme de Laval's salon.

In his memoirs, he makes no mention of this incident, but in her diary Mme de Laval does. After he described the invective to which he had been subjected, she exclaimed: "What? He said that to your face! You were with him! And you didn't seize a chair, the tongs, a log, I don't know what! You didn't launch yourself at him!" To which Talleyrand, lounging on her sofa, replied: "Oh! I really thought about it, but I am too lazy for that." All Paris was talking about "the incident" and naturally concluded that he was finished. When Talleyrand next saw Savary, he asked: "Which prison is it?" It is extraordinary that, although he had mentioned the word "treason", Napoleon obviously knew nothing about Talleyrand's many contacts with Metternich and Tsar Alexander. Why did the emperor overlook Talleyrand's dealings with the Austrians and the Russians? Was Fouché covering his back?

Somehow, Talleyrand always benefited from Napoleon's indulgence. He was not arrested, was not actually forbidden from attending the court and maintained his lucrative post as Napoleon's Vice-Grand Elector. Rather than taking refuge in his house, the following evening he turned up at the Tuileries for the regular Sunday reception wearing his most impassive face. The Duke de Gaeta, Minister of Finances, wanted to leave early so was one of the first to reach the Tuileries. To his astonishment, the former Bishop of Autun was already there leaning against the mantelpiece. Gaeta was curious to see what would happen and noted that, when the emperor appeared, he spoke to the people on Talleyrand's right and left, but ignored him. The Princess de Benevento was not so lucky. All Paris was amused to learn that she was forbidden from showing her face at court and banished to her property at Pont-de-Sains in the north of France. As the name of the unfortunate San Carlos had been mentioned in the altercation of the previous day, he too was exiled arbitrarily to Bourg-en-Bresse in the east of France.

A week later Talleyrand was back at court for the Sunday reception. The emperor passed in front of him without seeing him, but stopped to address a question to the man standing next to him. This gentleman hesitated to reply, so Talleyrand replied in his place, bowed deeply and, as the flawless courtier, took Napoleon's hand and kissed it. As a public relations exercise, it was a masterpiece that drew an appreciative murmur from the throng. An old Arab proverb says: "Kiss the hand that you cannot bite." Napoleon probably deeply regretted his loss of self-control and may have been grateful for the way the ice was broken.

The time had come for the women in Talleyrand's life to act. Mme de Rémusat was a lady-in-waiting at court and shared with Joséphine's daughter, Queen Hortense of Holland, the fact that the Prince de Benevento's disgrace was "clearly undeserved". When Hortense agreed to meet him herself, Talleyrand declared that, of all people, he was the person most attached to the emperor. He behaved with such cold dignity that Hortense had the impression that she was dealing with a visiting head-of-state. Later, she did her best to plead the cause of the fallen courtier to Napoleon. In fact, she said: "I lied so well that I almost burst out laughing." But it was Napoleon who was most amused. He was not deceived by Talleyrand's sincerity and devotion, accusing Hortense of being naïve. She defended Talleyrand further by saying that he never spoke about his political sentiments in public. "In any case, I will not hurt him," Napoleon concluded. "Only, I don't want him mixed up with my affairs anymore." A few weeks later he declared to Pierre-Louis

Roederer: "I will do him no harm; I will keep his other positions for him." Since he was incapable of listening to advice, Napoleon's justification is reasonable: "He can no longer tell me that he recommended or did not recommend one course of action or another."

Unbelievably, although Talleyrand was in disgrace, Napoleon would still consult him from time to time until the end of his regime, even at times when there was talk of sending him to prison. These strange interviews would take place as if nothing had ever happened between them. For instance, they held several late-night conversations in the early part of 1812, with Napoleon even offering Talleyrand the post of Governor of Poland during his Russian campaign. There is little doubt that, even before their first meeting at the Ministry of Foreign Affairs in 1797, Napoleon had a genuine liking for Talleyrand and was fascinated by his charm and his aristocratic bearing. Throughout the spring of 1809 Talleyrand kept Caulaincourt up-to-date about his evolving relationship with the emperor—from angry, to cold, to polite, to familiar but still distrusting.

While Talleyrand demonstrated a façade of unwavering fidelity to the regime, the irony was that behind the scenes he was the implacable enemy of an emperor who was doing irreparable damage to his country. During the early months of 1809 he still continued to meet Metternich, declaring his complete hostility to Napoleon, much to the Austrian ambassador's alarm. After war broke out between Austria and France in April, Metternich left France but they continued to communicate via a bank in Frankfurt and through Metternich's wife who remained in Paris. Talleyrand used foreign couriers to communicate with Vienna and St Petersburg, while he made sure that the private letters sent by post to and from his friends contained nothing but banalities designed to be read by the police. If his purpose was to undermine Napoleon's regime, it was necessary to throw informers off the scent: "I had to give an air of indifference and inactivity to my way of life that would not arouse Napoleon's suspicions." The Vice-Grand Elector also took every opportunity to write to Napoleon congratulating him on his victories in exaggeratedly approving terms. For instance, Napoleon received a nasty wound in the leg at Regensburg in Germany, once more highlighting the fragility of his regime, and received a grovelling letter of sympathy from

Talleyrand. In letters to Caulaincourt, he expressed, nevertheless, a lifetime bond to Napoleon and genuine gratitude for the generosity he had been shown in the past. However, he was indignant with Napoleon's Continental System that was causing ruin throughout Europe and the shameless military campaign going on in Spain that now served no purpose. Talleyrand had cautioned Napoleon not to cross the Spanish frontier with his army and, when he did so, his former foreign minister warned him: "Make war on the King of Spain, not on the Spanish people." Napoleon's own brother Joseph had written to him: "Your glory, Sire, will perish in Spain."

If Napoleon was now on the way out, then it was necessary to accelerate his fall. After the stormy meeting with the emperor, Talleyrand informed Vienna that he placed himself entirely at the service of Austria, with Metternich making it clear to his government that the information he supplied was invaluable. Having abandoned his post in the French Government and with restricted access to the court, his standing in the eyes of foreign capitals was diminished. He also told Metternich that, having lost part of his income, a few thousand francs would not go amiss. The answer came that Austria would pay him "all that he could reasonably demand". Austrian Foreign Minister Stadion sent 100,000 francs to Metternich to pass on to Talleyrand with the instruction that payments would be made depending on the usefulness of the information supplied. For instance, he warned the Austrians to keep a very careful watch on the troop movements of Marshal Nicolas Oudinot. It would have been undignified if Talleyrand had really only been interested in the money, but alongside these goals he also sought a higher goal: removing a dictatorship by restoring a pacific regime to France.

During Napoleon's absence fighting Austrian forces in central Europe, reports were received that the British had landed a large military force on the Island of Walcheren in the estuary of the River Scheldt in July 1809 in an attempt to take the pressure off the Austrians. By this time, the emperor was tied up in Vienna drawing up the Treaty of Schönbrunn with the Austrians and subject, once again, to fits of epilepsy. None of the ministers remaining in Paris dared to take action without instructions from the emperor, even the Minister of War. However, Fouché, who was at this time both Minister of Police and

Minister of the Interior, quickly mobilized an army of 30,000 men and appointed General Bernadotte to head it. Bernadotte, who had never been particularly loyal to Napoleon, happened to be in Paris at this moment because he had been sent home from Germany in disgrace. Fouché's rag-tag army contained a large number of nobles and royalists, including Talleyrand's brother Archambaud and his friend Montrond. However, the British were not defeated by the French but rather by "Walcheren fever", which affected tens of thousands of their troops and led to their withdrawal in December. For his initiative, Fouché was rewarded with the title of Duke d'Otrante by Napoleon. Nevertheless, this incident illustrated how easy it had been for one man to seize control and make war during the emperor's absence.

Talleyrand had a very clear view of what was happening. Napoleon had attacked Spain on a flimsy pretext that seemed to fly in the face of reason, motivating the Spanish people to participate in an uprising to resist the aggressor. Talleyrand was particularly annoyed with Napoleon since he had had the opportunity to establish a European-wide peace that would have rendered war impossible, allowing prosperity and civilization to spread throughout the continent. "Napoleon could have done these things and did not... It is on these outcomes that he must and will be judged... Posterity will say of him: this man was gifted with a very great intellectual power but he did not understand the true glory". Talleyrand believed that history would find Napoleon at fault for his shortcomings, but this did not happen as expected because the emperor's achievements eventually became the stuff of legend for the French people.

He no longer attended Napoleon's court on a regular basis, whose atmosphere and ephemeral luxury he found absurd, inviting mockery. The receptions at the Tuileries were often strained affairs attended by people who were uncomfortable with their new titles and official uniforms. In his former role of Grand Chamberlain, it had been Talleyrand's job to animate some of these occasions, which he did in his own way: "Gentlemen, the emperor is not messing about. He wants you to enjoy yourselves."

After sixteen years of war, Napoleon's enemies were beginning to learn how to combat him so that battles became more harshly fought with heavier casualties. The Franco-Austrian War of 1809, beginning with the Austrian invasion of Bavaria in April, was decided with victory for Napoleon at the Battle of Wagram in July and concluded with the Treaty of Schönbrunn in October. The new French Foreign Minister, Champagny, took his time over drafting the text of the treaty and Napoleon's patience began to wear thin. The emperor remarked that Talleyrand would have completed the task in half the time—no doubt becoming several million francs richer in the process. Faithful to the advice he had received from Talleyrand at Erfurt, Tsar Alexander I observed the military manoeuvres between the French and Austrian Armies in 1809 without becoming involved in them.

On 24 June 1809, Talleyrand's mother died. One could believe that, since he had already announced her premature death when he married Catherine Grand and makes no mention of this event in his memoirs, he had very little contact with her. Nonetheless, during his numerous changes of residence in Paris since the Revolution, he always arranged for his mother to live near him or he would move to be near her.

During this time out of favour, Talleyrand travelled to take the waters at Bourbon-l'Archambault, to visit Edmond and Dorothea in Paris and to survey his estate at Pont-de-Sains. His entourage consisted of Mme de Laval, his black maidservant Zoé and his adopted daughter Charlotte. At various points other friends would join him for a few days: Aimée de Coigny, the Duchess de Bauffremont or Choiseul. When in Paris he was a faithful visitor to Mme de Laval's salon, where he ceased to be the Prince de Benevento and became M. de Talleyrand. It was here that the full membership of his "harem" assembled: the Princess de Vaudémont, the Duchess de Luynes, Aimée de Coigny, the Countess de Jaucourt, not forgetting the Viscountess de Laval herself. While far from being in the first flush of youth, these ladies formed his faithful and devoted bodyguard, his guests at the dinner table and his partners at whist. When she was young and beautiful, Guyonne-Elisabeth-Joséphine, the Viscountess de Laval, had been Talleyrand's mistress but now her boudoir was the secret sanctuary where a group of old friends exchanged gossip and the usually monosyllabic Talleyrand let flow his caustic wit. She had herself the sharpest tongue, with Napoleon being the preferred target for her scorn, while keeping Talleyrand informed of what was happening in Paris. The Duchess de Luynes, whose mahogany wheelbarrow had contributed to constructing the embankments prior to the celebrations on the Champ-de-Mars on 14 July 1790, had become a passionate matron with a vulgar voice, a vulgar laugh, but who reserved her vulgar words exclusively for the emperor. A new recruit was the rich, one-eyed Polish Countess Tyszkiewicz, who was devoted to her idol and formed part of his whist table, losing money every night. When she died, the astonished Montrond saw Talleyrand cry for the first time ever. Also admitted to the Prince of Benevento's closed circle of former mistresses, soon to make the other participants jealous, was the 47-year-old Duchess von Courland, Dorothea's mother. She was intelligent, rich and had retained her beauty. In the summer, he stayed for long periods in the château she had rented at Rosny-sous-Bois, while in the winter she lived unambiguously under Talleyrand's roof in Paris. He paid great attention to her, sending her almost daily a little *billet doux* expressing love, tenderness, even passion. While one can never be sure of the true meaning of their relationship, Lady Yarmouth informed Montrond: "M. de Talleyrand is tumbled in a very violent love with D.C." One of his messages to the duchess reads: "Dear Friend. My wish is to spend my life with you; my wish is that you enjoy all the happiness that your lovable and sweet qualities merit... I love you, my Angel, with all my heart." After the Bourbon Restoration, the Duchess von Courland came to live at Valençay, where she occupied the principal suite.

Brought to Paris by the Duchess von Courland, one of the newcomers to his harem was Auguste-Charlotte, the extremely attractive German Countess von Kielmannsegge. She labelled Talleyrand as the "anaconda" while, as with so many others, succumbing to his charm and seeking a place in his circle of friends. In return, he called her "the great mare". Her husband had been arrested for involvement in a plot against Napoleon's brother Jérôme, King of Westphalia, but she had succeeded in securing his release through her personal intercession with Napoleon at the imperial court. One rumour suggests that she had a child by Napoleon. She became above all Napoleon's agent keeping him informed about the activities of the Saint-Germain set, a function she was able to perform while working with René Savary, once again Napoleon's Minister of Police. It can be noted that both the Duchess von Courland

and the Countess von Kielmannsegge came to Paris as devoted admirers of Napoleon but, due to the influence of Talleyrand, Courland rapidly changed her opinion about the emperor, while Kielmannsegge remained entirely devoted to Napoleon and his cause until the end of her life; he even wrote to her from Saint Helena. However, while Kielmannsegge was spying for the emperor, Courland was acting as the go-between for Talleyrand and the tsar. One may note that the troublesome Countess von Kielmannsegge was also a particularly close friend of the newly-wed Dorothea de Périgord.

Among Talleyrand's other acquaintances was Claire de Rémusat, the famous diarist and wife of Napoleon's first chamberlain. Twenty-six years younger than Talleyrand, she was the youngest of his devotees, enjoying a perfectly amicable relationship with the Prince. In 1812, Aimée de Coigny, another diarist and among Talleyrand's closest associates, was living with the Marquis Bruno de Boisgelin, an eager advocate of the Bourbon Restoration. Aimée eventually persuaded her lover that, if there was to be a leader of a faction opposed to Napoleon, Talleyrand was that person. She became a regular visitor at Talleyrand's house, where it was said of them: "The clacking of these two tongues kept us endlessly amused."

This is how Talleyrand kept himself out of trouble during this period, having considerable influence upon public opinion and certainly not forgotten by Napoleon. Invitations to the Prince de Benevento's dinners were considered as prestigious as those of the emperor. The meal would be served at 6 o'clock in the evening and upon leaving the table Talleyrand would often be at his most garrulous. Dinner would give way to a reception or sometimes dancing. He was also fond of chamber music, with his own group of musicians. Light refreshments would be served at midnight followed by conversation until 1 o'clock in the morning when the sacred hour would chime. Gauze-covered tables and dining chairs would be brought out for a game of whist, during which the host would be lost in silent concentration on his cards and huge sums of money would change hands.

In December 1809, Napoleon's marriage to Josephine was annulled so that he could marry a princess from one of the ancient European dynasties who might bear him a son. There were only three real potential sources of candidates: a member of the Bourbon family; one of the tsar's sisters; or a daughter of Francis I of Austria. Caulaincourt had been ordered to make yet another approach to Alexander I about his youngest sister Anna, when Metternich suddenly realized with alarm that a link between the French and Russian Empires would be extremely detrimental to the interests of the Austrian court. With great courage, he persuaded Francis I to sacrifice his daughter, the 18-year-old Archduchess Marie Louise, Marie-Antoinette's niece, as the bride of the Corsican tyrant. Napoleon was flattered, for the Austrians offered him the possibility of joining the European family of dynasties. A cabinet meeting was organized on 28 January 1810 to discuss the Austrian marriage proposal and Talleyrand, as Vice-Grand Elector, was present. When it was his turn to speak, he enthusiastically supported it because it was likely to lead to peace rather than war. He also felt, more than any of those present, that a Russian princess was unlikely to bring the same advantages. Marrying an Austrian princess would also be a way for Napoleon's regime to expiate any responsibility for Marie-Antoinette's death, throwing all blame onto a minor faction of the Jacobins. Despite the profound misgivings of the Austrian aristocracy, General Berthier, who had played a key part in the Austrian defeat at Wagram, was sent to Vienna to bring Marie Louise to Paris. Some people hoped that marrying an archduchess would satisfy the parvenu Napoleon's ambitions and encourage him towards moderation, but there was no way he would be satisfied until England had been conquered. In the spring of 1811, Marie Louise bore Napoleon the son and heir he sought. When the incredulous Tsar Alexander heard of Napoleon's marriage, his instant conclusion was that the emperor's next step would be to invade Russia.

The birth of Napoleon and Marie Louise's son, the King of Rome, gave Talleyrand an opportunity to visit the Tuileries, where he was still officially banned. A few days earlier, Talleyrand's own grandchild was born. What has aroused the interest of historians was that the baby's birth certificate states that he was born in Paris on 21 October as the son of a certain Auguste Demorny, while in fact he was actually born at St Maurice in Switzerland on 17 September of "unknown parentage". Research revealed that his parents were in fact not unknown at all: he was the fourth son of Joséphine's daughter Queen Hortense, the separated wife of Napoleon's brother Louis; and his real father was Talleyrand's son General Charles de Flahaut. He was therefore the half-brother of Napoleon III, Hortense's eldest son by Louis Bonaparte and the future dictator of France. The marriage between Hortense and Louis having collapsed, this child was brought up by his paternal grandmother Adelaïde de Flahaut/Mme de Souza and was granted the entirely fabricated title of the Duke de Morny. He would grow up to be a flamboyant, intelligent lady-killer, one of nineteenth-century France's richest and most talented businessmen.

Relations between Napoleon and Talleyrand had improved to the point that the Vice-Grand Elector was invited to the marriage ceremony at the Louvre on 2 April 1810. He had also arranged for his Spanish "prisoners" at Valençay to hold a firework display in honour of the emperor's wedding, the news of which made a good impression in the Tuileries Palace. Since one can never be too careful about what will happen in the future, he paid a visit to console Josephine at her Malmaison residence accompanied by the Duchess von Courland.

In January 1810, through the intermediary of the Dutch Government, Napoleon had made peaceful overtures to England but nothing came of it. At the beginning of June, Fouché without permission, made contact secretly with the government in London for exactly the same purpose. He was accused by Napoleon of making a grave error and summarily dismissed in an angry dressing-down at Saint Cloud. Fouché burned the papers concerning this affair and fled to Tuscany. He was replaced once more by the high-handed René Savary. In a move no doubt linked to this attempt to circumvent the disastrous Continental System, Talleyrand's financier friend Gabriel-Julien Ouvrard had made a mysterious visit to London. When he returned to Amsterdam on 3 June, he was arrested at the house of Mme Hamelin (Montrond's ex-mistress) when the energetic and faithful Savary burst in. By a very embarrassing coincidence, Talleyrand happened to be in the same house at the same time and, although he was not arrested, Napoleon required him to explain in writing why he was present and what his relationship with Ouvrard was. The emperor was not impressed with his Vice-Grand Elector's explanation but did not immediately pursue the matter. Napoleon asked, of all people, d'Hauterive to establish an official report on this affair, in which it was very soon concluded that Fouché had no ill intentions and his former boss was innocent. Ouvrard was imprisoned for two years. The fact that Fouché bolted in June 1810 and Talleyrand did not in January 1809 should not conceal the fact that he was at the mercy of a man who delighted in tormenting people like a cat playing with a mouse. Talleyrand flattered Napoleon mercilessly and the fact that he did not appear to be afraid of him no doubt served as a form of protection. The emperor called a meeting to decide on Fouché's fate at which Talleyrand was present. It was eventually decided to punish him with mere disgrace, while Talleyrand recommended that, while the Minister of the Police may have committed an error, he should be replaced as "by M. Fouché himself". Fouché's error was that he had sincerely desired peace and, now that he was gone, the tsar's agent Nesselrode for one realized that war with Russia was inevitable.

There remained the problem of how Talleyrand would continue to finance his extravagant life-style and avoid ruin. Not only did he live like a prince, but he paid pensions to his brothers Archambaud and Boson who had no other source of income, he maintained two large houses in Paris and had recently purchased further property and forests in the region of Valençay. After the angry scene in January 1809, Napoleon had stopped paying for the accommodation of the three Spanish princes at Valençay. He also refused permission for Talleyrand to sell the Principality of Benevento to the Kingdom of Naples. Even though he had his suspicions about Talleyrand's activities, kept him under observation and had his private mail surveyed, he could find no evidence of wrong-doing so that his only recourse was to make Catherine de Talleyrand's life a misery. If the continued existence of Talleyrand troubled the emperor, his absence from his government also left a vacuum. The former Bishop of Autun was conspiring to bring peace to Europe and the greatest warrior of the epoch could do nothing about it. Only in Austrian and Russian archives is there any trace of Talleyrand's resistance.

In May 1810, the emperor was once again in high dudgeon. The project on which he had placed so much faith to bring the United Kingdom to its knees—the Continental System—was failing. He was, perhaps, the only person in the whole of Europe who thought that such an absurd scheme was likely to achieve the desired outcome. In fact, he was asking each country, including France, to cease trading with the United Kingdom in the hope that it would harm the British economy. The whole idea seemed flawed since the Royal Navy ruled the seas, controlling who traded with whom. The only effect was that the United Kingdom's merchant ships roamed the world's oceans, increasing trade with foreign countries while European traders fretted as their businesses collapsed. Even Napoleon's brother Louis, King of Holland, established clandestine contacts with England seeking a way for his country to escape from the embargo on trade. In fact, the only country which could observe the Continental System with equanimity was Austria, which no longer had access to the coast.

Napoleon's Continental System was leading to economic collapse, with the Ouvrard affair resulting in the bankruptcy of Mme Simons' financier husband in Brussels, losing in the process another 4 million francs that Talleyrand had placed in his care. If Napoleon was not deliberately trying to ruin him, the former Bishop of Autun could have done himself a favour by reducing his expenses to correspond to his income. He turned to the tsar for help, but Alexander obviously felt that he had discharged his debt by allowing Talleyrand's nephew to marry Dorothea von Biron. When writing to the tsar, he requested that his begging letter should be destroyed. Alexander neither burnt the letter nor found it within his power to help him financially for he feared it would be impossible to keep such a matter secret. However, Talleyrand had not given up on the tsar, whose ambassador in Paris was Boris Kourakin. Metternich was no longer ambassador to France having been recalled to Vienna as Austrian Foreign Minister, his place in Paris being filled by Prince Schwarzenberg. Talleyrand considered both Kourakin and Schwarzenberg as nonentities and would have nothing to do with them. Fortunately, both the tsar and Francis I of Austria had appointed special envoys, not to Napoleon's Government but to the Prince de Benevento himself: Charles-Robert, Count de Nesselrode for Russia and Engelbert, Chevalier de Floret for Austria. The multilingual, modest and discreet Floret had lived in Paris and had been an acquaintance of Talleyrand for some time already. The young Nesselrode was charged with conducting secret correspondence between the tsar, Caulaincourt and Talleyrand, of which even the Russian Embassy in Paris remained ignorant. In earlier correspondence between Nesselrode and Dalberg, Talleyrand bore the pseudonym "Cousin Henry", Napoleon was "Sophie Smith", Caulaincourt "the Professor" and the tsar of Russia "Louise". With the departure of Fouché ("Natascha"), Nesselrode was despondent for it was from him that "Cousin Henry" obtained most of his information. It is evident that "Cousin Henry", in his hour of need, was stimulated to desperate measures for he now wrote to the tsar asking not for money but for Russian import licences that would allow him to circumvent the blockade and bring Russian wood and hemp to England in American ships commanding a high price and thereby making enormous profits.

The rich burgomasters in Hamburg begged Talleyrand to intervene on their behalf with the emperor in order to protect their ancient trading practices with England, offering him 4 million francs for his pains. In his present position of disgrace, he could do nothing for them but he did not refuse their money either. Eventually, the good citizens of Hamburg became impatient and approached Napoleon asking for their money to be returned. Despite another dressing down on the emperor's part and another indifferent non-reaction on Talleyrand's part, no trace of the money was ever found. Things would get worse before they got better. Once again, Talleyrand was obliged to sell his library but the sale, which took place on 30 April 1811, was once again a disappointment.

Things were going from bad to worse. The citizens of Hamburg wanted their money back and Mollien, the Minister of Finances, agreed with them. The Spanish princes at Valençay were costing a small fortune, while Napoleon's grant for their upkeep fell far short of the true cost. Talleyrand proposed to Napoleon that he should purchase the principality of Benevento from him, but the answer came back that the emperor would simply repossess it. Having almost ruined him, Napoleon now set out to humiliate him.

Mme de Rémusat describes the pleasure that Napoleon gained from persecuting his retinue by meddling in their private affairs. One day he reproached Dorothea for the extravagant lifestyle of her husband Edmond, which left her in tears. It should be said that even Napoleon thought he had gone too far this time and tried to make amends. The Duchess von Courland had hired the Châteauneuf de Saint-Germain as a summer residence, with the Prince de Benevento spending all his time there with her, riding on horses through the forest, composing letters to the tsar and sending her little *billets doux*—even though he saw her every day! Meanwhile, the Princess de Benevento had returned discreetly from her banishment at Pont-de-Sains and lived in the Hôtel de Monaco in Paris. One evening a gendarme appeared at Saint-Germain bearing a letter from Savary. It informed Talleyrand that his wife, dressed as a man, had returned to the Château de Valençay for a rendez-vous with her lover, the Duke de San Carlos. She had also been seen at the proscribed Mme de Staël's Château de Coppet in Switzerland. The emperor required her banishment to Pont-de-Sains to be renewed and, this time, her neglectful husband would accompany her. In a dictatorship, all matters called for the dictator's personal intervention—even the most trivial. The thought of leaving Paris and being obliged to live in the company of his wife was sufficient to inspire Talleyrand to write a letter. While the gendarme waited and after a number of false starts, he eventually wrote asking Savary for an interview. The next day he went to the minister's office and succeeded in persuading Savary that only the Princess de Benevento would suffer exile. To his satisfaction and relief, he was able to return to the company of his harem—without his wife.

Napoleon believed that Talleyrand would eventually be obliged to come begging at his feet: "I want Talleyrand, who has so often lacked loyalty and who has shown so many instances of immorality, to be reduced to living exclusively from my generosity." But Talleyrand had no faith in the emperor's generosity and also felt that he wanted as little contact as possible with a doomed regime. In fact, the Prince de Benevento was directing opposition activities on a European scale, betraying the emperor but serving the interests of France as a surrogate intelligence officer for the Austrians and the Russians. By the beginning of 1811, Nesselrode was in possession of so much information about the forthcoming invasion of Russia that he feared for his life and asked to be relieved—in fact, he had no need to be apprehensive for Napoleon looked upon him favourably. Recommended by Caulaincourt, a new Russian agent was dispatched to Paris to maintain liaison with Talleyrand. Rather like Montrond, Colonel Alexander Chernyshov proved to be a handsome, half-diplomat, half-soldier rogue, and soon established intimate relations with the beautiful Princess Pauline Borghese, Napoleon's sister and widow of General Leclerc. When he arrived in Paris, he renewed all the old spy networks organized by Markoff in the days of the Consulate and sustained by Dalberg. For a considerable time, he was feted in the salons and even received enthusiastically by Napoleon in whose army he had once served with distinction. Nevertheless, the police had him under observation since he seemed to have an unusual interest in confidential military information. Chernyshov left Paris suddenly on 14 February 1812, having been tipped off by Pauline Borghese that he was about to be arrested. In his apartment, the police found the fragment of a message from a certain Michel, a clerk in the Ministry of War, who, when arrested, confessed that he had been supplying the Russians with secret information for eight years!

Chernyshov was convinced that war was inevitable between France and Russia. The tsar had been building up his forces and was ready in February 1811 not for defence but to attack—a year before Napoleon. Napoleon wanted to recreate Poland as an independent kingdom, while the Russians were determined to stop it by occupying the whole country. Chernyshov recommended to the tsar that he should seize Poland and declare himself king. It was at this moment that Talleyrand was informed of what was going on and expressed his violent opposition to Chernyshov's proposal. His attitude was that, from a military perspective, the Russian Army should not attempt to enter or cross a hostile Poland exposing its long supply lines. It was also vital to wait for Napoleon's forces and his best generals to be inextricably tied up in Spain. It was equally important that Napoleon should be identified as the aggressor. By not attacking, the tsar could consolidate his forces, while all the blame for the impending war would then fall unambiguously on Napoleon. Furthermore, Russia should make peace with Turkey at once and establish a solid agreement with Austria. Tsar Alexander received Talleyrand's message on 27 April 1811 and decided not to go on the offensive. Caulaincourt agreed entirely with Talleyrand; the two men had been in perpetual contact with each other via Nesselrode.

When Caulaincourt returned to Paris at the end of his tenure as ambassador, he brought messages of peaceful friendship from Tsar Alexander for Napoleon. In a long meeting, Caulaincourt presented the tsar as full of good intentions towards France, but Napoleon was convinced otherwise, believing that Alexander was false, ambitious and ready to go to war. As usual, Caulaincourt was very honest with Napoleon, telling him that he understood exactly what were the motives behind the emperor's policies. However, either Poland would be independent or Russia was an ally—he had to choose which. He described exactly what would—and did—happen if Napoleon invaded Russia. Following the meeting, Napoleon delayed the preparation for the invasion of Russia and announced that he was no longer in favour of Polish independence.

There was never a complete understanding between Napoleon and Talleyrand but never a final rupture either. On the one hand, the emperor continued to consult him but, at other times, remained wary and kept him at a distance. As early as 1810, Floret, the Austrian agent, was astonished to learn that Talleyrand had once again the right to enter Napoleon's office at any time without an appointment and even dined with him. To what can be attributed this return to favour? Talleyrand had always opposed Caulaincourt's half-hearted efforts to secure the hand of the youngest Russian Princess Anna for Napoleon's wife. When the Austrians proposed the Archduchess Marie Louise instead, Napoleon believed that Talleyrand was the only person who could advise him on his negotiations with Vienna. At a meeting at the Trianon Palace in 1812, Talleyrand told the emperor to avoid entering into a war with Russia over Poland, to make peace with Russia and Austria and to withdraw from Spain. While completely ignoring this sound advice, Napoleon finished the conversation with: "Ah! You are the devil of a man! I can't avoid talking to you about my affairs, nor stop myself from liking you." Little by little Talleyrand's relationship with Napoleon improved, with his German-speaking niece Dorothea de Périgord being appointed lady-in-waiting to the Empress Marie Louise.

During the course of 1811, Talleyrand's financial affairs reached a critical phase. The idea of an imperial dignitary going bankrupt was too embarrassing even for Emperor Napoleon to contemplate and it was he himself who provided the solution to Talleyrand's financial crisis. First, he paid the backlog on the accommodation of the Spanish Princes at Valençay—2,697,000 francs. Then, on 31 January 1812, the government purchased the Hôtel de Monaco and his other Parisian properties for an inflated 2,180,000 francs. Napoleon also instructed Minister of Finance Nicolas Mollien to deduct the money he owed to the burghers of Hamburg from these sums. We do not know how but, during 1812 and 1813, Talleyrand's financial situation rebounded so dramatically that he was able to purchase the truly magnificent property of 2, Rue Saint-Florentin on the corner of the Rue de Rivoli opposite the Tuileries Palace—his final Parisian residence. In his will, Talleyrand admits: "The fortune I leave to my nephews came for the most part from [Napoleon]." Talleyrand always owned a country residence not far from Paris and it was at this same time he purchased the Château de Saint-Brice north of Paris. What appear to be simple purchases were in fact extremely complicated transactions involving the settlement of debts, borrowing money from front men and under-the-table deals—one can easily get lost.

When Nesselrode first took up his position in Paris as agent to Talleyrand, he asked what were Napoleon's true intentions towards Russia. Talleyrand told him that as soon as there was some kind of stability in Spain, Napoleon's troops would cross the River Vistula in order to invade Russia, so Tsar Alexander had every interest in making peace with Turkey "at any price" in order to be ready for war. Following "Cousin Henry's" strong warning, Nesselrode kept the tsar fully informed of French preparations to invade Russia. Talleyrand repeated what he had recommended at Erfurt: if European peace was to be achieved, it would be through an alliance of Austria and Russia against France.

In preparation for the invasion of Russia, there was a considerable amount of staff work to be accomplished. It was concluded that a force of some 600,000 men could be assembled, together with the necessary horses and supplies. The person who Napoleon appointed to be in charge of this task was Emmerich von Dalberg, who lost no time in sharing this information with the Austrian Government. It seems completely nonsensical that Napoleon would nominate d'Hauterive to conduct an inquiry into the clandestine activities of Fouché and Talleyrand, and place Dalberg in charge of confidential military preparations.

When, in the spring, Napoleon set off for Russia in what would become the War of 1812, Talleyrand's harem began to disintegrate. The

Duchess von Courland returned to her estates in Eastern Europe so as not to forfeit the tsar's pension; she was, after all, a Russian subject living in the enemy's capital. The Countess von Kielmannsegge left for Germany and the Countess Tyszkiewicz wanted to see what was going to happen in her native Warsaw. Every day another of his ladies would climb into her coach and set off for her provincial domains. It was time to look for a new recruit.

CHAPTER XIV
NAPOLEON'S FALL

After the Duchess von Courland had gone back to her family residence in Löbichau, her daughter Dorothea, the Countess de Périgord, stayed close to her "uncle" in Paris. To a 15-year-old girl, at first sight he must have been hideous. "Monsieur de Talleyrand is the most disgusting looking individual I ever saw," wrote the Duke of Argyll a few years earlier. "His complexion is that of a corpse considerably advanced in corruption." Another correspondent described him as: "An old, fuddled, lame, villainous schoolmaster with a deep and hoarse voice." Dorothea, now aged 20, adored him, while his verdict on her was one of equal satisfaction.

As a child, she had received a profoundly Prussian upbringing and upon arrival in Paris had disapproved strongly of the city's morals, fashion and ideas. Talleyrand's opinion was that a few years in the French capital would soon correct these faults. She was a solitary figure with no close female friends, while her strong personality gave her an air of disdain. After the birth of three children, her marriage with Edmond was on the point of collapse, since they were intellectually incompatible and he was more concerned with his own pursuits than with his wife. Born between two cultures, speaking several languages, she was a true European at a time when the word was unknown. Unable to exploit her numerous talents, she understood that her destiny was far more likely to be fulfilled in the Prince de Benevento's company than with her waster husband. With the passage of time and with her penetrating regard, the teenage waif turned into a beautiful woman. The first to notice this was Talleyrand's old friend Narbonne, which may have triggered some kind of awakening in the Prince de Benevento himself. German-speaking Dorothea had been appointed as a lady-in-waiting to the Empress Marie Louise, a post she carried out without great enthusiasm since she held Napoleon and his court in contempt. In writing to Caulaincourt,

Talleyrand explained that he appreciated this connection with the imperial court, although her presence was only required on formal occasions and she was never involved in the empress's private life. While she had received no meaningful religious education as a child, in 1811 Dorothea became a Catholic and, thereafter, lived a life of irreproachable virtue and purity—that is, up until the time of Napoleon's fall from power!

Edmond, now a colonel in Murat's army, was by no means a poor soldier and numbered among the survivors of Napoleon's winter campaign of 1812 in Russia. As frivolous as his father, addicted to gambling like his uncle, he spent his wife's fortune in a carefree manner and pursued dancers to his ruin. He liked to wear extravagant decoration and embroidery, such that many years earlier General Berthier once told him to get out of his presence since the gaudy outfit he was wearing could no longer be described as a military uniform. Edmond was captured by the Prussian cavalry following the Battle of Leipzig during a skirmish near Mühlberg in Brandenburg in October 1813 and released at the time of Napoleon's abdication in April 1814.

In 1812, Talleyrand was a courageous man living on tenterhooks. He knew that if any one of his secret letters to Metternich or to the tsar were intercepted by Napoleon's police the consequences would be fatal. Somehow, Dorothea discovered what he was doing and found it fascinating: "This bold temperament, this instinctive gallantry which inspired an irresistible taste for all forms of danger, which makes peril attractive and hazards fascinating." She not only admired him, she enjoyed the double game he was playing: "There was beneath the nobility of his manners, the slowness of his movements, the self-indulgence of his habits, an audacious foolhardiness which at times sparkled." Talleyrand's "audacious" character opened up for her a world of intrigue that she found irresistible.

Aware that his regular mail was intercepted and read, Talleyrand made sure that the letters he wrote to Caulaincourt in Saint Petersburg were full of uninhibited praise for Napoleon's victories, that they were enthusiastic about the potential reunification of Poland, and that he anticipated glorious peace negotiations in the very near future. The police found in them the words of a faithful subject deriving no pleasure from the military disasters befalling Napoleon in Spain. His secret letters to Metternich and the tsar were conveyed by more inconspicuous channels.

One of the surviving members of Talleyrand's harem left in Paris was Aimée de Coigny. When they first met at the salon of the Bellegarde sisters, Aimée was so put off by his expressionless mask that she was almost ready to stop her visits there but, little by little, they grew to become inseparable friends. Napoleon disliked Aimée's loose morals and at a reception at the Tuileries Palace asked her in public: "Well, Madame, are you still so fond of men?" Her riposte was: "Yes, Sire, when they are polite." Sometime during 1812, the 43-year-old Aimée formed a liaison with the 45-year-old Marquis Bruno-Gabriel de Boisgelin, one of Louis XVIII's agents in Paris and a sworn enemy of Napoleon. Coigny and Boisgelin decided to do everything in their power to hasten the emperor's downfall, believing strongly that only the restoration of the Bourbon kings could save France from further turmoil. Since the summer of 1812, Aimée had been making frequent visits to the Rue Saint-Florentin, which, due to her long-term acquaintance with Talleyrand and as a female friend, did not arouse suspicion.

Aimée de Coigny had spent her childhood at the Château de Vigny in the Val d'Oise, to the north-east of Paris. Passing some of the summer months there, she and Boisgelin became acquainted with the resident chaplain, the Abbé Desnoyelles. His parents were Belgian peasants and he had subsequently become a Franciscan monk, in other words, a mediocre priest. She labelled him as brave, coarse, licentious, lazy, stupid, honest and able but, above all, a devoted Royalist. He would become the messenger carrying secret communications between Boisgelin and the court of Louis Stanislas Xavier, also known as Louis XVIII, in England.

Louis Stanislas Xavier, the Count de Provence, had been an intelligent boy, excelling in the classics. His education was religious in nature—several of his teachers were priests—and of the same quality and consistency as that of his older brother, Louis Auguste. In May 1774, their grandfather Louis XV died of smallpox and Louis Auguste succeeded him as King Louis XVI. As the new king's younger brother and heir, Louis Stanislas received the official title of "Monsieur" and longed for a political role but was left in limbo. In the aftermath of the

304

French Revolution, on the night of 20-21 June 1791, the Count de Provence and his wife successfully fled to the **Austrian Netherlands** (nowadays Belgium) by separate routes at the same time as the royal family's failed **flight to Varennes**. Following the death of Louis XVI on the guillotine in 1793 and that of his son Louis Joseph (i.e. Louis XVII) in captivity in 1795, for the Royalist camp the Count of Provence became the rightful king. After several years of wandering throughout Europe, staying in Germany, Italy, Russia, Prussia and Sweden, Louis Stanislas and his wife finally moved **to Hartwell House** in Buckinghamshire, England, in 1807. The **Prince Regent** (the future George IV) of the United Kingdom was very charitable to the exiled Bourbons, granting them the permanent **right of asylum** and providing extremely generous allowances to support them and their over 100 courtiers. Significantly, in 1809, Louis appointed the **Count de Blacas** as his principal political advisor. Queen Marie Joséphine, Louis's wife, died childless in November 1810—there were rumours and counter-rumours that the marriage was never consummated. That same winter, Louis suffered a particularly severe attack of gout, which was a recurring problem for him at Hartwell, and he had resorted to a specially-constructed wheelchair— we shall meet this machine again!

Although Talleyrand sought peace, he found himself in a situation where he was actually advising Napoleon's enemies how best to make war. Once again, Talleyrand recommended that Russia and Austria should form an alliance, arming themselves rapidly for the forthcoming conflict. Russia occupied a large part of eastern Poland and was not prepared to relinquish it without a fight, while the central part of Poland—the Grand Duchy of Warsaw—was Napoleon's protectorate under the tutelage of the King of Saxony. Russia had also abandoned Napoleon's embargo on trade with the United Kingdom—the Continental System. Talleyrand forecast that the storm over these conflicting interests would break in 1812—he was right. As we have already seen, the tsar had been ready for action early and proposed taking the offensive in 1811, but Talleyrand had dissuaded him.

When performing his official duties as Vice-Grand Elector at the Tuileries Palace, Talleyrand was aware that the import of each word he uttered in public was noted and analysed. He craved a situation where what he said was "without significance and without consequences". Aimée de Coigny organized a whole programme of distractions for him. The attractive Bellegarde sisters, Aurore and Adélaïde, held weekly dinners where writers and artists were invited in order that the great diplomat should not become jaded. The Bellegarde sisters were also present at the Princess de Vaudémont's salon, where the conversation varied between the caustic repartee of Mme de Laval and the profound wit—or occasionally the meaningful silences—of the former Bishop of Autun. These evenings provided an unobtrusive opportunity for the meeting of those people who wished to see the end of Napoleon's regime, including Auguste de Saint-Aignan (Caulaincourt's brother-in-law), Pasquier, Molé and Vitrolles.

Dalberg had established a long-term friendship with a Royalist agent from the provinces who had fled France during the Revolution and joined the Royalist army, Eugène François d'Arnauld, the Baron de Vitrolles, a charming, honourable, modest but intelligent gentleman. He came to Paris in 1813 and was to play a significant role in the restoration of the Bourbon monarchy. Aimée de Coigny describes him as "clever, devoted and daring". Thanks to him, the discussions about Napoleon's successor began to turn seriously in the direction of Louis Stanislas Xavier, already known among the Royalists as Louis XVIII.

Napoleon considered England as his principal adversary, so the purpose of defeating the Russians and conquering Spain was to force the British Government, as the only remaining ally, to the negotiating table. Due to the Napoleonic Wars, the British had adopted tough measures at sea to isolate France, involving the seizure of American ships and their crews. Not surprisingly, this had severely irritated the American Government and in June 1812 war broke out between England and the United States, which Napoleon considered a blessing.

Soon after Napoleon's marriage proposal to Grand Duchess Catherine, the tsar's favourite sister, had gone unheeded, she had married her cousin George, Duke of Oldenburg. At the end of 1810 the tsar rejected the Continental System and, in retaliation, the Duchy of Oldenburg, located on the North Sea coast of Germany, was annexed by Napoleon on 22 January 1811. Oldenburg had been ruled as a regency by the Grand Duke Peter I, George's father and the tsar's uncle. This annexation was therefore a great insult on Napoleon's part towards the Russian royal family. Furthermore, given the unresolved Polish situation and the defunct Continental System, the relationship between Russia and France reached a low ebb.

At this moment, Russia was fighting the Ottoman Empire for possession of the provinces on the western coast of the Black Sea, so Talleyrand advised Nesselrode that the tsar should sign a peace agreement with the Sultan "at any price" leaving the Russian armies free to deal with the war with Napoleon that would inevitably come. Talleyrand's basic plan was that Russia and Austria should form a defensive alliance that would deter Napoleon—a north-south line would be drawn across Europe from the Baltic to the Alps and, if Napoleon crossed it, war would be declared by both countries. Only an alliance between Russia and Austria was strong enough to counterbalance the power of the French Army.

Napoleon's advisers at this time included the frank and forthright Caulaincourt, the zealous Maret and the frivolous Narbonne. Who better than Talleyrand could manipulate Austria, keep an eye on Prussia and deal with Tsar Alexander? In the meantime, the reconciliation between Talleyrand and Napoleon had reached a point where, one evening in March 1812, the emperor, swearing him to secrecy, proposed to appoint him as the future governor of Warsaw from where he could reorganize the Polish state while the French Army attacked Russia. This would also mean that Talleyrand would not remain in Paris plotting behind Napoleon's back. The prospect of becoming an important player in a gigantic exercise pleased him, while the linguistic assistance of the Duchess von Courland and Mme Tyszkiewicz would certainly facilitate his task. He might even be in the right position to conduct peace negotiations with the Russians! Another of Napoleon's forgiven courtiers was Fouché, who had returned to favour. In one of his first actions, he advised Napoleon not to go to war with Russia.

If Talleyrand were to take up his new post as governor of Warsaw, he would require ready cash, but there was no way of sending money to Poland. For this reason, Talleyrand transferred 60,000 francs to Vienna to avoid having currency problems when he reached Warsaw. Minister of Posts Lavalette informed Napoleon about this move, which could easily have been interpreted as a signal alerting the Austrians of Napoleon's intentions. Furthermore, Talleyrand had boasted to his harem that he was back in favour with the emperor. Before long, his appointment in Warsaw was a secret no more—and cancelled. Napoleon was furious and sent Maret and the Archbishop of Malines, the ex-Abbé de Pradt, to Warsaw instead—a decision he would come to regret bitterly during the retreat from Moscow. The idea of leaving Talleyrand behind him in Paris where he would find himself free to conspire was too much for Napoleon, so on two separate occasions he gave instructions to Minister of Police Savary to banish him from Paris—but nothing was done. Napoleon did not insist on Talleyrand's exile but, in August 1812, told Savary to keep a close eye on him and forbade the 22-year-old Empress Marie Louise from paying Talleyrand any favours, such as inviting him to her whist evenings. Savary and Caulaincourt noted Talleyrand's exasperation at once more falling out of favour and they recommended that Napoleon should meet him. "I do not wish to see him," declared the emperor. When it was far too late, Napoleon subsequently realized that Talleyrand, Courland and Tyszkiewicz would have succeeded in Warsaw where Maret and de Pradt failed.

Talleyrand knew that the Russians were ready for war and that Napoleon's army had ceased to be the same invincible body that it had been ten years earlier when it was composed exclusively of Frenchmen led by officers promoted from the ranks. By summoning his client kings and princes to provide troops, almost half of Napoleon's army was not French. The Count de Sémonville overheard Talleyrand at a reception one evening murmuring: "It's the beginning of the end." Mme de Coigny and Talleyrand both believed that the fall of Napoleon was imminent and had discussed the formation of some form of liberal government following his departure for Eastern Europe. The Russian Ambassador to Paris, Karl Nesselrode, explained the attitude of Talleyrand and Fouché to the tsar: "These men do not believe that they are betraying their master but protecting him from the fire of his passions by preventing him from undertaking endless wars which are culling the population, reducing it to poverty and could end in horrific disasters."

It was in this way that Napoleon, setting off to join his army at Dresden prior to the invasion of Russia, left Talleyrand and Fouché behind in Paris. This may have saved their lives but politically it was an error; it would have been far better to have taken them along, rather than leaving them to conspire in Paris. Napoleon's invasion of Russia in 1812 is remembered as one of the greatest military disasters of all time. While plunging into the wastes of Russia, Napoleon would learn that he was also losing control of Spain with Wellington's victory at Salamanca.

Why did Napoleon invade Russia? In order to achieve his strategy of European domination, he had introduced the Continental System in an attempt to bring the British economy to ruin. If it were to succeed, all European countries had to participate in a trade embargo, thus depriving the British of revenue to conduct military and naval operations. Already, Spain and Portugal had expressed their dissent and had been punished by the presence of the French Army. Alexander never seriously engaged with the Continental System and, while Napoleon had been distracted by combat in the Iberian Peninsula, the tsar abandoned the embargo and pursued his expansionist agenda in Eastern Europe. His edict of 31 December 1810 had cast aside Napoleon's blockade and thereafter he sought friendship with England. In doing so, he undermined Napoleon's whole strategy. Both Russia and France began to prepare for war in earnest, activities which could hardly be kept secret.

What triggered the war of 1812? The Russians had invaded the Aaland Islands and Finland causing a political crisis in Sweden leading to the overthrow of the monarchy. Jean-Baptiste Bernadotte, formerly one of Napoleon's marshals, was elected Crown Prince of Sweden. He was not a man who would obey Napoleon blindly and took his new responsibilities very seriously. Tsar Alexander offered to become Sweden's ally and, after Napoleon seized Swedish Pomerania (an isolated pocket on the north German Baltic coast), Bernadotte accepted. Napoleon could not tolerate this situation.

At the end of 1811, during the preparations for his Russian campaign, Napoleon wanted to remove from Tsar Alexander's mind any suspicion that Russia was about to be attacked by the biggest army in history. Ambassador Caulaincourt presented to the tsar a note from Napoleon stating that all the obvious preparations in Europe for a vast military campaign by the French Army were aimed at crushing the last traces of resistance among the Spanish people. Caulaincourt read the note twice to Alexander who listened with full attention. The tsar then replied that, unfortunately, although he would like to believe the assurances he had been given, the information that he had received from a multitude of other sources indicated that the content of the note was entirely without substance. He then said to Caulaincourt: "You see how many reasons I have not to believe one word of Napoleon's assertions. Nevertheless, I would begin to have confidence in them if you, M. de Caulaincourt, can tell me on your honour that you give them your full and entire conviction." Upon hearing these words, Caulaincourt turned on his heel and left the room without responding. To appreciate what kind of a man he was, when he returned to his office, he wrote a full report to his master of precisely what had happened, including its conclusion. Nevertheless, there was no doubt also that Caulaincourt would find out what the Russian tactics were and find it his duty to report them back to Napoleon.

Meanwhile, rumours began to circulate that Russia had plans to take over the Grand Duchy of Warsaw, one of Napoleon's most loyal enclaves in Eastern Europe. Prior to the invasion of Russia, Alexander and Napoleon were both clearly aware of each other's intentions. Early in 1812, Alexander concluded peace with Turkey, thus releasing troops and resources to face the French onslaught. In June 1812, Napoleon and his *Grande Armée* set out across Europe into the jaws of disaster. Although a supply system had been put in place, Napoleon's troops often fed themselves by pillaging towns and villages as they advanced. Due to bad or non-existent roads and the poor farmland across which they advanced, the supply system soon began to falter, while during the advance and subsequent retreat the Russians destroyed everything in the path of the French Army.

Napoleon was so sure of the success of the Russian expedition that he had already foreseen overwintering his army in Turkey with his headquarters located in Constantinople. He had even established diplomatic negotiations with Persia with a view to marching on to India with 200,000 men to overthrow the British domination of the sub-continent. However, upon Napoleon's forces reaching Moscow—significantly, the economic capital rather than the political one—the Russians set the city ablaze. The French were left without supplies or shelter, while Alexander refused to negotiate. As the winter closed in,

Napoleon's Army withdrew to the west pursued by the Russians. This resulted in the collapse of military order and enormous losses of men, horses and equipment. It is interesting to note that, up until the Battle of Borodino on 6 September 1812, Mme de Staël had been staying in Moscow but travelled to St Petersburg on the following days before moving on to Stockholm and London. In Sweden, she met the new King Charles XIV John, formerly General Bernadotte, whose ambition was to join Russia and England in a coalition to combat the French Emperor.

The course of Parisian life was overturned on 23 October 1812 when General Claude François de Malet (not to be confused with Napoleon's aide-de-camp General Hugues-Bernard Maret) decided to seize power by arresting Savary, Minister of Police, and Pasquier, the Prefect of Police for Paris, on the pretence that Napoleon was dead. However, he failed to arrest Archchancellor Cambacérès and General Henri Clarke, Minister of War. Finally, the plot was foiled when an incredulous Colonel Pierre Doucet recognized Malet as being someone he knew to have a history of mental issues. He was also aware of letters written by Napoleon after the date given for his supposed death. The plotters were executed. Talleyrand, who had nothing to do with it, could not take the plot seriously, sending a letter to the Duchess von Courland specifically for the attention of Savary's police: "This sort of little movement stimulated by this type of delinquent subject, General Malet, who was not sufficiently supervised". In another letter to Caulaincourt, he declared for public consumption that Paris should be garrisoned by more reliable troops. This incident was a further illustration of the fragility of Napoleon's regime, but equally that it was necessary for any dissidents to proceed with extreme caution. The time for Talleyrand to act had not yet come.

News of Napoleon's disastrous military failure in Russia reached Paris on 16 December. Two evenings later, Dorothea was on duty with the Empress Marie Louise at the Tuileries Palace when she heard a noise at the door. Two scruffy individuals dressed in furs entered, one short, the other tall; it was Napoleon and Caulaincourt back from the Russian front. Dorothea hastily scribbled a note to inform Talleyrand. At the end of each stage of the journey back to Paris, Caulaincourt had made copious notes of his conversations with the emperor. Later, General

Maret, Duke de Bassano, who was Napoleon's personal secretary, published an account of the invasion of Russia and retreat from Moscow. Caulaincourt was unhappy about Maret's description of events and subsequently wrote his own version based on his notes, although publication was seriously delayed and the work eventually lost. Over one hundred years later, the manuscript was re-discovered and published under the title *With Napoleon in Russia*. During the invasion of the Soviet Union in 1941, many German officers carried copies of Caulaincourt's book with them although, nevertheless, the final outcome was the same as in 1812.

In order to decide what to do after the failure of his Russian Campaign, Napoleon called a meeting of his advisers at the Tuileries on 3 January 1813—Talleyrand amongst them. The Russian Army would now obviously move westward, joined by the Prussians and the Austrians, with the prospect that the French Army's remaining isolated units would be crushed in their path or simply by-passed. At this moment, Napoleon could have retreated from Spain, brought back the 150,000 men manning fortresses in Germany, swelled the ranks of his army with new recruits while withdrawing to France's natural frontiers. In this situation, he would have presented a formidable front to his enemies. Talleyrand, Cambacérès and Caulaincourt recommended peace at any price, withdrawal without delay and Austrian mediation. With authority, courage and lucidity, Talleyrand told Napoleon: "Negotiate. You have in your hand at the moment assets that you can forfeit. If you wait, you may have lost them and with them the ability to negotiate will also be gone." If Napoleon had listened, perhaps he would have salvaged the remnants of his regime—but he had already made up his mind to pursue the continental war to the bitter end in an attempt to preserve his empire. He preferred to listen to the opinion of Maret, whom Talleyrand considered a vacuous wastrel. When Maret returned from the Russian front, Talleyrand crowed sarcastically: "Oh, look how they exaggerate! Didn't they say all the equipment was lost? But now Maret is back!"

Later that year, Talleyrand and Mme de La Tour du Pin each found themselves at a salon in Paris. The French retreat across Germany and the invasion of France was a cause of concern. What news did Talleyrand have of Napoleon? "Oh! Don't talk to me about your emperor! He's finished!" "How finished? What do you mean?" she asked. "I mean," he replied, "he is a man who would hide under his bed." He went on: "He has lost all his equipment. He's had it, that's all." He showed Mme de La Tour du Pin a British newspaper cutting that he had circled in pencil reporting a dinner that had been hosted in London by the Prince Regent in honour of the Duchess d'Angoulême—the daughter of Louis XVI and Marie-Antoinette, in fact, the only surviving member of her family. The dining room and the table were decorated in blue with the insignia of white lilies—the Bourbon emblems. The newspaper article bore a very clear message about the upsurge of the Bourbons without the need for any further comment.

Up until this time, the Allies had been defeated one by one, but now Portugal, Prussia, Russia, Spain, Sweden and the United Kingdom joined together in the Sixth Coalition together with a number of smaller German states. On 11 August 1813, Austrian troops joined the countries belonging to the Sixth Coalition, who had decided to implement the Trachenberg Plan, a campaign to disengage their forces when they knew that Napoleon was on the battlefield. The Allies planned to combat and defeat the French marshals and generals separately one by one, thus weakening his army, while eventually building up an overwhelming force that even Napoleon could not defeat. This tactic evolved after a series of defeats and near disasters suffered by the Coalition at the battles of Lützen, Bautzen and Dresden. The plan worked, such that at the four-day Battle of Leipzig in October 1813, where the Allies had a considerable numerical advantage, the emperor was soundly defeated and driven out of Germany, across the Rhine back into France itself, having to hack his way through the Bavarian Army at Hanau, which threatened to cut off his line of retreat.

On the Spanish border, on 7 October 1813, the Duke of Wellington with an army of 100,000 men, using completely different military tactics to those of Napoleon, had penetrated on to French soil after the Battle of the River Bidasoa. In the east, an Allied Army of more than 200,000 men crossed the Rhine in the middle of December.

Increasingly desperate, Napoleon wavered between offering Talleyrand his old ministry or having him exiled. Caulaincourt describes Napoleon pacing up and down in his office at Saint-Cloud wondering how he could best employ Talleyrand whom, at the same time, he distrusted above all others. While Napoleon was prepared to benefit from Talleyrand's prestige and skill, he would not follow his advice. Talleyrand stated indignantly: "I am not familiar with your affairs... Only you know them!" Napoleon retorted: "Do you want to betray me?" "No, Sire," replied Talleyrand: "I do not want the responsibility because I believe it contrary to my way of envisaging the glory and happiness of my country." This is what he had been thinking since 1805 and even before, but had waited eight years to express it. Mme von Kielmannsegge reported yet another dreadful scene between Talleyrand and Napoleon, where the latter threatened to shoot him or hang him, calling him a traitor and once again stamping on his unfortunate hat. The disgraced minister sailed calmly out of Napoleon's office with a remark for those waiting outside: "The emperor is charming this morning." The "squalls" between the two men became more frequent and it sometimes took the intervention of Caulaincourt, Cambacérès, Berthier, Savary, Fouché or even Talleyrand's son Charles de Flahaut to invoke Napoleon's clemency. A few days after offering him the ministry, Napoleon remarked scornfully that Talleyrand was worthless. It is remarkable that, despite all the hatred, wariness, contempt and bitterness, Napoleon readily admitted that he was "the most capable minister I ever had".

We have not finished with Napoleon's tantrums for another one took place at Saint-Cloud on 9 November 1813. Talleyrand had not been invited to attend a reception but turned up anyway. Napoleon was furious and in a boastful mood, declaring: "I tell you that if I were critically ill, you would be dead before me!" With his tongue firmly in his cheek, Talleyrand replied: "Sire, I did not need such a warning for my most ardent wish is asking Heaven to protect Your Majesty's days." With the imminent prospect of being arrested and executed, Talleyrand appeared neither intimidated nor able to forget his courtly good manners. He remarked to Savary that, instead of continuously scolding him with offensive language, it would have been far wiser for Napoleon to question the advice of his so-called friends, who represented a greater menace to him than his enemies. Talleyrand's conclusion on Napoleon was that he should be allowed to complete his own destruction: "There was never a more dangerous conspirator against him than himself."

Napoleon was obsessed with being betrayed, although he had made so many mistakes that the matter of betrayal was now of secondary importance. A few days later, Napoleon sought Talleyrand's opinion as if nothing had happened between them. Talleyrand told him: "There is only one solution. You have made a mistake. You must say so and try to say it graciously."

Talleyrand did not have any good words for those who succeeded him at the Ministry of Foreign Affairs. In 1811, Champagny had been replaced in this post by the unpopular Maret, who was one of the rare people who wanted to pursue the war. Napoleon realized that he would have to sacrifice Maret. Using Caulaincourt as a messenger, Napoleon threatened Talleyrand with punishment, imprisonment and/or exile if he did not accept the post of Foreign Minister. In November 1813, yet again, Napoleon offered Talleyrand the Ministry of Foreign Affairs—on condition that he gave up his wife ("that trollop"), his harem of countesses and his title of Vice-Grand Elector. Clearly, these unacceptable conditions were quite ridiculous—Talleyrand refused. Napoleon was attempting to persuade Caulaincourt that there was only one candidate to replace Maret on the Rue du Bac—Caulaincourt himself.

No-one had any doubt that Napoleon's government was finished—except for the emperor and his immediate entourage—so the big question was: What would replace it? Vitrolles, Coigny and Boisgelin had spoken of bringing the Bourbons back to the throne. One member of Louis XVIII's little court at Hartwell was well known to Talleyrand—his uncle Alexandre-Angélique, Archbishop of Reims. A conciliatory letter sent to his uncle made such a good impression that the archbishop read it aloud to Louis XVIII, who exclaimed: "Thank God! Bonaparte must be finished." He asked the archbishop to reply to his nephew recalling fond memories of their past acquaintance at Versailles—he exaggerated a little for they hardly knew each other. Louis XVIII understood that Talleyrand's abandonment of Napoleon signalled the end of his regime, so the Count de Blacas, Louis's councillor, asked the Prince de Benevento if he would like to become an agent, providing the exiled king with information. It would have been far too dangerous to enter into such an arrangement and in the early part of 1814 the restoration of

Louis XVIII was just one of many possible alternatives for a regime to follow Napoleon's Empire. When Hartwell House circulated a proclamation from Louis XVIII in Paris, Napoleon interrogated Talleyrand about it, who pretended complete ignorance. Although his Vice-Grand Elector found the document "clumsy", certain parts bore a striking resemblance to his own manner of thinking.

We enter a period of great turmoil, with Napoleon alternating between scenes of violent confrontation with Talleyrand and then vainly offering him a government post. "He who refuses to serve me today is inevitably my enemy," bellowed Napoleon at him in front of Cambacérès, Caulaincourt and Savary. He called for Maret to arrest Talleyrand on the spot but, strangely, he could not be found. Later, Napoleon calmed down and Talleyrand left. On 16 January 1814, another flare-up took place when the Prince de Benevento was accused of setting in motion a slide on the stock market. He took the precaution of asking Courtiade to burn a large quantity of his private papers—with the result that historians are faced with further gaps in the written record.

Although it was one of the coldest winters in living memory, on 25 January 1814, Napoleon left Paris to rejoin his army in the field; Talleyrand and the emperor would never meet again. During a reception at Fontainebleau the evening before, Napoleon remarked that, while combating the enemies of France, he knew that he was leaving other enemies behind him. During a council meeting, Napoleon accused Talleyrand of conducting a secret correspondence with Caulaincourt—everyone knew perfectly well that his letters to Caulaincourt were being intercepted and read by the police, for this reason he always included enthusiastic expressions of loyalty to the emperor in them. The Vice-Grand Elector replied without flinching: "I do not need to remind Your Highness to employ my private letters with the very greatest discretion!" With Napoleon gone, Empress Marie Louise remained in Paris acting as president of the Council of Regents, of which Talleyrand formed part. In order that Talleyrand should not dominate proceedings, Napoleon nominated his brother Joseph Bonaparte as lieutenant-general of the Empire. Napoleon probably thought that it was wise to appoint Talleyrand to a place where he could be supervised by Cambacérès and Joseph. The Vice-Grand Elector considered Marie Louise as a sensible person who represented a point of stability. His dear friend the Duchess von Courland had returned to France and he advised her that if Marie Louise ever left Paris, she should do the same. Fearing that at any moment he would find himself, amongst many others, standing before the firing squad, he asked the duchess to take care of Charlotte's education. Nevertheless, he was still the second most important political figure in France and, as Aimée de Coigny wrote: "All Paris came to see him in secret and in private," but he continued to sit on the fence regarding who would follow Napoleon as the ruler of France. In the meantime, Aimée began to visit the Rue Saint-Florentin more and more frequently using her powers of persuasion to convince Talleyrand to support the restoration of the Bourbon dynasty. One day, closing his office door to make sure they were alone, Talleyrand said to her: "Madame de Coigny, I myself would like the king but...". Before he could complete his sentence, the impulsive Aimée threw her arms round his neck and congratulated him for saving the country. The problem for Talleyrand was that, while he had known the unpretentious Duke d'Artois—Louis XVI's youngest brother—quite well, he was not so familiar with the intelligent, infirm and crafty Louis XVIII, and he could not be sure how his own involvement in the Enghien Affair would be interpreted by the Bourbons. Speaking about Talleyrand, Napoleon said to Caulaincourt: "If, one day, he succeeds in restoring the Bourbons, it will be them who take my revenge on him."

Aimée told Talleyrand that her lover Boisgelin was in contact with Louis and perhaps he would like to read their correspondence. She returned the next day and, when they were alone, showed him a copy of Boisgelin's draft letter to Louis XVIII, drawing attention to a paragraph that said it was impossible for the king to return without the involvement of Talleyrand. He was delighted with what he read—"That's it!"—but they agreed that the copy of the letter in his hands should be destroyed. "He twisted the paper, lit it from a candle, threw the flames into the fireplace and crossed the shovel and the tongs above it so as to prevent the ashes from flying up the chimney." Up to this moment Talleyrand had been in favour of a Regency but he now decided to support the Bourbon Restoration. Rather than Aimée coming to the Rue Saint-Florentin, in future he drove to her house in his carriage.

Even on the battlefield, Napoleon continued to harbour suspicions about his Vice-Grand Elector. He wrote to his brother Joseph, who lodged at the Luxembourg Palace, to keep a close eye on him. As a reflection of the times, it should also be noted that Napoleon had misgivings about the empress and especially the loyalty of his own brother Joseph! The emperor told Savary, the Minister of Police, to make sure that the comings and goings at Talleyrand's residence were observed. One day, Savary learned that the ex-Abbé de Pradt, the ex-Abbé Louis, Dalberg and a few others were all meeting at the ex-Abbé de Périgord's residence on the Rue Saint-Florentin. In their memoirs, both Savary and Talleyrand describe what happened. The clumsy Minister of Police burst in unannounced in the middle of their animated conversation and said half-joking: "This time, no need to deny it, I have caught you plotting." Although Talleyrand and Savary were not on friendly terms, they had worked together as close colleagues for a number of years. In February 1814, Napoleon had given Savary written instructions to arrest Talleyrand, but the Minister of Police protested to Lavalette: "Don't I have enough Royalists to look after in the whole of France [...] Talleyrand is the only person preventing him from making a fool of himself." Both Talleyrand and Savary detested Maret and sought peace. Savary must have been keenly aware that, if the Bourbons were restored to power, his position as the officer who had executed the Duke d'Enghien would be extremely delicate. While Savary was aware of everything that was going on, it was equally obvious to him that Napoleon was no longer the strong man of France, so there was no sequel to his intervention at Talleyrand's house. The philosophical Talleyrand's only comment was: "What an awful job it is to be the Minister of Police!"

Talleyrand had known the ex-Abbé Dominique Louis for a very long time since they had participated together at *La Fête de la Fédération* in July 1790. Louis had graduated from theology to finance and had been made a baron by Napoleon. Like Talleyrand, he always coveted a ministerial post and would be responsible for the French Ministry of Finance at various times until the 1830s. The ex-Abbé Dominique de Pradt had become a secretary to Napoleon in 1804 and had later been appointed Bishop of Poitiers until 1808, finally being promoted to the post of Archbishop of Malines, a diocese near Brussels. In 1812, by one of Napoleon's hasty, inexplicable and regrettable decisions, he had been appointed French ambassador to Warsaw.

Working with Dalberg and Roux-Laborie during this time, the Prince de Benevento attempted to know everything, to see everything, to hear everything. Bourrienne let him know about important letters passing through the postal service; Jaucourt was Joseph Bonaparte's chamberlain; La Besnardière was in contact with the Austrians. Aimée de Coigny tells us that Talleyrand and Caulaincourt were able to communicate with each other by secret code and one can be sure that d'Hauterive, who was temporarily manning the Ministry of Foreign Affairs, also kept him informed of events.

Louis de Bourrienne had been Napoleon's childhood friend and his personal secretary up until 1802, when he was dismissed for dishonest financial dealings. Now, rather than serving the emperor, Bourrienne served Talleyrand. It was Bourrienne who was good friends with Antoine de Lavalette, the Director-General of Posts, who knew at all times where everyone was located giving him access to the mail service, so that while Savary's men were browsing Talleyrand's letters, Talleyrand read Napoleon's. Earlier, one of Bourrienne's most enterprising strokes of genius was, when required to purchase a large quantity of military cloaks for Napoleon's Army, smuggled them in at great profit from England at a time when the countries were at war with each other and all trade prohibited!

While Napoleon was attempting to stall the Allied Armies to the east of Paris, the faithful Caulaincourt, now Minister of Foreign Affairs, was sent on a mission to negotiate with the leaders of the Sixth Coalition at the town of Châtillon. Before he left, Talleyrand informed him, to his surprise, that he should bear in mind the interests of the Bourbon regime that would inevitably follow Napoleon's collapse. Caulaincourt kept his mouth shut about the significance of this remark, for it implied that Talleyrand had secret contacts with Louis XVIII. The principal bone of contention in negotiations with the Allies was whether the northern border of France was the traditional, pre-revolutionary one of 1789 or whether it now ran all the way up the left bank of the Rhine to its estuary with the Scheldt on the North Sea. As far as Napoleon was concerned, it was the latter, whereas, if the Bourbons were restored to the throne, they would probably accept the ancient frontier without any qualms.

In the spring of 1814, the French population received exaggerated reports of Napoleon's successes, while his defeats were passed over in silence. With the end of Napoleon's regime imminent, a number of people were waiting for an opportunity to deal the final blow that would bring him down. Since the defeat of Napoleon would inevitably mean the defeat of France, it would be best if the choice of regime that would follow were decided beforehand. As regards his successor, there were a number of possibilities: one of Napoleon's marshals, or Louis-Philippe d'Orléans, or Napoleon's infant son or Louis XVIII. While none of them lacked drawbacks, it gradually became clear to Talleyrand that the latter was the least bad choice. In this case, the plotters proposed that Louis XVIII would be invited to assume the throne controlled by a constitution and parliament that would oblige him to issue laws in the people's interest. But would the formidable Louis allow himself to be restrained by a liberal constitution?

Whatever solution was found to the government of France after the fall of Napoleon, nothing would happen without the approval of the principal Allies. Dalberg was desperate to hasten the advance of their armies and sought a foolhardy messenger to cross the front lines to make contact with them. The ardent Baron de Vitrolles was so devoted to the Royalist cause that he was ready to die for it. He volunteered to go, leaving Paris on 6 March by regular mail-coach in the direction of Lyon, dressed in plain clothes as if returning to his home in south-eastern France, although his intention was to reach the Allies by passing through open country to the south of the front line. Without too many difficulties, he reached the Allied camp carrying a miniscule message written by Dalberg in invisible ink for the tsar's envoy Nesselrode. In a conversation with Vitrolles, Dalberg had warned him to be extremely cautious with the tricky Metternich, but also particularly with Talleyrand. "You don't know this monkey," he told him. "He would not run the risk of burning his fingers when all the chestnuts are for him alone." Vitrolles stumbled upon Stadion's headquarters, the Austrian Minister of Finance, at Châtillon. He was then directed to Nesselrode, Metternich, Tsar Alexander, Viscount Castlereagh, the British Foreign Secretary, and Karl August von Hardenberg, the Prussian Chancellor. They all received him with open arms, while the message he was carrying convinced the Allies to march at once towards Paris. Upon leaving the Allied camp, Vitrolles rode off in the opposite direction since the person with whom he most wanted to make contact was the Duke d'Artois, Louis XVIII's brother and emissary. He found him in Nancy, where Artois was astonished to learn that Vitrolles, who he had never met before, had passed through the front line, had spoken with the leaders of the Allied armies and carried a hand-written message from Metternich. When it came to discussing with Artois who should be entrusted with the provisional government of France before the king's arrival, Vitrolles declared: "The name of M. de Talleyrand was the first, and indeed the only one, that came to mind." Artois still referred to Talleyrand as "the Bishop of Autun". For Vitrolles, returning to Paris was by far the most dangerous part of the journey since he was obliged to cross the continually shifting front. He had hardly left Nancy before he was captured by a mob of peasants and handed over to Napoleon's cavalry. Some days later, he succeeded in escaping in the city of Troyes by running down a dark alley at night. He eventually arrived in Paris, where his friends had given him up for dead.

During the spring of 1814, Napoleon was fighting for the first time on French soil. From a purely military point of view, never had his generalship been more brilliant, but his faults in diplomacy and statesmanship had already completely undermined his position. He was faced with overwhelming numbers of Austrian, Prussian and Russian troops advancing irrevocably towards Paris from the east, while Wellington at the head of the British, Spanish and Portuguese armies was progressing steadily from the south-west. In November 1813, the Allies had actually made an offer to halt their advance and to respect the natural frontiers of France, but Napoleon so little appreciated the weakness of his position that he rejected it. Again, in February 1814, the Allies proposed to respect the frontiers of 1791 and Caulaincourt, as Minister of Foreign Affairs, urged acceptance. However, Napoleon had recently achieved some small military successes and, typically, was not prepared to listen to anybody. Since reaching any kind of peace agreement with Napoleon was obviously never going to happen, his behaviour had the positive effect of strengthening the resolve of the Allies to remain united until they achieved total victory.

The Battles of Laon, Arcis-sur-Aube and Saint-Dizier were the last combats fought by Napoleon against the Austro-Russian Armies. A letter from Napoleon to Marie Louise was intercepted revealing that there was now nothing in front of the Allied Armies' overwhelming force except some isolated and exhausted French Army units, while another seized letter from Savary to Napoleon requested that he should return to Paris at once if the city were to remain in his hands. Since Napoleon's forces in eastern France were gradually drifting southward, the route to Paris lay open, where a provisional government headed by Talleyrand would be waiting to receive the Allies. In this way, street fighting that might damage the city could be avoided. Napoleon said: "Ah! If Talleyrand had been here, he would have got me out of this mess." It was at this point that Baron Louis made the celebrated remark: "The man is a corpse but he doesn't stink yet."

On 12 March, Wellington's army reached Bordeaux with the city opening its gates to the 12,000 soldiers of General Beresford, while at the same time the Duke d'Angoulême, the son of the Duke d'Artois, landed from a British warship to cries of "Vive le roi!". For the first time in twenty years the Bourbons were proclaimed by the French people. Meanwhile, back at the Tuileries Palace and encouraged by Napoleon's express permission, Talleyrand had been playing whist with the Empress Marie Louise, Queen Hortense and Mathieu Molé, the Minister of Justice. On 28 March, Talleyrand and Pasquier, the Parisian Prefect of Police, could not agree as to whether Marie Louise and her son should stay in Paris or take refuge elsewhere. Talleyrand wanted them to leave, while Pasquier believed that it was the Regent's duty to stay in the capital where the Austrian-born empress's presence might guarantee clemency on the part of the Allied Armies. On this very same day, when the Council of Regents met, in what appeared to be a *volte-face*, Talleyrand now recommended that Marie Louise should stay in Paris! Finally, following Napoleon's explicit instructions, it was decided that the empress and her son should leave the city before it was too late. When asked why he had first encouraged her to leave and then changed his mind, Talleyrand replied: "I could see that the empress didn't trust me and if I advised leaving, she would stay. If I favoured that she stayed, she would leave." The departure of the imperial household would considerably facilitate the restoration of the Bourbons. In the event that Napoleon's were killed on the battlefield, Talleyrand was determined to prevent any of his brothers from being able to influence a regency.

The following day the empress and her infant son, the King of Rome, in the company of Savary left for the town of Blois. Talleyrand had already made sure that Dorothea, in her capacity as lady-in-waiting, was kept well away from Paris suffering from an "illness". Meanwhile, those military units remaining in Paris made a half-hearted effort to fortify the entrances to the city. On 30 March 1814, the sound of gunfire could be heard from the north of the city as a token resistance was mounted by the French Army. Talleyrand had been ordered by Savary to leave with the imperial court but, from his point of view, it was essential that he remain in the city in order to supervise the installation of a new interim government. As always in a critical situation, he was prepared "to let the women do the work". In the company of the well-rehearsed Mme de Rémusat, Talleyrand went to see Prefect of Police Pasquier, who was her cousin. The stratagem was to say that poor Talleyrand was torn between two duties. As a member of the Council of Regents, he should have left the city with Marie Louise and Savary but, with Paris about to be taken over by the Allies, who was better placed than he to deal with the foreign sovereigns, ministers, generals and ambassadors? Should not those politicians with responsibilities stay to defend the inhabitants? Was he not the best intermediary and moderator? In front of Pasquier, Talleyrand deliberately fumbled to find the words to describe his dilemma but Mme de Rémusat rushed to his rescue with a "solution". Her husband was in command of the guard at the city's gate at the Porte de Passy. Could Pasquier not organize a false departure whereby Talleyrand attempted to leave the city but was refused passage? Nothing could be easier!

Étienne Pasquier enjoyed a long and active career in French politics as a moderate reformer, first becoming involved in the *Parlement de Paris* prior to the Revolution. During the Terror, Pasquier tried to remain in obscurity but was arrested and imprisoned. His father was guillotined but Étienne was released after the fall of Robespierre at the end of July 1794. Thanks to the intervention of Cambacérès, Napoleon gave him a post on the State Council. In October 1810, the emperor made him Prefect of Police for Paris.

On the evening of 30 March, the Vice-Grand Elector and his secretary Gabriel Perrey duly arrived in their carriage with all their baggage at the Porte de Passy, where M. de Rémusat, well primed, invited them politely to turn back since their papers were not in order. For the onlookers' benefit, Talleyrand protested loudly about being the helpless victim of an absurd abuse of authority. Foolishly, he then tried to leave by another gateway where the officer in charge was only too keen to repair Rémusat's error by letting him pass. Talleyrand had great difficulties persuading this man that he didn't really want to leave at all. He returned to the Rue Saint-Florentin where a crowd of people were waiting to greet him—Bourrienne among them—having been informed of the evening's charade. Rémusat would, however, testify that passage had been refused—so if Napoleon were to suddenly reappear there would be no question of disloyalty. Talleyrand went to bed waiting for the tsar to arrive.

While the population of Paris was alternately seized with feelings of resignation, anxiety and panic, the moment had come for the Vice-Grand Elector to act. Generals Marmont and Mortier had been instructed to negotiate the surrender of the city with their Russian counterparts. The tsar's representative, Count Mikhail Orlov, had made himself Marmont's hostage and was taken to the general's house in the Rue de Paradis, where he met Talleyrand and Bourrienne. Talleyrand wanted the city to capitulate rapidly and allow the Allied Armies to enter so that there was no question of Napoleon making a last stand. At 3 o'clock in the morning of 30 March an agreement was signed allowing the remaining French troops to leave the city quietly. Talleyrand's parting words to Orlov were: "Sir, please be kind enough to convey to His Majesty, the Emperor of Russia, the Prince de Talleyrand's profound respect."

The Allies had issued a generous and magnanimous proclamation signed by the Austrian Prince Schwarzenberg, but actually written by Alexander I and his Corsican councillor Carlo Andrea Pozzo di Borgo. Neither Napoleon nor the Bourbons were mentioned, both of whom were despised by Alexander, but the text looked forward to "a beneficial authority in France, that can unite the union of all nations and all governments with it". Alexander's immediate ambition was to contrast Napoleon's miserable entry into a deserted and silent Moscow with his own triumphal arrival in Paris as a liberator rather than a conqueror. Talleyrand knew that Alexander wanted to be admired, so prepared to flatter him in his most elegant manner possible.

CHAPTER XV
THE ALLIES ARRIVE

At 6 o'clock on the morning of 31 March 1814, a small miracle took place at the Rue Saint-Florentin. Talleyrand was already out of bed and undergoing his morning toilette ready for the day's events when Count Nesselrode arrived. In his dressing gowns and towels, Talleyrand was helped to his feet in a cloud of powder and embraced the tsar's envoy. Having been primed by Vitrolles's visit to Allied headquarters, Nesselrode believed that Talleyrand was the person whom he needed to talk to about the procedure for the Allied sovereigns and their armies to enter Paris. Talleyrand called the ex-Abbés Louis and de Pradt as well as Dalberg to his assistance, whose task it would be to inform the population by edict that there would be no interruption in the maintenance of public order. Talleyrand, Nesselrode and Dalberg worked on the text of a declaration, while Antoine Roux-Laborie, secretary-general of the provisional government, wrote it down. In fact, Dalberg already possessed a draft document prepared by Talleyrand the previous day. Now, all it needed was Tsar Alexander's signature. When he arrived, he was about to sign it when Talleyrand suggested adding a phrase. The Allied Declaration was conciliatory, requesting the departure of Bonaparte and, as long as France chose a wise and moderate government, the country would be treated with fairness, while retaining its natural frontiers. The words that Talleyrand muttered in the tsar's ear read as follows: "It is necessary that *France should be great and powerful*." The purpose of this phrase was to ensure that France was not broken up into different regions awarded to each ally.

Even though the Allies were in a generous mood, Talleyrand was later reproached for not having obtained more concessions. While the victors were indeed prepared to be magnanimous, they were hardly beholden to Napoleon's former Vice-Grand Elector, while France itself was powerless. They would certainly not invite Napoleon to resume the throne, while his infant son and the Empress Marie Louise could easily have become Metternich's puppets. Furthermore, there was no reason to believe that the many military units cut off behind enemy lines formed part of French territory and should be ordered to fight to the last man for a lost cause.

The leaders of the Allied Armies rode into Paris as far as the Place de la Concorde through large but generally silent crowds. From the windows of his house fronting onto the Rue de Rivoli, Talleyrand could observe the head of the column with Tsar Alexander I in the centre, flanked by Frederick William III, King of Prussia, and Prince Schwarzenberg, representing the Emperor of Austria. A printer had been found who could produce the declaration by the end of the day, the text of which had been agreed that morning. This man made one important modification, changing the title to "Proclamation", which the tsar and Talleyrand accepted. In the meantime, an incident had occurred that forced the tsar into Talleyrand's arms. It had been foreseen that the Russian contingent would be housed in the Elysée Palace but a rumour, which Talleyrand found ludicrous, advised that it had been mined with explosives. Thus, this residence was declared unsafe and the Russians were invited to occupy the first floor of Talleyrand's house, placing himself in the advantageous position where he became the host and councillor to the victorious tsar. Nothing could have been more propitious for the tasks that lay ahead of them. Thus, Talleyrand's dining room became a place for decision-making, where Tsar Alexander, the King of Prussia, Castlereagh, Prince Schwarzenberg and, later, the Duke of Wellington enjoyed the most prestigious dishes prepared by "the king of chefs and the chef of kings", Antonin Carême.

During the afternoon of 31 March, the Tsar and Talleyrand met first alone, before meeting with the grand council in the main salon. The chairman was Alexander flanked by Nesselrode and Pozzo di Borgo, the King of Prussia with Schwarzenberg and the Prince von Liechtenstein for the Emperor of Austria. Talleyrand, seconded by Dalberg, only represented himself—he was no longer Vice-Grand Elector of a non-existent regime and he had no mandate to speak on behalf of the Bourbons. The matter before them was what type of regime would now govern France after more than twenty years of war. Talleyrand pleaded for the principle of legitimacy: the return of the Bourbons to the throne and a liberal constitution. The tsar did not share his enthusiasm about the restoration of the Bourbons, preferring a Council of Regents who would govern the country until Napoleon's son came of age. Evidently, the Empress Marie Louise and her father Francis I would not be opposed to such a plan, although the fact that she and her son were now located some distance from Paris made this solution less obvious. On the other hand, the British Government wanted nothing to do with Napoleon, nor his brothers, nor a regency, nor anybody associated with them—this included Talleyrand, Fouché and even Metternich. It wanted to restore Louis XVIII to the throne, since the Bourbons were viewed as representing peace, wisdom and legitimacy. With Napoleon located at this time at Fontainebleau, only about 60 kilometres from Paris, with some 45,000 loyal troops, and Marie Louise and her son taking refuge in Blois more than 150 kilometres away, the idea of a regency seemed very fragile and the threat of a civil war very real. Talleyrand's honourable intention for Marie Louise and her son was to send them to a safe haven outside France. After many months of doubts and hesitations, the moment had come to take a decision; Talleyrand favoured legitimacy, in other words, Louis XVIII.

The tsar, who had great faith in Talleyrand's judgement, asked how he could be certain that the population would accept Louis XVIII as the King of France, to which the former Vice-Grand Elector replied that the Senate would vote it. He sent his emissaries—Beurnonville, Jaucourt, Dalberg and de Pradt—across Paris telling the senators that they were required to attend the Luxembourg Palace at once in order to vote on a provisional government for France. In reality, he had no right to do so— Cambacérès had already informed the members of the Senate that they should only attend meetings that conformed to the terms of the Constitution of the Year X. However, Talleyrand knew that a large group of senators were opposed to Napoleon, particularly if their place on the Senate could be assured, and his own representatives would have a strong influence on them. Nothing was said about the type of future government nor its name. Some 64 of the potential 140 senators left their beds and voted during the night of 31 March as Talleyrand had predicted. The following day, Talleyrand informed the tsar that the Senate had elected a provisional government with himself as its head. Furthermore, it required the destitution of Napoleon, the restoration of the Bourbons and also expressed the desire for a new constitution. Later, when Louis XVIII arrived in Paris, the king's entourage tried to minimize Talleyrand's role in these proceedings. The exiled Royalists, now able to return to France, considered the former Bishop of Autun with the greatest distrust— nothing more than a priest who had renounced his calling and married a courtesan. However, with all the leaders of the Great Powers sitting at his dining table, it was difficult to avoid the fact that the most important decisions were taken there. The Royalist Vitrolles, who more than anybody knew what was happening, described Talleyrand's role: "He accepted the Restoration as a necessity and tackled it with all his might." The following day the senators voted for the dismissal of Napoleon and all the members of his family.

Evidently, if someone assassinated Napoleon, it would make the political situation much easier to deal with. Sometime later a rumour circulated that, on 2 April, Roux-Laborie and Dalberg introduced Talleyrand to a fellow who was prepared to send Napoleon into the next world. This man, a soldier of fortune from a pseudo-noble family called Maubreuil, turned out to be a thorough scoundrel. Not long afterwards, Maubreuil was arrested for attacking the Queen of Westphalia's carriage—the wife of Jérôme Bonaparte—during which he stole her very valuable jewels and her money. In his defence, after being arrested, Maubreuil accused Talleyrand of supplying him with a band of men dressed as hunters (costumes found in the storeroom of the École Militaire) and a supply of cash to assassinate Napoleon. It was very unlike the cautious Talleyrand to become involved in such a compromising and ill-conceived affair that would have been perceived badly by both the British and the Russians. Maubreuil's technique was to make the most preposterous declarations in the hope that they would be believed by some gullible person in a position of authority. Unfortunately for Maubreuil, he soon came into contact with Vitrolles who understood immediately that he was dealing with a hardened criminal and had him arrested. We have not heard the last of Maubreuil.

Napoleon and his remaining faithful troops still posed a threat since in Paris the only French soldiers were a small number of national guardsmen under the command of General Dessoles. It was necessary somehow to weaken Napoleon's position. Through an agreement signed with Schwartzenberg, General Marmont, who was holding a line to the south of Paris, agreed to move his two divisions westward towards Versailles on 4 April, leaving Napoleon's position hopelessly exposed. Marmont staggered back to the Rue Saint-Florentin to discover himself a hero. A big fuss was made of him since he had done precisely what Talleyrand wished—surrendering the last major cohesive unit of Napoleon's Army.

It was during this time that Talleyrand became one of France's greatest servants. Neither his troubled private life, nor his mercenary pursuit of riches, nor his relaxed attitude to morality could conceal the constancy of his patriotism. For Talleyrand, there would be no question of Napoleon being involved any further in the government of France, since the Bourbon family provided the only viable solution. Napoleon had steered Europe into chaos and his still unsatisfied ambitions meant that he would always be ready to continue where he left off. On the other hand, the Bourbons were believed to represent moderation and the respect by France of its traditional borders. It was the Count de Provence/Louis XVIII himself who had first pronounced the word "legitimacy" at the time of Napoleon's coronation. "Europe's primary need," wrote Talleyrand in his memoirs, "was [...] to bring back the principle of legitimacy." The ruler of a country epitomized the law, which had the greatest impact when the sovereign held supreme power. Even Napoleon realised that only the Bourbons could rule France after him. With Talleyrand insisting on the word "legitimacy", Tsar Alexander's attitude to a regency began to weaken. What everyone, including the tsar, wanted was for France to remain at peace within its natural frontiers, yet strong enough to stand up to England and Austria.

While the Champs-Elysées had become a camp for heavily armed soldiers, Paris was calm and the Allied Armies could not complain about the way they were received. The fall of Napoleon came not as a national calamity but rather as deliverance from a tyrant. The city did not sleep as Cossacks, Prussians and Austrians mingled with Parisians on the streets. Talleyrand took the foreign sovereigns to the opera, where the audience applauded them as liberators. That a French audience should spontaneously show their appreciation for the leaders of foreign armies on its own soil illustrated the level of discontent with Napoleon's regime. Afterwards, Talleyrand invited his guests back to a reception at the Rue Saint-Florentin where the staircases and reception rooms were heaving with people.

Talleyrand's house was rearranged so that he occupied the apartments on the ground floor or "entresol", the tsar and his aides-de-camp occupied the first floor, while Nesselrode and his staff were installed on the second floor. An indescribable confusion reigned. The staircases, courtyard and even the Rue de Rivoli in front of the main façade were overflowing with Russian soldiers. There was a steady flow of Austrian, Prussian and Russian officers, the traffic being directed by Roux-Laborie, whose carriage was parked permanently before the main gate to run urgent errands. Talleyrand had given up three of his six rooms to install the secretariat of the provisional government under the direction of Du Pont. Never before and never again would Talleyrand hold such power. The transitional government met almost continuously in his bedroom, where the new Constitution would be drafted. He was lucky if he managed three hours sleep at night, after which the ritual of his unavoidable morning toilette took place in the presence of princes and generals while he attempted to dictate to de Pradt. Even Pasquier, who disliked him, could not help admiring his industry. In the provisional government, as designated by the Senate under Talleyrand's presidency, the Treasury was handled by Dufresne de Saint-Léon; Finance by Baron Louis; the Interior by Beugnot; and War by General Dupont (defeated at the Battle of Bailén in Spain and recently released from prison). As the sharp tongue of Chateaubriand labelled it: "Talleyrand's whist table."

Between 30 March and 6 April 1814, Talleyrand attempted to abolish everything that made Napoleon's rule insupportable. He sent the latest conscripts for the army back to their homes; he liberated political prisoners and hostages; he exchanged prisoners-of-war; he restored the free circulation of the postal service; he told his Spanish prisoners at Valençay to go home to Madrid; and placed Napoleon's police under the responsibility of the departmental prefects. Particularly, he tried to give everyone confidence and prevented a bureaucratic vacuum by maintaining all officials in their posts. Money was borrowed from the banks so that the city never went without bread. Baron Louis found 10 million gold francs in the cellars of the Tuileries. The Count de Semallé took possession of the several million francs that the Empress Marie Louise had in her possession when she left Paris. There were difficulties, however, since Bavarian and Prussian soldiers stationed in Paris started to pillage the city. Furthermore, the Royalist enclaves that had started to erupt around the country refused to obey a government composed mainly of Napoleon's former senior officials.

On 4 April at Fontainebleau, Napoleon's marshals Ney, Lefebvre, Berthier, Oudinot, Moncey and Macdonald refused to fight on, forcing the emperor to sign a conditional abdication in the hope that his wife would be nominated as regent in favour of their infant son. He tried to commit suicide in the early hours of 13 April by taking a noxious concoction prepared by his doctor, although the only effect was to make him extremely ill. Following this incident, he said: "I forgive Talleyrand for I have treated him very badly; if I had won, he could not have stayed in France. The Bourbons would do well to employ him; he loves money and plotting, but he is capable. I have always had a weak spot for him. I don't know how it happened that I fell out with him in preference for Maret, for both of them were useful to me."

The Royalists now believed that Talleyrand had completed his work and would be released from his functions with an honourable reward for his services. Louis XVIII's younger brother, the Duke d'Artois (who had last met Talleyrand during a clandestine conversation on the night of 17 July 1789 some twenty-five years previously), sent his emissary, the Count de Semallé, to meet with the tsar in order to discuss the arrangements for the royal family's return. Talleyrand received Semallé politely, refused to allow him to meet Alexander and made it clear that, if he wished to discuss the affairs of France, he was already in the presence of the head of the country's provisional government. As an initial piece of guidance, Talleyrand recommended that the royal cortège should enter Paris bearing the tricolour flag that had been the country's standard for the past twenty years and not the Bourbons' white emblem covered with a pattern of gold fleurs-de-lis. The Revolution's tricolour flag had been created by combining the old royal white flag flanked by the red-and-blue colours of Paris. As a sign of things to come, Semallé indignantly rejected this advice.

Other visitors to the Rue Saint-Florentin included Caulaincourt. It may be recalled that he was a well-regarded and long-term friend of both Talleyrand and the tsar. He haunted Talleyrand's house as Napoleon's representative and, taking advantage of the tsar leaving a meeting, managed to attract his attention and passed Napoleon's message—the emperor was prepared to abdicate on condition that a regency was set up for his son. Alexander was not actually opposed to this idea but sought Talleyrand's advice. Talleyrand was sure that, whatever type of regency was created, in no time at all Napoleon would seize control of it and once more enter the field with his army. Alexander's answer to Caulaincourt was: "Too late!" Talleyrand could hardly conceal his satisfaction as the unfortunate Caulaincourt was shown the way out. The last vestiges of his fondness for Napoleon had now turned to complete contempt for, more than the insults he had suffered, he hated Napoleon for the disastrous mistakes he had made. At Fontainebleau, Napoleon had no choice but to sign his unconditional abdication and liberate his officer corps, who were keen to rush back to Paris to declare their allegiance to the new Bourbon regime.

On 1 April, Alexander addressed the Senate in person and laid out terms similar to the previous day's proclamation. As a gesture of good will, he announced that 150,000 French prisoners of war, who had been held in Russia since the French retreat eighteen months earlier, would be released immediately. The next day, the Senate agreed to the Coalition's terms and passed a resolution deposing Napoleon with an instruction to the various French Armies to lay down their arms while abandoning all fidelity to Napoleon. Army officers were dispatched to different parts of the country to tell the troops to cease fighting.

With the departure of Napoleon, the Parisian journalists—and particularly the caricaturists—were at last able to express themselves with liberty. A cartoon appeared showing Talleyrand in the form of a merry-go-round entitled "the man with six heads", illustrating how he had successfully managed to survive each new political situation—a state of affairs faced by a great many French people. Visitors flooded to the Rue Saint-Florentin to declare their allegiance to the new royal regime, among them Napoleon's marshals who only a few days earlier had been reviewing the emperor's troops in the courtyard at Fontainebleau. Other dignitaries who presented themselves included Napoleon's former judges who had condemned boatloads of dissidents to oblivion in Guyana and Jacobin politicians whose hands were stained with the blood of those who had defended Louis XVI. A religious service in favour of Louis XVIII took place at Notre Dame. Talleyrand asked Josephine if she wanted to attend—she was not well and refused. Josephine died in Rueil-Malmaison a few weeks later on 29 May, soon after walking with Tsar Alexander in the gardens of her house. In another piece of mischief, Talleyrand told General Marmont that General Jourdan's soldiers had attached the white Bourbon cocarde to their hats; and then informed Jourdan that Marmont's troops had done the same thing. The two generals rushed to distribute the change of emblem to their troops.

A commission under the chairmanship of Charles-François Lebrun met on 3 April 1814 at the Rue Saint-Florentin to prepare a new constitution intended to provide a balance between the sovereign's powers and the acquisitions of the population as a result of the French Revolution. Talleyrand's idea was that Louis XVIII's power would be confined in the same manner as that of the British monarchy. A constitutional monarchy would indicate that the restoration of the Bourbons was a consequence of changing the regime and not the purpose of the change. Talleyrand was aware that Louis XVIII was a political force to be reckoned with, while the commission's work was also hampered by the zealous Parisian Royalists led by the Count de Semallé.

The first draft of the new constitution drew largely on the one adopted in 1791, proposing a one-chamber legislature. When it was shown to Talleyrand, he immediately understood that neither he nor Louis XVIII could accept it and sent the commission back to work. In order to achieve a balance of power, a two-chamber legislature was required based on the British model. A week later it produced a document called the Constitutional Charter, which was unanimously accepted by the Senate. The civil guarantees brushed aside by Napoleon were restored: a free vote by parliament on taxes, trial by jury, permanent appointment of judges, freedom of conscience and of religion, freedom of the press—within certain limits. A key phrase of the Constitutional Charter described the Restoration of the Bourbons: "The French people freely call to the throne of France, Louis-Stanislas-Xavier of France, brother of the last king and, after him, the other members of the House of Bourbon in the ancient order." However imperfect this constitution, it would lay the foundations for the government of France for the next thirty-four years. Talleyrand received the congratulations of Benjamin Constant who had read the draft constitution and found the ideas of liberty it contained to his taste.

It remained to present the new constitution to Louis XVIII himself and obtain his agreement. However, Talleyrand had seriously underestimated the resistance of the autocratic king since the battle over the wording and interpretation of the charter had barely begun. The Duke de La Rochefoucauld was sent as an emissary to make contact with the court still located in England. This choice was not made by accident for, even though a member of the old aristocracy, he had an impeccable record as a revolutionary liberal. Louis XVIII refused to meet him.

Besides regulating state business, Talleyrand paid close attention to his own political survival. On the 7 April, he sent two of his agents, a M. de Villers and Gabriel Perrey, to the archives in the Tuileries Palace with instructions to destroy, without making a fuss, all documentation implicating the former Bishop of Autun in the affairs concerning the assassination of the Duke d'Enghien, the war in Spain and his doubtful financial dealings. M. Bary, the archivist in charge, refused to co-operate and was quickly dismissed, being replaced by M. de Villers himself. All the original documents concerning these affairs were destroyed—but several copies existed of some of them. We may ask for what reason Talleyrand desired the correspondence concerning the invasion of Spain to be destroyed—had he been initially in favour? The work having been completed, M. Bary was restored to his post to supervise the empty shelves.

There was a big dinner at Talleyrand's house on Easter Sunday 1814—a family dinner. He invited the Tsar of Russia, his brother Archambaud and the Duchess von Courland, while Edmond had not yet returned from captivity as a prisoner-of-war. Unexpectedly, the hostess was Edmond's wife, the twenty-year-old Dorothea de Périgord. This is the first time that Dorothea appears as the mistress of Talleyrand's household, a position she will occupy almost without interruption for the next twenty-four years. For the time being, he maintained his daily little notes to the Duchess von Courland but Dorothea was destined gradually to eclipse her mother's role.

The Treaty of Fontainebleau, established on 11 April 1814, was signed in Paris by the plenipotentiaries of the Austrian Empire, Russia and Prussia and ratified by Napoleon on 13 April. Although it was signed by Talleyrand, the terms of the treaty were actually arranged between Caulaincourt, Nesselrode and Tsar Alexander. It can be noted that Castlereagh, shocked by the leniency of its terms, would never sign it for the United Kingdom. In this way, the Allies ended Napoleon's rule as Emperor of France and banished him, at the tsar's suggestion, into exile on the island of Elba—much closer to the European mainland than many would have considered wise. Both Talleyrand and Fouché felt that Alexander's choice of the island of Elba was an undignified and probably unsafe destination. It would have been much better for everybody concerned if Napoleon had been exiled to a more distant refuge—Corfu, the Azores and Saint Helena had been mentioned. Even Metternich was ill at ease with Elba as a solution and predicted that there would be another war within two years. After consulting Talleyrand, Fouché wrote a letter to Napoleon suggesting that he would have found the United States of America a most congenial destination. Napoleon would not be executed or imprisoned but became sovereign ruler of Elba, maintaining his title of emperor and, in theory at least, receiving an allowance from the French Government and with permission to maintain a force of 400 soldiers—although, being Napoleon, this soon became 1,000. His mother and sisters also received a state pension. It was a humiliating outcome for the man whose armies had once dominated Europe from Madrid to Warsaw and from Hamburg to Rome.

Vitrolles set out for Nancy with a letter from Talleyrand to give to the Duke d'Artois. Of all the members of the Bourbon family, the one who Talleyrand knew best and liked the most was the Duke d'Artois— despite his complete absence of political skills. Talleyrand would have manipulated him like a puppet if Vitrolles had not warned the duke of the danger. On his way back to Paris, Vitrolles received a copy of the Constitutional Charter and, as a confirmed Royalist, considered it a calamity. Later, Talleyrand went to the village of Bondy, about

10 kilometres east of Paris, to meet Artois who would henceforth assume the title of the kingdom's lieutenant-general and be addressed as "Monsieur", the royal title applying to the heir to the throne. Despite the turbulent events of the intervening years, the two men received each other courteously, with memories of their earlier acquaintance. Even though the army and a great part of the French population were not ready to abandon the tricolour flag of the Revolution and despite Talleyrand's advice to the contrary, Artois entered Paris on 12 April preceded by the white emblem of the Bourbon family. That night, Monsieur slept in the Tuileries Palace and the tsar took up residence in the Elysée Palace, having borrowed Antonin Carême as his cook during his time in Paris. In his half-empty house, Talleyrand did not retire until 3 o'clock that morning being occupied with preparing a suitable summary of the day's events for publication in *Le Moniteur*. He asked the Count de Beugnot, Minister of the Interior in the provisional government, to prepare a draft since "a day like that is not complete without a statement". No-one had paid much attention to what the Duke d'Artois had muttered in reply to Talleyrand's greeting at Bondy and, furthermore, his words had certainly lacked import. "Make up a response," Talleyrand told Beugnot, who was, however, reluctant to place words into the mouth of royalty. The first draft was considered too eloquent; the second too long. The third draft was published in *Le Moniteur*: "No more divisions; peace and France. Finally, I see it again; nothing has changed except that *there is now one more Frenchman!*" The Parisian newspapers seized upon these concluding six words and no-one could be more pleased than the Duke d'Artois himself for not having uttered them!

The departure of Napoleon and the arrival of the Duke d'Artois put the clock back twenty years. Very soon, the first differences of opinion surfaced. The title of "Lieutenant-General of the Kingdom" assumed by the Duke d'Artois—from where did it come? Semallé, Vitrolles and Montesquiou declared that it had been granted to him by Louis XVIII. Talleyrand didn't agree. A provisional government ran the country in conformity with the Senate's directives and according to the terms of a Constitutional Charter. If Monsieur benefited from a political title, and since Louis XVIII was still in England, it can only have been bestowed on him by the Senate. Artois was required to attend the Senate and,

336

without good grace, request that this body should confirm his official title. More trouble was brewing; Artois let it be known that his brother did not accept the new Constitutional Charter and wished to make "certain alterations"!

As the Duke d'Artois had been making his way towards Paris, Talleyrand had sent an envoy to meet him—the banker Ouvrard. How could a government function without money, lots of money? The same applied to the former Bishop of Autun himself, who had the ability to attract money to his person, lots of money. Accusations were made that, during his first days in charge of the provisional government, he diverted vast sums of money into his personal accounts. Chateaubriand made a judgement about him: "When M. de Talleyrand is not plotting, he peddles." In fact, he was capable of doing both at the same time such was his enormous need for cash.

Despite the French Army's capitulation and the abdication of Napoleon, nothing had been done to bring the war officially to an end, so that communications across the lines of the different armies were difficult. On 19 April 2014, Metternich proposed that Talleyrand should sign an armistice with the Great Powers that confined France to its 1792 borders, meaning that the Treaty of Lunéville of 1801—where its territory had extended across northern Italy and into the Netherlands, including what is now Belgium and Switzerland—became null and void. The loss of these lands conquered by Napoleon seemed inevitable, with the result that, in terms of territory gained, the outcome of Napoleon's fifteen-year war with his neighbours was insignificant. These conditions may have seemed harsh, but without Talleyrand's presence the situation could have been much worse. His critics were particularly irritated that the fifty-three undefeated French garrisons holding out in isolated pockets scattered across Europe were obliged to surrender, but these fortresses had lost all of their military significance. Talleyrand was never particularly troubled by public opinion and considered these military outposts as points of weakness rather than strength. With France occupied by the Allied armies, Talleyrand could not resist their absolute power. As Napoleon's aggression had resulted in the entire French population being branded with hatred and suspicion, it was, above all, necessary to give the Allies confidence by presenting France as a peaceful country ready to assume its place in the community of nations. When the armistice was signed on 23 April, the conditions appeared severe even to Talleyrand but there were compensations: the Imperial Army would be demobilized, the requisitions by the Allied Armies would soon come to an end, prisoners-of-war would be released and the troops cut off behind enemy lines brought home. Another way of looking at it was that, in the middle of an economic slump, France benefited from a statesman respected by the victors and able to stand between their possible vengeance and the general population.

Following the Treaty of Fontainebleau agreed with Napoleon, in a different ceremony, a European-wide peace was signed in Paris with the four main Allies, thereby avoiding another continental conflict until 1914, a century later. After a period of over twenty years of fighting during which many European countries had been completely overrun and/or ceased to exist, France was defeated but remained intact. To understand Talleyrand, the French patriot, one has to recognize that he also believed that the interests of all European nations were very similar. For Talleyrand, Voltaire and the Prince de Ligne, borders arbitrarily divided up the countries that shared the same civilization—that of the Enlightenment. There was, however, a division between western and eastern Europe, which made the survival of Austria all the more important since it stood as a bastion between Europe and Asia. Throughout the Napoleonic Wars, Talleyrand had consistently sought to preserve the Habsburg Empire.

The Treaty of Paris, signed by Louis XVIII on 30 May 1814, restoring France to her 1789 borders, is incredibly moderate. The country had to pay no war indemnity; it did not have to return works of art stolen during the wars; several small territories that had not formed part of the country before the Revolution were now incorporated into metropolitan France; the remnants of the army were not required to disarm—while the Sixth Coalition's occupying armies would soon withdraw from French soil. The Treaty of Paris also contains some surprisingly modern measures: the rights of foreigners on French territory were guaranteed; the abandonment of the slave trade was scheduled; and the free circulation of international traffic on certain European rivers assured. There is even an innovative proposition that must have come straight from Talleyrand—disarmament! Much later a French general wrote: "After a war so completely lost, could one win a better peace?" In order to explain what happened in the following year, attention should be drawn to the fact that the Treaty of Fontainebleau foresaw an allowance being paid to Napoleon by the new French Government, while the Treaty of Paris failed to address this point—with disastrous consequences.

All of these events took place in the absence of the new king, who did not seem to be in any particular hurry to reach Paris. Unfortunately, he had been detained in England by another severe attack of gout. At least, he was kept informed of proceedings by a series of notes on the political situation from Talleyrand recommending, among other things, that he should accept the new Constitutional Charter, even if it had appeared rather too liberal to his brother, the Duke d'Artois. The king landed at Calais on 24 April 1814 and entered Paris a few days later escorted by the Imperial Guard.

Louis XVIII met Talleyrand at Compiègne five days later. The two men were about the same age, had known about each other at the old Court of Versailles, both had problems with their legs, both were politically astute—inevitably, they detested each other. Talleyrand's brother Archambaud is even believed to have shared Louis's mistress, the Countess de Balbi. He would have preferred a king not quite so politically shrewd, secretive, touchy and who was not convinced that he was an all-powerful God-given monarch. Louis was intelligent and well-educated with a taste for teasing people with practical jokes. The king's principal councillor and favourite was Pierre-Louis Jean Casimir, Count de Blacas, who Talleyrand could not stand either. To begin with, Louis wished to show Talleyrand, the ex-revolutionary and married former-bishop, that he received him only because he had no choice. He humiliated him by making him wait for two hours in an antechamber before Blacas conducted him into the presence of the king seated behind his desk. The king was a large man, extremely overweight but not lacking in dignity. He wore a blue costume of a bygone era with gold buttons and epaulettes over a long white waistcoat and with a blue sash. The king greeted him politely and remarked that their ancestors dated from the same epoch of history and each could so easily have occupied the place of the other. Nevertheless, by his attitude Louis established himself as standing on the political high ground. Years later, Talleyrand did not retain a happy memory of their meeting, summing Louis up as "a notorious liar... selfish, insensitive, greedy, ungrateful" and, one could add, profoundly confident of his inviolable claim to be monarch of France by the grace of God—and not by a decision of the Senate. The Marquess de la Tour du Pin once remarked about Talleyrand that, although his own standards of behaviour sometimes had little to recommend them: "He had... an abhorrence for other people's faults." While the king and his minister did not like each other, they were able to establish a working relationship.

Louis flattered Talleyrand that he had successfully weathered the Revolution, the Directory, the Consulate and the Napoleonic Empire, before realising that the nation's true destiny lay with the Bourbon Restoration. "My God, Sire," Talleyrand replied, "it was nothing to do with me. There is something inexplicable in me that brings bad luck to the governments that neglect me." Nevertheless, Louis distrusted Talleyrand and was determined that he should not have the last word about the government of his kingdom. He suggested that the title of Prince de Benevento should in future be modified into something more French, the Prince de Talleyrand for instance. However, he did not mention the Constitutional Charter or the members of the future government. He was adept at both changing the subject when sensitive issues were raised, of nonchalantly insulting his interlocutor and of dropping a serious proposition into the middle of a light-hearted conversation. It did not take Louis XVIII long to go back on his many promises. He and his newly-appointed Comptroller-General of Finance Baron Louis (Talleyrand's former colleague) were determined not to let the exchequer fall into deficit (a 75-million-franc debt had been inherited from Napoleon), and took fiscal measures to ensure this. Louis XVIII had assured the people that the unpopular taxes on tobacco, wine and salt would be abolished after his restoration, but once he took up the throne this did not happen, which led to rioting in Bordeaux. Expenditures on the army were sharply reduced in the 1815 budget—the military had accounted for 55% of government spending in 1814!

Talleyrand met the king again at Saint-Ouen the following day where he introduced him to the Senate's members and made a speech drawing attention to "the twenty years of ruin and grief" that had taken place before Louis's arrival. The king issued a declaration to the French people, written by himself with the help of Blacas and Vitrolles, which would form a preface to the new Constitutional Charter. Talleyrand had tactfully removed the words: "Given at Paris, in the year of grace 1814, and of our reign the nineteenth," which placed the beginning of his sovereignty in June 1795, after the death of Louis XVII, the son of Louis XVI and Marie-Antoinette. These words were subsequently restored to the document.

Although the Great Powers occupying Paris had demanded a new constitution, it was hard to believe that Louis XVIII would accept Talleyrand's package deal without a fight. Louis was determined that the Constitutional Charter would be granted as an act of grace from the throne and not be understood as reflecting the people's demands. The king and his entourage—Artois, Blacas, Vitrolles—would not accept the Constitutional Charter and started to tamper with it so that the new regime bore a stronger resemblance to a "limited monarchy" rather than a "parliamentary monarchy". It would have been better for Talleyrand to have outlined a few basic principles rather than spell out the details for this is where they focused their attention. The French Constitutional Charter of 1814 guaranteed rights that were common in most other Western European countries at that time. For instance, measures on taxation were to be adopted by both the Chamber of Deputies and the Chamber of Peers. These principles, together with the retention of the Napoleonic Code, represented the gains of the French Revolution. There was, however, special provision introduced by the Royalists for the Roman Catholic Church to be restored as the official state religion. Similarly, press freedom, in particular, was subject to harsh censorship laws, which threw doubt on the charter's whole purpose. Talleyrand was shocked that the freedom of the press, non-existent under Napoleon's rule, had not been reinstated, while the declaration of Roman Catholicism as the state religion disturbed this unfrocked priest, a firm believer in freedom of conscience. Of all the new ministers, Talleyrand found himself most opposed to Montesquiou, who favoured press censorship. Despite his protests, Talleyrand had no say in the final draft of the Constitutional Charter for he was excluded from the commission that drew it up. While the king was no doubt delighted with his tampering, the charter now contained all the ingredients that would lead to the downfall of the Bourbon regime fifteen years later. The liberal politicians of Paris were annoyed with the charter and presented their reproaches to Tsar Alexander, who held Talleyrand responsible for insisting on bringing back the Bourbons. The tsar had never wanted to see the Bourbons restored to the throne in the first place and blamed Talleyrand for the undemocratic elements now introduced into the charter. On 3 June, the King of Prussia and Tsar Alexander, accompanied by Metternich, left Paris for London without saying farewell, which upset Talleyrand. Alexander had several grounds to be annoyed. He had been received by Louis XVIII at Compiègne as the representative of a second-rate power. He had become convinced that he had been shown a liberal constitution as a bluff in order to obtain his approval for the return of the Bourbons and, once Louis XVIII had arrived, changes were introduced in favour of absolutism. He also felt that his disinterest in removing Napoleon from France had not been appreciated for he deserved to be rewarded by the acquisition of a large piece of territory—Poland, for example. In an attempt to redress the situation, a few days later Talleyrand wrote a long letter to Alexander regretting the coolness in their relations and explaining that he had had no say in the modifications to the charter introduced by Louis and his entourage. It is, nevertheless, curious that the tsar's quarrel with Talleyrand concerned an insufficiently liberal French constitution, whereas in his own country a harsh feudalism endured as it had done since the Middle Ages. Alexander had a weakness for Jacobinism—as long as it stayed in France. The tsar did not react to Talleyrand's letter. However, their rupture had more profound causes. When Napoleon had been in charge, Talleyrand and the tsar had a common enemy. Now that Napoleon had gone, they could each resume their former long-term ambitions: Alexander sought to move the Russian border westwards while Talleyrand attempted to frustrate him.

While the final version of the Constitutional Charter adopted on 4 June 1814 contained some of the "liberal" ideas proposed by the Senate and some of the Republican acquisitions of the Revolution, it placed the king firmly in charge. He would have the last word even if his power was constrained by a two-chamber parliament. The various ministers of the new government did not form a cohesive team and would be received by the king individually, only being summoned to cabinet meetings sporadically. Another proposed measure widened the breach between rich and poor: the members of parliament would receive no salary, meaning that only the very wealthy could envisage being elected. To be eligible for membership in the Chamber of Deputies, one had to pay over 1,000 francs per year in tax and be over the age of 40. The king felt that being a member of parliament was such an honour that people were prepared to do it for nothing, but Talleyrand objected strongly. The king would appoint nobles to the Chamber of Peers on a hereditary basis, or for life, at his discretion. Deputies would be elected every five years, with one fifth of them eligible for election each year. In a complete denial of the French Revolution, some 90,000 citizens were entitled to vote out of a population of nearly 30 million men, women and children (amounting to less than 0.3%). Talleyrand believed that the consequences of this ruling were likely to be very expensive. With Blacas as the Head of the Royal Household, the government seemed determined to return to the ways of the *Ancien Régime*. Louis was very partial to the stuffy procedures of favouritism and was continuously bombarded with petitions on the part of returning *émigrés* who considered they should be well rewarded for their suffering and fidelity. There was an enormous contrast between the last days of the Empire when the *émigrés* could return only when pardoned and the first days of the Restoration when they arrived as the victors and wore their exile as a badge of distinction.

Nonetheless, the achievements of Talleyrand during the spring of 1814, reconciling the restored monarchy with the Revolution and the Empire, were immense. He had suggested that the national emblem should be the tricolour flag and not the Bourbon fleurs-de-lis; he had insisted on a new constitution being written in a few days; he had successfully set up a legislature consisting of two chambers; the king's brother had been granted the title of lieutenant-general by the Senate; he had successfully maintained the administrative apparatus of Napoleon's Empire—all of this without paying one franc in indemnities to the Allies. Peace and reason had become once again the foundations of a new government which was amongst the most liberal in Europe. Although Louis XVIII had not made anyone prime minister, when he needed someone to fulfil this official role momentarily, he turned to Talleyrand.

Only Blacas had any influence on the king, while the foreign ambassadors noted that Talleyrand, despite his talents, had no say unless his role was absolutely inescapable. For instance, Baron Louis had prepared a financial law, which the king required Talleyrand to explain to the Chamber of Peers on 8 September. Some of the ideas on political and financial organization that had been upheld at the beginning of the Revolution were at last beginning to receive serious attention. Baron Louis was a remarkable financier and the Ministry of Finance's activities during the Restoration were almost revolutionary: the state should honour its debts—a problem that had caused the downfall of Louis XVI and which the Revolution had never been able to resolve.

Familiar with court etiquette, Talleyrand swore undying fidelity to the new monarch—we are already acquainted with the little importance he attributed to such oaths—while stating that he would be ready to assume once again the function of Minister of Foreign Affairs. Upon swearing this oath of office, he remarked to the king: "Sire, it's the thirteenth; I hope it will be the last." For the third time in his life, Talleyrand took up his responsibilities on the Rue du Bac. In fact, he spent as little time there as possible, passing through from time to time and maintaining contact with his staff from his headquarters at the Rue Saint-Florentin, where he continued to lead the life of a grandee. Not forgetting his family, he asked for his nephew Edmond to be considered as an aide-de-camp and for Dorothea to become a lady-in-waiting at the royal court. Edmond subsequently received a promotion to the rank of brigadier-general. Despite having known Dorothea as a child in Mittau, Louis XVIII had no wish to appoint former members of Napoleon's court to his own household.

Because of communication difficulties, Napoleon's forces in south-western France had continued fighting bloody battles for nearly a week after his abdication. This delayed the arrival of the Duke of Wellington, commander-in-chief of the British, Portuguese and Spanish Armies, who finally reached Paris and greeted Talleyrand as if he were an old friend. Relations had been restored with Mme de Staël, while even the Princess de Benevento (now Talleyrand) made a discreet reappearance. Talleyrand could be seen in all the most fashionable places in Paris together with the Count de Blacas, Louis XVIII's favourite. Talleyrand did not like Blacas but the latter had direct access to the king at all times and was therefore a contact worth cultivating.

The life that Talleyrand had been leading during April and May 1814 left him exhausted. He had been working rigorously day and night faced with a thousand urgent cares. He believed that, in the Revolution's aftermath, France could only be governed under a liberal constitution, which would serve the interests of both the French population and the monarchy. He longed for a moment of calm, but Louis XVIII would cause him more anguish than the Allied negotiators. A year later, in the second Treaty of Paris of 1815, following Napoleon's return to France during the Hundred Days and his defeat at Waterloo, the generous terms of 1814 would be forgotten. France would be punished for Napoleon's misdemeanours.

Now that the royal court could assume its true colours, its members felt at liberty to create as many enemies as possible. The daughter of Louis XVI and Marie-Antoinette, the Duchess d'Angoulême, reserved a reception for Talleyrand so cool as to leave him in no doubt about her sentiments. The Duke d'Artois and his friends expressed their hatred and contempt for anybody who had anything to do with the Revolution or the Empire. In the army, Napoleon's officers were systematically retired and new ones promoted from the within ranks of the Royalists.

The Treaty of Paris established the arrangements between France and the Allies, but what of the rest of Europe? The convening of the Congress of Vienna in the autumn of 1814 provided an opportunity for a long-term peace plan for Europe by reassembling the countries torn apart by the French Revolutionary and Napoleonic Wars. Already on 12 May, Talleyrand had asked for France to have a voice at this congress, which was destined to redraw the map of Europe. In Paris, he was feeling increasingly isolated and unable to place his friends in key positions, while the press continued to scorn him. A political battle raged between the new Royalists and those who were nostalgic for Napoleon's Empire; he was detested by both parties. Louis realized that he had in his service one of Europe's most skilled negotiators, while sending him to the Austrian capital removed his disturbing presence from Paris. Talleyrand decided that it was vital at Vienna for France to benefit from the support of the United Kingdom. He knew that both Castlereagh and Wellington were sympathetic to his cause but could he win over the Prince Regent and the British Government?

CHAPTER XVI
THE CONGRESS OF VIENNA

The 1814 Treaty of Paris had established the conditions for peace between the Four Great Powers and France. It had been decided that, soon thereafter, the European countries would meet in Vienna to examine how to reconstruct the rest of Europe from the ruins left by the Napoleonic Wars. The four most powerful nations—Austria, Prussia, Russia and the United Kingdom—were likely to impose their own solution on future borders. A number of other countries had been awarded the status of observers but were not expected to participate in the decision-making: Sweden, Spain, Denmark, Portugal, a number of German principalities, Switzerland... and France. They might benefit from the Great Powers' largesse or they might lose out if they were badly represented.

Before leaving Paris for Vienna, Talleyrand had a number of private meetings with Louis XVIII in the royal chambers at the Tuileries where they analysed together what could be anticipated during the congress. It should be said that, when not influenced by his court and particularly his brother, a good understanding seemed to exist between Louis and his minister. Unfortunately, this good understanding was not to last as both of these men were masters of behind-the-scenes scheming. There were four points that the king asked Talleyrand to defend: that no member of the Austrian royal family should reign over the Kingdom of Sardinia; that Naples should be restored to its rightful Bourbon king, Ferdinand IV; that the whole of Poland should not be occupied by Russia; and that Prussia should not acquire Saxony. The French monarch remained sympathetic to the cause of his cousin Frederick-August, the good king of Saxony, who had allied himself with Napoleon and had been so generous to Talleyrand. His kingdom was likely to be seized by the victorious Prussia. In this connection, a general objective was to limit any expansion of Prussia that would make it more powerful. The first task upon reaching Vienna would be, if possible, to establish France's position as an equal partner with the Great Powers, while declaring that the country was content to remain at peace within its ancient frontiers. The British representative, Lord Castlereagh, passed by Paris on his way to Vienna, meeting with Talleyrand and Louis XVIII. He was received with such enthusiastic expressions of friendship that he felt it necessary "to repress the exuberance" that was in danger of "exciting jealousy in other states".

Talleyrand left for Vienna with a team consisting of many old comrades: Dalberg to advise on the German question but also to spread secrets that would benefit from being more widely known; Alexis de Noailles to report back to Louis XVIII ("If I must be spied on," Talleyrand explained, "it's best that it's someone I have chosen myself."); the Marquis de La Tour du Pin-Gouvernet to sign passports; La Besnardière to be his assistant in the more serious work of negotiations; and his secretary Gabriel Perrey to draft letters. His old colleague from the days in exile at Juniper Hall, François de Jaucourt, took over the Ministry of Foreign Affairs in Paris. D'Hauterive was on leave and in semi-disgrace having been extremely outspoken during the first months of the Restoration. "It was also necessary," Talleyrand added, "to make the French Embassy as agreeable as possible." For this purpose, he took Carême with him, together with a team of chefs and a generous supply of pots and pans. Finally, the last member of the team would be the hostess for the French delegation in Vienna, Dorothea de Périgord, who had grown in beauty, dignity, elegance and self-confidence. Her three much older sisters would also be present in the Austrian capital: Wilhelmine von Sagan, Pauline von Hohenzollern-Hechingen and Johanna, the Princess Pignatelli.

When the Tsar of Russia had taken up residence in the Rue Saint-Florentin in April 1814, Dorothea had just suffered the loss of her 2-year-old daughter to measles. In the midst of all the important affairs of state that preoccupied him at this time, Talleyrand spent a few moments every evening to console her since her husband Edmond was quite incapable of sharing her grief. When Talleyrand proposed taking her with him to Vienna, the austere Dorothea willingly gave up her mourning and became transformed into a fascinating and elegant adventuress ready for anything. To do this, she rejected "the honest and regular happiness that some women enjoy", as well as her marriage in order to pursue a new career. The 60-year-old unconventional patriarch diplomat and this 21-year-old German-speaking mother of three would develop a partnership of destiny. Talleyrand did not consider taking with him to Vienna either his wife, who had now reverted to the title of Princess de Talleyrand, or the Duchess von Courland, to whom Talleyrand had addressed *billets doux* almost every day. Suddenly, she found herself replaced by her youngest daughter and had to seek solace in the company of the other members of Talleyrand's harem in Paris. He did, however, continue to send her his little notes, which have been a great source of information for historians. Edmond de Périgord could also quite easily have fulfilled the role of La Tour du Pin but the fact that he was left behind tells us that Talleyrand was weary of his folly and Dorothea had no wish for his company.

On 16 September 1814, everything was ready for the expedition to Vienna, where the French delegation needed to make a big impression. In contrast with the missions to London in the 1790s when he had no official status, Louis confirmed his new title of "Prince de Talleyrand". His political standing was further augmented by being awarded the coveted Golden Fleece by Emperor Francis I of Austria during a visit to Paris in August. But no title, rank, honour or award equalled the impact of Dorothea de Périgord, who became Talleyrand's trump card in the social and diplomatic dealings at the congress. She was not only his charming hostess at the French Embassy, but helped draft his dispatches to Paris. At the time of leaving for Vienna, there is no suggestion of any relationship between Talleyrand and Dorothea other than that of "uncle" and "niece". However, the gossips of Paris could not fail to draw attention to a 60-year-old libertine and womaniser leaving in the company of a 21-year-old woman. To Mme de Talleyrand, this was the final blow to her marriage.

It took them a week to reach Vienna, the French delegation installing itself in the splendid Questenberg-Kaunitz Palace on Johannesgasse, where the whole house needed a thorough cleaning and the mattresses and carpets had been attacked by moths. The process of purchasing new linen and decorations was made more complicated by the need to begin at once the official visits dictated by protocol. Before the French delegation's arrival, the Great Powers had already begun preliminary talks among themselves since they were the only ones whose opinions mattered—or so they believed.

In the autumn of 1814 and winter and spring of 1815, Vienna became an international centre celebrating the festival of peace after two decades of tumult that had shaken the continent to its foundations. During the previous twenty-two years, allies had become enemies and enemies allies, territories had changed hands, frontiers had disappeared or been redrawn, dynasties had been overthrown, monarchs sent into exile with new rulers taking their place at a bewildering rate. Now, the most important dignitaries of European diplomacy and their ladies had come to Vienna to reassemble the pieces. Alongside the meetings of the congress there was a hectic social round, with the headquarters of the French delegation rapidly becoming one of the most popular destinations with its series of banquets. A festival committee coordinated the numerous military parades, concerts, ballets, charades, sleigh rides, hunting parties and masked balls where one danced until dawn. Fortunes were spent on smart clothes and jewellery, while amateur theatricals were extremely popular.

The representative of the United Kingdom, Lord Castlereagh, was an aloof, handsome and seemingly imperturbable gentleman. Looking much younger than his 45 years, he had risen quickly in the British political hierarchy and was known to be confident and courageous. Britain's prestige was considerable at the congress for it had been at war almost uninterruptedly since 1793 and, furthermore, possessed the strongest economy. The British policy was that no single power should be allowed to dominate the Continent of Europe, so its government sought a "just equilibrium". The British delegation was housed in a twenty-two-roomed mansion on Minoritenplatz, which Castlereagh shared with his half-brother, the rambunctious Sir Charles Stewart.

In terms of power, Russia was also a giant, since it boasted by far the largest landmass and the largest army in the world. The Tsar of Russia, present in person, had appointed as his plenipotentiaries: Anstett, Nesselrode, Stackelberg and Stein from Germany; Czartoryski from Poland; La Harpe from Switzerland; Kapodistrias from Corfu; Pozzo di

Borgo from Corsica; and his foreign minister Count Andrey Razumovsky from the Ukraine. The most cosmopolitan in this cosmopolitan group was Karl Nesselrode, whose Jewish mother had given birth to him at sea near Lisbon, where his father was Russian ambassador. He had been baptized as a Protestant at the British Embassy in Portugal and educated in Berlin. Although Nesselrode would guide Russian foreign policy over the next four decades, he could neither read nor write Russian and spoke it badly. As a young man, the Corsican Carlo Andrea Pozzo di Borgo had been a political ally of both Joseph and Napoleon Bonaparte, with whom he had discussed the island's independence. He had been sent to Paris by the historical leader of the Corsicans, General Pasquale Paoli, in September 1790, representing his homeland at the Constituent Assembly. He subsequently became a dedicated Royalist and a sworn enemy of Napoleon, travelling all over Europe advising different governments on how to combat his belligerent one-time friend. In 1804 he entered the Russian diplomatic service and had been specifically named in the Treaty of Tilsit as a subject worthy of Napoleon's wrath.

Metternich, representing Austria, appointed Friedrich von Gentz as his personal assistant, who also became Secretary-General of the congress. For Prussia, the delegation consisted of the deaf Prince Hardenburg accompanied by Baron Wilhelm von Humboldt. Each delegation was, of course, equipped with teams of secretaries, translators, advisers, statisticians and messengers. Ninety-three ministers representing larger and smaller countries responded to the invitation, including minor royalties, the Papacy, the Sultan of Turkey, a number of religious groups (including the Jewish community) and the press. Naples had sent two rival delegations, one on behalf of the Napoleonic King Joachim Murat and the other for the Bourbon King Ferdinand IV. All of these delegations were under the impression that they would be granted an opportunity to speak, make their claims and assume their place in the new European order. On the contrary, the four Great Powers intended to keep the direction of affairs entirely in their own hands. However, as one writer put it, Talleyrand "seemed to dominate that illustrious assembly by the charm of his mind and the ascendency of his genius."

Upon arrival, Talleyrand faced some unpleasant surprises. He did not realise at first that Louis XVIII, very wary of his minister, had established confidential parallel contacts with Metternich via the Austrian ambassador in Paris, the Count von Bombelles. At least one of the opinions that Louis had shared with Metternich expressed exactly the opposite view to the one he had asked his minister to defend. A few days after the French delegation reached Vienna, Metternich wrote to Bombelles in Paris: "I believe the king is far from having undivided confidence in his minister... the Count de Blacas told me that the king did not require Austria to declare itself against Naples (Murat)." In fact, Louis XVIII had given precise instructions to Talleyrand that Naples should be restored to its Bourbon king, while in his secret dealings with Metternich he suggested a less firm position: as long as Austrian troops did not disturb the peace in Italy, Murat could remain the ruler of Naples—a little more than a year later Murat would be dead.

When writing to his king, Talleyrand informed him that, as the representative of the defeated nation, in the first instance he had not had the right to participate in the meetings and had therefore been unable to negotiate with the four Great Powers. If the Quadruple Alliance had been solidly united, then the chances of France making its voice heard were slight, but some of the victors sought territorial rewards for winning the war and this proved to be their undoing. If someone would frustrate their greed and stimulate their jealousy, then the seeds of discord might be sown. That someone was Talleyrand. "I will be gentle, conciliatory but positive," he wrote to Louis XVIII, "speaking only of principles and never deviating from them."

As a friendly gesture reflecting their past close relations, Nesselrode and Metternich invited Talleyrand to attend a preliminary meeting held on the afternoon of 30 September at Metternich's house. He then, as Gentz records, proceeded to harangue them for two hours. Why was Spain represented, not by the head of mission, but by Don Pedro, Marquis de Labrador? Because the head of mission had not yet arrived. Why did Prussia have two representatives at the meeting? Because, unfortunately, Hardenberg was deaf. Very well, said Talleyrand, "each of us has our infirmities" and he would bring Dalberg with him next time. A point won. Why were the Portuguese and Swedish representatives not present? This query met with an embarrassed silence. The document he was handed resumed the Allies' previous discussions. He seized upon the word "Allies". "What Allies? Allies against whom? Not against Napoleon; he is banished to Elba. Not against France; peace has been restored. And surely not against the King of France, the main guarantor of peace." Someone explained that the word Allies had been used for brevity. "Brevity," retorted the cantankerous Talleyrand, "should not be purchased at the price of accuracy." He added: "Gentlemen, let's speak frankly. If there are still any allied powers, my presence is not required. Yet, if I were not here, I would definitely be missed. I am perhaps the only one who asks for nothing. Great respect, that is all I want for France. I repeat that I want nothing from you, yet I bring you something important—the sacred principle of legitimacy." He then pointed out that this meeting, taking place on 30 September, was already discussing important matters on the agenda before the scheduled date for the congress to begin on 1 October, as had been stated on the invitations issued in Paris in the spring of that year. The Quadruple Alliance had ceased to exist upon the signing of the Treaty of Paris. Therefore, none of the deliberations during the preliminary meetings were admissible. The documents reflecting these discussions were withdrawn.

Regarding the way the congress would carry out its work, Metternich suggested that the subjects to be discussed should be divided into two categories and each category should be handed over to one of two committees. When these committees had made their report, the plenary meeting of the Congress would meet to adopt (or not) their recommendations. Talleyrand immediately understood that this was a way for the Great Powers to settle all the important issues among themselves. Somebody then mentioned the King of Naples. "Of which king of Naples are you talking?" he asked. When the name of Murat was mentioned, he stated: "We do not know the man in question." Considering that he was perfectly acquainted with Murat and had exchanged letters with him, those around the table were staggered by his impudence. The tireless and resourceful Secretary-General, Friedrich von Gentz, complained bitterly: "The intervention of Talleyrand and Labrador has badly upset our plans. It is a scene I shall never forget."

Friedrich von Gentz has been described as an influential, brilliant, cynical and clear-sighted journalist on historical, political and financial matters. He exercised a strong influence on European politics throughout this period, earning the label of "that wretched scribe" from Napoleon for his persistent hostility. Writing in English, French and German, he was recognized by various European powers as an ally whose pen had proved a potent weapon in their cause, with the result that he was showered with gifts and pensions in gratitude. After 1812, he became Metternich's assistant and inseparable companion, accompanying him on his journeys all over Europe. He was also devoted to the pleasures of society and gained an unparalleled reputation as a loose-living, disreputable, debt-ridden gambler and philanderer. Talleyrand also discovered that he had a weakness for flattery, chocolate, perfume and money.

The three greatest problems facing the congress were: the desire of Russia to take possession of Poland; the desire of Prussia to take possession of Saxony and the Rhineland in recompense for losing its part of Poland to the Russians; and the problem of Naples where there were two kings, Joachim Murat and Ferdinand IV. The smaller nations had also suffered at Napoleon's hands: Denmark, the Netherlands, Spain, Portugal, Sweden, Switzerland, Wurttemberg. The fact that they were small did not mean that they should suffer the same fate as the defeated nation. Spain, Portugal and Sweden had signed the Treaty of Paris and, therefore, could claim a place at the high table. By not according them this place, the four Great Powers had placed themselves at fault. With dignity and firmness, Talleyrand called them to order. That evening, he returned with a note for the four ministers pointing out that the only organ capable of directing the congress's work should consist of the eight signatories of the Treaty of Paris, and that their authority should be confirmed at a plenary meeting. The "Four" agreed that the congress should henceforth be directed by "Eight" countries. However, they refused to call a plenary meeting which meant, in fact, that the actual opening of the Congress was postponed indefinitely.

Despite their long association, Talleyrand did not like Metternich, calling him "the pallid one" and describing him in his letters to Louis XVIII as tortuous, vague, vain and false: "His main technique is to waste our time believing that it is the way to gain it." The outcome was that the work of the congress was delayed from one day to the next while the Big Four held informal discussions amongst themselves without informing Talleyrand, of whom they had become very wary.

There was a real danger that the four allies, under pressure from the aggressive Russia and Prussia, would impose their will on the whole proceedings and take decisions about European borders with impunity. The phrase Talleyrand introduced into the discussions with exquisite courtesy was "the rule of law", words that had not been heard for twenty years. The Prussian minister, learning that henceforth the negotiations would take place following the rulebook, exclaimed: "What is public law doing here?" Talleyrand's cool response was: "It is here!" Resorting to this principle changed the way in which the congress conducted its business and attracted the attention of the very annoying Spanish representative Labrador. He, in turn, assembled the smaller nations into a unified front. It was eventually decided that Labrador was out of his depth and excluded from the discussions. In this way, Talleyrand became the spokesman for the secondary powers advising them to exercise their rights by participating in all the meetings, which they were entitled to do as co-signatories of the Treaty of Paris. The Great Powers were obliged to admit the smaller nations and, as another signatory but for a different reason, France joined them. Having achieved his main objective, Talleyrand rapidly abandoned the minor powers. From Paris, Pozzo di Borgo wrote to Nesselrode: "His interest in other people depends on how much he needs them at that moment; even his politeness is an investment with interest payable before the end of the day… In any event, you know him better than me." Considering that France had been defeated by the four dominant European powers, Talleyrand had broken through their united front—a remarkable achievement. While they did not know exactly what they wanted, Talleyrand with his clear-cut principles, irrefutable logic and lucid persistence dominated the congress.

The United Kingdom sought no territorial gains on the continent of Europe, which made Castlereagh altogether a much easier person to deal with. The British Minister of Foreign Affairs was not devious and cunning, had only the vaguest idea about European geography and desired simply that the continental nations should settle their affairs amongst themselves. He disliked the tsar's intention to take control over the whole of Poland realizing that, if agreement was going to be reached, Russia would have to moderate its position. The British wanted the

Netherlands to occupy Luxembourg and Belgium, including the great commercial port of Antwerp, thus safeguarding England's continental trade. Once this objective had been achieved, in February 1815 Castlereagh returned to London, his place being taken by the British ambassador to Paris, the Duke of Wellington—one of Talleyrand's particular friends—who was received with great pomp.

In the eighteenth century, one of the largest populations in Europe had been that of Poland. However, with no natural frontiers and the national leadership in disarray, Poland had been easy prey to its three powerful neighbours: Russia, Austria and Prussia. Talleyrand always considered the progressive occupation of Poland by these three powers between 1772 and 1795 as a transgression. If an enlarged and independent Poland were to be recreated, it would involve Prussia and Austria ceding those parts that they governed, with the inevitable necessity of compensating them with territory elsewhere. Austria could look towards occupying northern Italy and the Balkans, but Prussia might then expect to take possession of Saxony and the Rhineland. The Prussian delegation was determined to emerge from the congress with its country as the largest and most influential Germanic power.

After the defeat of Prussia in 1807, Napoleon had created his protectorate of the Grand Duchy of Warsaw on a central part of Polish territory and placed it under the authority of the King of Saxony. Would this Grand Duchy become the core of an independent Polish state or would it be swallowed up in a Russian take over? The question of Poland was clearly going to be the major stumbling block since Russian troops already occupied the country. Castlereagh reproached the tsar for endangering the unity of the Great Powers by keeping his hold on Poland in violation of the Treaty of Reichenbach of 1813, where he had agreed to share Napoleon's Duchy of Warsaw with Prussia and Austria. Matters came to a head in mid-November 1814 when, in a confrontation with the tsar, Talleyrand told him that he could not simply occupy Poland and ignore the consequences. The tsar declared: "Poland is my conquest and I will keep what I occupy," and spoke of "those who have betrayed the cause of Europe". Since Alexander had signed a treaty with Napoleon in 1807 over the division of Poland, Talleyrand's stinging reply was: "Sire, it is just a question of dates." In the course of the Napoleonic wars, the

355

Austrians, the Prussians and the Russians had all been obliged to humble themselves before the power of the French emperor. Only England and King Louis XVIII had not compromised themselves at some stage. This scene ended with the tsar storming out of the room, slamming the door behind him. However, thereafter, Alexander was much more accommodating with Talleyrand. The tsar was equally surprised about Castlereagh's opposition to his plans to recreate an "independent" Poland under his tutelage. Alexander liked to give the impression that he was making a generous gesture by restoring the country's independence after it had been wrongly occupied forty years earlier and, furthermore, he would grant it an "enlightened constitution". Alexander wanted to create an enlarged Kingdom of Poland, but subservient to himself. What business was it of Castlereagh's to object? Indeed, Castlereagh was concerned that Polish independence under Russian tutelage would upset the whole balance of power in Europe and plant the seeds of another war. On the other hand, the Russian aristocracy opposed any democratic experiments in Poland that might inspire ideas of emancipation in the Russian peasantry. The preference of public opinion in Russia was for their country to expand southward in the direction of Constantinople and the Ottoman Empire.

Metternich did not play any significant part in this crisis for, unfortunately, at this moment he was consumed with Dorothea's eldest sister Wilhelmine, the Duchess of Sagan. The tsar desired to obtain all of Poland but Metternich was prepared to give up neither the southern part that Austria had occupied since 1772 nor his place in Wilhelmine's affections. Although this couple had known each other for ten years, their affair started in the spring of 1813 coming to an end in October 1814. The passion between the two is documented by over 600 letters written by Metternich to Wilhelmine containing details about the political wheeling and dealing taking place at the congress. Her rival for the affection of Metternich and the tsar was the Princess Bagration, who fanned the tsar's jealousy by feeding him the most intimate details of an earlier love affair with Metternich. Alexander began to resent Metternich with "an implacable hatred" leading to explosions of rage that considerably complicated negotiations.

What was to be done about Prussia's ambition to occupy Saxony?

Hardenburg, who felt he was being outmanoeuvred over Saxony, threatened to declare war until confronted with Castlereagh's icy stare. It was up to Talleyrand to find the solution. The King of Saxony was accused of being Napoleon's ally, but Talleyrand pointed out that practically every country around the table had this sin upon its conscience. Why should the King of Saxony be singled out for punishment? And could one country legally seize the territory of its neighbour? Was this any different from Napoleon's tactics? At this point, Saxony was occupied by the Russian Army. However, if the Russians fully supported the Prussian takeover of Saxony, even the Prussian delegation was alarmed at the consequences of being indebted to the Russians. At this point, Metternich sent a note to Prince Hardenberg suggesting that Prussia could occupy Saxony, but only on condition that it renounced all its other territorial ambitions and specifically prevented the tsar from gaining Poland. Talleyrand's solution to these different desires was that they should be declared openly during a plenary session of the congress, giving public opinion an opportunity to express its reservations.

In the early weeks of the congress, fractures began to appear between the ambitions of Tsar Alexander and Hardenberg on one side, and the reservations of Metternich and Castlereagh on the other. If the Great Powers became divided into two halves, the adhesion of Talleyrand to one camp or the other would give him a casting vote. After months of manoeuvring, Talleyrand's presence at the negotiating table became permanent, such that, during the course of January 1815, agreement was reached on the Polish and German questions.

The Polish problem was indissolubly linked to the question of Saxony. Talleyrand had envisaged Bavaria, Saxony and Württemberg as independent buffer states between Austria and Prussia, avoiding potential points of future conflict. Frederick-August, the King of Saxony, had backed the wrong horse in the Napoleonic Wars and was held as a prisoner in Berlin. Since the congress refused to recognize his representative, serious rear-guard action was required on this matter. He believed that Talleyrand could help him out of this dilemma and knew just how to motivate him; 6 million francs were provided as an incentive. Frederick-August could also count upon the support of Louis XVIII whose mother had been Marie-Josephine of Saxony—they were first cousins

Talleyrand had a quiet discussion with Metternich pointing out all the aspects involved in reconstituting Europe. Reviving arguments from ten years previously, Talleyrand reminded him that, if Russia occupied all of Poland, its frontier would move significantly in the direction of central Europe and share a common border—and point of friction—with Austria. Metternich grasped the significance. Talleyrand's attitude to Poland was either to grant it complete independence or, if the Russians insisted on taking it over, to reduce its size so that it did not border on Austria or Prussia. Exactly the same scenario applied to Prussia taking over Saxony, where Austria's border would be exposed again. Prussia and Russia were on such good terms that they had nothing to fear from each other and might very well support the other's territorial claims. Metternich now realized that such an arrangement was unlikely to bring peace to Europe, while the enemies of Austria were not in Paris but in Berlin and St Petersburg.

Another confrontation developed over the Kingdom of Naples and the fate of its Napoleonic King Joachim Murat. Louis XVIII had asked Talleyrand to support the restoration of the Bourbon King Ferdinand IV, but Austria was involved in political intrigues in Italy with the result that it was not actually opposed to Murat remaining in power. The tsar told Talleyrand that he could put pressure on Austria to remove Murat if, in turn, the French delegation would cease to place obstacles in the path of the annexation of Saxony by Prussia. The tsar's behaviour became increasingly erratic and he came to be regarded as the villain of the piece. Although Talleyrand was hardly a paragon of morality, he told the tsar: "It is your wish, your interest that determines [your attitude] but myself, I am obliged to follow principles and principles can never be traded." During November and December 1814, he feared that, without principles, international affairs would soon degenerate into a reckless scramble for territory to satisfy self-interest or, worse still, simply provoking armed conflict. However, the possibility that the Great Powers were prepared to come to blows finally served to improve the prospects for peace.

Tsar Alexander was aware that his power base at home had crumbled and he became increasingly irritable and impetuous in Vienna. He was described by various correspondents as rude, crude and unpredictable, prone to bullying and boasting—another Napoleon. When frustrated, he would threaten to use his army to gain his point, and thereafter the dust would settle and everyone would be invited to a ball at his residence. Increasingly, he tried to conceal his schizophrenia in a cloud of mysticism and sentimental words, seeking omens and supernatural guidance in the Bible. On one occasion, Metternich was invited to dinner with Alexander and his spiritual guide, Mme Julie von Krüdener—a fourth chair was left vacant "for our Lord Jesus Christ". During the military campaign that ended in the occupation of Paris in 1814, the fate of the world hung on the outcome of imperial prayer-meetings held in the presence of Mme von Krüdener. The other Great Powers were puzzled by the tsar, who saw himself as the epoch's Christian emancipator who had conquered a great military genius due to the tenacity of his own leadership. To sceptics like Metternich, he merely seemed to be masking his European-wide ambitions "under the language of evangelical abnegation".

The best way to frustrate the territorial intentions of Prussia and Russia was to divide the four Allies, so Talleyrand began to raise doubts in the minds of the Austrian and British negotiators over the aggressive intentions of Russia and Prussia in Eastern Europe. On 3 January 1815, Austria, France and the United Kingdom signed a secret defensive treaty of mutual protection. Rather than being an outsider at the Congress of Vienna, Talleyrand proclaimed proudly to his king that France was now an ally of the two most progressive and civilized nations of Europe. In fact, this treaty was a manoeuvre designed to intimidate Prussia and Russia and strengthen the hand of Austria. What had originally been the meeting of "Four" became in January 1815 the congress of "Five". It was not long before Tsar Alexander found out about the "secret" treaty and who its author was. Not surprisingly, he developed a profound distrust for Talleyrand but these events restored mutual respect at the congress.

In February, the Great Powers finally reached agreement on Poland and Saxony. Russia received only the Duchy of Warsaw to add to its possessions in eastern Poland. To the disillusionment of the Polish patriots, that part of the country was "irrevocably attached to Russia" and

Tsar Alexander became its king. Prussia obtained only the northern part of Saxony leaving the richest and most populous parts, including the great commercial and cultural cities of Leipzig and Dresden, in the hands of its former king. Once these two problems had been resolved, the remaining work of the Congress fell into place easily. Nevertheless, Talleyrand could not always win; Prussia was granted the right to occupy a considerable part of the Rhineland and Westphalia, as well as Swedish Pomerania on the Baltic coast. These Roman Catholic territories, peaceful, devoted to industry, study and the arts fell under the domination of a Protestant, militaristic and aggressive state. The border of Prussia, and therefore the presence of its army, would move significantly westwards and henceforth would be placed just 220 kilometres from Paris.

How could Talleyrand, who had been given specific instructions to avoid this outcome, concede this point? Regrettably, Castlereagh insisted upon it. Since Louis XVIII was determined to defend the Saxon throne of Frederick-August, and Prussia had expressed its intentions of taking possession of other territories—the Rhineland, Luxembourg and Belgium—Castlereagh suggested that Prussia might be satisfied by acquiring part of its territorial ambitions. There were limits to the degree that Talleyrand could oppose his chief ally so, in a choice between Prussia occupying either all of Saxony or the right bank of the Rhine, he chose the least bad solution. It took the Prussians some time to realize that they had gained considerably from this trafficking. The new German Confederation was given a constitution and a parliament at Frankfurt. It would be forty-eight years later that Bismarck would succeed in unifying the whole of Germany. The origins of the War of 1870 and the First and Second World Wars were created at Vienna in 1815.

In Naples, Murat found his throne under threat from Talleyrand and offered him 5 million francs to curb his enthusiasm. On the other hand, Ferdinand IV, the legitimate king of Naples now located in Sicily, sent Talleyrand a comparable sum to kindle his enthusiasm. It was clear that Murat, a brave and talented cavalryman, could only be dislodged by a powerful military intervention. Talleyrand was astonished to discover in February that Metternich had been negotiating the Naples issue directly with Louis XVIII and Blacas behind his back, demonstrating that the apparent confidence in the correspondence between the king and himself had been illusionary. Metternich's position was weakened by the fact that he had once been Caroline Murat's lover and still allowed his policy to be affected by this affair. However, in 1814, Metternich had signed an agreement with Murat guaranteeing his right to the throne if he deserted Napoleon. Metternich and Wellington reached a secret agreement allowing the Austrian Army to progress down the Italian peninsula restoring order as they advanced. When Napoleon returned to power on 20 March 1815, Murat decided that the moment had come for him to reunify Italy, so he started moving his army up the peninsula towards the Austrian forces—despite Napoleon's advice to the contrary—occupying Talleyrand's Duchy of Benevento on the way. It was a fatal error of judgement, with the flamboyant Murat meeting and being defeated by the Austrians, court-martialled and executed by firing squad. Ferdinand IV recovered his kingdom under the new name of the Kingdom of the Two Sicilies. The Pope repossessed his ancient domains, including the Duchy of Benevento, but continued to pay Talleyrand a modest annual pension for it.

But what became of Napoleon's wife, the Empress Marie Louise? In April 1814, there had been a race between the Austrian cavalry and Napoleon's cavalry to catch up with her in the French town of Blois. The Austrians had won and she was taken to her father's residence in Vienna, living in isolation, with the ancient Prince de Ligne playing toy soldiers with her son. Later, in August 1814, Metternich instructed the dashing, one-eyed General Adam von Neipperg, a notorious lady-killer, to escort Napoleon's wife to Aix-les-Bains to take the waters for the benefit of her health. The true purpose of this mission was simply to prevent the empress from joining Napoleon in exile in Elba "by any means whatsoever", a task that Neipperg carried out so commendably that, before long, Marie Louise fell into his arms, while the subject of Elba never arose again. In the final act of the Congress of Vienna on 9 June 1815, she was granted the title of sovereign Duchess of Parma. After Napoleon's death in 1821, Neipperg married Marie Louise.

Of all the women in Talleyrand's life, it was the intelligent and fascinating Dorothea who affected him the most. She dominated him and he liked it. Not only did he make her responsible for his household, she became his companion, supporter and councillor. He shared his intentions and his political secrets with her—and his heart. This 61-year-old despot fell in love and was made to suffer for it. At the many receptions held during the congress, the arrival of the Prince de Talleyrand and Dorothea de Périgord always caused a stir. As one of the most celebrated couples in Vienna, they brought with them an ambiguous air of scandal—not to say incest—that added to their notoriety. Remarkably beautiful, Dorothea had now succumbed to wearing the latest Parisian fashions, while her mother had provided her with some fabulous jewellery.

In Vienna, everyone spied on everyone else—as well as being spied upon themselves. Organized by Baron Franz Hager, the Austrian police were everywhere—eavesdropping at the receptions, snooping in the corridors, opening letters, driving the carriages—with Francis I receiving reports every morning. There was a genuine justification for all this activity—the security of the illustrious guests. Ever since Talleyrand's arrival, he had been the focus of particular attention. The police tried to introduce someone into his residence to spy on him but, as one disillusioned agent reported: "[His] house is nothing less than a fortress in which he stands guard only with those people of whom he is sure." They believed that he shared his meals late at night with a mysterious personality in a room where someone played the piano to conceal their conversation. Finally, Talleyrand explained to Metternich that his enigmatic companion, a harmless Austrian pianist called Sigismund Neukomm, had formed part of his household for a number of years. La Tour du Pin had installed a comfortable armchair in Talleyrand's salon and, while listening to Mozart, Beethoven and Haydn (and no doubt works by Neukomm himself), he would read the daily files assembled by Dalberg and prepare for the role he would play in the next day's discussions. Talleyrand and Dorothea were careful not to leave documents lying around, while Dalberg, on the other hand, was very careless. Talleyrand had also invited to Vienna Napoleon's now-redundant official court painter Jean-Baptiste Isabey, who set up his studio in the Leopoldstadt to paint portraits of notable personalities attending the congress. While creating his masterpiece of this great political assembly, his studio became a popular destination for people viewing his half-finished portraits and listening to his entertaining gossip about Napoleonic Paris. The glory of France was also represented by the ballerina Émilie Bigottini, who had accompanied Talleyrand to Vienna and entertained the public with her breathtaking performances.

A favourite target for police supervision was Dorothea's eldest sister, Wilhelmine von Sagan. Her ambitions and great wealth meant that she played an important role in Vienna's social life, but due to her lackadaisical upbringing she lacked any sense of responsibility, morality and particularly fidelity. In her heyday, the beautiful, flamboyant, wealthy Wilhelmine lived a shiftless, hedonistic existence as an international libertine, discarding lovers and husbands with casual zeal. Talleyrand liked to converse with Wilhelmine, who described the dreadful scenes that took place between Metternich and the tsar, including the threat of a duel. Francis I intervened and pointed out to the tsar "how very strange it would seem" for two such great men to fight to the death over a woman. Wilhelmine would die twenty-four years later as a lonely, stout old woman, "very partial to tobacco".

Dalberg, the only person in whom Talleyrand had entire confidence—mistakenly, as it turns out—played the part of Louis XVIII's ambassador extraordinaire, being on familiar terms with Austrian, Italian and German Protestant diplomats. Among his many tasks was keeping in touch with Jaucourt at the Rue du Bac in Paris. Before anyone was allowed to meet Talleyrand to discuss Prussian and Russian affairs, it was necessary to pass through Dalberg's office. As a public relations exercise, the Prince de Talleyrand invited the aristocracy and diplomats of Europe to a grand memorial service for Louis XVI on 21 January 1815 at St Stephen's Cathedral. On this same date only sixteen years previously, in the company of Napoleon Bonaparte, he had been at a Jacobin ceremony to celebrate the demise of Louis Capet.

The Prince de Talleyrand's daily routine respected the one already established in Paris. He went to bed late and woke up late. Then, like a seventeenth century monarch, the unchanging ritual of his morning toilette took place in public under the direction of Courtiade. His appearance always made a big impression with his powdered hair, his high cravat with the order of the golden fleece hanging over his shoulders and the hesitant walk setting him apart from the rest of humanity. His long silk coat with lace cuffs was worn above tight knee-breeches, white stockings and court shoes with red heels and diamond buckles. In society, he always kept his features impassive in what became known as "the sphinx mask". His legendary good manners and brilliant conversation were paralleled by the refinement of his dining table, where Carême still reigned supreme. When Louis XVIII inquired whether Talleyrand had sufficient staff, he thanked the king and wrote in reply: "Sire, I need more cooks than diplomats." He was also renowned for his partiality to Brie cheese.

In Vienna, Talleyrand met again one of the last great characters of eighteenth-century society: Charles-Joseph, the 79-year-old Prince de Ligne, whose ancestry comprised the same long generations of nobility as Talleyrand. However, far from being a member of the elite, he was a Bohemian who looked upon the Storming of the Bastille as "Europe's finest day". He had lived in so many different countries and spoke so many languages that he was known as "the most European of Europeans". He had had as many mistresses as Talleyrand but never lingered with them too long: "In love, only the commencement is charming. I am not surprised that one likes the pleasure of beginning so often." The incorrigible Prince de Ligne one day said something to Talleyrand which eventually filtered through to the Tuileries in Paris: "You are a little like the King of France. All Louis XVIII has to do is obey you." It came up in the conversation that Talleyrand had been accused of betraying Napoleon for seven years: "What?" said the Prince de Ligne in astonishment, "Only seven years! And I have had my suspicions about you for twenty years!" Reflecting the authority of Talleyrand at the Congress, he wrote that when Louis XVIII's minister entered the room, "Alexander keeps his mouth shut, Francis heads for the door and Frederick looks at his boots." Another of his epithets is: "Politics is the art of making war without killing anyone." One could say that the curtain fell on the eighteenth century on 13 December 1814 when the dying Prince de Ligne said: "The congress lacks one thing: the funeral of a field-marshal. Leave it to me." He left us with his last legendary caricature of the Congress of Vienna. Since a large part of the congress's work took place during salons, banquets and balls, he observed: "It doesn't advance, it dances."

There were two clouds on the horizon during the congress. The first was that the plague had broken out in Silesia and was advancing inexorably in the direction of Vienna. Nothing was known at that time about how the plague was transmitted except that it spared no-one. Fortunately, with the arrival of winter, the epidemic stopped upon reaching the suburbs of the city. The second peril was represented by Napoleon who, for some people's comfort, was located far too close to the French and Italian coasts. Castlereagh, Metternich and Talleyrand were all aware of the danger, but Francis I did not wish to discuss the subject further. As for Tsar Alexander, whose decision it had been, strongly influenced by Caulaincourt, to send Napoleon to Elba, Talleyrand found him alternately violent and tranquil. Then, one morning in late February 1815, Talleyrand had not yet risen while Dorothea sat on the edge of his bed eating her breakfast. That evening the usual reception would take place where she was looking forward to playing a role in a little comedy that had been arranged. An urgent letter arrived from Metternich. They both believed it was to give them the timetable of that day's meetings. "Bonaparte has left the Isle of Elba!" Dorothea read in horror. "And what about my rehearsal?" With his customary calm, Talleyrand replied: "It will take place, Madame."

A little more than a month later, Gentz, who had no particular sense of humour, was drinking his morning coffee when a copy of a poster printed in French was passed on to him from Metternich's office. It appeared that, upon his arrival in Paris, Napoleon's first task had been to offer 10,000 ducats in gold to anyone who would apprehend or kill Friedrich von Gentz. Fearing for his life, Gentz was alarmed until someone pointed out the date—1 April!

CHAPTER XVII
WATERLOO

Napoleon leaving Elba raised a number of questions. Why did he leave? How did he leave? But particularly, where did he go? There was nothing in the Treaty of Fontainebleau that actually forbade Napoleon from leaving Elba and, since the United Kingdom had never signed the treaty, why would it be the responsibility of the British if he left? The reason was that Castlereagh had placed a British commissioner on the island to keep an eye on the fallen emperor.

Not all of the dispositions in the Treaty of Fontainebleau concerning Napoleon had been respected. By this treaty's terms, he had been promised an annual income of 2 million francs from Louis XVIII's purse and pensions for the members of his family—but the money had never materialized. The problem was that France had not been involved in drawing up the Treaty of Fontainebleau between the Allies and Napoleon, where the financial arrangements had been detailed. Whereas the subsequent Treaty of Paris, established between the Allies and France, makes no mention of Napoleon's allowance. So, administratively, and no doubt assisted by some bureaucratic bloody-mindedness, there was no legal obligation for Louis XVIII to pay any money to Napoleon. Furthermore, the French Government had stripped Elba of all its resources and finances prior to Napoleon's arrival. He had his own private funds but maintaining the meaningless luxury of a large number of staff and troops meant that this money would soon be exhausted. Already, in November 1814, the British commissioner whose job it was to keep an eye on Napoleon, informed Castlereagh of the emperor's money problems. Even the tsar in Vienna was aware that the allowance had not been paid to Napoleon and reminded Talleyrand about it.

On the island of Elba, Napoleon had launched a range of ambitious schemes to improve its infrastructure: building roads, creating a fire brigade, a brick-works, aqueducts to bring fresh water, planting mulberry trees to found a silk industry, and oak, pine, olive and chestnut trees to stem soil erosion. He proposed a municipal service to remove the garbage that rotted on the filthy streets. He improved the island's defences since there was the ever-present danger that his enemies would attempt to capture and assassinate him. Napoleon took charge of the nearby island of Pianosa, where he envisaged sowing wheat to supply Elba with grain, setting up a stud farm to breed horses and building retirement homes for his loyal retainers. In fact, these were the actions of a dynamic and enlightened ruler, in total contrast with the reckless conqueror who had spread terror throughout Europe.

Talleyrand had taken the elementary precaution of placing informants on Elba to keep an eye on the former emperor. Aware that he would be spied on, Napoleon had his mail from the mainland addressed to a local fisherman, Signor Senno. In this way, he had learned that there was profound concern at the Congress of Vienna about his location close to the European mainland with "a strong body of opinion" wishing to banish him to a more remote location. Visitors to Elba informed him that he was still popular in France, particularly among his former troops, while the uncompromising Bourbons did not enjoy the same approval. A further blow was that his wife's secretary in Vienna, Claude-François de Méneval, informed him that the Empress Marie Louise was no longer at liberty to receive his letters or reply to them. Losing all hope that Marie Louise would ever visit the island, he was gratified by the visit of his Polish mistress Maria Walewska and their illegitimate son Alexandre. Yet another rumour reached him—there was a conspiracy to place the Duke d'Orléans on the throne of France. If this occurred, the morose, restless and bored Napoleon feared slipping into oblivion. The moment had come to take action.

Why had the 38-year-old Highlander, Colonel Neil Campbell, been chosen to become the emperor's minder? In fact, many prominent figures had been approached but had declined the opportunity of sharing a small, rocky Mediterranean island with Napoleon. Campbell had been severely wounded during the latter stages of the invasion of France while leading a cavalry charge during the Battle of Fère-Champenoise, when a Russian Cossack mistook him for a French officer. He had arrived in Elba with his head in bandages and his arm in a sling. His orders from Lord Castlereagh stated that he was in no way to act as a prison warder, but rather to facilitate the former French emperor in taking up residence on the island. Napoleon and the obscure British officer got on well together. Lord Castlereagh's instructions also clearly indicated that Campbell was not obliged to remain on Elba longer than he thought necessary, but at Napoleon's request he had promised to stay until the termination of the Congress of Vienna. Because it was believed that Campbell was permanently stationed on the island, the British Navy relaxed its blockade.

On 16 February 1815, Campbell set off from Elba to Livorno in Italy on *H.M.S. Partridge* carrying dispatches for Lord Castlereagh and Talleyrand in which he expressed his anxiety about Napoleon's intentions. Napoleon immediately issued orders to prepare the sixteen-gun brig *Inconstant* for sea painted like an English ship and furnished with supplies for three months. Otherwise, Napoleon was at pains to act as though life was continuing as normal on Elba. One week later, when the *Partridge* returned without Campbell, Napoleon ordered the *Inconstant* to put to sea and remain out of sight to conceal his intentions. On 24 February the *Partridge* left the island once again to pick up Campbell. Napoleon then placed an embargo on all shipping so that no-one could alert the outside world about his plans. At 8 p.m. on Sunday 26 February, the firing of a cannon signalled the 45-year-old ex-emperor's departure. His flotilla consisted of seven various-sized boats carrying 1,150 people. On their way to the French coast, they passed a couple of other ships without being troubled but particularly noteworthy was that the French frigate *Fleur-de-Lys*, patrolling northwest of the nearby islet of Capraia, did not observe them at all.

On the morning of 28 February, Campbell returned to Elba on the *Partridge* to discover the bird had flown. No one in Napoleon's household would tell him where he had gone. He sent a fishing boat with dispatches to Livorno to spread the news to the world, then sailed in the general direction of the south coast of France, on the way encountering the *Fleur-de-Lys,* whose captain told him that the imperial flotilla could not have passed him without being spotted. Although, to Campbell, France seemed the most likely destination, his conversation with the captain of the *Fleur-de-Lys* meant that he had to search in all directions.

On 1 March, Napoleon's little navy commenced disembarkation at Golfe-Juan, between Cannes and Antibes. He then set off for Paris taking a more tortuous road through the Alps rather than the direct route up the Rhône valley. Apart from evading troops sent to block his way, another justification for this decision was that he avoided much of the South of France, which had suffered particularly during Napoleon's rule and was a hotbed of resentment against him. He made it all the way to Paris without a shot being fired against him, since troops sent to block his passage rapidly transferred their allegiance to him and swelled the ranks. Louis XVIII was so unpopular that desertion and betrayal took place on a grand scale. On 20 March, Napoleon made a triumphal entry into the capital amidst an immense cheering crowd and began his second term on the French throne—Louis XVIII having fled to Belgium the night before. Once installed in Paris, Napoleon declared himself a changed man. He proclaimed freedom of the press—within certain limits—and told Fouché's police to protect the people rather than persecute them. He further declared that he would honour all existing peace agreements—although, after more than a decade of broken promises, no-one could possibly pay any credit to this one. Most remarkable of all, Benjamin Constant became one of his political advisers.

The deception for Napoleon was that, after twenty years of war, the nation's finances were in ruins and, in the short time since his abdication, the Bourbons had not been able to restore them. He could not possibly assemble the resources he required, so he would be obliged to fight and win a battle of desperation or his fate would be sealed. The royal army should have counted 200,000 men but consisted of less than one-third this figure. It was poorly equipped and led by inexperienced Royalist officers. However, by cancelling leave, rounding up deserters, pulling military cadets out of the classroom and bringing in sailors from the navy, Napoleon soon assembled a force of a quarter of a million men. He placed orders for muskets, pistols, cartridges, uniforms, boots and all the paraphernalia needed to conduct a military campaign but, since there was no guarantee that these items would be paid for, many disillusioned provincial authorities ignored the emperor's decrees. Some Royalist and Jacobin forces formed spontaneous resistance groups in parts of the country, the latter ferociously opposed to both Napoleon and Louis XVIII. In Paris, the press sympathetic to Napoleon mocked Talleyrand, who observed serenely: "It's a matter of weeks"—once again he was right.

In the short term, Talleyrand too was deprived of his post and governmental revenues and, furthermore, his properties in France, worth millions, were impounded by Napoleon. He sent part of his staff back to Paris from Vienna, while Castlereagh advised him that the Viennese banks would honour all his debts, although in the final analysis this assistance only covered the basics. Wellington left Vienna to take command of his army in the Low Countries, with the British delegation to the congress now under the responsibility of Lords Clancarty and Cathcart.

The consequences of Napoleon's return would be totally disastrous for France's and especially Talleyrand's position in Vienna in the eyes of the Great Powers. The tsar's decision allowing Napoleon to abdicate in 1814 and to be exiled on Elba was now clearly a monumental error; his most determined enemies would have been very glad to hang the former emperor. The terms of the Treaty of Fontainebleau covering Napoleon's abdication and the fate of his family were now evidently null and void. At first glance, it seemed as if the French population had welcomed him back to power with enthusiasm. Talleyrand reacted strongly to Napoleon's return, knowing that there had to be differentiation between Napoleon's intentions and the cause of the French people, who were not as keen about the return of the dictator as appearances suggested. The reaction of Austria, Prussia and Russia was to declare total war against France with the intention of conquering the country, breaking it up into pieces and distributing its various regions amongst themselves. The Austrian, British and Prussian Armies began to gather, while the Russian Army on its way home reversed course. The only troops immediately available to confront Napoleon consisted of the British Army in Belgium and Blücher's Prussian contingent in the Rhineland. The British Government announced that it was ready to finance an Allied Army of 1 million men.

During March 1815, the Vienna Congress met again several times, with Talleyrand taking advantage of the situation to hold individual meetings with the various Great Powers to plead the cause of France. The Duchess von Courland arrived in Vienna on 24 March having been chased out of Paris by Napoleon's return. Since all four of her daughters were in Vienna at this time, it is interesting to observe that she chose to stay with Dorothea and Talleyrand. Given her own relationship with Talleyrand, it is impossible to believe that she would have stayed in the Kaunitz Palace if there was any question of a liaison between the Prince and Dorothea. She would surely have discovered it within the space of a few hours. The minister set the mother and the daughter to work telling the great and the good that it was an injustice to associate Napoleon's actions and ambitions with the desires of the French people. On 13 March, he presented a draft declaration to the congress stating that the imminent war was not against France, the primary victim, but exclusively against Napoleon. He declared that it was France's destiny to remain geographically intact and to be governed by the Bourbons. Would the Allies sign a declaration condemning Napoleon as an outlaw? They would!

Since many members of the French king's army and government officials were deserting to Napoleon, this declaration was also an expression of support by the Great Powers for Louis XVIII so as to strengthen the resolve of all Frenchmen whose opinions were wavering. On 25 March, the four Great Powers renewed their determination to confront Napoleon and invited Louis XVIII to join them. Talleyrand urged the king, located in Ghent with his court and ministers, to call for the formation of a national army consisting of those Frenchmen who were opposed to Napoleon—whose defeat, according to him, was inevitable.

In the midst of these international affairs, Talleyrand met for the last time in Vienna the graceful, the beautiful Mme de Brionne, his former mistress who he had not seen for thirty years. As she lay on her deathbed, he found himself in tears unable to speak. Another disagreeable situation was waiting for him. In his company, Dorothea was keenly interested by the diplomacy going on around her and began to contribute to the dispatches addressed to Louis XVIII. However, the Prince de Talleyrand could not supply what she found in the company of handsome young men. Dorothea began to take more than an interest in them although, at first, her secret was kept well-hidden. The first person to be seen in her company was the young Prince Johann von Trauttmansdorff, the Austrian emperor's equerry. He was seductive and light-hearted but when Gentz introduced her to the 22-year-old Count Karel Jan Clam-Martinic, aide-de-camp to the Prince Schwarzenberg, matters became more serious. One of the most brilliant officers in the Austrian Army, handsome, witty, ambitious and from an ancient noble family, for Dorothea he represented something new and exciting. Soon he was paying visits to the Kaunitz Palace, riding with her in the Prater Park and dining with her in restaurants. Carême created a new dessert called the "Clam-Martinic Torte". For the first time in his life Talleyrand suffered the pangs of jealousy.

Another visitor to the Kaunitz Palace was the indefatigable Montrond. While all Europe was on the march, Montrond passed through the Allied lines wrapped in the disguise of the "Abbé Altieri". Charles de Flahaut, on the same mission to reach Vienna, had only got as far as Strasbourg before being arrested. Montrond had been charged by Napoleon to invite Talleyrand to become a member of his new provisional government with the promise of having his confiscated property returned. As the entire diplomatic corps had fled Paris upon his return to the city, Napoleon needed the presence of someone of Talleyrand's standing to provide a minimum of international credibility. A third messenger was authorized to approach Metternich and offer a huge sum of money if he would desert the coalition—but none of these enterprises were successful.

On 9 June 1815, the delegates gathered in the imperial palace to sign the Congress of Vienna's Final Act, although Napoleon's seizure of power appeared to render the whole exercise null and void. In fact, Francis I, Tsar Alexander, the Prussian King Frederick William and Wellington had all left Vienna in preparation for the coming confrontation with Napoleon. Of the main leaders, this left Metternich and Talleyrand to actually apply their signatures to the document, and the latter was only present because he had repeatedly disobeyed Louis XVIII's orders to join him in Ghent. Louis had already summoned him since the end of April to reach Ghent as soon as possible, but Talleyrand had had no trouble postponing his departure with a series of plausible excuses. Having destroyed all the remaining papers in the Kaunitz Palace, the following day Talleyrand set off to find Louis XVIII without any great enthusiasm since it involved coming into contact once again with the disagreeable *émigrés* who peopled the king's court. Both Alexis de Noailles, aide-de-camp to the Duke d'Artois, and Jaucourt had informed him that Louis was considering making him prime minister. He was in no hurry to reach the royal court, dominated by the abominable Blacas and where his advice had been disregarded. He did, nevertheless, address a memoir to the king which was a severe warning. By governing the country without taking account of public opinion, the nature of which had changed fundamentally over the previous twenty years, the king had taken the risk of alienating a large part of the population. By issuing decrees and placing himself above the law, by putting the fortunes of those who had purchased national property in jeopardy, by ignoring the army and the non-Royalist elites, he was in great danger of losing support for his regime. The ease with which Napoleon had seized power was an illustration of how divine right and absolutism were no longer sufficient defences for the throne. There were even those—Tsar Alexander among them—who thought the king's ineptitude had already disqualified him from ever returning to the throne and were looking for another solution. When and if Louis returned to France, he must respect the constitution; he had made a mockery of individual freedom, freedom of the press, an independent judiciary and the government and monarch working together as a team. To survive, he should create a legislature able to vote on the laws promised in the Constitutional Charter. On the contrary, the Royalist "Ultras" surrounding the king and his brother believed that the success of Napoleon's return was a sure sign of insufficient resolve in eliminating all those who had served the Revolution and the Empire. The Duke d'Artois, who had great influence upon his brother at this time, recommended a thorough reshuffle of the government, including the dismissal of both Blacas and Talleyrand, and a complete return to the monarchy as it had existed before 1789.

Upon reaching Frankfurt, Talleyrand fell ill with a cold and stayed with Archbishop Karl-Theodor Dalberg, where he met the Duke de Richelieu, a great, great nephew of Cardinal Richelieu, the first minister of Louis XIII in the early part of the seventeenth century. At their meeting in Frankfurt, the two Frenchmen held long conversations together—although Richelieu was perfectly aware of the former Bishop of Autun's reputation for straying from the straight and narrow path. Their mutual appreciation was to be short-lived.

Nine days after leaving Vienna, Talleyrand reached Aachen late at night, where he learned that a major battle had taken place the day before—18 June 1815—at a place called Waterloo in Belgium and that Napoleon was on the run. He then decided to reach Mons, where Louis was now staying, as quickly as possible. It took him another four days to cover the 150 kilometres—it was perfectly possible to travel that distance in a day by horse-drawn carriage. Louis XVIII, who was exasperated with waiting for him to arrive, announced that he had no wish to meet his disrespectful minister. Much of what we know about the relationship between Talleyrand and Louis XVIII during this period is gleaned from the pen of Chateaubriand, not an unbiased witness.

Chateaubriand and Talleyrand had crossed paths many times since the former resigned his post following the assassination of the Duke d'Enghien in 1804. When serving as Minister of Foreign Affairs, Talleyrand had tried to further the famous author's chaotic career. Although born only fourteen years apart, the two men were of entirely different generations. Chateaubriand, from Saint-Malo in provincial Brittany, had been born into a middle-class, Catholic family and had experienced at first hand all the frightful horrors of the revolutionary period, while Talleyrand, the aristocrat, remained a product of the Parisian pre-Revolutionary good life. Chateaubriand was ambitious, easily offended and unpredictable, with the result that Talleyrand had little confidence in his political abilities.

What Talleyrand had accomplished in Vienna was remarkable and he knew that in Louis's entourage he could count upon a number of allies: Jaucourt, acting Minister of Foreign Affairs, Baron Louis, Minister of Finance, and Jacques-Claude Beugnot, the acting Minister of Police. Chateaubriand, also present in Ghent as one of the editors of *Le Moniteur*, was at this moment also very sympathetic to Talleyrand; he too had mentioned to the king that his Minister of Foreign Affairs would make an excellent prime minister, believing that he himself might thereby be given a ministerial post—having missed his opportunity at the first Restoration. Metternich, who fully appreciated Talleyrand's qualities, instructed his ambassador in Brussels to consult him on all matters and on all occasions. However, under the influence of Blacas and the Dukes d'Artois and de Berry, Louis XVIII was under pressure to dismiss him.

When Talleyrand reached Mons, a situation arose between him and the king. As Chateaubriand describes it—if we can believe him—the Minister of Foreign Affairs was soon surrounded by a group of courtiers anxious to learn his news, announcing that he would not be ready to meet the king until the following day. Louis XVIII was annoyed at this cavalier attitude, while Chateaubriand asked Talleyrand to reconsider his position. The king announced that he would leave very early the next morning. The next day, someone woke Talleyrand up: "The king is leaving!" In a flash, Talleyrand was out of bed and rushed to the gate dressed as he was, where the king's coach was passing through. The coachman had to stop and the king, mystified, asked what was going on. "Sire, it's M. de Talleyrand." Louis XVIII did not believe this: "He's asleep." But no, his Minister of Foreign Affairs was really there at the gateway on foot. Louis leaned out of the window. Talleyrand excused himself for the delay in reaching the royal court, to which the king appeared to pay no heed. Louis quickly concluded the conversation with: "Prince, you are leaving us. Taking the waters would do you good. Send us your news." He then told the coachman to proceed, leaving Talleyrand rooted to the spot.

Rather than being appointed as prime minister, Talleyrand had been humiliated. He had poorly evaluated the influence of the Duke d'Artois and his friends. In the words of Fouché: "Don't make fun of idiots, in times of crisis they are very powerful." Despite his impertinent behaviour, Chateaubriand and the Duke of Wellington set to work to reconcile him with the king. A note was subsequently received saying that the king accepted a meeting. Louis XVIII and his Minister of Foreign Affairs disliked each other but Louis's government could not function without him and Talleyrand desperately needed to keep hold of a position of power. In the coming days, Talleyrand would become Prime Minister and Chateaubriand would be abandoned. For the rest of his life, Chateaubriand would take every opportunity to pay back this affront by pouring scorn on the former Bishop of Autun.

When Louis XVIII reached Cambrai on 27 June, he summoned Talleyrand, who arrived contrite. He presented a note that gave his opinion about the way the king should conduct himself in the coming days. Although they had not seen each other for nine months, the king received him as if they had met the previous day, paying no great attention to him at dinner and taking refuge behind the silence of court etiquette. After dinner Talleyrand did succeed in having a private interview with Louis. Before leaving Vienna, his long dispatch to the king had suggested that Louis was largely responsible for his own misfortunes. To sweeten the pill, Talleyrand gave the impression that these were not his own words but those of the Tsar of Russia. Indeed, it is worth recalling that Alexander had a range of recriminations aimed at Louis XVIII: a Blue Ribbon had been awarded to the British Prince Regent, but not to him; his pleas on behalf of Caulaincourt had been ignored; no concessions had been proposed when it was suggested to betroth the Duke de Berry to the tsar's youngest sister; and he was not at all happy with the way the French Constitutional Charter had been adulterated after he had approved it.

Talleyrand told the king that the leaders of democracy were not supporters of Napoleon, nor were they opposed to the return of the Bourbons, but they could not tolerate being excluded from political decision-making. The Bourbons had been restored to the throne due to the principle of legitimacy, but the Royalists had chosen to interpret the situation as absolutism. To avoid the crown being offered to the Duke d'Orléans, Louis should set up a government that respected the constitution and worked as a team. Talleyrand was prepared to assume the head of it. In the old days, the crown had benefited from the support of the clergy and the nobility, but these institutions had now lost the great power of protection they once provided. Furthermore, Louis was surrounded by men who had emigrated more than twenty years earlier and were quite out of touch with the France of 1815. Chief among these was the Count de Blacas, while the advice of the Duke d'Artois and his son, the Duke de Berry, had not served the king's interests in a positive way at all. Talleyrand recommended a public declaration of the faults committed during the first Restoration. When returning to Paris, it seemed to Talleyrand, to Chateaubriand and even to Metternich, that the king should not follow in the wake of the Allied armies proceeding under their protection but should travel independently. Their idea was to set up the government in Lyon and only regain Paris once the capital had been liberated. After a long and heated conversation, with Talleyrand threatening to leave for a spa in Germany, Louis agreed to separate himself from Blacas, who departed for London the next day. For the rest, Louis refused to follow Talleyrand's advice. Paris was still in Napoleon's hands, who might well attempt to convert the city into a fortress for his last stand. Finally, the matter was decided by the Duke of Wellington, who requested that the king should join him at his headquarters in the town of Le Cateau-Cambrésis. Talleyrand declared despairingly to the Duchess von Courland: "I am not satisfied with my first interview."

Napoleon did not attempt a last-ditch resistance on the streets of Paris having withdrawn on 29 June to Josephine's old residence at Malmaison to the west of Paris where he met his mother for the last time. When the royal cortège reached Le Cateau-Cambrésis on 25 June, Louis XVIII issued a clumsy proclamation which admitted that he was returning to power thanks to the action of foreign soldiers and drew attention to the harsh punishments he reserved for his unfaithful subjects. Even Wellington was worried about the political ineptness of this proclamation. Louis summoned all his ministers to a meeting at the nearby town of Cambrai on 27 June. Talleyrand was there with his allies, including Chateaubriand who was beginning to regret his association with the Minister of Foreign Affairs but believed he might succeed Blacas as master of the king's household. The meeting took place at 10 o'clock in the morning with Louis surrounded by Wellington and the entire diplomatic corps, including Pozzo di Borgo for Russia and Baron de Vincent for Austria. Louis was required to listen to a revised royal proclamation, written by Talleyrand and Beugnot, which accepted that errors had been committed during the first Restoration, that he intended to govern the country respecting the constitution and that he would pardon those misguided Frenchmen who had supported Napoleon during the 100 Days—except for the very worst offenders who would face trial. Furthermore, the Duke d'Artois and the Duke de Berry would be excluded from the governmental team. In short, the king was required to apologize for his mistakes and forgive his enemies.

Louis XVIII, who asked for the revised proclamation to be read to him twice, would have certainly taken this text as a cruel rebuke. The king's brother and his son protested that the king should not be required to admit that he had committed any errors. After another animated debate, it became clear that Talleyrand was not placing the blame for errors on the king but directly on "Monsieur" himself. The Duke d'Artois exploded: "The Prince de Talleyrand is forgetting himself," to which Talleyrand replied: "I fear it is so, but the truth was stronger than I." To the satisfaction of Baron Louis, Jaucourt, Beugnot and Talleyrand, the second declaration was issued using their wording. With a nudge from Wellington, Talleyrand was made Prime Minister as well as Minister of Foreign Affairs. However, Monsieur, the Duke de Berry and their associates were furious and decided that Talleyrand would have to go. It would take them three months to achieve their aim.

Those seeking to ingratiate themselves with the future government did not seek the king's presence but flocked to make themselves known to Talleyrand, even overflowing into his bedroom. He asked one claimant why the king should show him favour, to which the man replied that he had been with Louis at Ghent. Talleyrand could not conceal his disbelief: "Those who went with His Majesty to Ghent were perhaps 700 or 800. But those who came back from Ghent are, to my knowledge, more than 50,000."

The Allied Armies, followed by the royal cortège, reached the town of Roye about 100 kilometres north of Paris. The Prussian soldiers, in particular, began to make exactions and pillaged every village they came to. During another meeting of the king's council, Talleyrand proposed that the most capable people should be appointed to future ministerial functions, regardless of their past history—even if it so happened that they had signed Louis XVI's death warrant. He was, of course, referring to Fouché, who was at this moment keeping Paris under control prior to the king's return and therefore fulfilling an absolutely vital function. In this time of crisis, Fouché had obtained the conditional abdication of Napoleon, made sure the King of Rome would not inherit power and set the members of parliament to work preparing yet another constitution. Before the king left Mons, Fouché had sent Mme de Vitrolles as an emissary, whose husband was at this moment in prison in the South of

France, having been seized by Napoleon's police. Archambaud de Périgord, Talleyrand's own brother, was also sent to Cambrai with passports issued by Fouché to make contact with the king. The message was very simple: the Prefect of Police would ensure that Paris was peaceful in return for guarantees for his personal safety. Although Talleyrand could not be said to be an unconditional supporter of Fouché, he realized that a man capable of keeping Paris calm at this critical moment was vital. If Fouché were rejected as a member of the government and found himself in opposition, a catastrophic civil war could easily have erupted, for the former Minister of the Police was as capable of provoking resistance as he was in suppressing it.

Talleyrand reluctantly went to see Louis XVIII, who had now reached Saint-Denis on the outskirts of Paris, and explained the situation. Wellington too wanted Fouché to remain as the Minister of Police in order to satisfy the Jacobin elements and guarantee national reconciliation. He had written to Talleyrand in support of Fouché: "The king cannot at this moment refuse to employ him." The king understood immediately: "Do everything that you consider useful in my service." The Ultras were flabbergasted for, during the Revolution, Fouché had been one of the most ardent and blood-thirsty of Jacobins. When the recently released Vitrolles heard the news, he immediately rushed to Talleyrand's residence and burst into his bedroom at 4 o'clock in the morning. Having returned to France, Talleyrand had taken up his nocturnal habits again and, in the presence of Jaucourt and the Baron Louis, was just getting ready for bed. Vitrolles demanded to know what had been decided about Fouché, whose noble title was the Duke d'Otranto. "Your Duke d'Otranto has said nothing," yawned Talleyrand. "The Duke d'Otranto is far more your man than mine," replied Vitrolles irritably. In fact, Fouché had already accepted the position of Minister of the Police and was ready to take the oath of allegiance to Louis XVIII.

On 29 June, Wellington received a delegation from the two chambers asking for a regency to be established for Napoleon's son; he gave them no choice but to accept the return of Louis XVIII. He then negotiated with Marshal Davout for the peaceful surrender of the capital. Talleyrand was lost in admiration: "Wellington has arranged everybody's business. He is an admirable man. His character is good and straightforward." When the Allied advance reached Neuilly on the outskirts of Paris, Wellington invited Fouché to dine with Talleyrand and himself. Pozzo di Borgo, the tsar's ears and eyes, was also present. On 7 July, Chateaubriand was waiting to see the king in an antechamber, sitting in a dark corner, when the door opened and in came "vice leaning on the arm of crime, M. de Talleyrand supported by M. Fouché". Chateaubriand could not believe his eyes at this incredible sight. He concluded: "The trusty regicide, kneeling, placed the hands that had caused the head of Louis XVI to fall between the hands of the martyred king's brother; the renegade ex-bishop witnessed the swearing in." Pozzo di Borgo watched the former Jacobin and the former bishop drive away together in a carriage. "I would love to hear what these two little lambs are saying to each other," he remarked dryly.

It was now certain that Louis XVIII could return to Paris without fear of bombs, flying paving stones and a hostile crowd. On 8 July 1815, he entered Paris through the traditional Porte de Saint-Denis in a carriage identifiable as British made and was received by the Parisians without enthusiasm. On 8 July 1815, Louis slept in the same bed at the Tuileries Palace that Napoleon had vacated only a couple of weeks earlier. When Talleyrand arrived at the Rue Saint-Florentin, Courtiade was there to receive him. The seals had been removed from his residence and he quickly resumed his old routine, except that he was now Prime Minister for Louis XVIII.

There was then the problem of how to deal with those who had cooperated with Napoleon during the 100 Days. Talleyrand was anxious to avoid a witch hunt and, allowing time for passions to subside, proposed that the affair should be judged by the two future elected legislative chambers. Talleyrand likewise argued that those peers who had continued to occupy their seats during the 100 Days should be immune from prosecution because their positions were vital to the running of the country. Finally, with the king's approval, he managed to reduce the number of accused to twenty-six, while Fouché, anxious to show his zeal, had a list containing fifty-seven names. Talleyrand told him: "There are many innocent people on your list!" None of the names on Fouché's list was as guilty as the person who had compiled it. Finally, only two personalities were executed by firing squad—Marshal Ney and General de La Bédoyère—who had both been sent to block Napoleon's passage on his way to Paris and had joined forces with him. Talleyrand did manage to save the lives of some of his closest associates, including his son, Charles de Flahaut. It took the personal intervention of the tsar to save Caulaincourt. As for Savary, he had accompanied Napoleon to Rochefort on the Bay of Biscay and sailed with him to Plymouth. He was not allowed to travel to Saint Helena, but interned in Malta. After escaping, he travelled about Europe for some years in more or less distress, but eventually returned to France and regained his civil rights.

It was in the South of France, in particular, that the population carried out retaliation on Protestants and supporters of Napoleon associated with the 100 Days. The government was obliged to issue a proclamation stating that "private vengeance" was unacceptable and undermined the work of the law courts. Fouché was also spreading alarming rumours which disturbed the population such that Talleyrand was obliged to restrict the freedom of the press in order to limit them. It became obvious that, if Talleyrand were to survive, Fouché would have to go.

The ex-Emperor of France had reached Rochefort on 3 July with the intention of taking a boat for the United States, but to do so he needed a passport from the provisional government—which was unlikely. He transferred to the tiny offshore island of Aix and finally decided to give himself up to the British Royal Navy. He was taken aboard the third-rate ship of the line *H.M.S. Bellerophon* and sailed for Torquay and then Plymouth, where crowds gathered to catch a glimpse of the warship's infamous passenger. He learned that he would not be allowed to set foot on English soil and his ultimate fate was banishment. He boarded *H.M.S. Northumberland* on 7 August and reached Saint Helena in the South Atlantic two months later, eventually taking up residence in the former governor's bungalow. Talleyrand had been asked to name a French commissioner to act as a liaison with the English commissioner on Saint Helena and gained his revenge by choosing the Marquis de Montchenu, who Napoleon refused to have anything to do with already knowing him as an ignorant, pompous chatterbox. Surprisingly, Montchenu got on quite well with Napoleon's British custodian, the tactless Sir Hudson Lowe, of whom the Duke of Wellington said: "He was a man wanting in education and judgment. He was a stupid man. He knew nothing at all of the world, and like all men who knew nothing of the world, he was suspicious and jealous." Napoleon would have agreed with him.

CHAPTER XVIII
PRIME MINISTER

Despite the disapproval of the Royalist "Ultras", the new government assuming power for the second Bourbon Restoration on 9 July 1815 contained some of Talleyrand's most competent associates: Baron Louis was Minister of Finance, Fouché for the Police, Pasquier for Justice and the Interior, Jaucourt for the Navy and Molé for Transport. In contrast with what had taken place in 1814, the members of the second Restoration government would meet regularly with the king once a week and at Talleyrand's house every day. Talleyrand had asked the Duke de Richelieu to be responsible for the king's household, but this broad-minded and high-principled colleague had refused on the grounds that he had been absent from France for twenty-three years and was no longer familiar with the duties involved—in truth, Tsar Alexander had warned him about the difficulties of working alongside Talleyrand and he did not want to be involved in a government that also included Fouché. Pozzo di Borgo had refused the Ministry of the Interior for the same reasons.

Where had the Duke de Richelieu been all this time? After an early career in the French Army, he had subsequently been *premier gentilhomme de la chambre* to Louis XVI responsible for the morning and evening ceremonies of the king's *lever* and *coucher*. On 5 October 1789, he had been in Paris when the March on Versailles began during the French Revolution. Apprehensive about the safety of the royal family, he disguised himself as one of the crowd and, taking a shortcut through the woods, arrived just as the angry mob converged on the palace. He convinced Marie Antoinette to seek refuge in the king's apartments, thus saving her life. On the queen's suggestion, he left Paris in 1790 for the court in Vienna and later decided to volunteer for the Russian Army. Louis XVI invited him back to Paris but he soon returned to Vienna as a diplomat and, before long, was recruited into Catherine the Great's army again as a Major-General. He became friends with Tsar Alexander I, who appointed him Governor of Odessa, where the grateful citizens of this city erected a bronze statue to him in 1828.

To fill the role that the Duke de Richelieu had refused, the astute Talleyrand then proposed the Duke de La Vauguyon, who he knew Louis XVIII disliked. When Talleyrand persisted with this proposal, the king's resistance became more marked. So, Talleyrand then brought up the name of the person who he really wanted to fill this role—Alexis de Noailles, who had been with him in Vienna. Although appointed to spy on Talleyrand, Noailles had become one of his trusted associates; the king accepted this appointment at once.

Now that Fouché had become a minister again in the national government, the city of Paris needed a new Prefect of Police. Baron Louis proposed for this post a handsome, young lawyer from Libourne in south-western France called Élie-Louis Decazes. During the next four years, Decazes would rise to play a leading role in the French Government, quickly becoming a favourite of Louis XVIII.

The new government's task was not easy. It was opposed by the Ultras led by the Duke d'Artois, the Bonapartists had not given up the fight, while the Republicans still intended to defend the rights they had acquired during the Revolution. To reduce the threats to his government, Talleyrand excluded anybody belonging to the camp of the Duke d'Artois and his son, the Duke de Berry. Even though the United Kingdom and Austria supported the new government, the tsar had not forgiven the trials and tribulations that he had been subjected to in Vienna and favoured the Republican elements. In the south of France, the operations of the Ultras, led by the Duke d'Angoulême, bordered on anarchy and they would not let the new prime minister forget that he had once been the Bishop of Autun who had married a courtesan. His verdict on these people was: "They have learned nothing and forgotten nothing." Furthermore, he believed that the activities of the Royalist Ultras were so extreme that they were doing more damage to the royal family than the Republican opposition. In an effort to improve the image of the monarchy, Talleyrand proposed once more adopting the tricolour flag instead of the white Bourbon emblem but the Duke d'Artois and the Ultras would not accept it. In a bid to avoid controversy, the prudent Louis XVIII—"the impotent tight-rope walker", as Aimée de Coigny called him—had already forgone his coronation ceremony.

The country was occupied by several foreign armies looking for revenge and ready to commit arson, robbery and rape in a drunken rampage. The people of France were having to pay the price of Napoleon's brief return to power. Paris had once again become an occupied city. Prussian troops were encamped in front of the Louvre; British troops on the Champs-Élysées; elements of the Russian and Austrian Armies continued to arrive in France throughout the summer. The treasuries of departmental towns were plundered by the invaders, with the prefects who attempted to resist arrested. As head of the government, Talleyrand was not spared since his property at Pont-de-Sains in northern France had been sequestered by Napoleon and the Prussians now decided to sell it. He was obliged to intervene personally to halt the sale. The Prussian General Blücher, who did nothing to stop his troops' pillaging activities in the countryside, had a further grievance—he wanted to blow up the Pont de Jena, the bridge over the Seine in Paris that carried the name of one of Napoleon's victories over the Prussians. After a stand-off involving Talleyrand and the Duke of Wellington, a solution was found by renaming it "Le Pont de l'École Militaire".

We know that some of Talleyrand's habits were incompatible with the post of prime minister. There was, for instance, his well-known habit of deliberately delaying the signing of documents for days in case wiser councils prevailed. The king and the other ministers became frustrated that decisions were not being taken and important matters were not dealt with. For all his diplomatic skills, was Talleyrand the right person to be prime minister? Did he have the lucidity to take decisions and the time and energy to expedite affairs? Despite his self-possession and his impertinent tongue, he was more at ease carrying out the orders of a master than in being the master himself. Without the pressure that Napoleon placed on his ministers, he began to lose himself in self-indulgence. Pasquier remarked: "He succumbed to the idea that he was indispensable to France."

Despite his heavy timetable, the Prince de Talleyrand did not modify his long-standing routine. For instance, he went to bed very late, often playing cards for a couple of hours in the middle of the night, and woke up towards midday. Then there was the time-consuming ritual of his morning toilette involving a small team of people in the dressing of his hair, the donning of his clothes and the doing-up of his shoe buckles. Rémusat gave a detailed description of what happened after Talleyrand had woken up at 11.30 a.m. His bed was arranged in such a way that he slept sitting upright rather than laying down. He wrapped himself in an inordinate quantity of bedding, not because he was afraid of getting cold, but because he had a childhood fear of falling out of bed. Upon getting up: "The Prince came into a large bathroom... Upon his first appearance one saw only a large bundle of flannel, cotton, muslin and twill, a white heap that came staggering in, swaying, scarcely acknowledging those present, sitting down in front of the fireplace where three valets were waiting. One of them, a large man, powdered and dressed like his master, with black silk stockings, directed proceedings rather than participated in them (this was Courtiade); the two others in aprons, dressed in wig-makers' grey, paid particular attention to the dressing of his hair. They began at once by taking the woollen stockings and the flannel wrappings off his legs and plunging [his feet] into a small bucket of Barèges water [sulphurous water from thermal baths in the Pyrenees]. A cup of camomile tea was brought; he drank one or two more during the session; this was all he consumed. The rest of his body was swathed with underwear, waistcoats, dressing gowns, with all sorts of materials that tumbled down everywhere, and on his head a sort of cotton tiara tied with a pale-coloured ribbon; it was covered with a bonnet and a head-band coming down to his eyebrows over a bland face, agitated, with pale-coloured eyes, and cut off below by ample cravats hiding a small chin."

"Once the covering was removed it revealed a fine and abundant head of hair that had once been blond, more bleached by powder than by age. He was proud of it and it remained thick until the end of his life. It was the job of the two valets then to comb, to curl, to scent, to powder and, during this time, he was presented with a silver basin into which he plunged towels to wipe his face. As part of these preparatory procedures, so peculiar that one never tired of watching it, the most remarkable was the consumption of one or two glasses of warm water that he inhaled through the nose and blew out again like an elephant with his trunk. When the hairdressing was complete one finally had time to dry his feet, to put on his woollen hose, his white silk stockings, black silk trousers, and his long, buckled shoes. Then he would get up with difficulty, allowing the two or three dressing gowns to fall and at once a shirt was placed over him. The first valet then rolled several cravats of white muslin round his neck; at this moment, his hat was placed on his head, because he did not attain the same degree of elegance as he used to when the hairdresser had finished with his hair. Usually, rather than tuck his shirt into his black silk trousers, it hung outside and floated like a blouse, and he remained dressed like this, with his hat on his head talking with those present, among whom there were sometime ladies. It was said that this is how he had received the Emperor of Russia. By now it would be 1 o'clock in the afternoon and, since he did not like to rush or to change his habits, there were very few occasions during the Republic, the Empire or the Restoration when he would have considered the situation sufficiently serious to disturb this routine."

During this whole ritual, visitors would come and go. French and English newspapers would be piled on a table and people would read from them and make comments. Talleyrand would contribute to the conversation with words of wisdom or of humour. A future prime minister of France, Louis-Mathieu Molé, was also one of Talleyrand's acquaintances and gives us a less flattering view of his appearance at this time: "his pallid skin", "his arrogant expression and dead eyes", "his mouth, the only one like it of his race that expressed debauchery, satiety and disdain at the same time". Molé concludes his description with: "He has in him something of a great man, a woman, the priest and the cat; the great man and the priest dominate." Molé, Rémusat and Mme de Staël all addressed him as "the bishop".

In the afternoon, Talleyrand's first port of call was the Rue du Bac. With his faithful team of collaborators at the Ministry of Foreign Affairs, business carried on as usual. Dinner was at 5 o'clock, his main meal of the day. With guests such as Castlereagh, Metternich, Nesselrode and Wellington, his table was a miniature Council of Europe where important decisions were reached but he neglected the other ministries so that their affairs were often impeded by lack of direction. He may well have paid attention to the country's foreign policy, but the time left in the day was not sufficient to deal with the dossiers piling up on the king's desk. It was not until the early hours of the morning that Talleyrand began to deal with the most pressing affairs of the day, after playing cards with his harem. Louis XVIII began to reproach him because, despite his political savvy and negotiating skills, he was incapable of resolving difficult or long-drawn-out matters. As a member of the king's court, he was polite and diplomatic, but at the same time presented an air of indolence and superficiality, lacking the capacity of a government minister to expedite affairs briskly with precise instructions.

Even though the dinners taking place at the Rue Saint-Florentin included a number of illustrious foreign guests, France was not represented when the four Allies met to decide on the country's fate following Napoleon's final defeat. Remembering Talleyrand's independent stance at the Council of Vienna, he was unceremoniously excluded from participating in the daily discussions at the British Embassy. Particularly, Alexander I had played against Talleyrand in Vienna and lost, and was therefore keen to keep the Prince at a distance. Talleyrand tried to show that the French Government present at Vienna was exactly the same one that was now running the country, while the war of 1815 had been directed exclusively at defeating Napoleon. The Allies had, however, learned their lesson and were adamant. As their correspondence shows, Hardenberg, Humboldt, Stadion and Metternich believed that in 1814 they had been too generous, leaving France with too many of its resources intact, therefore: "A wise policy would be to place her in a position where she was incapable of causing damage." Some of the proposals suggested that the victors would annex parts of the country, but Castlereagh felt that the consequences were likely to upset the balance of European power and managed to resist their ambitions. Talleyrand was at pains to point out that Louis XVIII had been their ally during the Waterloo campaign, yet curiously he was now the victim of sanctions aimed at Napoleon!

It was obvious that the legislature as it had existed during Napoleon's 100 Days, consisting of a Senate nominated by Napoleon and a Chamber of Deputies elected in May 1815, would have to be replaced. For the election of the future Chamber of Deputies, it was decided to increase the number of seats and to lower the age of candidates to 25. Each departmental prefect was also allowed to nominate some twenty candidates to fulfil the local quota. Given the strong reaction among the provincial elites to Napoleon's 100 Days, it was hoped that the new parliament would contain a majority of Royalists. The reaction was indeed so strong that it gave exactly the result that Talleyrand feared most for these expectations were wildly exceeded by a large majority of Ultras who totally outvoted the Bonapartists, the Republicans and the Jacobins. Those new members taking their seats at the end of September 1815— labelled *La Chambre Introuvable* [the undiscoverable house]—consisted largely of men more Royalist than the king, who regarded the moderate men in the government with the gravest suspicions and whose unquestioned support for the monarchy rendered the country almost ungovernable. The new government ministers were caught between a sovereign who was unsympathetic to them and a hostile Chamber of Deputies. Many of those elected wanted simply to return to the days of the *Ancien Régime* and sought uncompromisingly to remove a government from power that was at best suspiciously Republican and at worst contained regicides. Their attention focused on Fouché whose presence in the Chamber of Deputies was likely to provoke a riot.

It would be necessary to make some concessions and the participation of Fouché in the government was obviously the sticking point. Although Louis XVIII had been able to return to a peaceful Paris largely thanks to Fouché's measures, the moment had come to find him an honourable position as far away from France as possible. Vitrolles tells us that, as a ministerial meeting was breaking up one evening at the Rue Saint-Florentin, Talleyrand began to talk of the prestigious roles played by France's ambassadors, particularly in distant countries. One country with which he was very familiar was the United States of America, of which he extolled the virtues—its rivers, its forests. Fouché, who was tidying up his papers, began to understand that these remarks were being addressed to him. A few days later, Fouché was appointed ambassador, not to Washington or Philadelphia but to Dresden. In January 1816, his troubled past caught up with him—his appointment was cancelled and he was banished as a regicide. By his first wife, Fouché had had five children who survived to adulthood, but she had died in 1812. No country would grant him asylum but Austria allowed him to live under police surveillance in Prague and Linz. He died in

Trieste in 1820. Just two months after becoming Prefect of Police for Paris, Élie Decazes took Fouché's place as Minister of Police in the national government.

The situation of a Chamber of Deputies dominated by the Royalists could be mitigated by filling the Chamber of Peers with Talleyrand's more moderate friends—Dalberg, Choiseul-Gouffier, Boniface de Castellane, Boisgelin, La Tour du Pin, Molé—while these people in their turn could nominate their own friends. As an afterthought and at the suggestion of Mme de Jaucourt, Talleyrand included the name of the king's former favourite Blacas and other faithful Royalists, such as the Count de La Châtre, Mme de Jaucourt's first husband. Louis XVIII would have preferred an assembly over which he could exercise a certain level of choice by nominating new members from time to time but Talleyrand, influenced by the British House of Lords, desired that these positions should be permanent and hereditary so as to guarantee their independence. The king was very surprised upon reading some of the names on the list, but accepted all the candidates without protest, while Vitrolles was amazed about the frivolous manner in which Talleyrand had drawn up the list of names.

It could have been believed that, with the departure of Fouché and having twice restored the Bourbons to the throne, Talleyrand was untouchable but he was soon to be disillusioned. When Roux-Laboric and Bourrienne informed the Chamber of Deputies about the departure of Fouché, its members showed far more interest in the dismissal of Talleyrand. He represented everything that the newly elected Royalist members detested so that his tenure as prime minister was in jeopardy and needed the support of the king. One of Talleyrand's maxims was: "A minister in need of support is a minister lost."

Matters came to a head when the Allies made known their harsh terms for the new Treaty of Paris following Napoleon's 100 Days. Talleyrand protested, but the Big Four confirmed on 22 September 1815 that they required France to accept unconditionally a number of guarantees. A particularly bitter pill for Talleyrand to swallow was that he would lose most of the concessions he had managed to squeeze out of the Allies in the previous year. France had to give up its long-term fortresses in Germany and lost the Saarland. The country had to pay an

389

indemnity of 800 million francs and finance the construction of a defensive line in the Low Countries facing towards France. An occupation force of 150,000 foreign troops on France's northern and eastern borders would also have to be financed for seven years. Among the other particularly disagreeable but perfectly understandable demands, the Allies now required France to return all the works of art looted during the Napoleonic Wars. The terms imposed on France bore a strong resemblance to those Napoleon presented to his defeated enemies in his heyday. Pope Pius VII sent his agent to recover all his masterpieces housed in the Louvre. One evening at the Rue Saint-Florentin there was an argument at the dinner table between Wellington and the Prince de Talleyrand, where the "Iron Duke" insisted on the morality of returning the King of the Netherland's stolen paintings. Talleyrand was obliged to accept this situation, but there was worse to come.

At a moment when Talleyrand was burdened with the heaviest political responsibilities, his mind continued to be tormented by Dorothea's affair with Clam. The Duchess von Courland had returned to Paris and brought sweetness into his life, but Dorothea was still occupied with Clam. This couple came back to Paris on 20 July 1815, when Edmond suddenly realised that she had not ceased to be his wife. He challenged Clam to a duel, the details of which were kept very quiet. However, we do know from an Austrian spy living in Paris that the Duchess von Courland and her four daughters were delighted when "Périgord received a sword blow through the face." Etienne Pasquier, one of Talleyrand's long-term friends, noted that at this time requiring the greatest concentration on government business, the Prime Minister had become involved "in a passion so intense as completely to absorb his mind". After Dorothea had left Paris again in the company of Clam, he was thrown into a state of despair. Chancellor Pasquier noted that at the age of 61 he was suffering from "both physical and moral despondency impossible to describe". Even August de Rémusat (who had "refused" to allow him to leave Paris in March 1814) explained that the suffering of desire, jealousy and melancholy of these recent months meant that Talleyrand was below par. During this period, the Prime Minister appeared distracted and the king displeased. Molé tells us that Dorothea was destined by nature "to govern some famous and really powerful man.

Nature had fitted her to play such a role, and to play it not without brilliance". Dorothea eventually gave up Clam to serve Talleyrand, but this move would take place far too late to save his government.

On 24 September 1815, Talleyrand, the Baron Louis and Dalberg went to see the king and requested his unconditional support in confronting the parliament dominated by the conservative Royalists. The Prime Minister also wished to inform the Allies that the terms of the new and unpopular second Treaty of Paris were totally unacceptable and he was not prepared to sign the document. Talleyrand had often acted in the king's presence like a craftsman dealing with an apprentice. He believed that the king would be afraid of losing him but Louis XVIII intended to be master in his own household. The Prime Minister had not intended to resign but the king, looking at the ceiling with an air of indifference, concluded after a short silence: "Well then, I shall take a new minister." Talleyrand said afterwards: "The king seemed enchanted to get rid of us." The official *Le Moniteur* did not mention his dismissal and there was, of course, no word of gratitude from Louis.

Talleyrand had found it more and more difficult to deal with the resistance of the parliament, which prevented him from implementing the policies he considered necessary. Both Metternich and Castlereagh were in Paris at this moment and begged him not to go. The tsar said nothing but had been drawing the king's attention to the Duke de Richelieu who he considered to be a far more promising candidate for the post of Prime Minister. The appointment of a personality recommended by one of the Allies could also be a way of obtaining concessions from them. Talleyrand would not be offered any further government role during the fifteen years that the Bourbons remained on the throne, although we are far from seeing the end of his career as the doyen of French politics.

If Louis XVIII no longer wished to benefit from Talleyrand's services, the former Prime Minister was still appreciated on a European scale. Even though Frederick Augustus now ruled over only two-fifths of his former kingdom, the King of Saxony rewarded Talleyrand liberally for his efforts in saving his realm. Ferdinand IV, King of the Two Sicilies, was equally grateful, granting Talleyrand the title and revenues of the Duchy of Dino. The recently retired minister declined the honour but asked if it could be assumed by his nephew Edmond. Although the marriage of Edmond and Dorothea was finished, as a newly converted Roman Catholic she had never sought a divorce; it was in this way that she became the Duchess de Dino, a title by which she chose to be known until 1838.

Metternich would continue as Austrian Minister of Foreign Affairs for the next thirty-three years, his career ending with the Revolution of 1848. According to an official Russian report, Tsar Alexander I died while on holiday in the Crimea in 1825 probably of typhus, although the circumstances have never been elucidated. There were many rumours about his death, including one in which he survived for another forty years as a Siberian hermit called Feodor Kuzmich!

Sadly, the most distressing fate was reserved for Lord Castlereagh, who had personified integrity and goodwill throughout the Congress of Vienna and its aftermath. Upon returning to London, Castlereagh became extremely unpopular for his European policies. A few years later, he began to suffer from some form of paranoia or anxiety with increasing bouts of inexplicable rages and forgetfulness. A link has been drawn between this little-explained ailment and syphilis. In an interview with King George IV at this time, he is also supposed to have remarked: "I am accused of the same crime as the Bishop of Clogher"—homosexuality. His friends and family became increasingly alarmed about his behaviour until one day in August 1822 Castlereagh, left momentarily alone, found a penknife with which he cut his own throat. Even his enemies acknowledged that, as a statesman and a gentleman, he had no equal.

CHAPTER XIX
THE POLITICAL WILDERNESS

After Talleyrand had been dismissed as Prime Minister in September 1815, his entire cabinet resigned in solidarity. The next day he sent an extremely firm message to the Allies suggesting that the terms of the proposed second Treaty of Paris following Napoleon's final departure should be renegotiated. It was not clear to people in Paris whether he had resigned because he disliked the terms of the treaty or whether he had been dismissed since he was made responsible for its harsh terms. In either case, his departure was understood as a victory for the Ultra-Royalists. The relationship between Talleyrand and Louis XVIII had been confrontational, with the Prince often imposing his decisions on the king by force but, in the end, Louis triumphed. It could also be understood as a victory for Tsar Alexander I and for the Duke d'Artois, who had both been seeking to remove the Prince for some time. The tsar also foresaw that his friend, the Duke de Richelieu, would be the ideal person to take Talleyrand's place as Prime Minister and, for this purpose, liberated him from all his responsibilities in Russia. In Richelieu, both the tsar and Louis XVIII would find a less troublesome partner. On 22 September, the tsar had an interview with Louis that lasted so long that the king's dinner had to be postponed for an hour-and-a-half—an event without precedent.

The following day, the king requested Pozzo di Borgo to write a letter to the Allies in which he threatened to abdicate if they did not modify the terms of their treaty—exactly what Talleyrand had asked the king to do some days earlier. Even though the Chamber of Deputies was dominated by the hot-headed Ultra-Royalists, Louis XVIII appointed the moderate Richelieu as Prime Minister on 26 September. One can imagine the frustration of Talleyrand who had asked him in vain to become a member of his government three months previously. Subsequently, the Prince claimed that, had he been Prime Minister, he would never have agreed to sign this second Treaty of Paris with the Allies, an event that took place in the following November.

Although he pretended to have left office without regret, Talleyrand's pride was deeply hurt and it would take a long time for his wounds to heal. He would certainly have accepted another ministerial responsibility had one been offered. Although no such proposal was forthcoming, Talleyrand was made Grand Chamberlain to the monarch and therefore, as at the time of Napoleon, would continue to have access to the royal court. Indeed, it granted him access to the king's private apartments and a generous salary of 100,000 francs.

His fall from grace does not reveal a favourable side to his character. He believed his absence from the government was a temporary situation, that it could not survive without him and that he would soon be recalled. However, the king was satisfied with the situation and found in Richelieu a simple, chivalrous and very competent minister. An indication of Talleyrand's state of mind is that he wrote a note to the Duchess von Courland declaring that he had "spent thirty years of [his] life thinking of nothing but how [he] could be useful to his country", but from now on would concentrate on his own affairs. Considering the vast fortunes he had accumulated by fair means and foul, it is difficult to accept that he had neglected his own affairs during these decades. He had the greatest difficulty accepting his political eclipse and his exasperation brought out spitefulness. In his private letters, he took the opportunity to pour scorn on the Duke de Richelieu, the Minister of Police Decazes and Louis XVIII himself. He was a member of the Chamber of Peers and therefore participated in the debates at the Luxembourg Palace, where he was equally scathing with his fellow peers. Wellington feared that he had lost his mind and when the king was advised of Talleyrand's troubled emotions he observed: "The wounded vanity, the frustrated ambition evident in his letters make very curious reading."

In his memoirs, never was the former Bishop of Autun so dishonest with himself than over his fall from grace: "I abandoned power without too many regrets." On the contrary, Pasquier wrote that the closing months of 1815 were "the most difficult period of his life." Talleyrand spoke about "the pleasures of the countryside" and decided to return to Valençay "to cultivate his garden", as Voltaire had recommended in his novel *Candide*.

He wrote a letter to the Duchess von Courland, residing at her Château at Löbichau in Thuringia, inviting her to share his life at Valençay: "We shall pass our lives, dearest friend, in the same place, in the same occupations, living exactly the same life. I can think of nothing comparable to the happiness of spending these days with you." She arrived immediately and was installed in her own private apartments, but by the end of the year she had gone back to her homeland, never to return, finding that she was competing with her daughter for his affections. Nonetheless, Talleyrand continued to send her little notes on an almost daily basis.

As for Dorothea, in November 1815 during her last visit to Paris with Clam, Talleyrand had made every effort to persuade her to stay, but she soon left with her lover for Italy. She was pregnant and by the end of the year lived with two of her sisters in the Austrian capital. Talleyrand wrote to his old adversary from the Congress of Vienna, Friedrich von Gentz, asking him to visit Dorothea and plead for her to come back to him. By a fortuitous coincidence, with the birth of a baby girl in February 1816, which she refused to recognize, she broke off her affair with Clam—much to his disappointment—and she returned to her uncle, never to leave him again. In April 1816, when he was no longer a government minister, Talleyrand and Dorothea made the journey together to Valençay with the Princess Tyszkiewicz after which he became a changed man. It has been suggested that, while she had not been Talleyrand's mistress in Vienna, the situation soon changed. The only surviving letter from Dorothea to Talleyrand dates from this epoch and leaves very little doubt about the evolution of their relationship. The constant presence of the Princess Tyszkiewicz gave a certain gloss of respectability to the household of Dorothea and Talleyrand.

The mutual admiration between Talleyrand and Dorothea de Périgord was remarkable since they enthusiastically appreciated each other's intelligence and company. She became his companion but also his eager impresario, directing his schemes and intrigues. Dorothea preferred living in isolated châteaux rather than among the Parisian crowds. She wrote that: "My long relationship with M. de Talleyrand made it difficult for me with the rest of the world. The minds that I met seemed to me slow, vague and easily distracted." There was another reason for Talleyrand to be content with this private life—he and the Princess de Talleyrand had agreed to a divorce. Talleyrand may have been incapable of severing the links with his wife, but the determined Dorothea had more than enough motivation and resolve to carry it through. During Napoleon's 100 Days in 1815, Catherine had fled to London, then to Brussels before returning to the property at Le Pont-de-Sains. When she arrived in Paris, Talleyrand wanted nothing further to do with her. Dorothea proposed that Mme de Talleyrand would not receive any money from her husband unless and until she was actually seen leaving on a boat for London by his secretary Gabriel Perrey. Catherine accepted the conditions—but never actually left Paris. Ultimately, she lived comfortably with a house in the outskirts of Paris and an apartment in town on the Rue de Lille.

Catherine de Talleyrand had found the *ménage à quatre* at the Rue Saint-Florentin not to her liking. Although her relationship with the Duchess von Courland was cordial, Dorothea made her life a misery. In return, Catherine had revealed embarrassing details about the relationship between the uncle and the niece. Even the king was perplexed by Talleyrand's rapport with his three women and observed mockingly: "Is it true that Mme de Talleyrand has returned? That should have given you something to think about." He replied: "I too had to undergo my 20 March"—it was not a good idea to tease Talleyrand on a sensitive issue. This was the date when Napoleon had returned and chased Louis XVIII out of Paris.

When in residence at Valençay, there was still one main meal a day served in the late afternoon, after which the Prince de Talleyrand would go for a drive in his carriage through the long avenues of his vast estate. The longer he stayed there, the more he came to like this domain in a corner of the Berry region, where he began a programme of almost continuous alterations to the buildings. It was also during these moments of calm that he began to dictate his memoirs. In the month of September, the principal occupation was hunting, for which purpose the château maintained some twenty horses and a pack of hounds formed into two hunts, one for wild boar and one for deer. In the hunting season, his gamekeeper would come to see him at the very early hour of 8 o'clock every morning. "It's unsupportable," he wrote jokingly to Bruno de Boisgelin. While Dorothea indulged in her favourite pastime on horseback, Talleyrand was content to follow along in his carriage. A few years later, their daughter Pauline would participate mounted on a donkey. Every year there would be a celebration on the feasts of St Maurice in September and St Charles in November, when the theatre constructed for the Spanish princes would come into use. The château required a multi-disciplinary staff to function—cooks, maids, grooms, gardeners and foresters, as well as a doctor for the hypochondriac Talleyrand and a chaplain for Dorothea, the born-again Christian.

Moving from Paris to Valençay every summer involved not only Talleyrand and Dorothea, but the three children who lived with her—two sons, Napoléon-Louis and Alexandre, fathered by Edmond, and a daughter, Pauline, believed to have been fathered by Talleyrand himself—their teachers and domestic staff. When visitors were invited to the château, he warned them of the presence of boisterous teenagers and the likelihood of disorder, although he himself enjoyed their liveliness. Napoléon-Louis soon became his great uncle's favourite, although the patriarch did not enjoy the same relationship with his younger brother Alexandre.

When Prosper Brugière, Baron de Barante, arrived at Valençay, he described his feeling as follows: "Here I am in this great château where everything is magnificently welcoming and where an aristocratically expended wealth reigns of which there is no longer or of which there is not yet another example in France." Barante was an ardent Royalist with liberal tendencies, well-known as a historian, writer, orator and statesman. As a young man he had formed an attachment to Germaine de Staël and later enjoyed a platonic relationship with Mme Récamier—as did nearly all her male friends, except Châteaubriand. Under both Napoleon and Louis XVIII, he had been appointed as head of various government departments and had also represented France abroad as an ambassador. Talleyrand had known him since Napoleon's Prussian Campaign of 1806; it would be Barante who pronounced Talleyrand's funeral oration in 1838.

It was at this time that the Prince arranged for his mysterious adopted daughter Charlotte to marry. However, in order to do so she needed a genuine name and status. Talleyrand obtained from a priest in London a birth certificate stating that a girl called Elisa Alix Sara had been born there on 4 October 1799. He then brought together a number of distinguished friends—Mathieu de Montmorency, Choiseul-Gouffier, Jaucourt and Du Pont amongst others—who testified that the girl born in London in 1799 was the same person who had been known as Charlotte de Talleyrand since 1803. Provided with a family name and a comfortable dowry, the 15-year-old Charlotte was married to Talleyrand's cousin, the 39-year-old Alexandre-Daniel de Périgord, and became the Baronne de Talleyrand. Her new husband followed a distinguished political career becoming successively a mayor, a deputy elected to parliament, a prefect of different *départements*, French plenipotentiary to Florence and a peer of France. Other members of Talleyrand's family would also be frequent visitors to the château: his brothers Archambaud and Boson, and the latter's daughter Georgine and her husband, the Duke d'Esclignac. In the autumn the cortège would return to the Rue Saint-Florentin in Paris, as the winters at Valençay were too cold and damp to be enjoyable. One could ask oneself how the Spanish princes had fared.

While maintaining the conservative and aristocratic way of life at home, on the political front Talleyrand remained faithful to the major social changes that had taken place since July 1789. He followed the government's affairs attentively, but his own life was also under scrutiny for Decazes was intercepting his mail. One day, the prefect of the Indre *département* and his secretary came to see the retired minister at Valençay—apparently an impromptu visit, but Talleyrand was not convinced of its innocence. In fact, the two visitors had an ulterior motive since the most preposterous rumours had been circulating that Napoleon was not really exiled on the island of Saint Helena but lurking somewhere in the vicinity. Furthermore, it was said that Talleyrand was plotting to place Napoleon's young son on the throne with himself as regent. The two visitors were received civilly and witnessed a scene of the most reassuring domestic bliss as Talleyrand stacked the books recently transferred from Paris on the shelves in his library assisted by two beautiful women—the Duchess von Courland and Dorothea. He had just sold off part of his collection in London for the sum of 220,000 francs—

by far the most profitable of his many book sales.

In the late summer of 1816, he set off with his ladies to take the waters at Bourbon-l'Archambault. The mayor of the town belonged to the Ultra-Royalists and treated his most illustrious guest as a suspicious Republican of doubtful pedigree requiring close supervision. Élie Decazes, who was kept regularly informed of Talleyrand's doings and sayings, was obliged to write to the mayor pointing out that the high rank of the Prince de Talleyrand in the king's court required that he should be shown respect at all times and wherever he went. Considering the scorn with which Talleyrand treated Decazes, perhaps he needed to revise his opinion about the Minister of Police—but not just yet.

Although Bourbon-l'Archambault was his preferred destination to take the waters at the end of each summer, he was also attracted to Cauterets in the Pyrenees and Aachen in Germany. Talleyrand always travelled with a large train of retainers: secretaries, servants and, inevitably, his partner at the card table, the Princess Tyszkiewicz. Throughout his later life he always had his own private doctor who accompanied him everywhere. In 1799 he had been advised that taking the waters would be good for his legs and feet, although with the passage of time the situation had not noticeably improved. He became increasingly obsessed with his health with rituals involving gargling, massages with eau-de-cologne and the application of poultices. The ex-Abbé de Pradt describes Talleyrand going to bed wearing no less than fourteen bonnets, while during the day he wore layers of wool and flannel beneath his clothes.

The duties of the Great Chamberlain obliged him to leave the pleasures of Valençay to be present at the marriage of Charles Ferdinand, the Duke de Berry, the second son of the Duke d'Artois—and third in succession to the throne after his father and the Duke d'Angoulême. Berry was the black sheep of the family, hot-tempered and always in trouble. While in exile in England he is believed to have actually married a young lady named Amy Brown and they had had two daughters—perhaps even two sons prior to their marriage. Later, after returning to France, the marriage with Amy was declared null and void, although in fact he had already installed her and her children in a house in Paris where she continued to live as his mistress.

The marriage of the Duke de Berry with Marie-Caroline de Bourbon-Two Sicilies, the grand-daughter of Ferdinand IV, the King of Naples, was partly the work of the Prince de Talleyrand. It had at first been proposed that Berry should marry the Grand Duchess Anna, the younger sister of Tsar Alexander I, but Talleyrand had advised against it on religious grounds and also because he thought a better alliance could be found elsewhere. Thus, Ambassador Blacas had successfully arranged with the Kingdom of the Two Sicilies for Caroline to marry the Duke de Berry. An initial marriage ceremony had been held in Naples, then celebrated again on 17 June 1816 in Paris where Caroline became Mme de Berry (not to be confused with Louis XV's mistress, Mme du Barry, who had died on the guillotine). Talleyrand was delighted to travel to Fontainebleau to greet the princess upon her arrival travelling in the company of Louis XVIII in the royal coach, no doubt listening to the king's malicious gossip about his court on the way there. The wedding itself was held at the Tuileries Palace with Talleyrand's uncle Alexandre-Angélique, Archbishop of Paris, officiating. The ceremony took place on a scale that put to shame Napoleon's attempts to celebrate the events of his reign. This politically arranged marriage turned out to be a happy one, despite Berry's numerous infidelities. Caroline and her husband lived at the Élysée Palace in Paris, nowadays the residence of the French president.

On 5 September 1816, Louis XVIII dissolved the *Chambre Introuvable,* considering its Ultra-Royalist tendency just too extreme for the good management of the country, and thereby considerably consolidating the positions of Richelieu and Decazes. It could have been expected that Talleyrand would be thrilled by such news but, still smarting from his dismissal in the previous year, he was determined to oppose anything that Richelieu, Decazes and the king were responsible for. With his harem, the Rue Saint-Florentin became the core of an opposition movement, although the qualities that had made his reputation—moderation, discretion, self-possession—sometimes deserted him. People flocked to see him, even his old friend Mme de Staël and those who had insulted him when he was in power. At his table, flowing with good food and quality wines, the conversation often became animated. Upon leaving the dining room table having drunk too much, regrettably he often let his tongue loose. There was such an occasion on 18 November 1816 at a dinner held at the British Embassy when Talleyrand made the most insulting remarks about Richelieu and Decazes in the presence of the ambassador, Lord Rothesay, the British politician George Canning and Pasquier, the newly elected President of the Chamber of Deputies. The assumption of this position by Pasquier meant that he had deserted Talleyrand and aligned himself with Richelieu and Decazes. The Prince could not contain his irritation about having been spied upon at Valençay and at Bourbon-l'Archambault, while he knew that his letters to Dorothea and the Duchess von Courland were intercepted and read even by the king. Once more, he criticized Richelieu loudly for having signed the second Treaty of Paris in 1815. His former colleague Pasquier was deeply embarrassed about such matters being aired vociferously in a foreign embassy and made for the door. Talleyrand cut him off, calling Decazes "a pimp" and shouting that the Chamber of Deputies degraded itself by having dealings with such a person. Pasquier responded that the members of the government could not tolerate being the subjects of such language from its Grand Chamberlain—and left. The next day all Paris was humming with accounts of this extraordinary event.

The Council of Ministers met to discuss the unpardonable behaviour of a member of the royal court. While some called for his dismissal and exile, Richelieu and Decazes, his most affronted victims, proposed that it would be sufficient to forbid Talleyrand access to the court in the Tuileries. After all, many of those present owed their positions to Talleyrand—perhaps he might be called upon again to assume a role in the government. Thus, M. de La Châtre, the king's equerry, handed Talleyrand a note written by Richelieu stating that he no longer had the right to enter His Majesty's court until further notice. In reply, Talleyrand reminded the king that he was his most faithful subject but would obey the instruction with the pained conscience of a man who has been wrongfully penalized. He apologized for his illegible hand-writing (but not his bad conduct), teasing the king by saying that he knew that he was perfectly able to read it.

Ambassador Rothesay informed the British Government of the incident. In an attempt to pour oil on troubled waters, Talleyrand wrote to his friend the Duke of Wellington explaining that the evening at the British Embassy had gone off rather well and that if people spoke about an incident, it was simply to pretend that one had taken place. Mme de Rémusat, who was in Toulouse at the time, regretted not being present since she had on previous occasions managed to stop his tongue from running amok. As for Dorothea, Molé describes her anger with him when he told her about the rupture with Pasquier. The outcome was that relations with both Pasquier and Molé were broken off for a number of years.

Chateaubriand spoke in Talleyrand's defence in the Chamber of Peers, for they shared one thing in common—bitterness. Despite the rupture with Pasquier and Molé, the salons of the Rue Saint-Florentin became as crowded as ever with visitors anxious to remain on good terms with the Prince in disgrace, who had become the icon of the opposition. Mme de Staël knew that his humiliation would not last long and such was his desire to be in the political limelight that he would inevitably come bouncing back. It was a time of dark conspiracies and impossible plots, and one way of allaying suspicion was to maintain contact with all of his ancient contacts, both enemies and friends: Blacas, Vitrolles, Boisgelin. Even the Ultras, who a year previously were ready to hang him, began to express an interest in closer contacts. Incredibly, he was once again on excellent terms with the Duke d'Artois, the Duke de Berry and other members of the royal family! The new leader of the Ultras, Jean-Baptiste Villèle, even made the extraordinary remark that Talleyrand was the only person with sufficient prestige to be head of a Royalist government.

An occasion presented itself for Talleyrand to find his way into the king's favour on 21 January 1817, when a great ceremony was held at the Saint-Denis Cathedral upon the anniversary of the death of Louis XVI. The Prince de Talleyrand had been forbidden from attending the court at the Tuileries, but not other royal events. He arrived in his full regalia ready to occupy the place of Grand Chamberlain standing near the monarch, but he was informed by the master of ceremonies, M. de Dreux-Brézé, that he was no longer admitted to the king's presence and it was preferable that he should find a seat among the other members of the Chamber of Peers in the nave of the cathedral. It may be recalled that

Dreux-Brézé had marched at the head of the procession for the opening of the States General at Versailles twenty-eight years previously on 4 May 1789.

Eventually, Richelieu, with great magnanimity, decided that Talleyrand had served his period of disgrace and should be readmitted to the court. Richelieu realized that keeping him away only encouraged his salon to become a hotbed of opposition. On 28 February 1817, Talleyrand was received by the king and a perfectly banal conversation took place. He wrote to the Duchess von Courland: "It is sufficiently good like this. We should consider ourselves satisfied and keep our mouths shut." From now on, Louis XVIII tolerated Talleyrand but did not trust him and would never accord him a government post. In future, when in Paris Talleyrand fulfilled his role as Grand Chamberlain rigorously, standing near the king, for instance, while his uncle Alexandre-Angélique conducted the mass.

Although Louis XVIII was never going to make him a minister, on 31 August 1817 he granted Talleyrand the title of duke and peer, which he was allowed to transfer to his brother Archambaud. The title of Duke de Talleyrand-Périgord later passed to Archambaud's son Edmond and subsequently to the eldest son that he had had with Dorothea—Napoléon-Louis. Talleyrand also asked Louis XVIII to convert Valençay into a duchy, but the king refused on the not unfounded grounds that the King of Spain might be affronted that his former prison would be so exalted.

In January 1817, he conjured up another shameless way of making money. During the period of the provisional government in April 1814, he had sent two men to remove and destroy papers from the state archives that might be an embarrassment in the future. Among these, he had retained intact the correspondence between himself and Bonaparte from 1799 to 1806. Using Mme de Souza as an intermediary, he offered this documentation to Metternich for 500,000 francs. Metternich was no fool; he asked to see the material, had the most interesting parts copied and sent it back without comment. Chateaubriand, who became Minister of Foreign Affairs some years later, knew all about this trafficking of state archives. This was not the end of the story for Perrey then took possession of a large part of the documentation and fled to London with it, selling parts off to collectors. After Talleyrand's death, some of these papers were salvaged by Dorothea and taken to her Château de Sagan in Silesia, where they were destroyed during the advance of the Russian Army in February 1945.

Dorothea and Edmond de Périgord had nothing in common but their name. The spendthrift Edmond had already disposed of his mother's fortune on gambling and the pursuit of women, among them Marie Walewska, Napoleon's former mistress. At the end of 1817, he decided to sell the Château de Rosny, which he had inherited from his mother. The money he obtained from the sale was barely enough to cover his debts and there seemed little hope that he would change his profligate ways. Talleyrand decided the moment had come to intervene so that Dorothea's fortune was not employed to finance his nephew's way of life. He proposed a legal separation that took place on 24 March 1818, although it only became final in 1824. Thereafter, Dorothea and her children shared the Rue Saint-Florentin and Valençay with the patriarch. She had a fiery temperament and her relationship with Charles-Maurice was often stormy. She was extremely beautiful and did not always live up to her title of Duchess de Dino [in French, Dino can be understood as: *say no*]. There were a number of lovers and a number of pregnancies as a result, although she did not recognize any of the children—except for one.

On 29 December 1820 Dorothea had given birth to a girl called Pauline. During that year, for the sake of appearances, Edmond had been persuaded to return to live at the Rue Saint-Florentin and Talleyrand had paid off his debts. Furthermore, when the nephew requested that he should be granted the title of Grand Officer of the *Légion d'Honneur*, the uncle took steps to satisfy this desire. These gestures resembled those of a troubled conscience intending to buy Edmond's silence. After Pauline was born, Edmond left for England, returning later to Paris to lead a bachelor's life, never meeting his wife again.

Was the 66-year-old Prince de Talleyrand the father of the child? In the absence of any other evidence, the gossips of Parisian society certainly did not hesitate to reach this conclusion, while Talleyrand did nothing to contradict their opinion. Writing her *Souvenirs* some years later, Dorothea suggests that she did not find the thirty-nine-year age gap between her and Talleyrand as repugnant as other women might have done. Despite the physical deficiency of his legs, he was known to be notoriously attractive to women. On the contrary, there is the intrinsic improbability of the liaison, Talleyrand's capability of fathering a child at his age and, finally, the reaction of Dorothea's mother, the Duchess von Courland, who could hardly have been ignorant of the circumstances—there was no coolness in the contacts between Courland and Talleyrand. One might feel that the big fuss to ensure the presence of Edmond pushes the evidence in favour of Talleyrand being the father, but the truth will never be known and any opinion will lie forever in the field of guesswork, although Dorothea's reputation suffered a blow that she would retain all her life. Talleyrand's behaviour towards Pauline, similar to that towards the adopted Charlotte, was always that of the doting father. This was not the last of Dorothea's pregnancies.

The year 1817 was marked by the death of Talleyrand's boyhood friend Auguste de Choiseul-Gouffier. A few weeks later, on 14 July Germaine de Staël passed away after a long illness at the age of 51. Among the most attentive visitors at her sick bed had been the Duke of Wellington, while Lord Byron's verdict on her was: "She was the best creature in the world." Despite her goodness, Germaine's life had been a perpetual but vain search for happiness. She and the former Bishop of Autun were too different to have a profound and long-lasting friendship: she was good-natured, faithful and generous; while he was inconstant, cynical and vindictive, particularly to his best friends, and the occasion of her death provided another opportunity to display this regrettable side of his character. Mme de Staël had always sought to idolize her father and his policies, although Talleyrand did not share her confidence in Jacques Necker's financial skills. Then, Du Pont de Nemours died, leaving Talleyrand as the last survivor of his youthful clique.

The Ultra-Royalists wanted to remove Richelieu from power and believed that Talleyrand could be their Trojan Horse. Vitrolles, the right-hand man of "Monsieur", had known the Duchess de Dino since she was a child and proposed to her that one of Talleyrand's acquaintances should go to the Allied congress in Aachen in the autumn of 1818 and place in the tsar's hands a memorandum describing the French political scene. The oblique idea was that this memorandum, written by Vitrolles on the instructions of the Duke d'Artois, would create a greater impact if it appeared to be presented by Talleyrand. Everyone was aware that Talleyrand knew all the ministers, princes and monarchs at Aachen personally but they were also aware that the tsar's greatest friend was Prime Minister Richelieu himself. To his dismay, Vitrolles could not get the Prince to understand what was expected of him. In truth, Talleyrand wanted nothing to do with the plan drawn up by the Royalists and did not want any of his friends to be compromised by being involved in it either. Equally, in the best diplomatic terms, he did not want to appear to reject Vitrolles's plan. Finally, it was Vitrolles himself who went to Aachen and, in consequence, was compromised and lost his position as Secretary of State at court.

The Congress of Aachen was a periodic high-level diplomatic meeting between France and the four Great Powers—Austria, Prussia, Russia and the United Kingdom. It produced an amicable settlement whereby France completed the payment of its reparations and the Allies withdrew all of their remaining troops from the country's borders two years before the date originally foreseen. For the Duke de Richelieu it was a major triumph since France regained its position as one of the principal European powers. Talleyrand was consumed with jealousy that Richelieu had succeeded, with much dignity, in obtaining from the Allies exactly what he might have expected to obtain himself. A further disappointment was in store—after the congress the tsar came to Paris but did not call in at the Rue Saint-Florentin for he would never forgive the Prince for what had taken place in Vienna in 1814 and 1815.

The nation remained split between those determined to consolidate the gains of the Revolution and those equally resolute to restore the monarchy to what it had been before 1789. There were also the soldiers and petty officials, drifting back to France from far-flung places, whose fidelity to Napoleon was unshaken. Year by year the Chamber of Deputies was gradually shifting to the left and there was discord among the members of Richelieu's government, particularly with Decazes. In November 1818, Mme de Rémusat, who missed nothing, could not believe her eyes when she saw the Duchess de Dino and the Baronne Alexandre de Périgord (i.e. Charlotte) making a courtesy visit to Mme Decazes. She wrote in her diary: "I saw M. de Talleyrand yesterday. He spoke to me about M. Decazes with a sort of praise, believing him to be the only good man in the government and describing him as clever." There was, of course, a reason for this abrupt change of heart. In December 1818, Richelieu had wanted to push through parliament a new electoral law that was opposed by Decazes—and by Talleyrand. Richelieu declared that he would resign if the new law was not adopted. Talleyrand seriously believed his hour had come and started drawing up lists of candidates to fill his ministries. He even invited Richelieu, who knew perfectly well what was going on, to a sumptuous dinner. Meanwhile, there was great confusion in the king's court as ministers criss-crossed each other alternatively giving or withdrawing their resignation. When Richelieu actually resigned himself, neither Louis XVIII nor "Monsieur" wanted anything to do with Talleyrand, so Decazes was nominated as Prime Minister.

Talleyrand's disappointment was made even more bitter as he saw the monarchy out of touch with reality and becoming unpopular, since the Ultras still believed that Louis XVIII ruled the country by some divine, infinitely powerful and indisputable right. On the other hand, having lived through the Age of Enlightenment, Talleyrand wished for *legitimacy*—the reasonable, moderate and controlled application of the law adopted by the parliament. "The legitimacy of kings, or rather the legitimacy of governments, is the safeguard of nations and it is for this reason that it is sacred." It was not the king's will or his whims that were sacred but the nation's laws of which he was the custodian. The king was only sacred because of this duty at all times to apply the law. Legitimacy, by guaranteeing public order, also guaranteed national contentment. The Bourbons and the Ultras did not accept this argument, believing that it was sacrilege to expect the godlike king to be restrained by laws voted by mere mortals such as the people's representatives.

On 13 February 1820, while leaving the opera, the Duke de Berry had been stabbed by a Bonapartist fanatic, Louis-Pierre Louvel. He died the next day, marking a turning point in the history of the Restoration monarchy. While his wife Caroline shaved her head and went into deep mourning, his death hastened the downfall and replacement of the Decazes government for she had pointed a finger at the former Minister of Police and said: "It is he who is the real assassin." The assassination of the Duke de Berry and the replacement of Decazes by Villèle as Prime

Minister resulted in further strengthening the power of the Ultras, eclipsing the liberals. On 29 September 1820, Caroline gave birth to Berry's posthumous son, who was called Henri, Duke de Bordeaux, later known as the Count de Chambord representing the unique male heir of the Bourbon dynasty. Henri was Caroline's fourth child, but the first two had died in infancy and her third child had been a daughter. By various mistresses, other illegitimate children were born after Berry's death. On his deathbed, he asked to see Amy Brown—her two daughters were subsequently brought up as members of the royal family. Louis XVIII was so delighted with the birth of his grand-nephew Henri that he nominated thirty-five new state dignitaries, among them Talleyrand, who donned his new regalia with its coat of black velvet with gold braid and a blue silk sash bearing the Order of the Holy Spirit. It was said that, in Europe, only the tsar and the Emperor of Austria wore more sumptuous insignia than the Prince de Talleyrand.

In the summer of 1821, Talleyrand returned to Paris and the Chamber of Peers to promote his latest burning issue: the freedom of the press. Following the assassination of the Duke de Berry, Richelieu's second government had quickly adopted severe restrictions on what could be printed, and what represented a violation of public morality, of religion and of the king's authority. It was strongly suspected by the paranoiac Ultras that a vast liberal conspiracy was afoot to overthrow the government. Talleyrand pointed out that the Chamber of Deputies, still dominated by the Ultra-Royalists, prevented any serious discussion of the issues facing the country and took no notice of the country's laws: "A government weakens itself when it obstinately refuses and for too long [to address] what the situation demands as necessary." In such circumstances: "The freedom of the press is a necessity of the time... In our time, it is not easy to deceive for long." While the liberties decided upon in 1789 had subsequently been seized and distorted by the Jacobins, he demanded that there should be a return to the enlightened decisions of the Constituent Assembly. Talleyrand concluded with these words: "There is somebody who is more intelligent than Voltaire, more intelligent than Bonaparte, more intelligent than all past and future directors and ministers; that person is Everybody!" At a time when Richelieu was about to fall again and the Ultras would inevitably decide the choice of the next prime minister, Talleyrand stated boldly his faith in freedom of religion, individual liberty, justice for all, trial by jury and freedom of the press. His words passed into oblivion, to be followed nine years later by the Bourbon dynasty.

The year 1821 was marked by the loss of a number of people who had played an important role in Talleyrand's life. By far the most momentous was the announcement of Napoleon's death at Saint Helena on 5 May. While Talleyrand tried to minimize the significance of this event, he could not stop the emperor's name from becoming mythical for the French. The British politician Lord Holland was at a dinner with Talleyrand when the news reached Paris in July and he noted what the Prince said on this occasion: "His genius was inconceivable. Nothing matched his energy, his imagination, his intelligence, his capacity for work, his ability to motivate... His career is the most astonishing one we have experienced for 1,000 years... He committed three cardinal errors: Spain, Russia and the Pope... In my opinion, [he is] the most extraordinary person who lived in our epoch and for many a century."

While Talleyrand was to a certain extent in awe of Napoleon, he was convinced that this notorious bad speller would be incapable of writing his own memoirs. Nevertheless, Napoleon had dictated a biography to his military aides in which Talleyrand appears from time to time: "I have never known anyone so immoral... But he has the gift of letting nothing show on his face, knowing when to say nothing." Even though Talleyrand was double-crossing him by keeping Tsar Alexander and Metternich informed of French policy over a period of seven years, neither Napoleon nor his police ever suspected him. Published in 1823, Napoleon's *Memoirs* rocketed to the top of the nineteenth century's list of bestsellers. In Napoleon's will, he also accepted full responsibility for the death of the Duke d'Enghien, although the stain of Talleyrand's involvement in this affair would never go away.

At the end of the summer of 1821, news reached him that the Duchess von Courland had died on 20 August. She had been ill since the month of June and they had exchanged letters in which, although he did not realise it at the time, his last words to her were: "Goodbye angel of goodness and sweetness." Although Dorothea had little reason to love her mother, in October she held a remembrance service for her at the

Lutheran Temple in Paris. At the same time, a grand ceremony took place for the burial of Talleyrand's uncle Alexandre-Angélique. Before he died, the 85-year-old archbishop had written to his wayward nephew begging him to assume once again his place within the church. His successor as Archbishop of Paris, Monsignor Hyacinthe Louis de Quélan, promised enthusiastically to recover the soul of the lost nephew for the church—it was not to be an idle promise.

It was to be a year of sadness with, in December, another loss. His dear and malicious confidante Mme de Rémusat died, who had known him so well since the glorious days of the Consulate. Their half-amorous, half-platonic relationship had never been troubled by unhappiness. Her verdict on him was: "Good grief! What a pity that you have spoiled yourself with pleasure! Because, finally, it seems to me that you are worth more than yourself." A year later the worthy Richelieu died, with no member of the ungrateful Bourbon family attending his funeral. Not only was it a time for losing people, but Talleyrand's political ambitions remained sadly unfulfilled.

Just as the French Revolution had been undermined by the extreme activities of the Jacobins, throughout this period, the popularity of the restored Bourbon monarchy was gradually eroded by its most passionate supporters—the Ultra-Royalists. However, their ranks produced no-one of political genius. Louis XVIII's efforts to restrain them were frustrated by the fact that his brother, the Duke d'Artois, was their most ardent devotee. The man most capable of supporting the king had been the avuncular, pipe-smoking Richelieu, who had been both extremely able and completely lacking in personal ambition. He had longed to be relieved of his heavy responsibilities, hated intrigue, was more than decent to his opponents and never asked his friends to face the temptations of high office. Whenever he threatened to resign, he was always persuaded to change his mind when told that he would be forcing the king to send for Talleyrand.

When Richelieu's second government was replaced by that of Villèle in 1822, the freedom of the press was further restricted by limiting what could be said about public morality, religion and the king's authority. Talleyrand seized the occasion to point out that this did not correspond at all to the Constitutional Charter drawn up in 1814 and signed by

Louis XVIII, where it was promised that legal disputes involving press freedom would be tried by a jury. Curiously, the Chamber of Peers started to attack the Ultra-Royalist tendency in the lower house for its stance on fundamental freedoms. Nevertheless, the Royalist government could always count upon a solid majority within the Chamber of Deputies. At the Rue Saint-Florentin, the only recourse was derision, in which the participants indulged with passion. From this time onwards, the monarchy was clearly out of step with society.

It was at about this time that Talleyrand and the Duchess de Dino made contact with their neighbour, the severe, honest and pure Pierre-Paul Royer-Collard, who lived fifteen kilometres from Valençay at Châteauvieux. Talleyrand must have known Royer-Collard from the early days of the Revolution since they had both been involved in politics in one way or another over the previous thirty years. Royer-Collard was loyal to the throne, sincere in his religious belief and did not pursue self-interest. They had nothing in common except for their independence of mind and their opposition to the Ultras. Unhappily, one of the virtuous Royer-Collard's well-known proclamations was: "There are two kinds of beings in this world that I cannot stand without a feeling of revulsion, they are a *regicide* and a married priest." Royer-Collard had not encouraged his neighbours to come and visit, but Talleyrand and the Duchess de Dino were determined to make the effort. Upon arrival after a difficult journey, the uncle and the niece took immense trouble to charm the recluse of Châteauvieux who, in a few hours, became their life-long friend sharing mutual esteem, admiration and a desire to meet again so as to support each other in the political arena. In 1815, Royer-Collard had taken over the chairmanship of the National Education Commission, managing to introduce free education in all village primary schools. By 1816, he had become the leader of the moderates and the "doctrinaires", who sought a constitutional monarchy, as opposed to the Ultras who wanted a complete return to the ways of the past. These two men were to form an unlikely partnership against a disagreeable affair when the Ultras decided to drag France into a Spanish war.

The King of Spain, Talleyrand's former "prisoner" Ferdinand VII, had been described as "cowardly, selfish, grasping, suspicious and vengeful". In 1820, he had been obliged to follow the political fashion and accord his subjects a constitution. A two-chamber parliament was established designed to limit his power—the Cortez. However, two years later Ferdinand was virtually a prisoner of his own government, while in the north of the country a Royalist insurrection rose up with the objective of abolishing the Cortez and annulling the new constitution. In France, the Ultras supported the cause of the Spanish Bourbons and demanded that the French Army should intervene to restore the absolute power of the Spanish king. When Talleyrand and Royer-Collard heard of this proposal they rushed back to Paris and tried to form a group of all those who opposed this Spanish adventure, seeking help in the most unlikely places—for instance, from the Russian ambassador to France, Pozzo di Borgo.

A conference was held in Verona on 20 October 1822 as part of the regular series of meetings among the Allies following the Napoleonic Wars. The two French representatives—Matthieu de Montmorency and Chateaubriand—were both fierce partisans of the French Army intervening in Spain, despite the fact that Louis XVIII had instructed them to act with moderation. The Duke of Wellington, representing the United Kingdom, was totally opposed to any Spanish adventure. Nevertheless, a majority at the meeting authorized the French to march on Spain with the military expedition led by the Duke d'Angoulême crossing the border on 28 January 1823. Napoleon's army had lived off the land by robbing the Spanish peasants of their produce, with the result that the whole population rose up against them. Angoulême's army had learned the lessons taught by Wellington and now paid for its supplies. The result was that, at relatively little cost, Ferdinand was restored to the throne. The campaign ended with a French victory at the Battle of Trocadero in Cadiz and—despite Ferdinand's promises of amnesty—was followed by mass executions among the rebels.

Meanwhile, in Paris, the opposition to this war centred around the residence of the Orléans faction at the Palais Royal. Talleyrand turned for help to a new journalist on the political scene. He was small, self-confident, ambitious, unscrupulous, ill-mannered, bursting with energy and spoke volubly with the southern accent of Marseille. His name was Adolphe Thiers and he contrasted sharply with the phlegmatic Talleyrand, renowned for his disdainful silences and piercing epigrams.

Under the tutelage of Talleyrand, who described Thiers as "an urchin of genius", he became an active member of those opposed to the Bourbon regime. Dorothea took longer to warm to him but they were allied by being members of the opposition and she soon came to appreciate his talent. Nearly fifty years later, in 1871, Thiers would become the first president of the Third French Republic.

Although Thiers was not at all the sort of person whose company Talleyrand sought, the Prince was remarkably tolerant of him. As soon as this young man got his foot in the door at the Rue Saint-Florentin, he became a regular visitor. He had just returned from a fact-finding mission to Spain, where Talleyrand feared that the French Army would once again become bogged down in guerrilla warfare as during Napoleon's time. On the contrary, Thiers was of the opinion that the Spanish were wary of becoming involved in another rebellion. While the two men did not necessarily agree, they appreciated each other's points of view.

Talleyrand wrote a speech against the Spanish War that he intended to read before the Chamber of Peers, although in fact it was never delivered because the government forbade anybody from taking the floor to oppose its policies. The text was, however, printed in the official record and contains two ground-breaking assertions. First: "People have the right to choose and to adopt by themselves the political regime under which they wish to live." And secondly, that their foreign neighbours have the duty—and also the interest—not to intervene by force in the internal political affairs of other states. He also declared that he had been strongly opposed to Napoleon's intervention in Spain (which is true) and that he made his opinion unambiguously clear to the emperor. Chateaubriand quickly pointed out that his "unambiguous opinion" was not without ambiguity. Talleyrand wanted Louis XVIII to understand that he was opposed to any involvement in a war guided by "crazy and reckless passions". Was France threatened by Spain? Did France want to obtain something from Spain? Talleyrand spoke for the whole nation: "The wish of France in its entirety is for peace." In his opinion, it was not a dynastic war but simply a decision by the Ultras to do in Spain what they had been unable to carry out in France—to succeed with a counter-revolution. The impact of Talleyrand's "speech" on public opinion was enormous, with the liberal opposition praising its author. Particularly,

Royer-Collard congratulated him in the most glowing terms, while the writer Stendhal pointed out that the simplicity of his arguments contrasted sharply with the empty words of Chateaubriand. Despite his forebodings, the military campaign in Spain was crowned with success and the local population did not rise up in armed insurrection.

In his *Mémoires d'outre tombe,* Chateaubriand who, as Minister of Foreign Affairs had launched the Spanish affair, painted Talleyrand as "the Prince of Evil" for having spoken out against this expedition. As we have already noted, Talleyrand never actually made the speech in the Chamber of Peers to which he refers. Talleyrand's verdict on Chateaubriand was that his example should not be followed: he did not understand people and he conducted his own affairs and those of the country very badly. Finally: "Chateaubriand wrote his works with a crow's feather!" The outcome was that Talleyrand's salon became an ever-more-fashionable place to be seen. Charles de Rémusat—Mme de Rémusat's son—was invited for the first time on 23 February 1823 to discover around the "Prophet's" dinner table all the big names of those who opposed the government: "There was between everybody a secret that was never pronounced, but which was understood in half-phrases."

In 1809, Louis-Philippe, from the Orléans branch of the Bourbon family, had married Maria Amalia de Bourbon, princess of the Two-Sicilies. The couple, who had ten children, had at first lived in Palermo but during the Restoration moved to the Palais Royal in Paris. Even before the Revolution, Talleyrand had had a weakness for the more liberal attitude of the Orléans family, believing that they would accept to rule the country as a constitutional monarchy. During his time as Prime Minister, he had been instrumental in restoring their family possessions confiscated during the Revolution. At about this time, the Orléans family suddenly became aware of Talleyrand's existence and invited him to dinner at their Parisian residence. He had already met Louis-Philippe's sister Adélaïde—known as "Mademoiselle"—in London in 1792 and knew that she had a strong inclination for politics. There was a similarity between the influence of Adélaïde over her brother and that of Dorothea over Talleyrand. The outcome was that the court of Louis XVIII became very nervous about the association between the Orléans family and Talleyrand, realizing that it was difficult to ignore his influence.

Talleyrand warned Vitrolles: "Beware. The Duke d'Orléans is treading on your heels."

It may be recalled, concerning the assassination of the Duke d'Enghien in March 1804, that it was Caulaincourt who had unwittingly facilitated his arrest, that the firing squad had been under the command of Savary, that Napoleon had accepted full responsibility for this event—but it had been Talleyrand's idea in the first place. In 1816, Talleyrand had met the old Louis V Joseph, Prince de Condé, Enghien's grandfather, at the royal court. A terrible scene was avoided because the elderly gentleman mistook—or pretended to mistake—the former Bishop of Autun for his uncle, the Archbishop of Paris. The Prince de Condé asked politely for news of the archbishop's strange nephew Charles-Maurice, this "yob", this "ne'er-do-well from Autun". It was Talleyrand's habit never to react to insults and this occasion was no exception. The old man retired to his Château de Chantilly and died there two years later. After his death, his son, Enghien's father, known up to this time as the Duke de Bourbon, assumed his father's hereditary title as Louis-Joseph, Prince de Condé. He took no action against those who were responsible for his son's death, although they were not forgotten and everyone knew who they were.

In 1818, Caulaincourt's wife, the Duchess de Vicence, the former Mme de Canisy, heard of these rumours circulating and wished to defend the honour of her husband, who had been deceived into playing a role in the Enghien Affair. As a preliminary, she sought the advice of the Prince de Talleyrand, who begged her to do nothing at all. However, the Duchess de Vicence wished to do something and reminded the Prince that the former Duke de Bourbon, now Prince de Condé, had a mistress called Mme de Feuchères. Upon hearing this, Talleyrand reacted strongly with: "Mme de Feuchères? What a shame! Do you really want to stoop that low?" Mme de Caulaincourt did not wish to stoop so low and dropped the subject.

Sophie Dawes, a London prostitute brought to Paris as the companion of the Duke d'Enghien's father, was pretty, clever and ambitious, and Condé gave her an education and a dowry. To prevent a scandal and to qualify her to be received at court, in 1818 she married the naïve Baron Adrien de Feuchères, an officer in the Royal Guard. The

Baroness de Feuchères then became a person of consequence at the court of Louis XVIII. Eventually, Adrien de Feuchères discovered the relationship between his wife and Condé and obtained a legal separation in 1827. She was banished from court for a time but before long made her way back into favour.

Long before these events and following his conversation with the Duchess de Vicence, in 1818, the former Bishop of Autun had decided that it would be an extremely good idea to make contact with Mme de Feuchères—but how to do it? He asked the Count de Durfort, who knew the Prince de Condé and Mme de Feuchères very well, to dinner where, with the greatest confidentiality, Talleyrand resuscitated his old story that before the fatal night of the Duke d'Enghien's arrest he had sent a note telling him to flee at once. Durfort was overcome with admiration for Talleyrand's reticence, believing he had become compromised in this sordid affair because he could never reveal his selfless act. Talleyrand encouraged Durfort in this illusion and invited him to share it with Mme de Feuchères, while expressing his lifelong devotion to the House of Condé. Mme de Feuchères duly accepted an invitation to the Rue Saint-Florentin. Upon her arrival, the Duchess de Dino curtsied before Mme de Feuchères as if she were the Duchess de Condé herself, after which their guest was ready to do anything for them. Mme de Feuchères was regaled with the same story as the Count de Durfort and performed her function so well that, before long, Talleyrand was invited to the Château de Chantilly. There was therefore only one last act to be performed—the Prince de Condé was invited to Valençay. Nobody could believe it!

In October 1823, Savary, who had returned to France, published an extract from his memoirs stating that he, the Duke de Rovigo, was the innocent victim of abominable accusations concerning the death of the Duke d'Enghien, while the true guilty parties strutted about concealing their crimes beneath their noble robes. Everyone immediately knew to whom he was referring. In the belief that Villers and Perrey had destroyed all the official files concerning the Enghien case in April 1814, up to now Talleyrand considered himself safe from repercussions, letting such accusations pass in silence. Never before had he lost any sleep over the allegations launched against him, however Savary's brochure represented a serious threat. Talleyrand left Valençay in a hurry on

3 November 1823, heading for Paris; Dorothea would follow a few days later with their luggage. One consolation was that he benefited from the support of Royer-Collard, who advised him "to go to the top"— Louis XVIII. Upon arrival, Talleyrand wrote to the king to oppose Savary's allegations and to give his own version of the Duke d'Enghien's death—the king's distant cousin. Overreacting, he asked the king to bring Savary to justice. This could easily have led to a nasty political showdown in court and rioting on the streets.

Louis XVIII behaved with serene majesty and came to Talleyrand's rescue. Shortly before he died, he refused to allow the affair to be submitted to the Chamber of Peers and expressed his complete confidence in his Grand Chamberlain. It could be said that in this way Louis settled his debt to Talleyrand for his efforts at the time of the Restoration. At the same time, a message was sent to the Parisian newspapers announcing that the Duke de Rovigo was forbidden from attending court. The Duchess de Broglie (Mme de Staël's daughter) wrote to Barante: "M. de Talleyrand comes out of this affair as white as snow; it would seem that it's a good thing for him to be slandered." Talleyrand himself wrote to Barante drawing attention to the fact that, in his will, Napoleon stated that he was himself uniquely responsible for the Duke d'Enghien's murder and, if he found himself in the same situation, he would have done the same thing again. This did not entirely erase the doubts circulating about Talleyrand's involvement in the crime, but doubts were something he could live with.

The ground floor of the Rue Saint-Florentin was an unparalleled hot-bed for political, diplomatic and worldly intrigue. Every evening the Prince de Talleyrand's salon was open for the diplomatic corps, distinguished foreign visitors, peers, deputies, friends and anyone who opposed the government, while a proper reception was held twice a week. As of 1 o'clock in the morning, the gaming tables would be set out for whist, with Talleyrand playing with his "sphinx" mask betraying nothing. Boniface de Castellane and the Princess Tyszkiewicz both ruined themselves for the pleasure of playing against the Prince.

Before he died, Louis XVIII must have been aware that the Prince de Talleyrand was intriguing again. The new Prime Minister Villèle wanted to reduce the interest on government borrowing, while Talleyrand managed to amass a majority in the Chamber of Peers to oppose him. He also recruited his devoted, financially independent and efficient assistant, the Duchess de Dino, to lobby for him. Abandoning her essentially Protestant background, she had become an ardent Roman Catholic with good relations with de Quélan, the new Archbishop of Paris, whom she persuaded to give instructions to his clergy opposing Villèle's proposal. Perhaps the archbishop thought that, in return, she would convince Talleyrand to return to the fold.

The year 1824 would mark the deaths of both Louis XVIII and Napoleon's former arch-chancellor Jean-Jacques Cambacérès. When the latter died on 8 March, the police burst into his residence and seized all his papers. Talleyrand did not require a second warning and quickly destroyed a great many of his own papers. The old king died of gangrene on 16 September. Dorothea was astonished that the Grand Chamberlain's duties involved, at the age of 70 and with his well-known lifelong infirmity, his almost permanent attendance at the dying monarch's bedside and the supervision of his bodily functions. She was assuming an ever-greater role in his life, particularly his intellectual life and, furthermore, he was beginning to tire of the Rue Saint-Florentin in favour of Valençay.

CHAPTER XX
CHARLES X

With the death of Louis XVIII at the age of 70, his younger brother—up to this time known as the Duke d'Artois or "Monsieur"—inherited the throne with the title of Charles X. Given his support of the Ultra-Royalists over the previous decade, it should not have been a surprise that he had an irresistible temptation to return to "absolutism". Between his accession in September 1824 and his coronation on 29 May 1825, the new king's authoritarian government had already begun to stray off-course by adopting measures that would lead to its downfall five years later. Even though Charles X's reign had been welcomed favourably by the public, after a year the political situation had already become very tense. The new king told Talleyrand that France would be grateful to the Ultras for saving the country, to which the Prince replied: "Sire, I never believed that the Capitol [of Rome] had been saved by a flock of geese."

Talleyrand observed with dismay that the government of Charles X adopted absurd policies—including the award of 1 billion francs to compensate the former *émigrés* for their property losses. Seeing himself as an absolute monarch and enjoying the support of the Ultras, the new king tried to eradicate the elements of democracy that had taken root since the Revolution in order to restore the nobility's privileges and Roman Catholicism as the state religion. These policies were now far out of touch with the evolution in society. Talleyrand's opinion was that unpopular measures would ultimately lead to violent demonstrations, that violent demonstrations would result in the introduction of greater censorship of the press, and this would trigger a revolution. He wrote: "It is the first link in the chain that will drag the whole edifice to the precipice." There was no doubt in Talleyrand's mind that this regime was doomed to failure, so the best thing that troubled politicians could do was to consider the government that would follow. In July 1830 he would have the answer.

It is worth recalling that, in 1815, Louis XVIII had decided to avoid a formal coronation to avoid controversy. In contrast, ten years later the Grand Chamberlain had to stand near the 68-year-old Charles X during the sumptuous enthronement ceremony held in Reims Cathedral. Following the centuries-old tradition of the *Ancien Régime*, the celebrations continued for several days leaving Talleyrand exhausted and exaggerating his physical deformity. It was at this time that he earned the nickname of "the limping devil". He decided to take some time off at Valençay with Dorothea, who was more relaxed in the countryside than in Paris. She detested his friends on the Faubourg Saint-Germain who made her feel like a foreigner.

Among the first guests to arrive at Valençay for the 1825 season was the bespectacled Adolphe Thiers, who was now a favoured acquaintance of both Talleyrand and the Duchess de Dino. She explained to him: "You know perfectly well that you are not only our best friend but our preferred one." Thiers had become the finest historian of the Revolutionary period, which had opened doors for him into the world of politics. An American visitor said of Thiers: "He was almost as good with witticisms as the old Prince de Talleyrand." Thiers felt that it was impossible to hope that Charles X would respect the Constitutional Charter and spoke openly of replacing him with someone from another branch of the Royal Family, namely Louis-Philippe, the Duke d'Orléans.

Upon their return to Valençay, the trio Talleyrand/Dino/Tyszkiewicz renewed their acquaintance with Royer-Collard at Châteauvieux, since it was rare at this stage for their apprehensive neighbour to make the journey in the other direction. In the autumn of 1825, the same trio decided to pass the winter in the South of France. Having experienced the long, cold and wet winters of Valençay, what could be more natural than to spend these months in the mild climate of the South of France, at that time a less-well-known part of the country? We now know that the voyage to the South of France was motivated by a completely different reason: Dorothea was pregnant again. Based on the child's date of birth (23 January 1826), it was conceived in the previous May when she and Talleyrand moved to Valençay. She would have become certain of the pregnancy in July. Due to the staff of the Château de Valençay often being in the pay of the police, it was essential to be discreet about this event because Talleyrand still had political ambitions. If the news of Dorothea's pregnancy reached his political enemies in Paris, they would certainly not miss the occasion to discredit him. Already his role during the Revolution and the Empire would prevent Charles X from ever employing him as a minister. A new scandal in which the 71-year-old patrician would be suspected of having sexual relations with his niece, thirty-nine years his junior, had to be avoided at all costs. He also felt obliged to accompany Dorothea, since her absence from him over the period of her pregnancy would also attract attention.

The trio went first of all to Geneva, travelling in separate carriages by different routes so as not to overwhelm the small hotels in which they stayed. This would certainly confuse anybody taking an interest in them and would conceal their final destination, since the whole purpose of this journey was to keep the Duchess de Dino out of the public's eye. If they had all travelled in a convoy together with their servants, the local authorities could not have failed to notice and inform Paris. Even their most faithful friends, such as Barante, knew nothing about the true purpose and there is, of course, no reference to Dorothea's pregnancy in any letters. They had intended to pass by the residence of the Baron de Vitrolles in the Alps, but were prevented from doing so by bad weather. Vitrolles eventually found out about the pregnancy because he passed through Marseille and met Talleyrand and Dorothea there but, being a perfect gentleman, kept his mouth shut.

Talleyrand and his two ladies were received like royalty in Marseille, being required to attend solemn masses, to unveil statues and to appear at the opera. The town of Nice was not, at that time, part of France so provided a suitably inconspicuous place to give birth, but all the properties for hire were occupied by English tourists. Finally, they arrived in Hyères, a small town not frequented by the high society people who flocked to Nice. It was the ideal place to bear a child because the local doctor had a very good reputation. It would be he who took care of the baby, baptized Julie Zulmé, and cared for her until his death. So, why did the birth of Charlotte de in 1820 take place in Paris in the public's eye, while the birth of Julie Zulmé in 1826 was concealed as a source of great embarrassment? Even if the Prince de Talleyrand had been the father of Pauline, it had not been too difficult to inveigle Dorothea's estranged husband Edmond to be present in the same house at a more or less convenient moment to explain the pregnancy. In the case of Julie Zulmé, however, Edmond had gone and, despite the efforts of historical researchers, no potential father has ever been identified—except Talleyrand himself. Apart from Pauline, Dorothea never had any contact with any of her illegitimate daughters.

After the birth of the baby, Talleyrand learned that during his absence he had been elected mayor of the village of Valençay, so in March 1826 they headed back north again. The first port of call was Paris where, with misgivings about the survival of the Bourbon dynasty, he brought himself up to date with political events. He believed that his influence was necessary to overcome the king's horror of liberalism and to deflect his temptation towards a totalitarian government. On the contrary, Charles X wanted to escape from the restraint of the Constitutional Charter imposed on his brother. However, whereas Louis XVIII had been a politically smart and clear-headed monarch, if devious, Charles was incapable of subterfuge and simply felt it was his royal obligation to bring France back to the situation that had existed forty years earlier. Later, Leopold I, King of the Belgians, wrote: "Louis XVIII was a clever, hard-hearted man, shackled by no principle, very proud and false. Charles X [was] an honest man, a kind friend, an honourable master, sincere in his opinions, and inclined to do everything that is right."

Talleyrand then returned to Valençay to carry out his new functions as mayor, which, rather than disappointing him by their humbleness, he fulfilled with great pleasure. He was a very good mayor, thoroughly appreciated by his citizens. The Prince conducted himself like a grand paternalistic and philanthropic squire, attempting to bring the village's isolation to an end by contributing to its infrastructure and economic development, as well as to its services. Influenced by his great-grandmother, he had a charitable mission constructed in the village where assistance and alms were distributed to the needy. A wool-spinning enterprise and an industrial forge were set up to promote the region's economic activity and improve the lives of its inhabitants. The prefect of the Indre *département* wanted to appoint Talleyrand to his general council since: "There are no beggars nor anybody in great need at

Valençay because the Prince de Talleyrand has set up workshops where there is employment for all ages. Those affected by illness are visited, supported and comforted by the sisters of charity that he has endowed and established in this small town. It is also in this way that the children of poor people, and particularly the girls, are brought up to appreciate work; the education they receive is both moral and religious." Even if his own faith was weak, he believed that religion was essential for the maintenance of social order.

On 20 January 1827, there was, once again, a religious service at Saint-Denis to commemorate the death of Louis XVI. In his capacity as Grand Chamberlain, Talleyrand stood behind Charles X in his official robes and, at the end of the ceremony, between two rows of armed guards preceded the Duke and Duchess d'Angoulême—heirs to the throne—down the chapel's steps in the drizzly weather to their carriage. Suddenly, while he stood still waiting for the carriage to leave, a fanatic burst through the guards and, slapping Talleyrand in the face, threw him to the ground and proceeded to kick him violently.

General Marmont, who was standing nearby, immediately gave orders for the attacker to be arrested who, when asked to explain his act, told his interrogators that: "I wanted to give the Prince de Talleyrand a thrashing. He did harm to me and my family." This was the Count de Maubreuil who we last met in 1814 when he claimed that Talleyrand had recruited him to assassinate Napoleon and had, between times, attacked and robbed the Queen of Westphalia. For the latter crime, he had received five years in prison. Finding himself once again under arrest, he gave as reasons for attacking Talleyrand that he wished to avenge the dishonour suffered by his family. He particularly disliked Talleyrand because he was an unfrocked priest.

His stunned victim was quickly placed back on his feet. Although no bones were broken, the 73-year-old had received a thorough beating with a swollen cheek, some bruised ribs and a stiff ankle. He was brought back to the Rue Saint-Florentin and put to bed. A register was placed at the entrance to his house where those people who came to express their sympathies could write their names. When the king came to see him at his bedside, he insisted that he had received a blow from a fist—to a Périgord, a slap in the face would have been completely unacceptable.

Pasquier, too, called to inquire about the patient's health and the two men became reconciled for the first time since the dreadful scene at the British Embassy eleven years earlier. The political climate was beginning to change and the Prince was assuming the image of a legendary figure in French politics.

Talleyrand tried to hush up the Maubreuil affair by telling the police that he was at Saint-Denis on a private visit—patently untrue—that he had suffered no serious injury and that he had never met Maubreuil in his life. This was almost true since the evidence seems to suggest that in 1814 they had merely been in each other's presence for an extremely brief and inconclusive moment. The case came before the court on 24 February 1827 as a criminal affair. Much of the Faubourg Saint-Germain came to hear the proceedings. The unbalanced Maubreuil embellished his earlier accusations saying that Talleyrand (or more probably Antoine Roux-Laborie) had offered him 200,000 livres, the title of duke and the grade of a general in 1814 if he would simply assassinate Napoleon and his family. Such claims were considered totally ludicrous and did not prevent Maubreuil from being sentenced once again to five years in prison with various fines. He appealed against the verdict asking that Roux-Laborie, Talleyrand's former assistant, should be called as a witness to the conversation that was supposed to have taken place in 1814, but the court would only consider the recent incident on the steps of Saint-Denis. When Maubreuil came before the appeals tribunal, he behaved like a raving lunatic, which only served to strengthen Talleyrand's position. The court was particularly shocked that Maubreuil had chosen a state occasion to commit an act of aggression during which the Prince de Talleyrand was carrying out his official duties of Grand Chamberlain in his regalia and in the presence of the heirs to the throne. With the assassination of the Duke de Berry in mind, the police realized that the Duke and Duchess d'Angoulême could quite easily have become the next victims, which set off alarm bells. It can be added that the Baron de Vitrolles was also a victim of Maubreuil's burning desire for vengeance.

Before the Maubreuil affair had been settled, Talleyrand was subject to another attack—this time blackmail. His former secretary Perrey had fled to England, taking with him various important documents recovered from the state archives, as well as the manuscript of Talleyrand's *Memoirs*. In London, no doubt in order to survive, Perrey sold these documents and had the *Memoirs* published. What made matters more complicated was that Perrey was able to imitate Talleyrand's handwriting and signature, since, when they worked together, he had often been asked to write letters on Talleyrand's behalf. Talleyrand let it be known that, to his great comfort, any documents being offered for sale were forgeries produced by a counterfeiter.

During the autumn of 1828, he returned once more to the South of France, not wishing to remain alone in his enormous Château de Valençay, where no visitors could be expected during the winter months. He travelled without Dorothea, who had recently purchased the Château de Rochecotte and had remained behind to supervise the building improvements. She also wanted to be alone with her new lover, Théobald Piscatory, a future ambassador of France, by whom she had already given birth to a daughter called Antonine-Dorothée Piscatory, brought up by the paternal grandparents. Talleyrand's journey to Hyères was rendered agreeable by a period of calm in French politics. Following a general election with negative results for the government, Prime Minister Villèle had resigned in January 1828. The major winner was Talleyrand's friend Royer-Collard, who became leader of the Chamber of Deputies, while a liberal government was formed under Prime Minister Martignac.

The former Mme de Talleyrand, aged 70, her beauty faded and her body grown heavy, lived in Paris on the Rue de Lille, just across the River Seine from the Tuileries. Her house did not receive many visitors, but one in particular was the Duchess d'Esclignac, who was Talleyrand's niece, his brother Boson's daughter. When the three members of the Spanish royal family imprisoned at Valençay returned to Spain after Napoleon's defeat in 1814, to her great satisfaction the Queen of Spain awarded Mme de Talleyrand the Grand Ribbon of the Order of Marie-Louise for her hospitality. Another faithful presence at her house was her lover, the Duke de San Carlos, equerry to the Spanish princes and now Spanish Ambassador to France. In July 1828, Talleyrand would learn with great sorrow of the death of San Carlos. He explained to Dalberg: "He was an honourable man and gave [Mme de Talleyrand] the wise advice that she needed. I do not know into whose hands she will now fall."

In Paris, the Prince de Talleyrand, now aged 74, was set in his ways: going to bed at dawn, the public ceremony of the *lever* at midday, a ceremonial dinner with guests in the early evening, after dinner conversation and card games until the small hours of the morning. He was still renowned for his expressionless "death mask" which intimidated those who met him in an official capacity. To Dorothea's dismay, Montrond was still his companion, taking rude liberties permitted of no-one else.

Dorothea's two boys were now in their late teens. Napoléon-Louis, the elder nephew, was sent on a grand tour of Germany and Italy; the younger, Alexandre, went to Brest to start a naval career. Only Pauline remained at Valençay. Charles, his son by Adélaïde de Flahaut, had been one of Napoleon's aides-de-camp and had remained faithful to the emperor until the very end. At the Restoration, he was spared exile due to Talleyrand's intervention but was placed under police surveillance. Flahaut eventually chose to leave for Germany and thence to the United Kingdom. In 1817, while in Edinburgh, he met and married the intelligent and ambitious heiress Margaret Mercer Elphinstone, a lady of considerable character and daughter of the crusty Admiral George Elphinstone. The rich old admiral stipulated that he would only leave his fortune to the male heirs born of this marriage—they had five daughters. The couple returned to France in 1827, when a reconciliation took place between the father and son.

By August 1829, Charles X could no longer tolerate the liberal policies of Prime Minister Martignac, dismissing him and appointing the extremely unpopular fanatic Jules de Polignac in his place. Polignac had complete faith in his master's divine right to be king but almost immediately lost his majority in parliament. Convinced that royal authority was under serious threat, that the press scorned religion and that a vast liberal plot was brewing not unlike that of 1789, Polignac decided to challenge the two chambers by not recalling them and governing without their approval. At this point, three journalists, Adolphe Thiers, François Mignet and Armand Carrel (later to become yet another victim of duelling), were invited by the Duchess de Dino's lover, Théobald Piscatory, to her residence at Rochecotte, where, as luck would have it, they met Talleyrand. Despite his strong protestations of innocence in his memoirs, he arranged with his banker friend Jacques Laffite to provide the deposit for these three journalists to found the opposition newspaper *Le National*, which first appeared in January 1830—its motto was "The king reigns but does not govern." This daily contributed much to unrest among the population. The idea began to circulate that social peace would never be achieved until the last Bourbon king was removed from power. Dorothea also invited her Ultra-Royalist friend the Baron de Vitrolles to visit her. He wanted to be her lover, while she wanted him to abandon his allegiance to Charles X and transfer it to the Orléanists. They were both to be disappointed for this was the end of their relationship.

Once again, announcements of Talleyrand's death began to circulate. Even if these rumours turned out to be false, he had still been written off as a spent force in the political arena. In the meantime, at the royal court Talleyrand continued to fulfil his role of Grand Chamberlain, one of whose duties was to play whist with the king. Since the king had become an immovable object, the liberal opposition began to assume the form of an irresistible force. There were two dangers: first that, as resistance to the king's regime mounted, it would strengthen his resolve thus delaying the outcome, and second that if the Orléans solution was mentioned prematurely the appropriate moment would pass and the population would no longer find it attractive. Talleyrand resorted to the tactic he had employed so often—to let time pass.

Montrond was required to do the rounds of the political corridors in order to find out which way the wind was blowing, making contact in the process with Mademoiselle Adélaïde, Louis-Philippe's sister. Talleyrand sent out his harem to ascertain the mood of the Faubourg Saint-Germain, the court, the ministries and the embassies. The leaders of the liberal opposition—Thiers, Mignet, Foy, Sebastiani—were invited to dinner on the first floor of the Rue Saint-Florentin, where Talleyrand disillusioned them as to whom was the host: "No, it's not me, it's my niece." Would he dare to invite the members of the opposition to his apartment on the ground floor? No, but the Duchess de Dino dared on the floor above and, what luck, Talleyrand was invited too!

In April 1829, Talleyrand had been able to arrange the marriage of

Dorothea's 18-year-old son, Napoléon-Louis, to Alix de Montmorency, linking two grand aristocratic families. The groom was at last given the title of Duke de Valençay and became the proprietor of the château, although Talleyrand would have the right to inhabit it for the rest of his life. In his will, he left a special annex addressed to Napoléon-Louis asking him to take care of the family's long-term fortunes: "It is a great comfort at my age to think that it is you who I leave as head of the family." Within two generations, Talleyrand's faith in a long and illustrious family history would turn out to be an illusion. In February 1830, his brother Boson died who, despite his many failings, had been richly rewarded by the Bourbon Restoration.

As for his nephew, the 40-year-old Edmond, uncle Charles-Maurice had bailed him out for his debts on numerous occasions, but the financial crisis that had begun in 1825 and the failure the following year of a bank set up by his friend Dalberg meant that he was facing problems himself, to the point that he was considering selling some of his paintings. In December 1829, Edmond was arrested in England for debt, having already fled France to hide from his creditors. It would be Talleyrand's old friend the Duke de Laval, Ambassador to London, who paid 60,000 francs to liberate him from prison and put him on a boat for Brussels. There remained his debts in France. One day, two bailiffs appeared in Talleyrand's courtyard who proposed to recover the money Edmond owed by seizing his uncle's property. Indeed, up to now he had always paid off his family's debts, granted pensions to his brothers, bought property for them, provided dowries and almost ruined himself for Napoléon-Louis's wedding. Montrond remarked that: "He never received anything in return but ingratitude." While Edmond continued to distract himself with gambling and prostitutes, Dorothea pursued her passionate affair with Piscatory with Charles-Maurice showing signs of jealousy. Edmond was eventually packed off to Florence and remained there in exile for the rest of his life.

When Talleyrand returned to Paris in February 1830, he did not conceal how he saw events unfolding. What the country needed was a monarchy that represented the continuity of power, while consolidating the political advances that had been realised since 1789. The person who united these principles in the most satisfactory way was Louis-Philippe, the Duke d'Orléans. However, those in favour of this outcome were, not surprisingly, seen as enemies of the Bourbon monarchy, such that the Ultras accused Talleyrand of plotting the downfall of Charles X in favour of Louis-Philippe.

Dorothea and the Prince de Talleyrand left Paris for Valençay in April 1830. He believed that the final collapse of the Bourbons was imminent and he did not want to be caught up in the predictable turmoil. He would, nevertheless, return to Paris in late July and be present during the final moments of Charles X's regime. On 11 June, he wrote to the Princess de Vaudémont that the situation was hopeless: "Nothing can prevent a shipwreck." A few days later, a letter addressed to Flahaut in a similar tone said: "We are advancing towards an unknown world without a compass and without a pilot." Even though he had no sympathy for the Ultras, he was hardly enthusiastic about what was likely to happen when the Bourbon regime collapsed. Indeed, everyone was worried about the prospects of a new social upheaval. What was certain was that there would be a run on the stock market, so Talleyrand speculated on a drop in the value of state funds, which turned out to be an excellent investment!

On 2 March 1830 the parliament had met again, but Charles X's opening speech received a negative reception. Even though the king appointed his ministers from among the ranks of the Ultras, they could never be Royalist enough for the extremists. The Ultras now allied themselves with the more liberal elements to make the country ungovernable. On 18 March, the deputies voted a measure requiring the king's prime minister to obtain the support of both chambers for the adoption of any new laws. Charles X quickly called for a general election hoping to obtain a clear majority of Royalists, which, unfortunately for him, did not happen. He then brought together a new council of ministers containing some of the most unpopular politicians in the country, whose particular value to him was their unconditional support for the obstinate king's right-wing policies. The king and his ministers decided to suspend the constitution and on 25 July, from the royal residence in Saint-Cloud, he issued four ordinances that severely censored the press, dissolved the newly elected chamber before it could meet, called for new elections in September and limited those who could vote. These measures were to prove terminal, provoking Thiers, in his opposition newspaper, to publish a call to revolt, which was signed by forty-three journalists. Louis XVIII once said of his younger brother: "He conspired against Louis XVI; he conspired against me; someday he will conspire against himself."

The ship of state finally struck the rocks on 27 July when rioting began on the streets of Paris and barricades were erected. In defiance of the king, the Chamber of Deputies continued to meet. The next day, the rioters took possession of the city hall and Talleyrand had the gold letters inconspicuously removed announcing that the house on the corner of the Rue Saint-Florentin (fronting on to the Place de la Concorde) belonged to him. When La Fayette heard what was going on, he raced into the city from his country residence, being acclaimed leader of the revolution. Fearful that the excesses of the 1789 Revolution were about to be repeated, deputies made La Fayette head of a restored National Guard and charged him with keeping order. They were also willing to proclaim him as ruler—but, sensibly, he refused. Prime Minister Polignac declared that what was happening on the streets of Paris was merely a riot and he was prepared to lose his head if he were wrong. "Not much of a present that," commented one lady of the court. Lord Rothesay, the British Ambassador, Pozzo di Borgo, the Russian Ambassador, and the Papal Nuncio went to Saint-Cloud and urged the elderly king to withdraw the four ordinances before it was too late. In the event that the monarchy collapsed, Talleyrand's initial preference was for the king's young grandson, Henri, to assume the throne under the title of Henri V with a regency governed by Louis-Philippe, Duke d'Orléans, which would have the advantage of presenting a semblance of legitimacy.

Meanwhile, on 28, 29 and 30 July, the insurrection ran amok and the royalist troops under the command of General Marmont were forced to leave the city, abandoning it to the revolutionaries. The tolling of a bell announced the departure of Charles X. The preliminaries of Charles X's abdication were that a few minutes after midnight on 31 July, he was warned that the Parisian mob were planning to attack his residence at Saint-Cloud. He decided to leave for Versailles with his family and the court, with the exception of the Duke d'Angoulême, who stayed behind with his troops, and the Duchess d'Angoulême, who was absent taking the waters at Vichy. The governor of the Palace of Versailles told him that this building was not safe, so the royal cortege moved on to the nearby Trianon arriving at 5 o'clock in the morning. When the Duke d'Angoulême arrived from Saint-Cloud with his troops, Charles X ordered a departure for the town of Rambouillet, some 30 kilometres to the south-west, where they arrived shortly before midnight on the same day. It was here for the first time that the king grasped the dimensions of the insurrection.

The Duchess d'Angoulême, or Marie-Thérèse, was the only surviving child of Louis XVI and Marie-Antoinette. After being released from the Temple Prison in December 1795, she eventually joined the court of her uncle Louis XVIII, who was living in exile in present-day Latvia. She agreed to marry her cousin Louis Antoine, the Duke d'Angoulême, the eldest son of the Duke d'Artois, on 10 June 1799. Neither of them was particularly intelligent and both were extremely pious. The Duke d'Angoulême was probably a disappointing husband and there was a good chance the marriage was never consummated. He was small, ugly and awkwardly built, unambitious, lacked his father's charm and manners, and was widely believed to be impotent or homosexual. Nevertheless, in September 1824, when Louis XVIII died and the Duke d'Artois became Charles X, the Duke and Duchess d'Angoulême became heirs to the French throne.

On 2 August, Charles X abdicated, bypassing his son the Duke d'Angoulême in favour of his grandson Henri, Duke de Bordeaux, the Duke de Berry's posthumous child who was not yet 10 years old. At first, the Duke d'Angoulême refused to countersign the document renouncing his rights to the throne of France but eventually acquiesced. On 16 August, the royal family reached Cherbourg on the Channel coast before embarking for England on steamships provided by Louis-Philippe.

On 29 July, with the sound of musketry in the vicinity of the Tuileries, Talleyrand had already sent his secretary Édouard Colmache to Neuilly with a letter addressed to Mademoiselle Adélaïde, Louis-Philippe's sister, since she was more ambitious and determined than her brother. The letter merely stated that she should listen to Colmache who was charged with conveying to her Talleyrand's recommendations, which were that Louis-Philippe should enter Paris without delay and assume leadership of the revolutionary movement since, without this action, there was a danger that the situation would soon deteriorate into anarchy. Although he had no constitutional right to replace Charles X, with his title of Lieutenant-General of the kingdom, Louis-Philippe "can place himself at the head of everything without upsetting anybody". He was warned, however, to adopt a prudent approach by agreeing to negotiate. Adélaïde had great confidence in Talleyrand and believed the crown was simply there for her brother to pick up. Louis-Philippe himself would never have taken this initiative if he had not been pushed by his sister and Talleyrand. Once he learned that Charles X had left Paris, he passed by Talleyrand's house before reaching the Palais Royal where a group of deputies urged him to assume the throne. He asked for time to think it over, sending Sebastiani to consult Talleyrand, who replied immediately: "Accept!" Fortified by this directive, Louis-Philippe went to the city hall where he was acclaimed king by the crowd and where La Fayette kissed his hand. He appeared on the balcony waving the tricolour flag and was proclaimed "King of the Barricades" by the insurgents massed below. The Chamber of Deputies and the Chamber of Peers met on 3 August, ignoring the deposed king's ordinances. La Fayette went back into retirement, happy to do so. At the age of 76, Talleyrand, "the cat who always falls on his feet", was back in business. It had been forty-one years since the French Revolution and sixteen since the first Bourbon Restoration.

CHAPTER XXI
AMBASSADOR TO LONDON

Without leaving his residence and without his name being mentioned in public, with the aid of Thiers, La Fayette and Mademoiselle Adélaïde, Talleyrand had contributed to bringing the Duke d'Orléans to power. It was not the first time that the country's ruler owed his place to him. Louis-Philippe assumed the new title of King of the French—rather than King of France—and became the symbol of wisdom, peace, liberty and respect for the law. In the evening of 31 July 1830, Talleyrand was driven to the Palais Royal where, as the first noble of France, he came to pay homage to the new king.

The Constitutional Charter of 1814 was revised from a more liberal perspective, the two chambers accepting whatever they were asked to vote for. In his memoirs, Talleyrand plays down his role in the establishment of the new regime. It is believed that, at this moment, France could very easily have become a republic rather than a monarchy and he wished to minimize his role in this choice. Perhaps it was because in Louis-Philippe he found someone like himself that Talleyrand described him as "the most enlightened king of Europe". The new king and the old diplomat had respect and esteem for each other and this clearly opened up a new phase for Talleyrand's political career. Both were excellent actors capable of hiding their true feelings, they were both patient in politics, had a good business sense, were devoted to their families and had a keen appreciation of people and political events. The new king was a simple man who walked the streets of Paris with his furled umbrella at the ready, and yet he had a very high opinion of his own destiny, was infatuated with his royal birth and was immensely proud to have married Maria Amalia of Naples and Sicily, the daughter of Ferdinand IV. As he had stood on the balcony of the Parisian *Hôtel de Ville* waving the tricolor flag and singing *La Marseillaise*, it was not forgotten that he was the son of a *regicide,* Philippe Égalité. For thirty years he had been on the fringes of power and during the Bourbon Restoration had endured a number of minor humiliations at the courts of Louis XVIII and Charles X but now took his revenge over his royal cousins.

The first task of any revolutionary government is to obtain the recognition and, if possible, the support of friendly powers. If the government of the new King William IV of the United Kingdom recognized the House of Orléans as the legitimate regime ruling France, Louis-Philippe could feel confident that other governments would follow suit. The ambassador to London therefore fulfilled an important function. He needed to be someone of great political experience, a recognised diplomat, an aristocrat who was familiar with the prominent politicians in London—in fact, it was a more important post than the Minister of Foreign Affairs. Talleyrand united all of these qualifications. In the first instance, he refused to go, saying that he was too old, too tired. However, the king "demanded" that he should accept and, with the help of his sister, managed to convince him that the embassy in London was the key to French foreign policy or, to put it another way, to the maintenance of peace in Europe. Even his enemies—even the new Tsar Nicholas I of Russia—acknowledged that his presence in London would be an unambiguous sign of France's peaceful intentions and a guarantee of the new government's permanence. On a personal level, Talleyrand was flattered to be playing a major role in diplomacy once more, while the salary that accompanied this appointment was certainly another attractive feature. Furthermore, despite his expulsion at the hands of William Pitt in 1794, he still liked London and the British, and from the early days of the Revolution he had consistently promoted an alliance between England and France. His appointment was approved by all the new ministers and announced in *Le Moniteur* on 6 September 1830. The opposition in Paris expressed its disgust at the new ambassador's appointment for the Parisians who had manned the barricades felt disillusioned that an old diplomat who had never sought popularity should be appointed to such an important post. Nevertheless, Talleyrand's nomination was viewed as a most reassuring move by foreign governments, and particularly for the British Prime Minister, the Duke of Wellington. Thiers continued to support the Prince in the

Chamber of Deputies and, in return, Talleyrand passed on to him the lessons he had learned from experience: take no notice of insults; have the courage to be unpopular. Despite the enormous difference in their origins, Talleyrand had nothing but praise for "dear Thiers", who he described as flexible, subtle and shrewd. The Ministry of Foreign Affairs on the Rue du Bac was assigned to Louis-Mathieu Molé.

The nations of Europe had seen a new regime come to power in France as the result of a street revolution and had, at first, feared that they were about to witness a repetition of the catastrophic events of forty years earlier. Bearing in mind what had happened in the aftermath of the French Revolution, the other European powers seriously considered whether it was necessary to descend on France with their armies and nip this revolution in the bud. Indeed, during the few days of turmoil at the end of July 1830, the anarchists in Paris had announced that it was their intention to launch a new revolutionary crusade to liberate the peoples of Europe by force from the yoke of their oppressors. In London and Vienna these words had created alarm since people could still remember the long period of armed conflict originating in 1793.

Before leaving Paris on 22 September 1830, Talleyrand went to see the new king, who was still ensconced in the Palais Royal while the Tuileries was made ready for him. He appeared before Louis-Philippe as if for an investiture, bearing his most sumptuous robes with all his decorations and, of course, with his hair dressed and powdered. While many Parisians were glad to see the back of him, upon reaching Dover he was received like a head of state with the guns of the castle firing a salute at twilight and a troop of cavalry commanded by Wellington's son waiting to escort him to London. Before his departure from Calais, he learned that the Belgian nation had just risen up against their masters and thrown the Dutch troops out of their country. There was little doubt that the British would consider the Belgian uprising as a direct consequence of the July Rebellion in Paris and the beginning of a new upsurge in European turmoil. Already, the Revolutionary and Bonapartist elements in France were prepared to come to the aid of the Belgians. Finding a satisfactory solution to the Belgian situation would occupy Talleyrand for the next year.

Upon reaching London three days later, he was greeted by a

boisterous crowd that surrounded his carriage calling out to "Old Tally". To waves of applause, he made a speech before them wrapped in a French flag with a tricolour cockade on his hat. The Duchess de Dino arrived on 30 September with their luggage, while the Duke of Wellington made a trip to London simply to offer a grand dinner in their honour. Talleyrand was already on good terms with the country's leaders, particularly those of a liberal disposition. Thirty-six years previously the former Bishop of Autun had been chased out of England by Pitt. When invited to the Duke of Wellington's country residence, he now had his revenge by sleeping in Pitt's bed and printing a description of this event in the Parisian newspaper *Le Constitutionnel*. Although she was not particularly appreciated in Paris, Dorothea was much more at ease in London and, from the very first reception given by the Duke, people seemed to accept that her relationship with Talleyrand was quite normal, being received at the royal court as if she were the official ambassadress. Wherever they went, their arrival drew cheering crowds, while the morning newspapers reported their every deed and gesture. When Talleyrand visited the British Parliament on 2 November, the public waited outside to give him an ovation upon leaving. Gone were the days in 1792 when Londoners out walking gave the French delegation a wide berth.

Since he had not occupied a position of power since 1815, the majority of Talleyrand's former collaborators had died or had become dispersed. He had little contact with the existing embassy staff, so Dorothea became Talleyrand's principal private secretary drafting all of his letters, while he brought over Adolphe Fourier, Count de Bacourt, to be his obliging, modest, honest and faithful assistant. As usual, Montrond—who has been described as Talleyrand's jackal—lived at the embassy, was paid using secret service funds and employed in a non-official capacity to maintain contacts with the British ministers, benefiting from the information they supplied to play the stock market. He also spent his time between Paris and London keeping the court of Louis-Philippe informed of his master's activities. And there was, of course, Courtiade.

What distinguished British and French society was that in London there was a marked hierarchy in the social order. Although a significant middle class had begun to develop, the country was still effectively controlled by the hereditary aristocracy whose wealth and power seemed immutable. In contrast, visitors from France represented a strange potpourri of personalities that sometimes brought with them amusement and sometimes embarrassment. Ambassadors presenting their letters of accreditation to the not-very-bright but essentially good-natured King William IV, who had just succeeded his brother George IV, were normally expected to make a short speech. When Talleyrand met the king on 6 October, a special chair was provided so that the ambassador could sit down, which was taken as an exceptional mark of courtesy and respect on the part of the monarch. Talleyrand thanked the king but refused the seat, remaining standing throughout the whole ceremony. His speech, written at the very last minute by Dorothea, emphasized the fact that the new French Monarchy of July 1830 had been voted unanimously by the parliament (which was not entirely true) and took the opportunity of reminding the British king that the Hanoverians had usurped the Stuart family as rulers of the United Kingdom in 1714—as a way of saying that it was not at all unusual for regimes to change. He was able to give Louis-Philippe and Mademoiselle a glowing account of the ceremony at the British court and provided a further snippet of information: having been granted asylum, the exiled French King Charles X was obliged to live fifty miles from the English coast so as to render contact with France as difficult as possible. Later, in the winter of 1832/1833, at the invitation of Francis I of Austria, the members of the Bourbon family moved to Prague. Finally, Charles took up residence in Gorizia near the Mediterranean coast of Italy, where he caught cholera and died in November 1836.

The government in London was under the authority of the Duke of Wellington. As well as being concerned about maintaining peace in Europe and laying the foundations for the Entente Cordiale, signed some seventy years later, Talleyrand turned his attention to the subject of Belgium. He behaved as if the real direction of foreign policy lay in his hands since, in fact, the most important events were taking place in London. If Talleyrand met Wellington for dinner, all the ambassadors in the city wanted to know the outcome of their conversation. With reference to the Belgian revolt against the Dutch, Talleyrand believed that he could resolve this sensitive issue himself together with Wellington and his friend Bertin de Veaux, the French ambassador to The Hague. He asked Bertin to send his reports of what was taking place between the Dutch and the Belgians directly to him in London without informing the ministry in Paris. The first thing that Bertin did was to ask for the approval of this measure by his minister in Paris. Not surprisingly, Molé could not tolerate this situation, requiring Bertin to send all of his reports to Paris and expecting Talleyrand to do the same thing before proceeding at every stage of the negotiations. For his part, Talleyrand only sent Molé insignificant notes on unimportant matters. The lack of communication brought the danger that Talleyrand would not necessarily implement French governmental policy, which was all the more probable since he intended to impose his own solution. On the contrary, he felt that it was not right for Molé to interfere in his negotiations in London since he believed that he knew best where France's interests lay. If there were to be a disagreement between France, Prussia and the United Kingdom over Belgium, only Talleyrand in London was in a position to find a solution. Thus, while the relationship between Ambassador Talleyrand and the British Government was on good standing, that with Minister Molé deteriorated. Molé had made it known that France would only intervene militarily in Belgium if provoked to do so by the presence of another country's army. Lord Aberdeen, responsible for Foreign Affairs, expressed the attitude that the United Kingdom wanted to remain neutral.

The strikingly handsome Louis-Mathieu Molé had seen his father arrested and dragged away to the guillotine when he was 12 years old and then had walked by his mother's stretcher as she was carried to prison. Later, upon his mother's release he took refuge in England and Switzerland. Upon his return to France, a volume of essays he had written attracted Napoleon's attention, whom he had subsequently served without enthusiasm as an advisor on Jewish affairs. Both his health and his mentality were seriously impaired by the hardships of his upbringing and he was now exasperated to learn that a private correspondence was taking place behind his back between the new king, the king's sister and his ambassador to London. The first confrontation with the proud and sensitive Molé took place over the French invasion of Algeria. Talleyrand wanted the conquest of this country to be abandoned so as to demonstrate good faith to the United Kingdom when drawing up a treaty of alliance.

Molé reacted strongly and said he would resign if the French Army pulled out of Algiers. Following this incident, the relationship deteriorated further. Another bone of contention was that Molé and Louis-Philippe did not publish the little speech that Talleyrand had made when presenting his credentials to William IV. It was believed that the words he addressed to the King of Great Britain and Ireland, while drawing no reaction in London, would not go down well with French readers. Tallcyrand was concerned that Molé had deliberately blocked the publication of his speech, so Mme de Dino sent a copy of it to her journalist friend Thiers who published it in *Le National* newspaper. For his part, Talleyrand dealt directly with Louis-Philippe through Mademoiselle Adélaïde or indirectly through her friend the Princess de Vaudémont. In retaliation, Molé then began to communicate directly with the Duke of Wellington who, of course, showed any correspondence concerning this affair to Talleyrand. Molé began to be exasperated with Talleyrand's behaviour and offered his resignation to Louis-Philippe.

Talleyrand wrote to Molé—who was, after all, one of his long-term acquaintances—trying to restore relations, the message of the letter being basically: "Be reasonable. Do it my way." The lack of respect shown by Talleyrand and Mme de Dino for Molé soon reached new levels of contempt. In her self-appointed role of deputy ambassadress, Dorothea wrote to Mademoiselle Adélaïde: "We are not happy with the dispatches of M. Molé." Her attitude was that Molé ought not to interfere in Talleyrand's affairs, which were inescapably in the best interests of France. Such a situation could not continue and the Minister of Foreign Affairs, indignant at seeing his role eclipsed, finally threw in the towel on 17 October, being replaced by the old General Sebastiani, who just allowed his ambassador to do as he pleased. The policy of the United Kingdom, recovering from an economic crisis and having reduced the size of its army, was to maintain the present balance of power in Europe.

During the Congress of Vienna in 1814, Talleyrand had already opposed the annexation of Catholic Belgium by Protestant Netherlands. However, Castlereagh had insisted that Belgium should be merged with the Netherlands to create a country that was strong enough to be independent of France but unlikely to pose a threat to England. It had been no surprise when, on 25 August 1830, the Belgians rose up and threw their Dutch oppressors out. One simple solution to the crisis was for France to take possession of the country, but this would be opposed by Prussia, which did not want to see France occupying all of the left bank of the Rhine, as well as by the United Kingdom, which feared that the commercial city of Antwerp would fall into French hands. Talleyrand understood the Belgian crisis to be an obstacle to good relations between France and England, for the former country sympathized with the Belgians while the British were traditionally the allies of the Dutch. The courts of Europe watched anxiously to see how the British Government and Talleyrand would resolve this affair. To begin with, Talleyrand declared the principle of "non-intervention" and managed to convince the British to do the same. Non-intervention was a new concept and, when asked to define it, Talleyrand explained laconically that "it meant much the same thing as intervention". Towards the middle of the month of October 1830 and in perfect harmony, Wellington and Talleyrand proposed a European conference to be held in London, rather than in Paris as Molé had wished. The main purpose of the conference was to avoid a European war, which would have been certain if France had unilaterally invaded Belgium to keep the Dutch at bay.

The conference on the fate of Belgium began on 4 November 1830 with Talleyrand appearing at first alone, without his retinue and employing the phrase: "I am simply a man with some experience who sits down among his old friends to discuss ways of maintaining peace." The fact that France was represented as an equal with the other powers was an undeniable success for the Prince, whose authority and experience enabled him to act as chairman. On the first day, hostilities between the Dutch and the Belgian forces were brought to an end, which was equivalent to recognizing the existence of an independent and neutral Belgian state. Then came the question of who should rule the potential new country. To preserve the peace, Louis-Philippe withdrew the candidature of his son, the Duke de Nemours—a decision with which Talleyrand agreed. However, to represent France at the conference, Louis-Philippe sent a surprising emissary, Talleyrand's son Charles de Flahaut, bearing a secret message from Sebastiani. Most unfortunately, Talleyrand considered Sebastiani's proposition—splitting Belgium into four by giving a part each to the Netherlands, Prussia and France and the port of Antwerp to the United Kingdom—as nonsensical. "I would rather cut off my fist than sign a deed that brought the English back," he told Flahaut. He sent his son back to Paris with a letter explaining that maintaining peace with England was far more important than carving up Belgium. Talleyrand wrote to Sebastiani: "This leads us naturally to consider England as the power with which we should choose to maintain the closest relations... England is the only power which, like us, really wants peace." Many of the other European powers believed that they had the right to behave as they pleased, enforcing their God-given desires with artillery. Talleyrand wrote: "We support public opinion with principles... the limited range of canons is well known." Nicholas I, the Tsar of Russia since 1825, proposed sending an army of Cossacks to "resolve" the Belgian crisis. The Poles chose this moment to revolt against Russian rule, which fortuitously tied up the Cossack soldiers.

In London, the Tories had ruled the country for sixty years and had always resisted the clamour of those championing political reform. Wellington's government fell on 15 November 1830 and was replaced by the Whig Government of Lord Grey, a conscientious and incorruptible aristocrat. Grey's term as Prime Minister was an outstanding one, finally seeing the introduction of several notable reforms: the poor law was updated, child labour restricted, slavery abolished in nearly all of the British Empire and the British electoral system thoroughly refashioned. If Talleyrand had a good understanding with "the Iron Duke", he had an even better one with Lord Grey, having shared a cup of tea with him on several occasions. A month later, Grey and Talleyrand managed to obtain a vote in favour of "the independence of Belgium". The conference then began to lose its way—was its purpose to settle the affairs of the Netherlands, which lived by trade, or those of the rebellious Belgians, whose economy was based on industry? Louis-Philippe once again sent Flahaut to London with orders to carry out his decision on the division of Belgium. Talleyrand and the British representatives refused categorically to support his son and, on 20 January 1831, decided upon "the perpetual neutrality of Belgium and the inviolability of its territory". It should be noted that Ambassador Talleyrand had overruled—or one might say ignored—the direct instructions of his king, his minister and his son.

As regards his son Charles, Count de Flahaut, over a period of thirty years Talleyrand had addressed affectionate letters to him, but these feelings were not always reciprocated. Flahaut's mind had been turned against his father during his childhood by his mother Adélaïde and, in the present circumstances, by his wife. In the aftermath of the Battle of Waterloo, where he had been an aide-de-camp to Napoleon, Flahaut ended up in the United Kingdom and, penniless but extremely attractive to women, had succeeded in winning the hand of the heiress Margaret Mercer Elphinstone. It could easily have been predicted that between "Meg Mercer", as her friends called her, and the Duchess de Dino there would be a battle of wills. Talleyrand had been dismayed by Louis-Philippe's plan to resolve the Belgian crisis by dividing the country up, while Flahaut had been annoyed at the failure of his mission to London. Thereafter, Talleyrand forbade his son to come to London. Flahaut thought that Dorothea was responsible for this decision, calling her "a horrid little serpent" and "a lying little devil", although the Prince had clearly acted upon his own assessment of his son's abilities. This situation was partly resolved when Flahaut was appointed French ambassador to Berlin, although during this period his wife was intriguing against her father-in-law since she had decided that her husband ought to be the next French ambassador to London. The hostility and calumny of this couple towards Talleyrand and Dorothea is quite remarkable.

Talleyrand had always favoured Prince Leopold of Saxe-Coburg and Gotha as his preferred candidate to be the new King of the Belgians—who, despite his Germanic origins, happened to be a British subject living in England. In a meeting with Foreign Secretary Lord Palmerston, the former Bishop of Autun so manipulated the conversation that it appeared as if Palmerston himself was the first to propose this idea. Talleyrand pretended to be pleasantly surprised and enthusiastically endorsed the suggestion. In what was thought to be the final act of the conference, Leopold I was elected King of the Belgians and entered Brussels on 21 July 1831. His first wife, a member of the British Royal family, having died during childbirth, he married one of Louis-Philippe's daughters, Louise-Marie d'Orléans, thus ensuring the support of the French monarchy. The treaty concerning Belgium was not actually signed until 15 November 1831, more than a year later than the date when Talleyrand thought it might come into effect. Louis-Philippe and Mademoiselle Adélaïde sent lukewarm congratulations, while the French press printed a torrent of insults and sarcasm.

These attitudes can be contrasted sharply with the highest esteem with which Talleyrand and France were held in London. The reputation of France had been fortified without having to go to war and the stability of the Orléans regime had been confirmed with the added prospect of a bright economic future. While there was widespread deception in Paris, the agreement was celebrated as a triumph in London, with the Lord Mayor giving a special dinner to honour this victory of intelligence and peace. Talleyrand proposed a toast to "the spectacle of liberty protected by the law", which was received with a thunderous ovation. However, neither France, Prussia nor the Netherlands were content with the outcome of the conference. The king of the Netherlands had from the very beginning been a troublesome partner and had brought the negotiations to a halt on several occasions. When the Dutch wrote a long, complicated and procrastinating proposal to the conference, Talleyrand made the remark: "When you are right, you do not write forty pages!" However, this was not the end of the affair since there were a few border issues to settle. In the first instance, Belgium attempted to annex Luxembourg, while Talleyrand required the new Belgian king to demolish the fortresses marking the border between Belgium and France. Then, on 2 August 1832, to Talleyrand's disgust, William I of the Netherlands invaded Belgium again. Since the British and French Governments demonstrated a united front, the Dutch retreated rapidly from Antwerp after the threat of French intervention and a blockade of its ports by the British fleet. With the recapture of Antwerp, the war was effectively over but William I continued the struggle for another eight years, with the conflict becoming a burden on the Dutch economy. In 1839, William was forced to abandon the war and he abdicated a year later. The very existence of Belgium—its independence, neutrality, frontiers and ruling family—and the fact that it was created without a full-scale European war, are almost single-handedly the achievements of Talleyrand. Never again would France and the United Kingdom make war on each other.

The Polish disaster continued. Talleyrand attempted to persuade the

United Kingdom, Prussia and Austria to intervene on behalf of the uprising in Warsaw—in vain. Russian troops crushed the Polish revolt mercilessly, leading Foreign Minister Sebastiani to make the infamous remark: "Order reigns in Warsaw." For a number of years, the Tsar of Russia's representative in London had been Prince Khristofor Liéven, although it was his wife Dorothea who established herself as a major political force, totally eclipsing her husband. In England's vibrant political environment, the Princess Liéven exercised a secret and intimate charm over the British Prime Minister, Lord Grey, with which Talleyrand could not compete. Through her ambition, wit and knowledge of the world, she became a leader of society; invitations to her house were most sought after and she introduced the waltz to England. The Duchess de Dino was younger and more beautiful, so at first the two ladies began to compete on both a personal level and on behalf of the two countries they represented. However, as Wellington's secretary wrote: "Mme de Dino was so intelligent and Talleyrand so remarkable that Mme de Liéven was irresistibly attracted to them." It was not long before the two Dorotheas became friends, although Mme de Dino was not entirely swayed by her Russian namesake, treating her like a spoilt child and describing her as a little bit vulgar, incapable of thinking for herself and unable to remain alone for five minutes. Like the Princess Liéven, Dorothea came to know all the important personalities in the British Government and kept Mademoiselle Adélaïde informed of any events that would contribute in a positive manner to Talleyrand's image. Adélaïde remained a particularly valuable channel for communicating with Louis-Philippe.

The French Embassy in London was located at this time at 50 Portland Place, which rapidly became the fashionable place to be seen, although Talleyrand's mobility was seriously challenged by the grand staircase leading up to his first-floor apartments. By October 1830, he moved to 21 Hanover Square with his bedroom easily accessible on the ground floor. After they had moved in, the owner, Lord Grey, informed him that the premises were haunted! Even if the court of Louis-Philippe in Paris was considered somewhat bourgeois, the French Embassy in London impressed with its magnificence. The writer Prosper Mérimée wrote about Talleyrand's life in London: "Wherever he goes, he creates a court and lays down the law." Dorothea wrote proudly to Barante that Talleyrand's dinners were a landmark in the capital's gastronomy, but the cost was likely to ruin them. Louis-Philippe had guaranteed to maintain his former Grand Chamberlain's salary at 100,000 francs, but if he continued with his entertainment programme, he was likely to bankrupt himself within the year. Dorothea wrote to Adélaïde asking for supplementary financial support.

People were fascinated by the French ambassador's costume of yesteryear, his conversation which was a never-ending source of anecdotes and his age; this "uncommon man" was treated with respect and admiration by all levels of society. One British journalist wrote: "He has here the world at his feet; all the English nobility keenly seek his company; the diplomats of every country kneel before him." One of his regular guests was the French poet Alphonse de Lamartine. It is a mystery how the most upright and romantic of poets and the most obdurate and cynical of diplomats established a friendship of mutual admiration. Lamartine was perfectly aware of Talleyrand's reputation with money, women and the truth—but perhaps chose to focus on the services he had rendered to his country. With his incredible intuition, Talleyrand predicted that Lamartine was destined for a career in politics as a great orator and tried to entice him into supporting Louis-Philippe— without success. He gave a stunning description of himself: "They say I am immoral and Machiavellian; I am merely unmoved and scornful. I have never given false advice to a government or a ruler, but I do not collapse when they do. After the shipwreck, one needs pilots to save the survivors. I remain composed and bring them to any port." Lamartine told him to his face that certain of his past actions were generally considered as profoundly dubious—particularly the episcopal letter he had written to the diocese of Autun in the early months of 1789. He replied: "For statesmen there are several ways of being honest; I see that my way is not yours, but one day you will appreciate me more than you think. My suspected crimes are the dreams of idiots. Does a clever man ever need crime? It is the resource of political idiots… Some people say vice, but crime? Shame on them…" The meaning would seem to be that both crime and war are committed by thoughtless people because they do not know how to negotiate and convince, only how to kill. These remarks might also be placed under the heading of "changing the subject".

Alongside his political success, Talleyrand was also feted in London society and invited everywhere. William IV requested his presence at the Court of St James, at Windsor Castle and at the Royal Pavilion in Brighton, while the French ambassador looked upon these invitations "as an order". The king had spent his formative years as an officer in the British Navy and had the habit of making rather risqué toasts after the ladies had left the dinner table. In the autumn, Talleyrand would be found in the country residences of the aristocracy, while evenings in town were spent playing whist at the Traveller's Club on Pall Mall or at White's on St James's Street. All the London salons were open to him and he was particularly keen on attending that of Lord and Lady Holland, whose company he appreciated. When he left London, he thanked the Hollands for having welcomed him in their household and for making him feel at home.

If relations with Lord Grey were close and confident, the same could not be said for those with Lord Palmerston, the Secretary of State for Foreign Affairs. Palmerston did not have the same unswerving admiration for Talleyrand as Wellington and Lord Grey. One day a satirical cartoon appeared bearing an astonishing resemblance to Talleyrand and Palmerston entitled "The Lame Leading the Blind", after which the flamboyant young minister distanced himself from the flattery and charisma of the French ambassador. Questions were raised in Parliament by the Marquess of Londonderry about the spell that Talleyrand exercised over the British Government. "That ass Londonderry," as one of his colleagues called him, was Lord Castlereagh's half-brother. Wellington, who belonged to the same political party as Londonderry, came to the Prince's rescue noting that he had been described as "an illustrious personality", not least by Londonderry's own half-sibling. Lord Holland, who had been present with Talleyrand when the news of Napoleon's death reached Paris, described him as a victim who had been "shamefully traduced... and misrepresented". The old man was brought to tears by the esteem in which he was held, particularly on the part of the Duke of Wellington. Never in his own country had he received such appreciation.

Casimir Périer was a prominent French banker and businessman who had become president of the Council of Ministers and Minister of Interior in the spring of 1831. In March 1832, during a cholera outbreak in Paris, Périer visited the sick, fell ill the next day and died six weeks later. Following this incident, Charles de Rémusat came to London to ask Talleyrand if he would form a new government. Rémusat had lunch with Dorothea, who told him: "M. de Talleyrand is much too determined not to become involved in any administration to allow himself to be moved on this matter." To make herself quite clear she added: "I would not permit it." Talleyrand felt that he could best serve his country's interests in the position he was already occupying. Despite Royer-Collard and Henri Guizot urging him to accept, he showed no enthusiasm, for Louis-Philippe had not personally asked him to assume this function.

These events took place while his health had been surprisingly good but, later on, Dorothea wrote to Mademoiselle Adélaïde that he was exhausted by the Belgian affair and in need of a respite from the weather and pollution of London. Bacourt was momentarily bedridden and the new assistant Laborde knew nothing. But it was not until 20 June 1832, leaving the reliable and newly recovered Bacourt in charge of the embassy, that Talleyrand left London for consultations with Louis-Philippe, before going on to Bourbon-l'Archambault to take the waters, to care for his legs, to eat only when necessary and "not to have to speak a word on any subject whatsoever". It was not an enjoyable experience as Dorothea had retired to Rochecotte, the wave of cholera was advancing across the country and he caught a bad cold. He soon abandoned the spa town and sought refuge with Dorothea in her château. He returned to London on 14 October. At the beginning of 1833, he learned with great sorrow of the death of the Princess de Vaudémont, the daughter-in-law of the Countess de Brionne, both of whom are believed to have been his mistresses in those radiant days before the Revolution. Another of his closest colleagues who passed away in April was Emmerich Dalberg, while Gilbert du Motier, General de La Fayette, died in May 1834. Despite the fact that La Fayette was a revered hero on both sides of the Atlantic and had played a role in French politics on-and-off for over fifty years, Talleyrand scorned him as "Gilles le Grand". His cruel verdict on La Fayette was: "Mediocrities play a part in great events simply because they happen to be present."

Against the background of these irreplaceable losses, Talleyrand did not weaken but continued with his sumptuous dinners, his brilliant receptions, his programme of investments and his heedless gambling. Prosper Mérimée, the author of *Carmen,* noted: "There is nothing so amusing as to see around him the most influential members of the House of Lords obsequious, almost servile." He also gives a detailed account of Talleyrand's habit of rinsing his nose with two glasses of warm water and expelling it—according to Mérimée—through his mouth, with an audience of the most noble male and female members of the British aristocracy observing the scene with rapt attention. Mérimée describes Talleyrand: "A great mound of flannel wrapped in a blue costume and dominated by a death's head covered in parchment." His limp had become so marked that he appeared to be in danger of falling at each step.

And then Talleyrand began to feel that he had strayed into a world where he no longer belonged. Sebastiani was replaced by the Duke de Broglie as the French Minister of Foreign Affairs, a man who required his ambassadors to do as they were told. Palmerston's behaviour became more offhand and arrogant, and he made life difficult for Talleyrand by dealing directly with the French Government through the British Embassy in Paris. Lord Grey had resigned and, under the new electoral laws, the membership of the British Parliament had changed. Furthermore, the king of the Netherlands continued to harass the Belgians. At 79 years of age, Talleyrand had had enough. In September 1833, he asked to be given a break and suggested that it should become permanent. However, the king and the Duke de Broglie, now the new French prime minister, were not in agreement, believing that his presence in London was indispensable. He spent four months at Valençay, returning to London on 13 December, stating that he would retire definitively in April 1834. Then his assistant Bacourt suddenly began to benefit from Talleyrand's ill-humour. Was he jealous? Had Dorothea succumbed to the charms of this "tall, thin young man, with such a handsome figure, of an extreme elegance and very amusing"? Indeed, Bacourt and Dorothea had established a very close relationship which was to last until her death in 1862. Meanwhile, Thiers had committed the cardinal sin of getting married to a 16-year-old young lady and Dorothea asked herself whether he was still such a desirable political ally and friend.

The summer of 1834 marked a major change in London's diplomatic life. Palmerston had appointed Sir Stratford Canning as British ambassador to St Petersburg, the one man whom he knew the tsar would not receive. For twenty-two years, the Princess Liéven had been one of the leaders of British society but, due to this diplomatic incident, her husband, the Russian ambassador, was recalled. She was horrified about the prospect of leaving her comfortable existence in London and refused to return to Russia. The Duchess de Dino too liked living in England—except for the climate and the cost of living—but to remove Talleyrand from Palmerston's conceit, she also believed that the moment had come to leave. Their mission was accomplished.

Throughout his career Talleyrand had sought a formal political and economic alliance between France and the United Kingdom, believing that this was the foundation of European peace and progress. In the months before his departure from London he attempted to bring this to fruition. Palmerston, while not refusing, preferred a quadripartite alliance including Spain and Portugal, both of whose governments required support. Such a treaty was signed on 22 April 1834, but Talleyrand found it gave liberties to the United Kingdom that were denied to France. This proved to be his swansong. On 18 August, at the age of 80, he placed his signature for the last time on an official document and four days later found himself in Paris. His secretary Colmache returned to him the key of his briefcase which he had left behind and his association with the French Embassy in London ended.

CHAPTER XXII
THE BELL TOLLS

Talleyrand, whose reputation was admired in political circles throughout Europe, returned to Paris to face a storm of abuse from the press. He was accused by a younger generation of journalists of the most nonsensical crimes against France: of being a "Jacobin", a *regicide*, a "Royalist conspirator". Even Chateaubriand, who should have known better, had no good words for him—did he for anyone? It took someone like Metternich to understand his true contribution: "M. de Talleyrand as a man and as a conscience represented the true France", for every one of his changes of allegiance had been in the interests of his country. He believed that constitutional monarchy, the liberty of the people, an alliance with the United Kingdom and peace in Europe were more important goals than satisfying the parade of regimes whose transient ambitions he had served.

Upon the couple returning to France from London, Talleyrand's only ambition was to return to Valençay. Dorothea had gone on ahead, realising that the Prince could very easily be detained in Paris by Louis-Philippe, by Mademoiselle Adélaïde or by the new Prime Minister Broglie, who all treated him with great deference. Dorothea was sure that he should retire now at what could be understood as a positive moment in his life, before the situation deteriorated and he was forced to go, although it was still not clear to everyone whether his departure from London was definitive. The king's son, the Duke d'Orléans, visiting Valençay in October (despite being discouraged from doing so by Charles de Flahaut), stated that Talleyrand's presence in London seemed as necessary as ever. Doubt about his future plans was removed when he sent his letter of resignation. Dorothea drafted it; Talleyrand introduced a few corrections and then it was passed to Royer-Collard for comments. When judged complete, he signed it and sent it to the Ministry of Foreign Affairs on 13 November 1834. Dorothea informed Thiers of his decision to retire and Talleyrand also wrote to the king and to Mademoiselle separately. The message in all these letters is much the same: the fear of no longer being equal to himself. Louis-Philippe realised that he was losing one of the great pillars of his regime: "I feel the need to have the support of your experience and, above all, the advice of that friendship that is so valuable to me." Dozens of letters arrived from both France and England expressing disbelief and stating that affairs could not be carried out successfully without him. Talleyrand named as his successor in London a career diplomat, Maximilien Gérard, Count de Rayneval, in whom he had the greatest confidence, but his opinion was disregarded and Sebastiani took his place. As an omen of the changing times, the Palace of Westminster, the home of the British Parliament, was accidentally destroyed by fire three days after submitting his resignation.

At Valençay, a château of almost royal splendour, he turned his attention to his people, the village and his domain concentrating on all that was liberal and humane in his nature. He rebuilt the town hall and restored the church tower, copying the style of the Church of St Martin in Vevey, Switzerland, and on which one can still read the date in Roman numerals MDCCCXXXVI—1836. Influenced by his childhood experience with his great-grandmother in her château at Chalais, he became the generous and kind-hearted patriarch who provided a pharmacy where his people could receive medicines. At times, there would be the free distribution of bread, wood, linen and money. This was hardly the same person who lived in Paris and had the popular reputation as the very personification of a self-indulgent and venal political schemer.

Returning to Paris from his château in December, he received an incessant series of visitors at the Rue Saint-Florentin. All society presented itself before the stiff-legged figure seated with his club foot resting on a stool for all to see. He did not always enter into conversation with the stream of visitors but, when he did, he could be brilliant and profound while his audience listened with delight. He was suspected of preparing his witticism beforehand, but they were too spontaneous for this to be true all the time. Once back in the capital, he was attracted again to political intrigue since he wanted to find a place in the government for his protégé Adolphe Thiers. He attended the court, meeting Louis-Philippe and Mademoiselle again. One of those present has left us a description of the scene: his costume was too big, his hat too large. He walked with the aid of a cane which, at each step, struck the iron support on his right leg, so that this tapping noise announced his arrival and departure.

Since the king continued to consult him on matters of state and twice proposed that he should go as ambassador to Vienna, he still did not have the air of a man who had withdrawn from political life. On 13 December 1834, Adolphe Thiers was received as a member of the Académie Française. Talleyrand, attended by a flotilla of elegant ladies, came to listen to his acceptance speech and to confirm his support for this candidate. As the patriarch entered the auditorium, those present rose spontaneously to their feet, confirming that many highly placed people did not share the popular press's opinion of him. In his speech, Thiers paid particular attention to two men seated before him in the room: Talleyrand and Royer-Collard.

In the summer at Valençay, he took great interest in the vegetable and flower gardens, and had espalier fruit trees planted along the garden walls. The farmyard and the surrounding forests were stocked with domestic animals and game that could be served at his table. He asked Bacourt in London to send him some seeds of the Scots Pine so that he could create a forest of them in the vicinity. He was still faithful to Brie cheese, whose reputation he had extolled in Vienna in 1814, naming it "the king of cheeses". As one visitor remarked unkindly: "The only king he did not betray."

From 1831, Dorothea had begun to keep a journal and from 1834 onwards wrote in it nearly every day. It confirms that they spent the winter at the Rue Saint-Florentin and the summer at Valençay, with shorter periods spent at the Château de Rochecotte. Whether in Paris or in the countryside, they entertained on a lavish scale. Among the stream of visitors to Valençay were old political allies, such as Noailles, Montmorency and La Besnardière, while harmony now reigned between himself and Élie Decazes. Adolphe Thiers and his wife were, of course, always welcome. Other distinguished visitors included Harriet, the Marchioness of Clanricarde, a great favourite and daughter of his old British acquaintance George Canning, and John Hamilton, the son of

Alexander Hamilton who had been such an agreeable host in Philadelphia in 1794. An unexpected guest was the Princess Liéven's stormy personality, the former Russian leader of London society. After her husband was recalled to St Petersburg, she had refused to return to her homeland and conducted an aimless existence around Europe until in 1837 she met and began to share her life with the liberal politician and author François Guizot, a situation that would continue until her death. Relations with Charles de Flahaut, who was now an equerry to the Duke d'Orléans, had deteriorated since Talleyrand had vetoed his son's visit to London in 1831. Forgetting his earlier reluctance, his neighbour and political ally Pierre-Paul Royer-Collard frequently made the journey to Valençay from his nearby residence at Châteauvieux.

An attaché at the British Embassy in Paris, Henry Greville, brother of the famous British political diarists of the time, was a regular visitor at the Rue Saint-Florentin and enthusiastically praised Talleyrand for his manners, his conversation and his kindness. In the autumn of 1834, he visited Valençay, giving a detailed description of the routine at the château: breakfast at 11.30; conversation in the salon until 2 p.m.; dinner at 5.30 p.m.; every evening the Prince went for an hour's carriage ride; the end of each day was marked by a glass of Madeira wine in which the Prince soaked a biscuit; a card table would be brought out for a game of whist; the post arrived from Paris at 11 p.m. When there were no visitors, he shut himself away with his books. At times the guests hunted deer with a pack of hounds, while on other days there might be a shooting party.

Since Dorothea owned the charming Château de Rochecotte in the Loire valley, they often spent periods living there. One day in the early autumn of 1834, Talleyrand and the Duchess de Dino returned to Valençay from Rochecotte to find it heaving with a group of unknown and uninvited visitors. The domestic staff told them that it was a Mme Dudevant, a M. de Musset and their retinue. They discovered that Mme Dudevant was better known as the famous author Georges Sand, who also owned a château in the Berry region. The visitors were received coolly in the main salon… and left. Three weeks later, on 15 October, an article appeared in the *Revue des Deux Mondes* signed Georges Sand which caused consternation. It described both Talleyrand and Dorothea in the most vulgar and insulting language, insinuating that they were monsters of impurity, debauchery and arrogance, and she hoped that Talleyrand would die a long and painful death. Georges Sand dismissed the article as a passing whim, but both of her victims were dumbfounded. As was his long-standing policy, Talleyrand did not react publicly, although he let his friends know that he was shocked by such rudeness, which perhaps told us more about the character of Georges Sand than that of her astonished hosts.

Not long after his installation at Valençay, the most faithful member of his harem died, Marie-Thérèse Poniatowska, the Princess Tyszkiewicz. She had her own apartment in the château and could also quite easily have lived at the Hôtel Talleyrand in Paris, but preferred to stay in her own premises further along the street. Of legendary generosity, she is buried in the Chapel Saint-Maurice in the village, alongside her idol whose company she had shared for twenty-seven years. Her death was a cruel reminder of his own declining health, which resulted in experiments with all sorts of remedies for the treatment of his long-suffering legs. No longer trusting himself to walk in the gardens, he was pushed around in the fancy wheelchair rediscovered in the basement of the Tuileries Palace that had once belonged to Louis XVIII. His fidelity to the Roman Catholic religion had always been a subject of doubt but, surprisingly, he attended mass every Sunday for he appreciated the church as the upholder of moral and social values in the community. One of his favourite authors was Bishop Jacques-Bénigne Bossuet, a French theologian, considered as one of the most brilliant orators of all time and a masterly French stylist. Court preacher to Louis XIV, Bossuet had been a strong advocate of the divine right of kings, who, according to him, received their power directly from God.

It should come as no surprise that, following the return from London, the intrepid Montrond came to live at Valençay. He was a vestige of a period in Talleyrand's past life and drew out the puritan in Dorothea. Unfortunately, with old age he had become less charming and harder to please. He poured criticism in coarse language on Talleyrand's neighbours, his guests, his domestic staff, his food, his wine, his horses. While the Prince suffered these reproaches in silence, Mme de Dino, who had been trying to get rid of Montrond for years, let him know quite bluntly that his presence at the château was irksome and that he would probably find life more agreeable in Paris. In October 1834, he was expelled unceremoniously from the château expressing disgust at the treatment reserved for an old friend. The next time Montrond met Talleyrand during one of his visits to Paris, he cut the Prince dead. Nevertheless, relations were soon re-established between the inseparable "child Jesus from Hell" and the "limping devil".

In December 1835, the Princess de Talleyrand died in her house on the Rue de Lille. Talleyrand had not seen his wife for twenty years. The Prince had been very concerned about what would happen to her following the demise of the Duke de San Carlos, but she had behaved with intelligence and discretion. In death she achieved a dignity that she had not always known in life, since it was the Archbishop of Paris himself, Monsignor de Quélan, who administered the last rites. Apart from informing people and arranging her funeral, Talleyrand seemed quite indifferent to her death, merely remarking offhandedly that: "This simplifies my position a lot." He was no longer a married priest and hypocrisy was not one of his vices.

Although he maintained his mental alertness to the very end, his agreeable life at Valençay was sometimes troubled by insomnia. Rather than wake up the other residents in the middle of the night for a game of whist, he would either read his dear Bossuet or write some pages of his memoirs. Another distraction was to add to his large collection of maxims, which he entered in a large red notebook kept in his pocket. Here, among many other gems, we find the following Voltairean phrase: "My course is run. I have planted some trees; I have built a house; I have done a lot of other stupid things; is it not time to stop?" On the subject of good manners, he wrote: "Elegance and simplicity together are in every situation and for every person the distinguishing feature of the nobility." He remarks that one cannot govern a country while ignoring the opinion of the general public, but that while public opinion is a vital reference, it is dangerous for governments to base their policies on it. In other words, in politics people's opinions matter and may indicate how far one may go, but not in which direction. Another epigrammatic phrase: "I forgive those people who do not share my opinion, but I do not forgive them for not having one of their own." While he had often been accused for changing his allegiance, he had never been reproached for steadfastly maintaining his opinion through each change of regime.

In January 1836, the unpopular government of the Duke de Broglie lost its majority in the Chamber of Deputies and the king chose as Prime Minister a man he was certain would soon fail—Adolphe Thiers. During the summer, the relationship between Thiers and Louis-Philippe became more and more strained since, in order to conduct his own foreign policy, the king blocked many of Thiers's diplomatic initiatives. Thiers suggested to the king that it might be better for France to follow the British model, giving the Prime Minister the power to decide on all diplomatic and military affairs but Louis-Philippe insisted that he was the chief of diplomacy and head of the army. Surprisingly, Thiers wanted to invade Spain. When it became clear that Talleyrand no longer supported Thiers, he had no alternative but to resign as Prime Minister, which took place on 29 August 1836—his place being taken by Molé. Even more surprisingly, given their abrasive relationship in 1830, Molé's first action was to write a letter of gushing admiration to Talleyrand seeking approval for his appointment. Dorothea wrote in her journal: "The friendship of the king for M. de Talleyrand… forbids any minister to be on bad terms with him."

In the autumn of 1836, Talleyrand was staying at Rochecotte when, among other visitors, the author Honoré de Balzac came to stay. He was enchanted by Talleyrand who asked him to visit him at Valençay. We owe to Balzac the following quotation from *Le Père Goriot,* where one of his characters, the criminal "Vautrin", seems to speak the mind of Talleyrand: "A man who prides himself that he never changed his mind is a man who undertakes always to follow a straight line, a fool who believes in infallibility." And he adds the political leitmotif: "There are no principles, there are only events; there are no laws, there are only circumstances… The superior man accepts events in order to direct them." Dorothea was not particularly captivated by Balzac's presence, finding him "clever no doubt" but vulgar.

In December 1836, Pauline de Talleyrand was 16 years old. The Prince treated her with a special tenderness and, whenever she was away from him, sent her charming little letters. They would take carriage rides through the streets of Paris together, particularly to the places where he had spent his childhood and youth. He made sure that she received a religious upbringing conducted by her confessor, the Abbé Dupanloup, while, in total contrast, her education was influenced by Voltaire's enlightened ideas. He described to her the life of his uncle Alexandre-Angélique, the late Archbishop of Paris, and asked her to treat the present archbishop, Monsignor de Quélen, as if he were her grandfather. Pauline repeated what he said to Dupanloup and eventually his sympathetic words reached the ears of de Quélan.

Returning to Valençay feeling very tired, Talleyrand decided to rewrite his will. He took the opportunity to retrace his life giving a rapid, simple explanation of his political career since he resigned from the bishopric of Autun: "My position ordained that I must find my own path. I looked for it alone because I did not want my life to depend on any party... I thought for a long time and halted at the idea of serving France as France in whatever situation; a great deal of help was needed everywhere. Thus, I did not blame myself for having served all the regimes from the Directory until the time I am writing." He then lists the governments that he has assisted, concluding with: "I did not abandon any of them until they had abandoned themselves." He emphasized that his political position had never been influenced by the interests of any political party nor even his own, only "the true interests of France which are furthermore, in my opinion, never contrary to the true interests of Europe". He acknowledges that he owes his wealth particularly to Napoleon and that his descendants should never forget it. The emperor had been generous it is true, but never to such a degree as to satisfy the enormous appetite of his profligate minister. At the end of Napoleon's reign, Talleyrand owned nothing other than the properties at Valençay, Pont-de-Sains and the Rue Saint-Florentin, so the greater part of his wealth had to have been assembled after the departure of Napoleon. No satisfactory explanation has ever been offered as to where the great fortune came from that allowed him to live in comfort for the last decades of his life. Stating that all of it came from Napoleon may have been a ploy to give a plausible explanation to a situation difficult to explain, such as the rumours of misplaced government revenue in the spring of 1814. When Talleyrand died, he left a considerable sum of money to Dorothea, to Pauline and to his nephews, but this is only a tiny amount compared to what he had spent on living in luxury, on simple generosity to his family and on gambling. Expenditure on his houses and his dining table corresponded to the expected idea of his social rank. "Opulence for M. de Talleyrand," wrote Alphonse de Lamartine, "was a policy as much as an elegance of his life."

Further on in his will, he placed the manuscript of his memoirs in the hands of Bacourt, requesting that it should not be published for thirty years. By that time, both Bacourt and Dorothea had died. Bacourt had passed the manuscript to other trustees asking them to delay publication until 1888 (fifty years later), by which time they too had died. It was the younger Duke de Broglie, Albert, grandson of Mme de Staël, who issued the memoirs in 1891 fifty-three years after Talleyrand's death. As a source illuminating the details of his life, this document is not particularly helpful because his memory was not always accurate nor his pen truthful, and it is strongly suspected that both Dorothea and Bacourt felt called upon to rewrite some passages to reflect the social mores of the mid-nineteenth century rather than what actually happened. By the time they came to be published, Napoleon's reputation had soared and Talleyrand's had sunk almost into oblivion.

At the château, Talleyrand liked to show visitors his large collection of paintings and marble busts, as well as his library containing 10,000 books. One of the paintings on display represented the tomb of Charles X, who had died in November 1836 and was buried in a monastery in Slovenia. Dorothea had won the painting in a lottery and presented it to the Prince in the hope that he would appreciate it. "You are quite right," observed Talleyrand profoundly. "It is true that Charles X was the most hopelessly incapable king and the one who made the greatest possible number of mistakes. However, I always looked upon him and liked him as the most loyal and agreeable person I ever knew."

When in Paris, Talleyrand called every day on Montrond, who had fallen ill. He could no longer climb the stairs to Montrond's apartment but asked for news while waiting outside in his carriage. However, one day Louis-Philippe wanted him to convey to Montrond the news that his son was engaged to be married, so Talleyrand asked to be carried into the house to deliver the message in person. Why should the king show such interest in an old rascal like Montrond? According to the diarist Thomas

Raikes, Montrond possessed information about the early life of the king that was best kept between themselves.

The question of whom Ferdinand, the Duke d'Orléans, Louis-Philippe's eldest son, should marry had been preoccupying French politicians and ambassadors for some time. Finally, in 1837, the negotiators' choice for his wife came to rest on the German Protestant Duchess Hélène von Mecklenburg-Schwerin, the King of Prussia's niece. The elder Duke de Broglie was sent to Germany as ambassador extraordinary to present the official request and bring the princess back to France. Since Monsignor de Quélen, the Archbishop of Paris, would not marry a Protestant princess in Notre Dame Cathedral, the marriage was celebrated on 30 May 1837 at the Château de Fontainebleau. Despite suffering from a profound lassitude, Talleyrand participated in the ceremony with Dorothea and Pauline, spending four days in Mme de Maintenon's former apartment at the château. Also present was his son's wife, Margaret de Flahaut and her daughter. Following the recent death of another of Flahaut's daughters, normal family relations had been re-established with Dorothea, although with "Meg Mercer" it was never going to be plain sailing. Talleyrand and Pauline did not remain for the full celebrations that continued for several days but returned to Valençay, where he held a grand dinner for all the local notables followed by a village fête. In the autumn of 1837, Dorothea allowed Montrond to be invited back to the château knowing that he was Talleyrand's preferred companion. At the end of the autumn, the Prince left Valençay for Paris for the last time with "an excessive and extraordinary pang of regret".

CHAPTER XXIII
RECONCILIATION

Talleyrand only had a few more months to live. Dorothea reminded him from time to time that he had never reached a satisfactory settlement with the Roman Catholic Church and might die without showing sufficient signs of remorse. In the eyes of Rome, the way he had led his life was immoral. The death of his wife had improved the situation but his status as a wayward bishop remained unresolved. One solution to avoid a scandal at his funeral would have been for him to die outside France. As early as 1835, Monsignor de Quélan, who had promised Talleyrand's uncle to take an interest in the nephew, contacted Rome to determine under what circumstances the Prince would be granted a proper Christian burial. The reply came back from Pope Gregory XVI: "A public retraction of his errors." Such an act of submission would be a major political victory for the church.

It was evident that Talleyrand had interpreted in his own way the Pope's message of 29 June 1802 liberating him from all of his ecclesiastical responsibilities and there was every chance that renewed negotiations with the church would be convoluted. The list of Rome's reproaches was long: it was he who had suggested the nationalization of the church in France and selling off its property to overcome the country's debts; he had signed the civil constitution of the clergy in December 1789; he had consecrated bishops after having resigned his post and without the authorization of Rome; he had married without being released from his vows of celibacy as a priest and bishop; finally, his nonspiritual behaviour had served as a role-model for other people. There was one more sin that the church could reproach him for: he had formed part of the government of an emperor who had humiliated two popes. He could claim with a clear conscience that he had played no part in Napoleon's treatment of Pius VI and Pius VII, which, moreover, certainly counted as one of the emperor's greatest blunders.

The fate of all those who opposed the church's doctrines was a furtive burial and oblivion. At the time of the Revolution, the upper classes had become deeply sceptical about religion. However, doubt and atheism among the upper classes had proved to be the trigger for anarchy and social disorder among the lower classes. Since the Revolution, the church had lost a great deal of its prestige—the Archbishop of Paris's residence had been ransacked by the mob as recently as 1830. Nonetheless, by 1838 the church had begun to regain some of its prestige, with the aristocracy rallying to its cause. It became clear that a return to the ancestral religious faith of France was the surest way of guaranteeing social order. By the mid-1830s it was no longer fashionable to be dubious about religion and Talleyrand was a loyal follower of fashion. Dorothea believed that the Prince should not be allowed to die without accepting some kind of reconciliation with the Catholic Church for the family name and its social standing required that the relationship with the church should be legitimized. However, any direct broaching of the subject with Talleyrand was likely to stimulate resistance.

He remained silent. He intended to choose the moment of any admission of guilt or act of submission and, at all costs, to avoid having to grovel. He had seen that Sieyès had died unrepentant in 1836 and was refused a religious funeral. Talleyrand had never shown himself as hostile to the clergy, while his indifference to religion could be contrasted with his confidence in its role in terms of social harmony and order. His political entourage, including Thiers, believed that he was simply teasing Archbishop de Quélan. However, thanks to the devout Pauline, an important step was accomplished—he became acquainted with the Abbé Dupanloup, Pauline's confessor. The Duchess de Dino and Pauline had often spoken with enthusiasm of this eloquent 36-year-old priest, so Talleyrand decided to meet him. Félix Dupanloup was invited to dinner on 6 February 1838 but, wary both of Talleyrand's sincerity and his intellectual superiority, and prejudiced about the prospect of being seen in the presence of "the limping devil" in person and ruining his reputation, declined. Talleyrand was astonished, a sentiment Dorothea shared with Archbishop de Quélan, who then insisted that Dupanloup should accept a second invitation. The archbishop proposed visiting the Rue Saint-Florentin himself but, although the Prince announced that he

461

was flattered by the prospect, it soon became clear that he had no wish to discuss the state of his soul with the head of the French church.

Dupanloup was a motivated, ardent and straightforward Christian and a fashionable priest among the Parisian intelligentsia; he pleased Talleyrand enormously. He kept a complete record of their meetings: "I do not know if kings are kinglier in their courts than M. Talleyrand appeared in his salon." The former Bishop of Autun was at his charming best; everything that the Prince said delighted Dupanloup and the priest soon abandoned his prejudices. In fact, rather than persuading the Prince to make peace with the church, Dupanloup rapidly became one of Talleyrand's disciples. Over dinner they discussed religious subjects, with Talleyrand describing his memories of Saint-Sulpice and his meeting with the Pope in 1804. Upon leaving the Rue Saint-Florentin, Dupanloup said to himself: "That was certainly one of the most edifying conversations that has taken place in Paris today; it only lacked a cross upon his chest to convince me that I was talking to one of the most venerable bishops of France." While Talleyrand's public image inspired censure and contempt, Dupanloup was astonished to discover that he was full of benevolence for the world and, in his own household, beloved by all those around him. The priest was carried away with eagerness and admiration, feeling that he was perhaps on the point of saving a soul. He asked if he might return to the Rue Saint-Florentin, where he held another long conversation with Talleyrand in private—without broaching the subject uppermost in the minds of the two men. Dupanloup would later become Bishop of Orléans and one of the major ecclesiastical figures of nineteenth century France.

The Prince de Talleyrand's last public appearance was on 3 March at the Institute of Sciences and Arts, where the room was packed by a public ready to listen to him deliver a eulogy in honour of Charles Frédéric Reinhard, who had recently died. A Wurttemberger who became a naturalized Frenchman, Reinhard had briefly taken Talleyrand's place as Minister of Foreign Affairs in the autumn of 1799, interrupting his career as French ambassador in different European cities. Since travelling to London together in 1792, Talleyrand had worked closely with and appreciated Reinhard, so that giving a funeral oration was an opportunity to pay tribute to a worthy colleague and an excellent occasion to present himself before the public for the last time. Since Reinhard had studied for the priesthood and then served the Revolution, the Directory, the Consulate, the Empire and the Bourbon Restoration, what Talleyrand said reflected his own career.

Disregarding the opinion of his doctor, the infirm figure of the Prince made his way slowly into the auditorium as the public rose to its feet on what was evidently an historic occasion. Present were all the familiar faces from the Rue Saint-Florentin: Royer-Collard, Pasquier, Thiers, Noailles, Barante, Molé, La Besnardière. He spoke for half-an-hour reading without glasses the eulogy that had been written for him by the Duchess de Dino. He listed the many different posts that Reinhard had filled and described the qualities needed to carry out those functions. He then presented the characteristics of the perfect Minister of Foreign Affairs: "A sort of instinct, always present, should prevent him from compromising himself in any conversation. He must have the faculty of appearing open, while remaining impenetrable; of masking reserve with the manner of careless abandon; of showing talent even in the choice of his amusements… Diplomacy is not a science of deceit and duplicity… People have made the mistake of confusing reserve with deceit. Good faith never authorizes deceit but it admits of reserve; and reserve has this peculiarity that it increases confidence."

In the play *The Marriage of Figaro* (1778) by Beaumarchais—who has made a couple of appearances in this narrative—"Figaro" describes how a diplomat should behave. One can make a delicious comparison between Talleyrand's description of the perfect diplomat and Beaumarchais's wonderful caricature: "Pretend to be oblivious of what everyone knows, and to know what others do not; seem to understand what no-one understands, not to hear what all are hearing and, in particular, appear to be able to do the impossible. Pretend to great secrecy when there is nothing to conceal. Shut yourself away in order to sharpen your pens and say that you are too busy to be approached. Seem profound when one is only hollow."

Talleyrand's oration was subsequently printed and distributed as a pamphlet to his circle of acquaintances, including the Abbé Dupanloup and Monsignor de Quélan. The copy sent to Adolphe de Bacourt, serving as Ambassador to Baden, included a note announcing that he was not well. Dupanloup came to thank him personally for his copy of the eulogy and sent his own recent theological work accompanied by a letter. Talleyrand asked Dorothea to read the letter to him and, when she had finished, he asked her: "Do you think that Dupanloup would come if we called him for my last moments?" She was sure that he would. The Prince admitted that he had considered a reconciliation with Rome, upon which Dorothea revealed that she had already drafted a letter on this same matter. He feared that, if he left it to the last minute to arrange his affairs with Rome, it would be interpreted as the feeble gesture of a senile old man. Particularly, he did not want the church to create a scandal by refusing him a funeral. The Abbé Dupanloup was invited to pass by once again. Behind these polite overtures lay the matter of the exact wording that the Prince might be prepared to sign as a public retraction. On one side, Dorothea and, on the other, Dupanloup and de Quélan began to draft different versions which they shared with each other. Although he must have been aware that the end of his life was near, Talleyrand appeared to be indifferent to reaching a fitting conclusion.

Another of his great colleagues, the Baron Louis, who he had known at least since 1790, passed away in August 1837. Although Joseph-Dominique Louis had been made a baron by Napoleon in 1809 and was his minister of finance in 1814–1815, he nevertheless supported the Bourbon restoration. It is remarkable that Baron Louis was subsequently given the portfolio of finance by Louis XVIII in 1815, again in the Decazes ministry of 1818 and became Louis-Philippe's minister of finance in 1831–1832.

On 28 March 1838, Talleyrand's brother Archambaud died suddenly. Since he had benefited from being addressed by the title of the Duke de Talleyrand, his son Edmond now inherited this title, which meant that his separated wife Dorothea could abandon being the Duchess de Dino, passing this inheritance to her son Alexandre, so as to become the Duchess de Talleyrand. Dupanloup came to express his condolences to the Prince and had a long conversation with Talleyrand, but no progress was made on the burning issue of his reconciliation with Rome. Eventually, Dorothea went to see Monsignor de Quélen bearing a hastily scribbled retraction which Talleyrand himself had written on both sides of a sheet of paper for the archbishop's consideration. De Quélen was touched to have been consulted yet felt the proposed text would gain if written in a more ecclesiastic language. During the month of April, the draft was passed backwards and forwards, edited and corrected by the archbishop's secretariat and by Talleyrand himself with obsessive attention, until he agreed to stop fiddling with it in early May—but would not sign it.

On 12 May, he fell ill with fever and his doctor, Jean Cruveilhier, diagnosed a tumour on his thigh and abscesses in the lumbar region. It was serious enough to call for immediate intervention by a surgeon, a cruelly painful business. Totally exhausted by this operation, Talleyrand could no longer lie down. He asked to be brought into his salon where Bacourt was present, stupefied by his self-control in the face of unimaginable discomfort. Abbé Dupanloup reappeared and raised once again the possibility of signing the letter of submission. The prince said that he had included in his draft text to de Quélan all that he wished to say and those who read it would understand his feelings on the matter, to which Dupanloup proposed that a second letter should be prepared— shorter and more succinct—and then produced such a letter written by the archbishop's staff, including parts of Talleyrand's text. In fact, the text consisted of two documents: a letter to the Pope and a request for forgiveness. The Prince announced that he was satisfied with the archbishop's version and was ready to sign it but, just as Dupanloup believed the matter settled, he quibbled saying: "Would you be good enough to leave the paper with me? I wish to read it one more time." The priest left without the signed paper and without any indication of what would happen next.

During the night of 15/16 May, Talleyrand's health deteriorated dramatically and Cruveilhier told him that, if he intended to put his affairs in order, the moment had come. The Duchess and Dupanloup were now seriously alarmed that, if he were to die without signing the letter of submission, there would be the unacceptable scandal of being denied a Christian burial. They decided to play their trump card—18-year-old Pauline. Fully aware of the importance of her mission, she came to the dying man's bedside accompanied by Dupanloup and begged him to sign the letter fearing that he would soon be too weak to hold a pen. The Prince insisted that he would only sign it when he was ready to do so. He called Dorothea and asked her to read the archbishop's text out loud once again. He was visibly weakening, but repeated: "Be calm, I won't delay." Dupanloup left disappointed once again.

Like Louis XVIII, Talleyrand would die in public. The courtyard, staircases and antechambers of the Rue Saint-Florentin were thronging with blue-blooded visitors waiting for news and ready to place bets as to whether he would or wouldn't sign. Since he had already accepted that he would sign, why did he not do so? Even on his deathbed Talleyrand created controversy. He treated his fate with the same stalling tactics he had used in international negotiations. "The submission," wrote Archbishop de Quélan, "encountered obstacles worthy of Satan." Montrond, sitting alone in gloomy silence, described the situation: "He was motivated by two feelings: to avoid the scandal of a funeral conducted without a religious ceremony and to accept at the very last minute in order to evade people's sarcasm." Royer-Collard reassured the anxious onlookers: "Fear nothing. He who has always been the peacemaker will not refuse to make his peace with God before he dies." Dupanloup had returned to the bedside during the day of 16 May and asked again if he would like to sign the declaration, since the archbishop was waiting for it. Talleyrand replied: "Thank the archbishop and tell him that everything will be done." Now Pauline was sent back in: "When will it be, uncle?" The answer was precise: "Tomorrow morning, between 5 and 6 o'clock." Dupanloup asked: "May I, Prince, take this as a hope?" "Do not say hope," the dying man responded, "say a certainty. It's positive." In the middle of the night a further deterioration brought Pauline to his bedside with a pen, the retraction and the letter of submission to the Pope. He spoke firmly: "It is not yet 6 o'clock."

On the early morning of 17 May, five worthy witnesses entered the bedroom to attest the validity of the signing: the Prince de Poix, for the aristocracy, the Count de Saint- Aulaire, French ambassador to Vienna, Barante, now ambassador to Saint-Petersburg, Royer-Collard and even Prime Minister Molé. Talleyrand's most long-serving valet Hélie was also present. Unable to sleep and still in possession of his mind, he asked what time it was. Someone replied 6 o'clock, but Dupanloup would have no deception: "It is not yet 5 o'clock." Suddenly, a girl in a gossamer dress entered the bed-chamber; it was Marie-Thérèse de Périgord,

Charlotte's daughter, coming to request Talleyrand's blessing before attending her first communion. She kneeled by his bed, he muttered some kind words and she left in tears.

Towards 6 o'clock Pauline brought him a pen to sign the papers and Dorothea asked if he wanted her to read the two letters one more time. He agreed. The first one reads:

Increasingly influenced by solemn considerations, obliged to judge serenely the consequences of a revolution that dragged everything with it and which has lasted fifty years, at the end of a long life and, after a long experience, I have come to find fault with the excesses of the century to which I belonged and to condemn in a forthright manner the serious errors in which I had the misfortune to participate which, through this long succession of years, have disturbed and distressed the apostolic Roman Catholic Church.

If it pleases the respectable friend of my family, Monsignor Archbishop of Paris, who has been kind enough to confirm to me the Pontifical Saint Peter's benevolent attitude towards me, to communicate to the Holy Father, as I wish, the deference of my respectful gratitude and my entire acceptance of the doctrine and the discipline of the church, to the decisions and judgements of the Holy See concerning the ecclesiastical affairs of France, which I dare to hope that His Holiness deigns to accept with indulgence.

Subsequently relieved by the venerable Pius VII of carrying out ecclesiastical functions, I sought throughout my long political career opportunities to render to religion and the many members of the Catholic clergy all the services that lay within my power. I have never ceased to consider myself as a child of the church. I deplore once again the actions in my life that have saddened it, and my last wishes are towards it and its supreme head.

No specific transgression was mentioned and no forgiveness asked. He signed the document "Charles-Maurice, Prince de Talleyrand", but observed that the document did not contain everything that he wanted to say. Dorothea replied that a second document addressed directly to the Pope contained the missing sentiments. In this second text, he recalled the dramatic circumstances of his life and the general disorder of the epoch through which he had lived without, once more, specifying exactly the faults concerned. He then addressed the circumstances that had destined him for a life in the church: "The respect that I owe to those who gave me life does not prevent me from saying that throughout my youth I was directed towards a profession for which I had no calling." He signed the second paper. At his request, the two documents were then dated 10 March 1838—over two months earlier—for the doyen of diplomats wanted to avoid the impression that he had signed them at the very last moment—even though he had. They were conveyed to Monsignor de Quélen, who dispatched them immediately to Rome. Dorothea's appraisal of de Quélen describes him as: "Kind, charitable, affectionate, grateful, sincerely attached to his duties and always ready to face martyrdom." His bust still stands in the Château de Rochecotte.

At 8 o'clock that morning, a commotion outside the Rue Saint-Florentin had announced the arrival of King Louis-Philippe accompanied by his sister Mademoiselle Adélaïde. Their visit was necessarily brief but, aware of the enormous honour that this visit represented to him and his family, etiquette demanded that he should name every person present in the bedchamber, including Hélie. The two royal visitors left and, when the room was empty, at 11 o'clock Dupanloup appeared at his side for the last confession. The previous one had been in 1789, forty-nine years previously. When it came to sprinkling the holy oil on his hands, he turned them palm downwards, murmuring: "Do not forget that I am a bishop."

He died in public like a king at 3.35 p.m. on 17 May 1838. The news spread, the crowd departed and peace fell on the Rue Saint-Florentin. A dispute over his retraction would now begin with Thiers pouring scorn on it, with the result that Dorothea refused to meet him ever again. In total contrast, Pope Gregory XVI found the text of the retraction far from satisfactory and had sent a much more severe set of instructions, which fortuitously arrived too late. Neither the Papacy nor the French royal court were prepared to publish the text of his signed retraction—Prime Minister Molé, André Dupin (President of the Chamber of Deputies) and Horace Sebastiani (Ambassador to London) told the Papal Nuncio that its publication would give rise to "distressing and scandalous" arguments in the two chambers.

The funeral took place on the morning of 22 May. All roads leading to the Church of the Assumption were lined each side by rows of soldiers presenting arms, with the long procession led by the clergy, preceding the immense hearse pulled by six horses bearing ostrich-feather plumes and draped in black silver-bordered drapes almost reaching the ground. Wary of a demonstration, at the last minute the government changed the route leaving a large part of the crowd dissatisfied. The hearse was followed by the diplomatic corps, members of the peerage and the Institute of Sciences and Arts, six carriages containing the Royal Family and a train of other vehicles. The mourners filed in front of his two nephews, the sons of Edmond and Dorothea: Louis, the Duke de Valençay and Alexandre, the Duke de Dino.

Dorothea did not like Paris and lost no time in arranging her affairs. She knew that, without the Prince, she was nothing at all and even her friendship with Adolphe Thiers was finished. There was a last farewell with Montrond during which the old scoundrel burst into tears. On 3 July, she sold the mansion on the Rue Saint-Florentin to James de Rothschild for the relatively modest sum of 1,181,000 francs. One week later, Talleyrand's library followed suit.

Some months after the ceremony, the bodies of Charles-Maurice and Archambaud de Talleyrand were transferred to a tomb in the crypt of the chapel at Valençay, together with that of his grandniece Yolande de Périgord, the daughter of Louis, Duke de Valençay, who had died aged 3. The coffins were transported on a gun carriage which, in the previous year, had served to bring back to France the body of Josephine's daughter, Queen Hortense, the mother of his grandson, the Duke de Morny. The entire population of Valençay and its environs came to pay homage to the great man, who they considered almost as a saint and whose departure was signalled by a volley of musketry. By this time Dorothea had returned to Germany, so the small number of personalities present counted Montrond, Dupanloup and Alexandre de Talleyrand.

Thus passed away one of the representatives of the Age of Enlightenment. There probably never was a statesman whose ideas were so right and who, for most of his life, was so misunderstood by public opinion. History reflects favourably on Talleyrand to the same measure that his contemporaries spoke ill of him. With his far-sighted talent, and his predominantly wise and moderate political conduct throughout a long and difficult career, it must be acknowledged that it is impossible not to admire him and to overlook his numerous peccadillos.

SOURCES

Andlau, B. d'. (1975.) *Madame de Staël.* Coppet, Switzerland.

Boigne, Comtesse de. N.d. *Mémoires de la Comtesse de Boigne.* 2 vols.

Caulaincourt, A. de. (2013.) *En traineau avec l'Empereur.* Paris: Arléa.

Chateaubriand, F.-R. de. (1989.) *Mémoires d'outre-tombe.* 2 vols. Paris: Garnier.

Colmache, E. 1850. *Revelations of the life of Prince Talleyrand.* London: Henry Colburn. (Kessinger Legacy Reprints.)

Cooper, D. 1932. *Talleyrand.* London: Phoenix.

Dard, E. 1935. *Napoléon et Talleyrand.* Paris: Fallois.

De Coigny, A.; Lamy, E. n.d. *Mémoires de Aimée de Coigny.* Paris: Calmann-Lévy.

De Souza, A. 1821. Adèle de Sénange. In: *Oeuvres complètes de Mme de Souza.* Paris: Eymery. (Dunda Books Classic.)

Dwyer, P. 2002. *Talleyrand.* London: Longman.

Forgues, E. (2018.) *Mémoires et relations politiques du Baron de Vitrolles.* 3 vols. London: Forgotten Books.

Goodden, A. 2008. *Madame de Staël: The dangerous exile.* Oxford, United Kingdom: OUP.

Grand, G.F. 1814. *Narrative of the life of a gentleman long resident in India.* Cape of Good Hope, South Africa.

Greenbaum, L.S. 1970. *Talleyrand: Statesman priest.* Washington, DC: Catholic University of America Press.

King, D. 2008. *Vienna, 1814.* New York NY: Broadway Paperbacks.

Larsen, E. 1968. *Carlo Andrea Pozzo di Borgo: one man against Napoleon.* London: Dobson.

La Tour du Pin, Marquise de. (1979.) *Mémoires de la Marquise de La Tour du Pin: journal d'une femme de cinquante ans.* Paris: Mercure de France.

Lawday, D. 2006. *Napoleon's master: a life of Prince Talleyrand.* London: Pimlico.

Morris, A.C., ed. 1888. *The diary and letters of Gouverneur Morris*. New York, NY: Charles Scribner's Sons.

Nicolson, H. 1946. *The Congress of Vienna: A study in Allied unity, 1812-1822*. New York, NY: Harcourt, Brace.

Orieux, J. 1970. *Talleyrand ou le sphinx incompris*. Paris: Flammarion.

Poniatowski, M. 1967. *Talleyrand aux Etats-Unis, 1794-1796*. Paris: Presses de la Cité.

Seward, D. 1991. *Metternich: the first European*. Harmondsworth, UK: Viking Penguin.

Waresquiel, E. de. 2003. *Talleyrand: le prince immobile*. Paris: Fayard.

Waresquiel, E. de. 2017. *Fouché: dossiers secrets*. Paris: Tallandier.

Ziegler, P. 1962. *The Duchess of Dino: chatelaine of Europe*. London: Collins.

INDEX

Bertin de Veaux, Louis François, 438
Bessières, Jean-Baptiste, 260
Beugnot, Jacques Claude, Count de, 330, 336, 374, 377, 378
Bigottini, Émilie, 363
Biron, Armand Louis de Gontaut, Duke de, 35
Biron, Dorothea von, *see* Dino, Dorothea,
Bismarck, Otto von, 360
Blacas, Pierre-Louis Jean Casimir, Count de, 305, 315, 339, 344, 351, 376
Blacons, Henri d'Armand de Forest, Marquess de, 99
Blücher, Gebhard Leberecht von, 370, 384
Boisgelin, Bruno-Gabriel de, 291, 397
Boisgelin, Thomas de, 41
Boissy d'Anglas, François-Antoine de, 109
Bombelles, Charles-René, Count von, 351
Bonaparte, Caroline, 267, 281, 361
Bonaparte, Jérôme, 247, 328
Bonaparte, Joseph, 193, 199, 221, 231, 246, 259, 276, 316, 319
Bonaparte, Louis, 240, 293
Bonaparte, Lucien, 173, 174, 175, 184, 187, 211
Bonaparte, Napoleon, *see* Napoleon I
Bonaparte, Pauline, 196
Boniface de Castellane-Nojean, Louis André, Marquis de, 63, 129, 144, 389, 417
Bordeaux, Henri, Duke de, 408, 431
Bossuet, Jacques-Bénigne, 454
Bougainville, Louis-Antoine de, 148
Bourrienne, Louis Antoine Fauvelet de, 319
Brienne, Étienne Charles de Loménie de, 50

Brionne, Louise de Rohan, Countess de, 29
Brissot, Jacques Pierre, 84
Broglie, Albert, Duke de, 458
Broglie, Albertina, Duchess de, 417
Broglie, Victor, Duke de, 448, 456, 459
Brown, Amy, 399, 408
Bruix, Étienne Eustache, 166, 174, 204
Brune, Guillaume, 171
Buffon, Marguerite Françoise Bouvier, Countess de, 47
Buonaparte, Letizia, 280
Burney, Frances (Fanny), 92, 193
Burr, Aaron, 13, 106
Byron, George Gordon, Lord, 405
Cabarrús, Thérésa, 102, 110, 118, 119, 120
Cadoudal, Georges, 213
Calonne, Charles Alexandre de, 43, 48, 49, 50, 80, 183
Cambacérès, Jean-Jacques de, 178
Campbell, Neil, 367, 368
Canisy, Adrienne de, 265, 415, 416
Canning, George, 82, 248, 401, 452
Canning, Sir Stratford, 449
Caprara, Giovanni Battista, 191, 203
Caraman, François-Joseph-Philippe de Riquet, Count de, 120
Carême, Antonin, 326, 336
Carnot, Lazare Nicolas Marguerite, Count, 117, 122, 123, 129, 140, 141, 144
Carrel, Armand, 426
Casanova, Giacomo, 229
Caselli, Carolus, 191, 203
Castlereagh, Robert Stewart, Viscount, 320, 326, 335, 345, 347, 349, 354, 355, 357, 360, 365, 366, 368, 370, 386, 387, 391, 392, 439, 446

Catharina von Württemberg, 256, 328, 423
Cathcart, William Schaw, Lord, 370
Catherine the Great, 81, 229, 382
Catherine, Grand Duchess, 270, 306
Caulaincourt, Armand-Augustin-Louis, Marquis de, 159, 214, 215, 247, 248, 250, 251, 264, 265, 266, 267, 268, 269, 270, 271, 274, 286, 287, 292, 295, 297, 298, 299, 302, 303, 306, 307, 308, 309, 311, 312, 313, 315, 316, 319, 321, 332, 335, 365, 376, 381, 415, 470
Cavanac, Anne Couppier, Marquess de, 42
Cazenove d'Arlens, Constance, 205
Cazenove, Théophile, 99
Chalais, Marie-Françoise de Rochechouart-Mortemart, Princess de, 22
Chamfort, Sébastien-Roch Nicolas, 46
Champagny, Jean-Baptiste de Nompère, Count de, 235, 251, 257, 266, 289, 315
Charlemagne, Mlle, 22, 23
Charles IV, 200, 258, 259
Charles X, 27, 64, 311, 419, 420, 421, 422, 423, 426, 429, 430, 431, 432, 434, 437, 458
Charles XIV John, see Bernadotte
Charlotte, Queen of England, 81
Charron, Pierre, 113
Chartres, Philippe, Duke de, see Orléans, Philippe, Duke d'
Chateaubriand, François-René, 192, 212, 330, 337, 374, 375, 377, 380, 402, 403, 412, 413, 414, 450, 470
Chatham, 1st Earl of, see William Pitt
Chauvelin, François-Bernard, Marquis de, 83, 89, 167

Chénier, André, 121
Chénier, Marie-Joseph, 124
Chernyshov, Alexander, 297, 298
Choderlos de Laclos, Pierre, 47
Choiseul, Étienne-François, Duke de, 23, 29, 45, 47, 48
Choiseul-Gouffrier, Auguste de, 34, 46, 389, 398, 405
Clam-Martinic, Karel Jan, 372
Clancarty, Richard Le Poer Trench, Lord, 370
Clarke, Henri-Jacques-Guillaume, 311
Coigny, Aimée de, 14, 35, 121, 193, 205, 215, 276, 280, 289, 291, 304, 306, 317, 319, 383, 470
Colbert, Jean-Baptiste, 181
Colmache, Édouard, 164, 431
Condé, Louis V Joseph, Prince de, 27, 415, 416
Condorcet, Nicolas de, 75
Consalvi, Ercole, 192, 237
Constant, Benjamin, 76, 114, 124, 126, 127, 129, 175, 200, 202, 206, 334, 369
Cornwallis, Charles, Marquess, 193
Courland, Anna Dorothea, Duchess von, 244, 272, 273, 274, 275, 290, 293, 296, 301, 302, 307, 311, 317, 334, 348, 371, 377, 390, 394, 395, 396, 398, 401, 403, 405, 409
Courland, Wilhelmine, Duchess von, see Sagan
Courtiade, Joseph, 29, 34, 89, 96, 97, 100, 138, 205, 237, 316, 363, 380, 385, 436
Cruveilhier, Jean, 465
Czartorisky, Prince Adam, 272, 274
D'Hauterive, Alexandre-Maurice Blanc, 45
Dalberg, Emmerich von, 216, 237, 238, 239, 300
Dalberg, Karl-Theodor von, 237,

Lebrun, Charles-François, 178, 333

Leclerc, Charles, 196, 199, 298

Lefebvre, François Joseph, 331

Leopold I, Prince of Saxe-Coburg and Gotha, 422, 442

Leszczynska, Marie, Queen of France, 22

Letourneur, Étienne-François, 123, 125

Liéven, Dorothea, Princess, 267

Liéven, Khristofor, Prince, 444

Ligne, Charles-Joseph, Prince de, 20, 28, 229, 338, 361, 364

Londonderry, Sir Charles Stewart, Marquis of, 446

Louis XIII, 373

Louis XIV, 46, 47, 258, 454

Louis XV, 415

Louis XVI, 15, 27, 29, 32, 33, 48, 50, 51, 52, 53, 55, 59, 64, 65, 66, 67, 70, 71, 72, 78, 79, 82, 83, 84, 85, 86, 87, 90, 104, 117, 120, 129, 139, 154, 155, 169, 171, 182, 185, 212, 213, 214, 218, 221, 273, 277, 304, 306, 313, 315, 317, 319, 320, 321, 327, 329, 331, 333, 334, 336, 338, 339, 340, 341, 343, 344, 345, 346, 347, 350, 351, 353, 356, 357, 358, 360, 363, 364, 366, 369, 370, 371, 372, 374, 375, 376, 377, 378, 379, 380, 382, 383, 387, 388, 389, 391, 393, 394, 396, 397, 400, 402, 403, 407, 408, 410, 411, 412, 413, 414, 416, 417, 418, 419, 420, 422, 423, 430, 431, 434, 454, 464, 466

Louis XVIII, 15, 27, 120, 169, 171, 182, 185, 218, 273, 304, 306, 315, 317, 319, 320, 321, 327, 329, 331, 333, 334, 336, 338, 339, 340, 341, 343, 344, 345, 346, 347, 350, 351, 353, 356, 357, 358, 360, 363, 364, 366, 369, 370, 371, 372, 374, 375, 376, 377, 378, 379, 380, 383, 387, 388, 389, 391, 393, 394, 396, 397, 400, 403, 407, 408, 410, 411, 412, 413, 414, 416, 417, 418, 419, 420, 422, 430, 431, 434, 454, 464, 466

Louis, Dauphin de France, 19, 71

Louis, Joseph Dominique, Baron, 318, 464

Louise of Prussia, 249

Louis-Philippe, 34, 104, 113, 320, 414, 420, 427, 428, 430, 431, 433, 434, 435, 436, 437, 439, 440, 441, 442, 444, 445, 447, 450, 452, 456, 458, 459, 464, 468

Louvel, Louis-Pierre, 407

Lowe, Sir Hudson, 381

Lucchesini, Girolamo, 222

Luynes, Guyonne-Élisabeth-Josèphe de Montmorency, Duchess de, 28, 70, 71, 205, 206, 223, 289

Macdonald, Jacques, 171, 331

Mack von Leiberich, Karl, Baron, 224

Mademoiselle, see Orléans, Louise-Adélaïde d'

Magallon, Charles, 156

Malet, Claude François de, 311

Malmesbury, James Harris, Lord, 121

Mannay, Charles, 26

Marat, Jean Paul, 104

Marboeuf, Yves-Alexandre de, 53

Maret, Hugues-Bernard, 125, 140, 204, 224, 256, 307, 308, 311, 312, 315, 316, 318, 331

Maria Amalia of Naples and Sicily, 433

Maria I, Queen of Portugal, 133

María Luisa of Parma, 258

Maria Theresa, Empress of Austria, 30

Marie Joséphine of Saxony, 358

Marie Louise, Empress of France, 299, 302, 308, 311, 316, 322,

403, 426, 428
Périgord, Yolande de, 469
Perregaux, Jean-Frédéric, 116,
  136, 163
Perrey, Gabriel-Antoine, 137, 216,
  323, 334, 347, 396, 403, 416,
  424
Philippe-Égalité,
  Orléans, Philippe d' 67, 124
Phillips, Susanna, 92 92
Piattoli, Scipione, 272
Pichegru, Jean-Charles, 114, 139,
  213, 214
Pictet-de-Rochemont, Charles, 7
Pignatelli, Johanna, Princess, 347
Piscatory, Antonine-Dorothée, 425
Piscatory, Théobald, 425, 426
Pitt, William, 13, 45, 81, 83, 94,
  95, 96, 167, 184, 189, 222, 233,
  434, 436
Pius VI, 73, 74, 190, 192, 219,
  221, 258, 390, 460, 467
Pius VII, 190, 192, 219, 221, 258,
  390, 460, 467
Poisson, Abel-François, Marquis
  de Marigny, 49
Poisson, Julie, Marquess de
  Marigny, 49
Poix, Just de Noailles, Prince de,
  466
Polignac, Jules de, 426
Polignac, Yolande de Polastron,
  Duchess de, 208
Pompadour, Jeanne Antoinette
  Poisson, Mme de, 29, 47, 49
Potocka, Anna, 244
Pozzo di Borgo, Carlo Andrea,
  Count de, 70, 324, 326, 350,
  354, 377, 380, 382, 393, 412,
  430, 470
Pradt, see De Pradt
Priestley, Joseph, 82
Prince Regent, see George IV
Provence, Count de, see Louis
  XVIII 15, 27, 67, 181, 182, 304,
  329
Quélan, see De Quélan

Radix de Sainte-Foy, Maximilien,
  46, 71, 76, 89, 99, 116, 119,
  134, 136, 144, 163, 176, 204,
  206, 210
Raikes, Thomas, 459
Ramel, Dominique-Vincent, 132
Rayneval, Maximilien Gérard,
  Count de, 451
Razumovsky, Andrey Kirillovich,
  Count de, 350
Récamier, Juliette, 14, 14, 136
Regnaud de Saint-Jean d'Angély,
  Michel, 194
Reinhard, Charles-Frédéric, Count
  de, 83, 115, 132, 169, 177, 462,
  463
Rémusat, August-Laurent de, 223,
  390
Rémusat, Charles de, 414, 447
Rémusat, Claire Élisabeth de
  Vergennes, Mme de, 193, 202,
  218, 219, 223, 279, 285, 296,
  323, 402, 406, 410, 414
Rensselaër, Elizabeth, 101
Rewbell, Jean-François, 117, 119,
  123, 125, 127, 133, 139, 140,
  144, 145, 146, 149, 165, 166
Richelieu, Armand de Vignerot du
  Plessis, Duke de, 98, 373, 382,
  383, 391, 393, 394, 406
Richelieu, Armand Jean du
  Plessis, Cardinal, 373
Ris, Clément de, 186
Robespierre, Maximilien, 17, 46,
  75, 78, 88, 89, 98, 103, 104,
  108, 118, 119, 122, 126, 154,
  163, 170, 323
Roederer, Antoine, 175, 176
Roederer, Pierre-Louis, 109, 116,
  124, 172, 175, 176, 286
Rohan, Louis René Édouard,
  Cardinal de, 29, 30
Rothesay, Charles Stuart, Lord,
  401, 430
Rothschild, James de, 469
Rousseau, Jean-Jacques, 10, 20,
  229